Eckardt Buchholz-Schuster | Daniel Herbe [eds.]

Applied Philosophy of Law – Orientation in a Nervous World?

Thoughts and Concepts

Nomos

The Deutsche Nationalbibliothek lists this publication in the Deutsche Nationalbibliografie; detailed bibliographic data are available on the Internet at http://dnb.d-nb.de

ISBN 978-3-7560-2014-0 (Print)
978-3-7489-5551-1 (ePDF)

Onlineversion
Inlibra

1st Edition 2026

We dedicate this volume to our esteemed doctoral supervisors: Prof. Dr. Joachim Rückert and to the memory of Prof. Dr. Rainer Schröder, who sadly passed away far too early. The idea for this book came to us on March 1st, 2024 during a walk along the beach under a bright blue sky on the beautiful North Sea island of Norderney. It was gently picked up, carried home and developed into the concept for this anthology that evening.

The Editors

Wir widmen diesen Band unseren verehrten Doktorvätern: Herrn Prof. Dr. Joachim Rückert und dem Andenken an Herrn Prof. Dr. Rainer Schröder, der leider viel zu früh verstorben ist. Die Idee zu diesem Buch fiel am 1. März 2024 während eines Strandspazierganges aus einem strahlend blauen Himmel auf die schöne Nordseeinsel Norderney. Sie wurde behutsam aufgefangen, nachhause getragen und noch am gleichen Abend zum Konzept der vorliegenden Anthologie fortentwickelt.

Die Herausgeber

‚Herbststimmung am Meer, 2025', © Lars Wiggert, Hamburg

Foreword

Stephan Kirste

With the dawn of the second quarter of the 21st century, new horizons are opening up for legal philosophy. New challenges are joining old ones to create an exciting new era full of new opportunities. These challenges affect all areas of legal philosophy, from its self-image to the theory of jurisprudence to legal theory and legal ethics.

Even though the democratic 'backsliding' towards authoritarian regimes has pushed the pressing issues of anti-discrimination, technological consequences for law and environmental justice into the background, legal philosophy must not allow itself to be distracted by this. Legal philosophy is once again facing significant institutional and theoretical challenges. Contrary to the recommendations of academic councils, the trend towards reducing the number of legal philosophy chairs and diminishing its importance in legal studies continues, particularly in Central Europe. Nevertheless, legal philosophy remains as essential as ever for building bridges to relevant discussions in professional philosophy, critically accompanying legal developments and training young lawyers who can make difficult decisions and deal with new legal challenges rationally and critically. An extraordinary diversity of theoretical approaches emerges when we examine current global trends in legal philosophy. These range from postmodern and postcolonial ideas to analytical theories, drawing on feminist and ecological philosophies, as well as political science, economics and sociology. Some further develop concepts of systems theory. A vibrant philosophy of law will therefore always observe developments in general philosophies and adopt approaches that offer fresh insights into law and potential solutions. Conversely, it is striking that, after years of leaving questions of justice to legal philosophy, practical philosophy and ethics have been discussing classic legal philosophical questions for several years now. Are they better off there? In recent years, agencies, research communities and foundations at European and national levels have rightly promoted interdisciplinary projects. Legal philosophy must participate in exploring the possibilities of intra-, inter-, and multi-disciplinarity.

With law remaining the backbone of society, unable to be observed outside of influences, social interests, values and processes, in the same way legal philosophy cannot regard jurisprudence as an isolated science. Legal philosophy must explore how jurisprudence can preserve its identity while contributing to the rationality of law by establishing connections with other relevant sciences. However, this identity has been severely challenged in recent years. The core of the identity of jurisprudence is formed by legal knowledge, interests and methods. Large language models pose theoretical and practical challenges to legal methods. How can the creative and innovative function of legal argumentation be ensured despite the increasing use of AI? Empirical methods produce impressive results in other sciences. Since 2000, there has been more intensive discussion in legal philosophy about the extent to which these methods can and should be incorporated more strongly into legal studies, for example through interdisciplinary co-operation with the humanities.

No one would claim that the question of what law is, or how it can be distinguished from other systems such as morality or custom, has already been answered. However, since the turn of the millennium, ecological and technological developments have raised new questions about the structure of law and its elements. Fundamentally, in a society that increasingly communicates virtually, the question arises as to whether the concept of norms can still be the basis for legal order. Technical imperatives that prevent undesirable behavior through technical means are increasingly replacing norms, which establish duties, prohibitions, or permissions. After World War II, human and fundamental rights expanded. Since Hugo Grotius, natural law theory and legal philosophy have sought to clearly outline the boundaries of law and war. However, hybrid forms of warfare are blurring these boundaries, and legal philosophy has yet to develop criteria for them. Should AI systems be recognized as moral agents in law, with rights and obligations? Many problems previously discussed in philosophical terms of natural law have become accessible to legal philosophy and jurisprudence. As a result, the level of protection of basic human needs and interests has reached an unprecedented level worldwide.

But have we gone too far? Discussions about the justification of humanitarian intervention and the demand for a return to the 'core content' of human rights are expressions of these developments. Populists who herald authoritarian systems call for politics to take precedence over law. Should we reinterpret the concept of law to distinguish it from politics?

Since its inception, legal philosophy has been challenged by questions about law's contribution to justice. In the 21st century, new topics have emerged in legal ethics or been explored in greater depth, both in terms of methodology and content. For example, postcolonial approaches are not only concerned with paternalistically granting justice to oppressed minorities, but also with allowing them to participate in debates about justice while bringing their cultural backgrounds to the table. Environmental and Global justice cannot be achieved without the participation of the Global South.

In terms of content, technical and political developments have raised new problems that legal philosophy is addressing. The first and most pressing issue is the unpreparedness not only of medicine but also legal ethics in the face of the challenges posed by the ongoing global pandemic. These include questions of distributive justice relating to medical services and products, the prioritisation of these services and products, how far autonomous decisions about one's health can be restricted in connection with mandatory vaccinations, and how health policy measures are democratically legitimised. The aging of society, the widening social divide, and the continuing high level of global migration raise the question of how the law can ensure a dignified existence without doing so at the expense of future generations. At the same time, it cannot be said that existing discrimination based on gender, religion, and minority status has been conclusively overcome. Legal philosophy must also work on fair solutions despite of conservative backlash. Even if growing global unrest distracts public attention from environmental issues, the question of climate justice and protecting future generations has not been resolved. Would granting certain natural entities legal status and subjective rights help to achieve justice? Can redistribution favor future generations? The law has always been concerned with securing the future. With man-made climate change, securing the future of this planet has become a matter of human action. In this respect, identifying conceptual deficits and proposing fair norms for sustainable human action is one of the most important tasks of legal-philosophical ethics.

Table of Contents

Stephan Kirste
Foreword 9

Introduction by the Editors 19

I. Legal Thought in Global and Critical Perspective

Oche Onazi
Re-imagining Disability Justice: African Legal Philosophy in a Global Context 27

Leonor Suárez Llanos
The Innocence of Crypto-Positivism: Dismantling Myths and Constructing Legal Fictions 57

Eckardt Buchholz-Schuster
Taking Stock: Philosophy of Law in the Age of the "Great Regression" 87

II. Legality and the Rule of Law

Adela Gasiorowska
Legality vs. Extreme Injustice by Omission: Normative-Legal Aspects of Local Authorities' Disobedience 115

John Murungi
Thinking about Law and its Rule at our Time 137

III. Human Rights and Social Contexts

Hyungjoon Jun
Universal Human Rights and the Ethics of Cultural Diversity. Toward an Intercultural Legitimacy of Human Rights 159

Hyun Jung Lee
Reconsidering Age Discrimination: Intersectional, Contextual, and Comparative Perspectives 187

Daniel Herbe
The Significance of Legal Philosophy for German Social Law 213

IV. Environmental and Technological Challenges

Heidi M. Hurd
Competing Conceptions of Sustainability 239

Jordan Pascoe
A Relational Approach to Regulating A.I.: Lessons from Environmental Law 271

V. International and Transnational Law

Win-chiat Lee
Universal Jurisdiction in the Absence of a World State: The Legitimacy of International Criminal Law 293

Veronica Rodriguez-Blanco
What Makes a Transnational Rule of Law? Understanding the Logos and Values of Human Action in Transnational Law 319

VI. Legal and Judicial Training

Juan Pablo Sterling Casas
Communicational Theory of Law and Legal Text: An Interdisciplinary Approach for Legal Education 343

Derk Venema
Philosophy of Law in Professional Ethics Training for Judges 367

List of Authors 391

...

2. We are at a time of profound global transformation. We are confronted by rising catastrophic and existential risks, many caused by the choices we make. Fellow human beings are enduring terrible suffering. If we do not change course, we risk tipping into a future of persistent crisis and breakdown.

3. Yet this is also a moment of hope and opportunity. Global transformation is a chance for renewal and progress grounded in our common humanity. Advances in knowledge, science, technology and innovation could deliver a breakthrough to a better and more sustainable future for all. The choice is ours. ...

United Nations, Pact for the future, 2024

Introduction by the Editors

'In view of globalization and the problems it poses for national and international law, the philosophy of law is becoming increasingly important'[1] - this thesis was put forward in 2008 in the introduction to the anthology *Rechtsphilosophie im 21. Jahrhundert* (Philosophy of Law in the 21st Century), edited by Winfried Brugger, Ulfrid Neumann and Stephan Kirste. Would this thesis still be formulated in the same way today?

Perhaps it would now make sense to make certain modifications or shifts in emphasis.[2] Certainly, in all areas, including in the humanities and natural sciences, we continue to feel the growing pressure of current global challenges and questions of justice.[3] However, in view of the numerous acute problems with national, international and even global dimensions in recent years[4], the question arises as to whether the importance of legal philosophy can keep pace with what might be described as an increasingly dramatic global situation. It also raises the question of how this significance actually manifests itself - or should manifest itself - in view of the sometimes catastrophic and regressive developments of the 21st century that are insufficiently contained by national and international law.

What, for example, is the normative significance of contemporary non-positivist legal philosophy in relation to state and supranational laissez-faire in the face of anthropogenic climate change or the mass migrant deaths in the Mediterranean that have been tolerated by European states for over

1 Winfried Brugger / Ulfrid Neumann / Stephan Kirste, *Rechtsphilosophie im 21. Jahrhundert* (1st ed. Frankfurt a.M. 2008) 2 ('Angesichts der Globalisierung und der von ihr aufgeworfenen Probleme für das nationale und das internationale Recht gewinnt die Rechtsphilosophie immer stärker an Bedeutung'), translation into English by the editors.

2 See also Stephan Kirste's foreword to this anthology in this context.

3 cf, eg, the relevant research area 'Connect4Transformation' at Coburg University of Applied Sciences and Arts < https://www.hs-coburg.de/en/research/research-profile/connect4transformation/ > accessed 5 November 2025.

4 In this context, see, eg, the policy briefs discussed at the UN Future Summit in New York in September 2024 with a focus on justice and human rights, including in the area of policy brief 1 ('Future Generations') and 9 ('A new Agenda for Peace'), < https://www.un.org/sites/un2.un.org/files/our-common-agenda-policy-briefs-a-quick-summary.pdf > accessed 5 November 2025.

a decade? Is this philosophy audible in relation to civil disobedience or democratic fatigue? Is it heard in relation to armed conflicts and nuclear deterrence?[5] Does it have anything substantial to contribute with regard to the various forms of international terrorism in which the end seemingly 'justifies' any means? What contributions can it make to strengthening human rights and international or transnational law?

Of course, good politics and active action cannot be replaced by legal philosophy. Moreover, to a certain extent, several contributions to the philosophy of law in recent decades appear to belong to a branch of philosophy which, when viewed in the light of day, could be alternatively described as a 'philosophy of lawyers', with content primarily tailored to their own specialist academic community.[6] Nevertheless, it is well known that every epoch, every turning point raises fundamental questions that have an impact on society, politics, philosophy and the philosophy of law. In this regard, important 20th century works on the concept of law by Lon Luvois Fuller, Herbert Lionel Adolphus Hart and Gustav Radbruch are just a few examples.[7] Could it not also be important for a present, and future, oriented philosophy of law to contribute more application-oriented analyses and concepts, that serve as normative orientation in the face of pressing challenges, aiming to feed these into (trans-)national, social, legislative and politically effective discourses?

As indicated above, there is no shortage of current questions and challenges for the philosophy of law. Against this background, this anthology is dedicated not least to promoting a discussion on whether and how the relevance of legal application and perhaps also the social and political impact of the contemporary philosophy of law could be strengthened with

---

5 For corresponding research approaches in the field of nuclear deterrence see, eg, *Ethics, Law and Nuclear Deterrence*, Oxford-Stanford project, < https://www.elac.ox.ac.uk/research/values-and-multilateralism-2/ > accessed 5 November 2025.

6 cf the critical characterization of this category by Hubert Rottleuthner, 'Juristen-philosophie' [1970] Kritische Justiz (KJ) 476.

7 Herbert Lionel Adolphus Hart, 'Positivism and the Separation of Law and Morals' (1958) Harvard Law Review, Vol. 71 No. 4, 593; Lon Luvois Fuller, 'Positivism and Fidelity to Law: A Reply to Professor Hart' (1958), Harvard Law Review, Vol. 71, No. 4 630; Gustav Radbruch, 'Gesetzliches Unrecht und übergesetzliches Recht', Süddeutsche Juristen-Zeitung 1 (1946) 105. English translation: G. Radbruch, 'Statutory Lawlessness and Supra-Statutory Law' (1946 / 2006), trans. Bonnie Litschewski Paulson and Stanley L. Paulson, Oxford Journal of Legal Studies (OJLS) Vol. 26, No. 1 1.

regard to national, international and in some cases existential challenges.[8] The anthology brings together international contributions that engage with the role of legal philosophy in the advancing yet crisis-ridden 21st century on various levels. It spans a wide range of topics, from fundamental reflections on the position and purpose of legal philosophy to rule of law, human rights, and environmental perspectives, and further to the concrete challenges posed by technological developments, inter- and transnational law, as well as aspects of legal education.

Three contributions in Section I, 'Legal Thought in Global and Critical Perspective', explore possible functions and positions of legal philosophy in the twenty-first century, each pursuing a distinct approach. Oche Onazi's contribution 'Re-imagining Disability Justice: African Legal Philosophy in a Global Context' uses the example of disability justice to illustrate the potential of African legal philosophy, often seen as a tool for preserving cultural traditions, for addressing the global challenges of our time. The essay argues for the relevance of African thought in shaping ethical and legal commitments worldwide, including the proposal of a global disability tax fund. In her article 'The Innocence of Crypto-Positivism: Dismantling Myths and Constructing Legal Fictions-Positivism', Leonor Suárez Llanos describes the limits and risks of a traditional and naive positivist legal thinking at a time when global realities are increasingly problematic. In terms of its coherence, she analyzes the conditions and key elements of a formalist normative theory of law, based on an analysis of the theory of knowledge and the possibilities of truth in legal knowledge and action. This contrasts with progressive approaches to egalitarian models and the protection of equality, which could also contribute to a change of perspective in contemporary legal philosophy. Her proposal focuses on research in terms of coherence and conceptual and dynamic retrointegration. In his contribution 'Taking Stock: Philosophy of Law in the Age of the "Great Regression"', Eckardt Buchholz-Schuster examines how the crises of the

8 For preliminary considerations in this direction, see Eckardt Buchholz-Schuster, 'Rechtsphilosophische Horizonte und die Globalisierung'; in: Bärbel Frischmann / Christian Holtorf (eds), *Über den Horizont. Standorte, Grenzen und Perspektiven* (De Gruther Oldenbourg 2019) 191; Eckardt Buchholz-Schuster, *Extreme Wrong Committed by National and Supranational Inactivity: Analyzing the Mediterranean Migrant Crisis and Climate Change from a Legal Philosophical Perspective / Extremes Unrecht durch national- und überstaatliches Unterlassen: Eine Analyse der Migrantenkrise im Mittelmeer und des Klimawandels aus rechtsphilosophischer Perspektive* (2nd edn, Berliner Wissenschaftsverlag 2023).

2020s, such as threats to democracy, human rights, international law, and planetary health, create new tasks for an applied legal philosophy. This affects both substantive issues, such as the legal-ethical assessment of state inaction and civil disobedience, and methodological challenges in decision-making and argumentation theory. At the same time, it advocates for a practice-oriented approach to legal philosophy that focuses on legal, but also social and political relevance.

Section II is devoted to the principles of 'Legality and the Rule of Law'. Adela Gąsiorowska's contribution 'Legality vs. Extreme Injustice by Omission. Normative-Legal Aspects of Local Authorities' Disobedience' addresses, in the context of migration, a normative conflict that may become increasingly characteristic of democratic societies in the twenty-first century. Drawing on an empirical assessment, Radbruch's formula, and considerations of civil disobedience, she develops differentiated normative analyses and conceptual approaches, sketching their possible implications at the level of local authorities. John Murungi, in his contribution 'Thinking about Law and its Rule at our Time', adopts a postcolonial perspective within his philosophical analysis of the conventional understanding of the rule of law. From this point of view, shaping the world in the postcolonial era requires a new understanding of law and its rule, a new metaphysics situated beyond both the Leibnizian focus on external relations and the fixation on legal actors.

Three authors in Section III engage from different perspectives with the overarching theme 'Human Rights and Social Contexts'. Hyungjoon Jun, in 'Universal Human Rights and the Ethics of Cultural Diversity. Toward an Intercultural Legitimacy of Human Rights', expands the understanding of justice in culturally pluralistic societies by systematically integrating insights from procedural, psychological, and substantive approaches. He ultimately argues for a practice of justification that is both institutionally grounded and aimed at intercultural validity, one that embraces cultural diversity as enriching while resisting relativism. Hyun Jung Lee's contribution, 'Reconsidering Age Discrimination: Intersectional, Contextual, and Comparative Perspectives' offers a critical analysis of relevant cases from the European Court of Human Rights. Drawing, amongst other examples, on the jurisprudence of the South African Constitutional Court and the Inter-American Court of Human Rights, she formulates proposals for a more effective protection of age-related rights within the European human rights system. In his contribution 'The Significance of Legal Philosophy for German Social Law,' Daniel Herbe explores the special position of social law within the German legal system as the framework governing the relationship between citizens and the social state throughout life. By analyzing the constitution-immanent 'social constitution' and its grounding in values such as human dignity, autonomy, and equality, he develops the foundations for a legal-philosophically informed approach to social policy within the liberal-democratic order.

Section IV, 'Environmental and Technological Challenges', begins with Heidi M. Hurd's 'Competing Conceptions of Sustainability'. According to her analysis, both 'weak' utilitarian and 'strong' deontological theories of sustainability lack sufficient legitimating force when it comes to the protection of the global environment. Thus, moral and legal philosophy continue to face a profound challenge in this domain. How can or should the law respond to the far-reaching transformations brought about by the A.I. revolution? Within this thematic field, Jordan Pascoe's contribution 'A Relational Approach to Regulating A.I.: Lessons from Environmental Law' explores this question through a comparative and relational lens. Her essay argues that A.I. is rapidly transforming society in ways that current regulations fail to address, posing risks to jobs, access to services, and social equity. It proposes using environmental law, especially invasive species management, as a model for developing relational, ecosystem-based approaches to A.I. regulation.

Two further contributions comprise Section V on the topic of 'International and Transnational Law'. In his contribution 'Universal Jurisdiction in the Absence of a World State: The Legitimacy of International Criminal Law', Win-chiat Lee outlines a philosophical basis for the legitimacy of international criminal law (ICL) and its universal jurisdiction. He points out that ICL's claim to prevent impunity for atrocities in the interests of justice could be limited if it fails to fully systematize and standardize the exercise of universal jurisdiction. In her contribution, Veronica Rodriguez-Blanco outlines a concept that is particularly relevant in an age of globalization that threatens to get out of hand: 'What Makes a Transnational Rule of Law? Understanding the Logos and Values of Human Action in Transnational Law'. Her chapter analyzes the nature of the 'structure' of a transnational rule of law and reflects, not least, the moral concern for protecting citizens at a transnational level from the arbitrariness of other people.

Section VI finally turns to legal philosophical aspects of 'Legal and Judicial Training'. Juan Pablo Sterling Casas' article 'Communicational Theory of Law and Legal Text: An Interdisciplinary Approach for Legal Education', argues that legal education should place linguistic and textual analysis at its core, recognizing legal order as a complex network of texts. Consequently, it proposes an analytical-hermeneutic and narratological approach to teaching law. Derk Venema presents an exemplary concept from the Netherlands that focuses on ethical dilemmas in his contribution on the 'Philosophy of Law in Professional Ethics Training for Judges'. Ethical 'correctness' appears in this concept as a pragmatic category rather than an objectively calculable or measurable fact.

Such an anthology is always the result of successful collaboration. First and foremost, we would like to thank all of the authors involved for their contributions to this anthology project. The submitted articles have impressed us not only individually but also as a whole, both in terms of their thematic and perspectival diversity and their high potential for application within and beyond the legal community. The manifold challenges facing today's world and legal philosophy that are addressed in the contributions are also reflected in the foreword by Prof. Dr. Stephan Kirste, for which we are very grateful. We would also like to thank Prof. Dr. Johannes Rux and Ms. Anja Reuter from Nomos Verlag for their valuable guidance and assistance in this project. Furthermore, we would like to express our gratitude to Coburg University of Applied Sciences and Arts, especially to the Dean of the Faculty of Social Work, Prof. Dr. Claudia Lohrenscheit, and the Vice President for Research, Prof. Dr. Martin Synold, for their support of this publication. Last but not least, we are also very grateful to our faculty colleague Prof. Dr. Veronika Hammer, who shared her valuable experience with anthology projects.

In conclusion, we hope that this anthology will stimulate further discourse on the role of an applied legal philosophy and future research collaborations on the topics covered here and related areas. It is our firm conviction that an applied legal philosophy can provide substantial guidance in the face of the manifold challenges of our time and enrich the chorus of voices that advocate for respect for human dignity, planetary health, and international law in the 21st century.

Bamberg / Coburg, November 2025

Eckardt Buchholz-Schuster / Daniel Herbe

I.
Legal Thought in Global and Critical Perspective

Re-imagining Disability Justice: African Legal Philosophy in a Global Context

Oche Onazi[*]

Abstract

African legal philosophy is presumed to be primarily relevant in the context of globalisation for reviving and preserving African cultural traditions, beliefs, and practices, preventing their erosion by global forces. However, its potential to address contemporary global challenges — including legal, political, economic, and social justice issues — remains underexplored. This chapter examines the problem of disability justice through the lens of African legal philosophy, examining how it is relevant to this domain. Building on my previous work, I will argue that African legal philosophy potentially offers a relational conception of disability justice, essential for prioritising much needed but frequently neglected obligations toward people with disabilities. Originally proposed to inspire a new culture of public obligations within African states, this chapter explores the possibility of extending these proposals to the global scale by considering the feasibility of a global hypothecated disability tax fund to support disability justice. By situating African legal philosophy within this domain, the chapter underscores the importance of obligation-based frameworks in reshaping and enriching the broader global conversation on disability justice. In doing so, it makes a case for the relevance of African legal philosophy to diverse audiences by offering a new perspective on how ethical and legal commitments to people with disabilities can be meaningfully upheld on a global scale.

1. Introduction

Given its recent history, along with prevailing prejudices and scepticism about its very existence, the literature on African legal philosophy (itself a much-contested concept) — though still emerging and relatively sparse — has largely focused on foundational questions regarding its existence, iden-

* Senior Lecturer in Law, Division of Law and Philosophy, University of Stirling, UK.

tity, nature, and meaning. This focus often takes precedence over examining its relevance to both historical and contemporary challenges, especially legal, political, economic, and social problems of global significance. The recent and evolutionary nature of the discipline may explain why African legal philosophy is skewed towards foundational questions. Nevertheless, it can be argued that foundational questions are not simply a preliminary issue but central to any legal philosophy or philosophical tradition. There can never be a time when such foundational questions about the nature of law and legal institutions seize to be important, especially considering the changing conditions or developments of law in contemporary societies.

Grounded in African philosophy, much of the existing literature emphasises the existence of African law prior to colonialism and its postcolonial transformation. This body of work largely emerges as a reaction to the profound disruptions caused by colonialism, which redefined nearly all aspects of African societies. Colonial rule imposed foreign legal frameworks, relegating African laws — deeply intertwined in local traditions — to a secondary status. In response, African legal philosophy has frequently adopted an introspective approach, aiming to reclaim lost heritage and authenticity or address historical injustices. Much like colonialism, globalisation has provoked comparable concerns regarding the existence and evolution of African legal philosophy, prompting deeper introspection about its approach and trajectory. Although there is no consensus on whether globalisation represents a break from or a continuation of colonialism, both phenomena undoubtedly share significant similarities. Both processes have entailed a substantial transfer of laws, legal principles, institutions and technologies, catalysed by strong forces of unification or homogenisation. These transfers were (and still are) shaped by interrelated economic, political and cultural factors, aiming to establish the legal foundation for wealth extraction, commerce and investment, or to promote social transformation. While globalisation is sometimes seen as fostering pluralism rather than the homogenisation of law, the limited body of literature on African legal philosophy often portrays it as a threat to indigenous African cultural traditions, beliefs, and practices.[1] This introspective approach has meant

1 See, for example, Adeyemi Akinsola, 'Impact of Globalization on African Culture: The Nigerian Example', (2020) 1(2) *Journal of African Social Studies* 47; Artwell Nhemachena, Tapiwa Warikandwa and Samuel Amoo, *Social and Legal Theory in the Age of Decoloniality: (Re-)Envisioning Pan-African Jurisprudence in the 21st Century* (Langaa Research and Publishing Common Initiative Group 2018); Bonny Ibhawoh,

that African legal philosophy is rarely recognised as a valuable contributor to the broader field of legal philosophy or to global problems. However, embracing a more globally engaged approach, as this chapter aims to demonstrate, is crucial not only for fostering an inclusive and intellectually diverse discipline of legal philosophy,[2] but also for advancing a fundamental African philosophical precept on a global stage: The importance of rendering obligations to others.

The broad aim of this chapter is to demonstrate how African legal philosophy can offer unique perspectives and solutions to critical global challenges across legal, political, economic, and social spheres. Specifically, I focus on the issue of disability justice, examining how African legal philosophy is relevant to this domain. Building on my previous work[3], I will argue that African legal philosophy potentially offers a relational conception of disability justice, essential for prioritising much needed but frequently neglected obligations toward people with disabilities. Originally developed to cultivate a new culture of public obligation to people with disabilities within African states, this chapter examines the potential for extending these proposals to a global scale. The chapter revisits my previous work on taxation as a practical mechanism for discharging obligations to people with disabilities, exploring whether this approach could facilitate the creation of a global hypothecated disability tax fund dedicated to disability justice. This fund could facilitate investments in poverty alleviation, accessibility infrastructure, assistive technologies, healthcare services, and education and employment opportunities, ensuring sustained global support for people with disabilities. By situating African legal philosophy within

'Historical Globalization and Colonial Legal Culture: African Assessors, Customary Law, and Criminal Justice in British Africa' (2009) 4(3) *Journal of Global History* 429; Jacques Vanderlinden, 'What Kind of Law Making in a Global World? The Case of Africa' (2007) 67 (4) *Louisiana Law Review*.

2 For a similar question about legal theory, see William Twining, *Globalisation and Legal Theory* (Cambridge University Press 2000).

3 Oche Onazi, 'Duties of Persons with Disabilities under the African Disability Rights Protocol: A Sceptical Argument' (2025) 25(2) *Human Rights Law Review* 1; Oche Onazi, 'Decolonising Disability Studies: Conceptualising Disability Justice from an African Relational Community Ideal' in Karen Soldadic and Robel Afeworki (eds), *Disability Intersectional Colonialities: Embodied Colonial Violence and Practices of Resistance at the Axis of Disability, Race, Indigeneity, Class, and Gender* (Routledge, 2024); Oche Onazi, 'What Obligations should be owed to [African] People with Disabilities' (2022) 18(1&2) *Review of Disability Studies: An International Journal* 1; Oche Onazi, *An African Path to Disability Justice: Community, Relationships and Obligations* (Springer 2020).

this domain, the chapter underscores the importance of obligation-based frameworks in reshaping and enriching the broader global conversation on disability justice. In doing so, it not only highlights the relevance of African legal philosophy to diverse audiences but also offers a new perspective on how ethical and legal commitments to people with disabilities can be meaningfully upheld on a global scale.

In the following section, I examine the intersections of globalisation, global justice, and disability justice, outlining the key contours of the debate and tracing how people with disabilities have been represented, or overlooked within this discourse. Drawing on African legal philosophy, I then develop a normative foundation for a relational approach to disability justice in the subsequent section. Building on this conceptual grounding, I advance the proposal for a global hypothecated disability tax fund as a practical manifestation of collective obligation and global solidarity next. This chapter concludes by summarising and reflecting on the implications of this proposal for disability justice.

2. Globalisation, Global Justice and Disability Justice

Despite recent global developments such as the Covid-19 pandemic, the rise in trade wars and the prioritisation of national interests indicating a potential retreat from globalisation, it remains a defining feature of modern international relations. Globalisation encapsulates the processes that create and sustain a unified global economy, an interconnected ecological system, and a global communication network, albeit one that does not equally penetrate all regions.[4] While globalisation has deep historical roots, its acceleration and complexity have significantly increased since the Second World War, interweaving economic, cultural and technological dimensions. Though earlier instances of globalisation predate the emergence of the nation-state, the scale and speed of these processes in contemporary times are unprecedented, transforming the ways people and societies interact. Often described as the shrinking of time and space,[5] globalisation has altered perceptions of distance, bringing disparate parts of the world into close interaction. Technological innovations, the movement of goods, ideas, and

4 William Twining, 'Globalisation and Legal Theory: Some Local Implications' (1996) 49(1) *Current Legal Problems* 1, 3.

5 David Harvey, *The Condition of Postmodernity: An Inquiry into the Origins of Cultural Change* (Wiley-Blackwell 1991).

(to a lesser extent) people, and advances in communication have made the world feel smaller, fostering deeper global connections.

The complex processes of globalisation have transcended geographical boundaries, borders and jurisdictions, enabling transnational relations and actions that extend beyond the sovereignty of nation-states. This interconnectedness has intensified global social relations, linking local events to broader global dynamics in profound and transformative ways.[6] Globalisation processes have increasingly interconnected the world, fostering interdependence among nations. However, this has not led to progression toward a singular world government or the dissolution of nation-states.[7] While globalisation trends have leaned toward centralisation or homogenisation, there has been a notable revival of smaller forms of nationalism and a renewed emphasis on local identities.[8]

Globalisation's impact has been undeniably twofold. On the one hand, it has accelerated global connectivity, facilitating trade, cultural exchange, and technological advancements; on the other, it has brought challenges such as the unequal distribution of benefits, poverty and the erosion of local identities, thus generating debates about the need for a fair global economic and political order[9]. Significantly, globalisation has disproportionately benefited wealthier nations — typically Western countries — and their transnational corporations (TNCs), often at the expense of nations in the global south, especially the more vulnerable communities amongst them. TNCs, as primary agents and major beneficiaries of globalisation, are frequently accused of exploiting low-wage labour markets in the global south while disproportionately retaining profits in the global north, thereby intensifying global inequality. Countries in the global south are predominantly seen as raw material suppliers, yet the unfair terms of international trade prevent them from achieving equitable exchanges. Moreover, access to the opportunities presented by globalisation has strikingly been uneven. Limited access to technology, education and infrastructure has left many populations unable to compete effectively, or fully participate exacerbating existing disparities.

In the field of political philosophy, and to a lesser extent legal philosophy, considerable literature has emerged in response to the challenges and inequities stemming from globalisation. This body of work has sought to

6 Twining (n 4).
7 Ibid.
8 Ibid.
9 Joseph Stiglitz, *Globalization and its Discontents* (Penguin 2002).

address the uneven distribution of resources and opportunities as well as the systemic issues globalisation presents, while exploring frameworks for envisioning how justice might be achieved in an increasingly unequal and interconnected world. Literature on global justice not only aims to provide analytical tools for clarifying and addressing the challenges posed by globalisation, but also to investigate the duties individuals owe to one another beyond national borders.[10] It examines the foundations of these obligations, probing their moral and philosophical underpinnings.[11] At its core, this field applies moral, legal and political philosophy to the global scale, shedding light on critical issues and potential injustices that transcend territorial boundaries.

The literature is dominated by two perspectives on whether global justice is achievable within the complexities of globalisation. Cosmopolitans[12] argue that globalisation fosters a global society where justice is realised through human rights and cooperation, prioritising individuals over local affiliations.[13] Communitarians,[14] nationalists and statists,[15] however, critique this view, emphasising the importance of national and communal identities. They contend that justice is grounded in political communities with shared traditions, not in an abstract global society. Garcia[16] offers an alternative that bridges the divide between cosmopolitanism and commu-

10 Kok-Chor Tan, *What is this thing called Global Justice* (Routledge 2017) 1, 2, 3; Mathias Risse, 'What We Owe to the Global Poor,' (2005) 9 *The Journal of Ethics* 81.

11 Tan (n 9).

12 Thomas Pogge and Darrel Moellendorf (eds), *Global Justice: Seminar Essays* (Paragon House 2008); Charles Beitz, 'Cosmopolitanism and Global Justice' (2005) 9(1/2) *The Journal of Ethics*; Thomas Pogge (ed), *Global Justice* (Blackwell Publishing 2004); Darrel Moellendorf, *Cosmopolitan Justice* (Westview Press 2002); Gillian Brock, *Cosmopolitanism: A Cosmopolitan Account* (Oxford University Press 2009); Martha Nussbaum, *Frontiers of Justice: Disability, Nationality, Species Membership* (Harvard University Press 2006); A Sen, *The Idea of Justice* (Penguin Press 2010).

13 Frank Garcia, 'Between Cosmopolis and Community: Globalisation and the Emerging Basis for Global Justice' (2013) 46 (1) *NYU Journal of International Law and Politics*, 1, 7.

14 Michael Walzer, *Spheres of Justice: A Defense of Pluralism and Equality* (Basic Books 1983).

15 David Miller, 'The Ethical significance of Nationality' (1988) 98 *Ethics* 647; David Miller *On Nationality* (Calderon Press 1995); David Miller, 'In Defense of Nationality' (1993) 10 (1) *Journal of Applied Philosophy* 3; David Miller, 'Cosmopolitanism: A Critique' (2002) 5(3) *Critical Review of International Social and Political Philosophy* 80; David Miller, National Responsibility and Global Justice (Oxford University Press 2007).

16 Garcia (n 13).

nitarianism, asserting that globalisation cultivates relationships that can support justice at a global scale. He argues that while it does not create a fully realised global community, it facilitates interconnectedness and shared awareness, fostering the conditions for global justice. Drawing on Rawls' idea of the circumstances of justice,[17] Garcia highlights globalisation's capacity to generate solidarity through both mutual assistance and the potential to cause harm, thereby making global justice not only plausible but necessary.

Despite its significance, disability justice has often remained on the periphery of discussions on globalisation and global justice, often overshadowed by dominant concerns such as global poverty, economic inequality, global trade, war, migration, climate change and human rights. When disability is addressed, it is often in connection with these broader issues, particularly through the lens of human rights, following the adoption of the United Nations Convention on the Rights of Persons with Disabilities (CRPD). Alternatively, disability justice has appeared in efforts to expand the scope of leading classical theories of justice beyond the boundaries of the nation-state. In this context, disability justice is understood as an umbrella term for the diverse attempts to expand the scope of various theories of justice to include people with disabilities. Similar to the broader discourse on global justice, classical theories of justice – most notably the social contract – have undergone revisions to account for their initial omission of disability as a critical aspect of justice.[18] Among these revisions, Martha Nussbaum's capabilities approach stands out for effectively bridging the concerns of global justice and disability justice.[19] By focusing on enabling individuals to flourish and achieve a life of dignity, the capabilities approach shifts the framework of justice from the distribution of resources to what individuals are able to do and become.[20] Nussbaum's list of ten central capabilities

17 Ibid, 15.

18 See, for example, Mark Stein, *Distributive Justice and Disability: Utilitarianism against Egalitarianism* (Yale University Press 2006); Richard Arneson. 'Equality and Equality of Opportunity for Welfare' (1998) 56(1) *Philosophical Studies* 77; Elizabeth Anderson, 'What is the point of Equality?' (1999) 109 *Ethics* 287; Eva Kittay, *Love's Labor: Essays in Women, Equality and Dependency* (Routledge 1999); Jonathan Wolf, 'Fairness, Respect and the Egalitarian Ethos' 27 *Philosophy and Public Affairs* 97; Ronald Dworkin, 'What is Equality? Part 2: Equality of Resources' (1981) 10 *Philosophy and Public Affairs* 296.

19 Nussbaum (n 12) 76-78.

20 Ibid, 70.

provides a benchmark for assessing whether all individuals, including those with disabilities, have the opportunities to lead fulfilling lives.[21] Aligned with the cosmopolitan orientation of her work, Nussbaum supports global cooperation and policies aimed at addressing disparities in capabilities across nations.[22]

In one of the few works examining disability justice within the context of globalisation, Häyry and Vehmas[23] endorse approaches such as Nussbaum's capabilities approach as a justification for international aid to mitigate the negative impact of disability in the global south. They carefully avoid generalising the experiences of individuals, acknowledging that not all people with disabilities are necessarily worse off in their societies. Nonetheless, they argue that disability, together with ill-health, gender inequality, and poverty serves as a critical measure of justice in any society. Using the example of river-blindness – the second most common cause of blindness worldwide, particularly in Africa – they explore which theories of justice would support humanitarian aid to address both the physical and social factors that hinder daily functioning by this impairment.[24] They conclude that the outcome-oriented theories, specifically preference utilitarianism and the capabilities approach, are best positioned to establish a governmental duty to initiate and support aid programmes abroad addressing river-blindness. Relational feminists and communitarians while limiting the scope of their justice obligations to specific communities, would generally support altruistic, voluntary or solidarity-driven initiatives that extend across national borders.[25] Responsibility sensitive (or luck) egalitarians, though divided on cosmopolitan duties, endorse the welfare functions of the state and can often be persuaded to support global welfare programmes.[26] In contrast, Häyry and Vehmas identify libertarianism as the theory that fundamentally opposes government-led initiatives for disabled people globally.[27] While libertarianism does not explicitly object to voluntary or charitable efforts, such as corporate social responsibility (CSR),

21 Ingrid Robeyns, 'The Capabilities Approach in Practice' (2006) 14(3) *Journal of Political Philosophy* 351.

22 Martha Nussbaum, 'Beyond the Social Contract: Capabilities and Global Justice' (2004) 32(1) *Oxford Development Studies* 3.

23 Matti Häyry and Simo Vehmas, 'Disability as a Test of Justice in a Globalising World' (2015) 11(1) *Journal of Global Ethics* 90.

24 Ibid, 93-96.

25 Ibid.

26 Ibid, 97.

27 Ibid, 96-97.

it remains sceptical about state intervention in matters of justice, particularly disability justice. The authors highlight the significant problem that, although globalisation lacks a uniform ideological foundation, it has predominantly been shaped by libertarianism, raising concerns about whether the rights and needs of disabled people will be taken seriously. Ultimately, Häyry and Vehmas question the capacity of CSR or voluntary charitable initiatives to effectively address disability justice, citing their undemocratic and unpredictable nature as key limitations.

As mentioned in the previous paragraph, the adoption of the CRPD provides a lens through which to explore the relationship between disability justice and globalisation. The global disability rights activism that resulted in the CRPD, represents a positive facet of globalisation. Similarly, technological advancements, particularly in assistive devices, underscore the transformative potential of global innovation to enhance the lives of people with disabilities. Some have argued that the CRPD has been leveraged by disability rights movements in the global south to resist neoliberal economic policies associated with globalisation.[28] Many of these movements in the global south advocated for the CRPD, believing it would elevate the issue of disability within the international development agenda and influence efforts of organisations such as the International Labour Organisation (ILO), the World Bank and International Non-Governmental Organisations (INGOs). On a national level, the CRPD now serves as a form of "international moral authority",[29] empowering advocates to challenge and resist neoliberal economic policies that disadvantage disabled people. However, scepticism persists regarding the CRPD's ability to address the inequities inherent in globalisation, particularly as the weaking of the state – traditionally the primary duty-bearer of human rights – continues. Another concern lies in the CRPD's implicit neutrality regarding injustices that produce or cause impairments.[30] By conceptualising impairments as an inherent aspect of human diversity within the social model of disability,

28 Karen Soldadic and Helen Meekosha, 'Human Rights and the Global South: The Case of Disability' (2011) 32(8) *Third World Quarterly* 1383, 1385.

29 Ibid, 1386. These perspectives can be contrasted with the sceptical literature about the co-option of human rights by forces of globalisation, or too weak to challenge the neoliberal economic forces. For some important examples, see Samuel Moyn, *Not Enough: Human Rights in an Unequal World* (Belknap Press 2018) and Upendra Baxi, *The Future of Human Rights* (Oxford University Press 2008).

30 Julie Maybee, 'Em 'body' ment and Disability: on taking the 'Body' out of Em 'Body' ment' (2017) 48(3) *Journal of Social Philosophy* 297; Karen Soldatic and Shaun Grech, 'Transnationalising Disability Studies: Rights, Justice and Impairment' (2014) 34(2)

the CRPD not only refrains from addressing the systemic production of impairments but also limits its efficacy in tackling contemporary disability injustices, especially those prevalent in Africa and the global south.

Nevertheless, a common characteristic of theories of global justice and disability justice, including the capabilities approach – arguably the most inclusive perspective due to its openness to cross-cultural conceptualisations – is their near-exclusive reliance on Western cultural reference points, experiences, beliefs, perspectives, traditions and understandings about both disability and justice.[31] This reliance may stem from the derivative nature of these theories which often draw from classical accounts of justice. The literature demonstrates limited engagement with alternative experiences, belief, or intellectual traditions, particularly those from the global south, including the African philosophical tradition. There is limited effort to explore other conceptions of justice outside Western paradigms or to examine how these alternative views might influence conventional understandings of disability justice. While the core objective of global justice literature is to emphasise the obligations of affluent regions toward poorer ones, it would be inaccurate to claim that African and other global south perspectives are absent from the discourse.[32] Nonetheless, the literature remains dominated by a form of universalism that often portrays Africa as a region lacking agency, dependent on replicating Western legal and political institutions for its transformation.

Human-rights approaches face similar critiques, despite the potential of regional human rights frameworks to foster culturally diverse and sensitive practices in disability rights. The opportunity to enrich human-rights discourse with attractive and compelling African ethical and moral insights has largely been overlooked. While human-rights and anti-discrimination laws are undeniably important, equal attention must be given to how African ethical and moral values can contribute to advancing disability justice.[33] Although negative cultural perceptions and practices should right-

Disability Studies Quarterly; Michael Oliver, 'The Social Model of Disability: Thirty Years On' (2013) 28(7) *Disability and Society* 1024; Tom Shakespeare, *Disability Rights and Wrongs Revisited* (Routledge 2013).

31 Onazi *An African Path to Disability Justice* (n 3) 81.

32 Uchenna Okeja, *African Philosophy and Global Justice* (Routledge 2019); Katrin Flikschuh, 'Should African Thinkers Engage in the Global Justice Debate?' (2017) 46(1) *Philosophical Papers* 33; Odera Oruka, *Practical Philosophy: In Search of an Ethical Minimum* (East African Educational Publishers 1997).

33 Onazi, *An African Path to Disability Justice* (n 3) 11.

ly be challenged through human-rights mechanisms, the failure to engage with them from ethical and moral standards internal to Africans has left the cultural domain insufficiently unaddressed.

The criticisms outlined above may seem unwarranted, as disability and disability justice have historically been underexplored in African philosophy. It is reasonable to argue that Western philosophers are limited to engaging with forms of knowledge accessible to them. While much of the written scholarship on African philosophy remains unavailable to Western audiences – due in part to challenges like the digital divide – it is difficult to identify a comprehensive body of work within the African philosophical tradition that extensively addresses disability and disability justice. Nevertheless, a growing body of scholarship is beginning to explore disability from African philosophical perspectives. While some writers have started to address the challenges disability poses to traditional notions of community and personhood,[34] the field still remains underdeveloped. The current literature is still in its infancy, with only a limited range of perspectives available. There are no dedicated, nor a substantial body of articles or books, making it difficult to assert that a significant paradigm shift is underway. Against this backdrop, my research seeks to contribute to the growing body of literature by offering a distinct African legal philosophy of disability justice, grounded in the relational concept of community associated with a certain strand of African communitarian thought.[35] It examines the epistemic gaps surrounding disability and disability justice

34 Julie Maybee, 'Disability and African Philosophy' in Shelly Tremain (ed), *The Bloomsbury Guide to Philosophy of Disability* (Bloomsbury Academic, 2023); Edwin Etieyibo, 'African Metaphysics and Disability' (2022) 41(2) South African Journal of Philosophy 159; Nompumelelo Manzini, 'The Othering of Persons with Severe Cognitive Disabilities in Elvis Imafidon (ed), *Handbook of African Philosophy of Difference* (Springer 2020); Elvis Imafidon and Kenneth Abudu, 'Some Epistemological Issues in the Othering of Persons with Disabilities in Africa' in Elvis Imafidon (ed), *Handbook of African Philosophy of Difference* (Springer 2020); Nompumelelo Manzini, 'Menkiti's Normative Concept of Personhood as Gendered, Ableist and Anti-Queer' (2018) 37(1) *South African Journal of Philosophy* 18; Julie Maybee, Unmaking Disability: The Three-Body Approach (Rowman and Littlefield 2019); Julie Maybee, 'Philosophy, Disability and the Social Conception of the Self' in George Hull (ed), *Debating African Philosophy: Perspectives on Identity, Decolonial Ethics and Comparative Philosophy* (Routledge, 2019); Elvis Imafidon, *African Philosophy and the Otherness of Albinism: White Skin, Black Race* (Routledge 2019.).

35 Onazi, *An African Path to Disability Justice* (n 3); Onazi, 'Duties of Persons with Disabilities under the African Disability Rights Protocol: A Sceptical Argument' (n 3); Onazi, 'Decolonising Disability Studies: Conceptualising Disability Justice from

in African legal-philosophical discourse. In this regard, my work should be understood as a contribution to an emerging yet vital conversation in this area, providing a framework that establishes a foundation for further inquiry and development in the field. Before exploring how these ideas are relevant to global disability justice discourse, I first elaborate on African legal philosophy to establish the foundational principles underpinning the approach in my research.

3. African Legal Philosophy

By primarily defining itself as an extension of African philosophy, the emerging scholarship in African legal philosophy has largely focused on existential, identity and meaning-related questions. However, it has paid insufficient attention to its relevance in addressing historical and contemporary challenges across social, economic, political, and legal domains. African philosophy can be understood in two ways, depending on perspective. It may be seen as a reflective exercise rooted in the culture and belief of Africans "...which rigorously and critically explicate a life-world".[36] Alternatively, it can be regarded as a relatively recent academic or professional discipline, characterised by a nascent body of literature along with "...codes, standards, recognised practitioners, and customs".[37] These two definitions are not mutually exclusive, as the academic discipline often draws its insights from cultural reflections. In developing an African legal philosophy of disability justice, my approach has primarily relied on written texts in the English language. I have aimed to extrapolate philosophically compelling concepts from this body of work rather than claim to reflect the culture and beliefs of any specific African people or community. This approach allows me to avoid relative conclusions in favour of abstract and universal principles of disability justice.

A substantive portion of the emerging literature on African legal philosophy is introspective, focusing on the doctrinal aspects of African law and legal systems. This focus often comes at the expense of a universal

an African Relational Community Ideal' (n 3); Onazi, 'What Obligations should be owed to [African] People with Disabilities' (n 3).

36 Bruce Janz (2007) 'African Philosophy' in Constantin Boundas (ed), *The Edinburgh Companion to 20th Century Philosophies* (University of Edinburgh Press 2007) 690.

37 Ibid.

or general theory of justice.[38] While concepts of justice are not entirely absent from this literature, they are primarily examined within the context of particular ethnographic or anthropological studies on legal doctrines and laws specific to African states. For example, the studies on traditional or indigenous justice systems[39] demonstrates that justice is often oriented toward maintaining social harmony,[40] restoration,[41] reconciliation,[42] or community participation.[43] While this body of work holds relevance for the development of an African and universal theory of justice, its conclusions remain too specific to provide a comprehensive theory. Furthermore, these studies have not been systematically applied to the fundamental structure of society.[44] Although anthropological and doctrinal studies of African law cannot be completely discounted, their particularistic and relative nature limits their ability to contribute to the development of an abstract and universal concept of justice within the African context, let alone a global context.

A theory of justice grounded in a pluralist conception of African legal philosophy, while appealing for its reflection of the continent's cultural diversity and values, faces challenges in achieving abstraction, generality, or universalism. While legal pluralism offers a compelling descriptive frame-

38 Gordon Woodman, 'Legal Pluralism and the search for Justice' (1996) 40(2) *Journal of African Studies* 152.

39 Jacob Arowosegebe, 'Indigenous African Jurisprudential Thoughts on the Concept of Justice: A Reconstruction through Yoruba Proverbs' (2017) 61(2) *Journal of African Law* 155; Joseph Agbakoba and Eyinnaya Nwauche, 'African Conceptions of Justice, Responsibility and Punishment' (2006) 37(3) *Cambrian Law Review* 33; Tom Bennet et al (eds), *African Perspectives in Tradition and Justice* (Intersentia 2012).

40 Abiola Ayinla, 'African Philosophy of Law: A Critique' (2002) 6 *Journal of International and Comparative Law* 147.

41 Christian Gade, 'Restorative Justice and South African Truth and Reconciliation Process' (2013) 32(1) *South African Journal Philosophy* 10; Jare Oladosu, 'Choosing Legal Theory on Cultural Grounds: An African Case for Legal Positivism' (2001) 2(2) *West African Review.*

42 Phil Clark, The Gacaca Courts, Post-Genocide Justice and Reconciliation in Rwanda: Justice without Lawyers (Cambridge University Press 2011); Mark Sanders, *Ambiguities of Witnessing: Law and Literature in the time of a Truth Commission* (Stanford University Press 2007); Coel Kirkby, 'Rwanda's Gacaca Courts: A Preliminary Critique' (2006) 50(2) *Journal African Law* 94; Desmond Tutu, *No Future Without Forgiveness: a Personal Overview of South Africa's Truth and Reconciliation Commission* (Random House 1999).

43 Augustine Park, 'Community-Based Restorative Transitional Justice in Sierra Leone' (2010) 13(1) *Contemporary Justice Review* 95.

44 Woodman (n 38) 164-165.

work for understanding the complexity of African law and legal systems — making it a more nuanced alternative to legal positivist theories — it struggles to provide a normative account of law that adequately addresses the concept of justice. Its scope remains largely confined to specific legal orders or domains, limiting its capacity to propose a universal conception of justice. This issue is pronounced in the African legal pluralism literature[45], but is also evident in general discussions on the subject. A key justice-related issue concerns how legal pluralism navigates conflicts between distinct legal orders, each governed by its own norms — some of which may be incompatible. Because every legal order asserts its own sources of authority, clashes inevitably arise when their underlying principles contradict one another. For example, tensions may emerge between international human rights law and state legal systems or when state laws conflict with customary legal practices. Such disputes often reveal power imbalances between legal orders, as well as their differing capacities to assert authority over specific issues and populations.[46]

The ability to resolve these conflicts depends on the particular conception of legal pluralism being applied. Weak legal pluralism posits that such disputes can be addressed through an overarching principle or dominant framework such as the repugnancy doctrine in African customary law, international human rights law, state legal systems, or mechanisms like the margin of appreciation, subsidiarity, and proportionality in European Union law.[47] By contrast, strong or radical interpretations of legal pluralism[48] pose greater challenges for conflict resolution, rejecting reliance on any meta-principle or external mechanism to mediate disputes.[49] Tamanaha's non-essentialist legal pluralism illustrates this tension by rejecting hierarchical prioritisation among legal systems or legal orders. Instead of presuming the normative value or effectiveness of any specific legal order,

45 Berihun Gebeye, 'Legal theory in Africa: between Legal Centralism and Legal Pluralism' (2017) *Queen Mary Law Journal* 37; William Oke, 'Multiculturalism, Legal Pluralism and the Separability Thesis: a Postmodern Critique of 'An African Case for Legal Pluralism' (2008) 2 *Law, Social Justice and Global Development*; Werner Menski, *Comparative Law in a Global Context: the Legal Systems of Asia and Africa* (Cambridge University Press 2006).

46 Brian Tamanaha, 'Understanding Legal Pluralism: Past to Present, Local to Global' (2008) 30 *Sydney Law Review* 375.

47 Sionaidh Douglas-Scott, *Law After Modernity* (Hart Publishing 2013) 123.

48 Onazi, *An African Path to Disability Justice* (n 3).

49 Douglas-Scott (n 47) 123.

this approach treats all legal systems as equally valid and insists they be evaluated empirically and within context.[50] However, this strong view of legal pluralism introduces a critical limitation: It lacks a mechanism for resolving conflicts or establishing justice standards.[51] While weak legal pluralism appears more inclusive and mindful of justice, its primary shortcoming is the absence of an internal mechanism for resolving conflicts between legal orders. Conflict resolution mechanisms tend to be external to the weak legal pluralist framework, highlighting its limitations as a foundation for a universal model of disability justice. To avoid these shortcomings, I draw on the African relational conception of community in the next section, using it as a foundation to develop a legal philosophy of disability justice that offers a more comprehensive and ethically grounded approach.

3.1. An African Legal Philosophy of Disability Justice

Building on the previous section, I argue that African legal philosophy should be understood not merely as a reflection of the continent's pluralism and diversity, but as a critical framework for interrogating the normative foundations of law and justice. While recognising the distinct legal traditions across Africa – whether received laws, customary practices, or plural legal systems – is essential, African legal philosophy must go beyond mere description. Its strength lies in its ability to critically scrutinise legal principles, ensuring they align with the ethical and relational community values central to certain strands of African communitarian thought. Rather than serving as a categorisation of legal structures, African legal philosophy should function as a critical tool for shaping laws in ways that advance relational human dignity, collective well-being, and social justice.

John Murungi[52] makes a pivotal contribution to African legal philosophy, avoiding the limitations of customary and pluralist approaches, which, despite their descriptive appeal, introduce a form of heterogeneity that makes it difficult to establish a coherent conception of justice. This fragmentation makes it challenging to unify Africa's legal diversity while also ensuring uni-

50 Brian Tamanaha, 'A Non-Essentialist version of Legal Pluralism' (2000) *Journal of Law and Society* 318.

51 Douglas-Scott (n 47) 135.

52 John Murungi, *An Introduction to African Legal Philosophy* (Lexington Books 2013) 136.

versal applicability. Murungi differentiates African legal philosophy from broader studies of African law, framing it as a branch of African philosophy – one that cannot be properly understood without engaging with philosophy more broadly.[53] Drawing from the African humanistic tradition, he asserts that the core of African legal philosophy is the protection and preservation of human beings, a principle intrinsic to African morality, thought, and lived experience. To be human, he contends, is to be part of a community – "a community in which no human being lives at the expense of another human being, and in which no one human community lives at the expense of another human community".[54]

Murungi's conceptualisation of African legal philosophy closely aligns with his definition of African jurisprudence, which he views as an inquiry into the essence of being human, an aspect insufficiently addressed by leading jurisprudential figures, legal theorists and/or legal philosophers such as Austin, Hart, and Dworkin. This perspective also challenges longstanding prejudices, particularly the assertion that Africans lack legal consciousness, a claim that underscores the importance of African legal philosophy in reclaiming its own foundations. [55] Murungi argues,

> "Each path of jurisprudence represents an attempt by human beings to tell a story about being human. Unless one discounts the humanity of others, one must admit that one has something in common with all other human beings. To discount what one has in common with other human beings is to discount oneself as a human being. What is essential to law is what secures human beings in their being. The pursuit and the preservation of what is human and what is implicated in being human are what, in a particular understanding, is signified by African jurisprudence."[56]

From the passage above, there is a clear parallel between African jurisprudence and African legal philosophy in their inherently relational nature, both emphasising that human existence derives meaning from connections with others. Consequently, laws, legal concepts, and institutions must be designed to uphold and sustain this relational foundation, recognising that

53 Ibid, 7.

54 Ibid, 24.

55 Georg Hegel, *The Philosophy of History* (James Sibree tr, Dover Publications 1959) 93.

56 John Murungi, 'The Question of African Jurisprudence: Some Hermeneutic Reflections' in Kwasi Wiredu (ed), *A Companion to African Philosophy* (Blackwell Publishing Ltd 2004) 425.

individuals cannot be fully understood outside the context of relations with each other. Not only does this relational dimension shape the concept of law, but it also fundamentally defines the concept of justice. Murungi's work illustrates this by framing injustice as the antithesis of justice, which is closely linked to the concept of obligation. He defines injustice as the violation of the obligation to exist as a social being.[57] In his view, injustice is "primarily the negation of the personal responsibility to be a social being"[58]. Although Murungi does not explicitly address disability justice, he nonetheless connects his broader conception of justice to this framework in the foreword to my book. He articulates that disability justice

> "entails an obligation to what ought to be done to ensure that no member of the human community is cast out of the human community because of his or her disability… . Disability injustice knows no religious, ethnic, national, racial, class, gender, cultural boundaries or historical boundaries. It is thoroughly intersectional. It is palpable. It cannot be avoided."[59]

Murungi's conception of African legal philosophy shares a clear affinity with the arguments I have advanced in my work regarding the centrality of horizontal relationships and obligations in the African philosophical tradition. Unlike approaches grounded in customary law and legal pluralism, Murungi's framework offers a robust foundation for developing an account of disability justice centred on the relational community ideal. While community is often understood as a collective or group-based entity in the literature, in this context, it represents an ethical and relational ideal grounded in intrinsic and asymmetrical obligations among those who may or may not be its members. This relational perspective defines community not as an abstract metaphysical construct or an entity that supersedes individual existence, but as a dynamic web of connections between individuals, that is, connections that form its very essence.[60]

Drucilla Cornell similarly conceptualises this relational ideal as a type of ethical community. She asserts that "… it is inseparable from how we are both embedded in and supported by a community that is not outside

---

57 Ibid, 523.

58 Oche Onazi, 'Before Rights and Responsibilities: An African Ethos of Citizenship' in Oche Onazi (ed), *African Legal Theory and Contemporary Problems: Critical Essays* (Springer 2014) 166.

59 Onazi, *An African Path to Disability Justice* (n 3) ix.

60 Ibid, 17.

us, something 'over there,' but is inscribed in us".[61] Through the lens of the Southern African concept of Ubuntu, she further describes this as "an interactive ethic, or an ontic orientation in which who and how we can be as human beings is always shaped in our interaction with each other".[62] Thus, relationships are not only foundational to the concept of community but also the source of its ethical and moral significance. Individuals are intrinsically intertwined, bound by mutual obligations, and serve as extensions of one another, enriching the relational ideal at its core. Cornell's work is particularly significant for its articulation of the ontic dimensions of community, which distinguishes it from Western political communitarianism, where community is often conceived as a pre-given, hierarchical, or external entity. Crucially, she underscores Ubuntu's universal applicability, presenting it not merely as an indigenous tradition but as a fundamental ethical framework that transcends local, national, regional and cultural boundaries.[63] However, scholars in African philosophy remain divided on whether the field leans towards a universalist or particularist orientation. This ongoing tension is one I return to in the penultimate section, where I explore a persuasive approach to reconciling these perspectives.

In my work[64] I have proposed the African relational ideal of community – along with its associated ethical values of relationships and obligations – as a framework for assessing disability justice in different countries across Africa. As previously highlighted, my approach centres on the notion of community as the highest ethical value, aiming to understand how people with disabilities are embedded within the relationships and obligations that define it. Disability justice, in this view, is grounded in the African relational conception of community, understood as an intrinsic ethical and horizontal ideal that encompasses individuals both within and beyond its immediate membership. This relational community ideal provides a critical lens for evaluating whether people with disabilities are meaningfully included within the web of social and institutional relationships that shape diverse societies. Framed in this way, disability justice functions as a prism for identifying the environmental, social, and cultural barriers that hinder

61 Drucilla Cornell, *Law and Revolution in South Africa: Ubuntu, Dignity, and the Struggle for Constitutional Transformation* (Fordham University Press 2014) 161.

62 Drucilla Cornell and Karen Van Marle, 'Exploring 'Ubuntu': Tentative Reflections' (2005) 5 *African Human Rights Law Journal* 205.

63 Ibid, 125.

64 Onazi, *An African Path to Disability Justice* (n 3) 117-133; Onazi, 'Obligations to [African] People with Disabilities' (n 3) 11-14.

people with disabilities from fully participating in and experiencing community relationships.

Achieving disability justice necessitates a range of interventions, including structural changes to societal institutions to facilitate the inclusion of people with disabilities in communal life. These interventions span legal reforms such as the introduction of new anti-discrimination measures or the enforcement of existing protections, to broader efforts addressing societal attitudes, poverty, inaccessible infrastructure, and inadequate public transportation, all of which constitute barriers to community participation.

The scale of necessary interventions underscores the centrality of obligations, long regarded as fundamental to the African relational community ideal. Sharing community with others not only entails forming relationships but also fulfilling a set of ethical, reciprocal obligations as a condition of personhood and belonging. While obligations are often conceived as mutual and reciprocal, such definitions risk excluding people with disabilities. A more inclusive approach recognises obligations as asymmetrical, acknowledging the heterogeneous composition of communities, where individuals possess differing talents, abilities, and needs. Asymmetrical obligations are particularly attuned to the ways individuals support and rely on each other, especially in cases of illness, injury, disability, or age-related vulnerability[65]. This framework places greater responsibility on individuals capable of caregiving and fostering concern for their community's most vulnerable members, as it is premised on the fundamental ethical imperative to care for, assist, and relate to others.

Collectively, these principles serve as a foundation for evaluating, critiquing, and revising existing laws, policies, and institutional practices to enhance their inclusiveness for people with disabilities. As a result, the proposed approach to disability justice carries both contemporary and forward-looking dimensions; it provides a critical perspective for assessing whether current legal and policy structures embody the ethical ideals of community, relationships, and obligations, while also serving as a guiding principle for the design of future laws and institutions.

65 Ibid.

3.2. The Application: The Primacy of Obligations

While this approach primarily involves criticising, evaluating or reshaping existing laws, policies, practices, legal and political institutions — or creating new ones — it also emphasises the importance of prioritising obligations toward people with disabilities. This objective is grounded in the other-regarding nature of obligations within African communitarian philosophy. However, there is a significant gap in practical guidance on how to effectively translate this principle into action. Obligations underscore the importance of helping others or desisting from harming others, especially the most vulnerable, as a condition of community membership. Drawing on the influential work of African philosopher Kwame Gyekye, an obligation is "a caring attitude or conduct that one feels one ought to adopt with respect to the well-being of another person or other persons"[66]. Gyekye further categorises obligations into three key principles: The obligation to help others in distress,[67] the obligation to show concern for the needs and welfare of others,[68]and the obligation not to harm others.[69] Gyekye's perspective underscores that obligations are not supererogatory acts, they are not optional moral gestures but rather stringent duties.[70] African philosophy rejects the distinction between voluntary moral obligations and supererogatory acts, arguing that obligations carry an inherent moral weight, imposing sanctions or criticism on those who fail to assist individuals in need. Under this framework, factors such as limited capacity, practicality, social rules and individual rights of autonomy do not justify exemption from one's moral duty to support others. This strict and binding nature of obligations arises from a fundamentally compassionate or altruistic civic order, which seeks to orient all individuals, especially those with the capacity to do so, to care and show concern for vulnerable members of society.

To incorporate this perspective (and as outlined in the previous section), I have proposed an asymmetrical conception of obligations,[71] emphasising the inherently compassionate and caring foundations of African communi-

---

66 Kwame Gyekye, *Tradition and Modernity: Philosophical Reflections on the African Person* (Oxford University Press 1997) 66.
67 Ibid, 66.
68 Ibid.
69 Ibid.
70 Ibid, 71-72.
71 Onazi, *An African Path to Disability Justice* (n 3) 128 - 133.

tarian morality. This approach recognises that obligations should extend to all individuals, regardless of their ability to reciprocate, thereby fostering inclusiveness and equality. Tangwa's[72] work on the Nso people of Cameroon exemplifies this inclusive view by defining personhood in a way that values all human beings equally, without a rigid criteria or capabilities for reciprocity. This perspective ensures that obligations are extended to everyone, including those with disabilities, reinforcing the altruistic and moral foundations of African communitarian philosophy.

In the context of the modern African nation-state, taxation has been proposed as a means to extend these obligations to people with disabilities.[73] Traditionally, such obligations were deeply rooted in small scale traditional precolonial societies or kinship groups in contemporary African communities.[74] Given this historical context, it remains complex to determine how they could be effectively practiced across a broader more diverse population within African states. One proposal to address this complexity is the introduction of a hypothecated tax scheme[75] — a targeted fiscal mechanism that concretely expresses the obligations of people without disabilities toward those with disabilities.[76] Taxation, in this context, becomes a tool for institutionalising and systematising collective obligations, thereby enhancing the quality of life for people with disabilities.[77] A strong version of hypothecation is envisaged, in which income from a designated tax is exclusively allocated to national disability services. This approach aims not only to guarantee sustained funding for disability-related programmes but also to provide an ethical framework through which non-disabled citizens fulfil their social obligations to those with disabilities. By securing long-term financial support, sucha system promotesa vision of collective obligations, centred on the dignity and well-being of society's most vulnerable members. In countries without a national disability service, the creation of such an institution would be a concrete expression of these collective

72 Godfrey Tangwa, 'The Traditional African Perception of a Person: Some Implications for Bioethics' (2000) 30(5) *Hastings Center Report* 39.

73 Onazi, *An African Path to Disability Justice* (n 3) 153-158; Onazi 'Obligations Owed to [African] People with Disabilities' (n 3) 11-14.

74 Ibid, *An African Path to Disability Justice* (n 3) 5.

75 On the hypothecation of taxes, see J Barret, Democratic Discourse, Taxation and Hypothecation (2012) 89(14) *Journal of Australian Taxation* 89.

76 Onazi, 'Obligations Owed to [African] People with Disabilities' (n 3) 158-160.

77 Onazi, *An African Path to Disability Justice* (n 3) 160-162; Onazi, 'Duties of African Persons with Disabilities' (n 3) 17-20.

commitments — responsible for administering funds, conducting research, and shaping policy. In contexts where national disability services already exist (for example, national disability commissions), hypothecation can be used as an additional revenue stream.[78] More broadly, these services would oversee public infrastructure improvements, fund healthcare, education, housing, assistive devices, and welfare programmes, as well as provide financial support to families and caregivers. The section that follows explores how these proposals might be adapted to the global stage. The aim is not to present an exhaustive blueprint, but rather to outline foundational ideas around which future collective action might be organised.

3.3. A Global Hypothecated Disability Tax Fund

These proposals have naturally been suggested for application in African countries, where they can be expanded and adapted to align with local needs and contemporary realities. It could also be argued that such initiatives hold particular significance for people with disabilities in Africa, more so than in other regions, given the continent's comparatively lower economic standing in global comparative terms. Africa is home to a substantial portion of the world's poor, and deep poverty is disproportionately prevalent among disabled Africans compared to their non-disabled counterparts. As a result, Africa is arguably where such measures are most urgently needed.

However, the widespread poverty across the continent raises questions about the feasibility of implementing these proposals on a meaningful scale. The success of a hypothecated tax scheme depends on the economic stability of individual countries, rendering it unsuitable for the majority of economically disadvantaged African states. Even in relatively strong and stable African economies, hypothecated taxation may be unviable due to the predominance of informal economic activity, which constrains the tax base.[79] Furthermore, across Africa, taxation remains a weak institution, often vulnerable to mismanagement and corruption.[80]

While taxes on alcohol, sugar, fuel, natural resources, property or corporations could theoretically be leveraged to support disability-related assistance, such an approach may be inconsistent with the underlying

78 Onazi, 'Duties of African Persons with Disabilities (n 3) 24.
79 Ibid.
80 Onazi, 'Obligations Owed to [African] People with Disabilities' (n 3) 19-20.

philosophical principles that inform the proposal. African relational communitarian ethics emphasises non-supererogatory collective obligations, where all individuals who are able should contribute to the care and support those in need. Any consideration of alternative revenue streams must not overlook this fundamental element. Although obligations have an individualistic element, they are not merely disaggregated or optional duties. Instead, they function as collective obligations, requiring individuals to contribute to others and the broader well-being of society. This necessitates not only opportunities for individuals to fulfil their duties across different domains of life but also institutional structures that connect these obligations into a cohesive framework for collective welfare, particularly for the most vulnerable. As argued in the previous section, taxation is one of the most effective tools for transforming individual obligations into a unified social commitment. By designing tax structures that align with African relational community principles, societies can establish a formalised system of collective obligations, ensuring that care and support are not left solely to voluntary goodwill but integrated into a sustainable economic framework. Hypothecated taxation offers a mechanism to institutionalise asymmetrical obligations, creating a structured means through which individuals contribute according to their ability, reinforcing the ethical principles of relationality, community and shared obligations.

Although corruption and fiscal management present complex challenges that require robust participatory democratic and accountability structures, one potential approach to ensuring economic viability and long-term sustainability of the national hypothecated tax schemes is the establishment of a global hypothecated disability tax fund. A dedicated fund designed to support individuals worldwide could be justified (as I will elaborate below) by the emphasis on obligations to support people with disabilities, drawing on the arguments and justifications presented in the previous section. By pooling resources from affluent individuals and states, it could serve as a mechanism to address disability-related inequalities on a global scale. Such a fund could provide a range of support from accessibility infrastructure in Africa and the global south, assistive technologies and healthcare services to education and employment opportunities for people with disabilities.

A global hypothecated disability tax fund could be a transformative step toward dismantling systemic barriers and fostering the inclusion of people with disabilities worldwide. However, its justification and implementation present significant challenges. Prominent among them is the difficulty of scaling national hypothecated tax schemes to a global level. As noted, such obligations originate in small-scale, precolonial societies and remain partially embedded within kinship structures in contemporary African communities. If these practices are complex to implement across diverse populations within African states, the challenge is even greater on a global scale, where no centralised mechanism akin to a state exists. A potentially feasible approach to establishing a global hypothecated disability tax scheme could be through an international agreement, most likely a convention among states.[81] Each member-state would raise the tax through its national tax authority or, if necessary, establish a national hypothecated tax scheme to facilitate collection. States would then contribute an agreed percentage or amount to an international organisation or body responsible for distributing funds to national disability services and similar bodies supporting people with disabilities in states worldwide.

This international organisation would be open to membership from all states; however, only those that have signed and ratified the convention would be eligible to access its resources to support disabled people within their countries. This ensures commitment to the agreed principles and financial obligations underpinning the scheme. Meanwhile, poorer countries in Africa and the global south — where the prevalence of poverty among disabled people is higher — should retain a greater share of the funds raised, while more affluent nations should receive a smaller share to support their disabled populations. After all, recent trends in some Western countries, such as the United Kingdom,[82] indicate a decline in financial support for people with disabilities. While these disability benefit cuts may be driven by narrow economic priorities such as austerity or fiscal responsibility at the expense of societal obligations to disabled individuals, they highlight the financial pressures faced even by the most affluent nations, reinforcing the relevance of a global hypothecated disability tax fund.

81 For a similar idea but broadly related to the creation of a unified international tax system, see Gillian Brock, 'Taxation and Global Justice: Closing the Gap between Theory and Practice' (2008) 39(2) *Journal of Social Philosophy* 161, 175. For an alternative global tax model, see Jagdish Bhagwati, 'Taxing the Brain' (1976) 19(3) *Challenge* 34.

82 Kiran Stacey, Pippa Crerar and Jessica Elgot, 'Up to 1.2 million Disabled People Will Lose Thousands in UK Welfare Overhaul, Experts Warn' *The Guardian* (London, 18 March 2025) Up to 1.2m disabled people will lose thousands in UK welfare overhaul, experts warn | Welfare | The Guardian accessed 3 May 2025.

A global hypothecated disability tax fund can serve as a powerful mechanism for reinforcing national efforts by providing supplemental, predictable financing to under-resourced disability support programmes. It enhances global equality by redistributing resources from wealthier nations to those with limited tax bases, thereby promoting shared responsibility and solidarity. Moreover, its presence could incentivise national governments to establish or strengthen their own disability-specific funds, aligning domestic priorities with global norms of inclusion, accessibility, and obligation-based support. This approach on multiple scales ensures a more coherent and coordinated response to disability justice across jurisdictions.

There is no shortage of ideas or proposals — including emerging practices in global taxation — that may offer useful precedents for implementing a hypothecated disability tax fund on a global scale. Several existing models provide valuable insights. For instance, carbon taxes[83] have been successfully implemented in countries such as Sweden, Finland, Germany, the Netherlands, and Norway. Similarly, the air-ticket or solidarity tax,[84] introduced by former French President Jacques Chirac to support global health programmes under the auspices of the World Health Organization (WHO), has gained traction among 66 countries and several international organisations across the world.[85] An alternative approach to hypothecation could involve adapting the air-ticket or solidarity tax model to fund critical disability support initiatives in Africa and the global south. Much older adaptable proposals that have garnered support but remain unimplemented include the Tobin tax (currency transaction tax),[86] e-mail

83 The Carbon Tax Center Carbon Tax Center – Pricing carbon efficiently and e quitably accessed 3 May 2025; Zhong Zhang and Andrea Baranzin, 'What Do We Know About Carbon Taxes?: An Inquiry into Their Impacts On Competitiveness and Distribution of Income' (2003) 56 *Environmental Change, Vulnerability and Governance Series.*

84 Anna Segerstad, 'Airline Tickets Taxes: Innovation or Idiocy' (2006) 26(4) *Economic Affairs* 68; Frank Gardner, Jr., 'Globotaxes: Financing an Unfriendly Supranational Government by International Taxation without Representation' (2006) 2 *Yale Journal of International Affairs* 77.

85 Ministere De L'Europe Et Des Affaires Etrangeres, Innovative Financing For Development Innovative financing for development - Ministry for Europe and Foreign Aff airs accessed 3 May 2025.

86 Mahbub Ul Haq, Inge Kaul and Isabelle Grunberg (eds), *The Tobin Tax: Coping with Financial Volatility* (Oxford University Press 1996); James Tobin, *The New Economics, One Decade Older. The Eliot Janeway Lectures on Historical Economics in Honor of Joseph Schumpeter,1972* (Princeton University Press 1974).

taxes, world trade tax, international arms trade tax, aviation fuel tax, and taxes on luxury goods and consumption.[87]

Another proposal closely aligned with concerns about disability justice — given the high global incidence of poverty among disabled populations — is Thomas Pogge's Global Resources Dividend (GRD).[88] His model suggests a 1 per cent tax on the use or sale of resources worldwide, which could generate approximately $300 billion annually to alleviate global poverty. Although not explicitly designed for disability-related concerns, it signals the realm of possibilities for a global disability tax framework. Similarly, Gillian Brock's[89] work underscores that any global tax proposal must be preceded by radical reforms to the global tax system in order to achieve meaningful poverty alleviation. Brock does not fundamentally disagree with Pogge's justification for the GRD, particularly the claim that existing international arrangements are complicit in perpetuating global poverty.[90] Nevertheless, she argues that the failure to reform the international order prevents affluent nations from adequately fulfilling both positive and negative obligations toward poorer states.[91] Unlike Pogge, Brock prioritises the restructuring of global tax and accounting institutions including measures to increase transparency in oil transactions, prevent tax evasion, and curb manipulative pricing practices as a more pragmatic approach to addressing global poverty and, in parallel, the depletion of the global commons. More importantly, she seeks not only to assist the global poor but also to empower them to help themselves, fostering long-term economic sustainability and self-reliance. Brock further advocates the introduction of taxation on global public goods, such as peace and socio-political stability, which can be implemented through existing global tax initiatives. However, she is also open to the creation of a harmonised international tax regime — established by inter-governmental agreement and administered under an

87 For a good discussion of these proposals, see G Brock, 'Global Taxation' in Deen Chatterjee (ed) *Encyclopaedia of Global Justice* (Springer 2011) 443.

88 Thomas Pogge, *World Poverty and Human Rights: Cosmopolitan Responsibilities and Reforms* (Polity Press 2007) 202-220; Thomas Pogge, 'Eradicating Systematic Poverty: Brief for a Global Resources Dividend' (2001) 2 *Journal of Human Development* 59, 60.

89 Brock (n 81).

90 Pogge, 'Eradicating Systematic Poverty' (n 88) 67-68.

91 Ibid.

international tax organisation — to work alongside national tax authorities in coordinating efforts and allocating resources for poverty alleviation.[92]

Both Pogge and Brock rely on variations of cosmopolitanism to justify obligations toward the global poor, particularly in the global south. Pogge argues that Western and affluent countries —including their citizens — benefit from a deeply unjust international order. This system not only contributes to the impoverishment of populations in the global south but also undermines the ability of wealthier nations to fulfil both their positive obligations to assist poorer countries and their negative obligations to avoid perpetuating harm. By contrast, Brock grounds similar obligations in cosmopolitan principles aimed at ensuring that all individuals can meet their basic needs, safeguard their fundamental liberties, and establish the social and political structures necessary to support these objectives.

This emphasis on global obligations raises important questions when considered alongside African legal philosophical traditions. As a communitarian philosophy, it remains unclear whether and how it can substantiate duties beyond immediate communal boundaries. The existing African philosophy literature has not extensively explored its capacity to address obligations toward distant others. This tension is particularly significant in global justice debates, where obligations or duties often extend beyond localised relationships. A potential way to navigate this tension lies in the debate over whether African philosophy primarily prioritises partial obligations[93] — such as those owed to family and close-knit communities — or impartial obligations,[94] which extend to all human beings irrespective of special affiliation.

Thaddeus Metz offers a perspective that may help reconcile these concerns, arguing that African philosophy embraces both partial and impartial elements.[95] Rather than treating them as conflicting, he suggests they are

92 For a good discussion on the need for an international tax organisation, see Vito Tanzi,' Is There a Need for a World Tax Organization?' in Assaf Razin and Efraim Sadka (eds), *The Economics of Globalization: Policy Perspectives from Public Economics* (Cambridge University Press 1999).

93 Motsamai Molefe, 'An African Perspective on the Partiality and Impartiality Debate: Insights from Kwasi Wiredu's Moral Philosophy' (2017) 36(4) *South African Journal of Philosophy* 470; Motsamai Molefe, 'A Critique of Kwasi Wiredu's Humanism and Impartiality' (2016) 48 *Acta Academica* 108.

94 Kwasi Wiredu, *Cultural Universals and Particulars: An African Perspective* (Indiana University Press 1996) 237.

95 Thaddeus Metz, *A Relational Moral Theory: African Ethics in and Beyond the Continent* (Oxford University Press 2021) 117-119.

mutually reinforcing.[96] Metz's relational moral theory provides a framework for addressing this balance. He posits that dignity is conferred upon individuals based on their capacity for community, which is defined by their ability to foster friendly relationships or be befriended by others. Full moral status is granted to individuals who exhibit both traits, while those demonstrating only one element receive partial moral status. According to Metz, impartiality aligns with an individual's capacity to engage in communal relationships, as this ability is universal and inherent to all human beings. Partiality, on the other hand, pertains to actual communal or friendly relationships, which individuals have compelling reasons to preserve, enrich, and actively participate in. Metz insists that this perspective is best appreciated when partiality is not regarded as a non-moral consideration that conflicts with moral reasoning. Instead, he maintains that partiality and impartiality are two interconnected dimensions of morality, both stemming from his foundational principle of communality or friendliness. On one hand, the capacity to engage in communal or friendly relationships grants moral reason to interact with others; on the other, having established communal or friendly relationships with a particular individual creates additional moral grounds for sustaining and deepening those relationships.[97]

Metz offers a valuable framework for navigating the delicate balance between special obligations and duties to distant others. His approach helps address the tension between universality and particularity, a theme highlighted in Section 3.1. However, a key concern with his approach lies in its gradations of human dignity, which grant full moral status to individuals capable of being both subjects and objects of communal or friendly relationships, while assigning partial moral status to those who can only be objects of such relationships.[98] This distinction raises ethical concerns, particularly regarding certain categories of people with disabilities, who may fall into the latter classification. If their moral status is perceived as diminished due to their limited capacity for communal engagement, the theory risks undermining the principle of equal moral worth, potentially leading to unjust treatment or exclusion. In my work, I have sought to be more inclusive by engaging with Tangwa's non-essentialist conception of personhood, which is not only non-prescriptive but also more reflective of

96 For a different way of reconciling both concepts, see Motsamai Molefe, *Partiality and Impartiality in African Philosophy* (Lexington Books 2021).

97 Metz (n 95)106 – 109.

98 Ibid.

the asymmetrical, dependent dimensions of human nature, and the ethical obligations that arise from them. Combined with the relational community ideal — an expansive framework that extends beyond close-knit relationships — it effectively grounds far-reaching ethical commitments without positioning them in opposition to special and personal affiliations.

Nevertheless, Metz's argument shares similarities with prominent cosmopolitan perspectives, which seek to balance special obligations to loved ones, family and local communities with global obligations. Although critics argue that such views often fail to fully acknowledge the relational nature of human beings,[99] it should be emphasised that cosmopolitanism does not necessitate abandoning local obligations; rather, it provides a framework for integrating them into a global ethical structure. Nussbaum's seminal work[100] articulates this idea arguing that a cosmopolitan's preference for their local community is not based on its inherent superiority but rather on its practical effectiveness in advancing the common good.[101] She acknowledges that classical cosmopolitan theories often overlook this perspective, which, in her view, is addressed by her capabilities approach. Without necessarily endorsing the capabilities approach itself, the underlying strategy for reconciling particularistic and universal obligations may offer a valuable resource for African legal philosophy in navigating similar normative challenges.

4. Conclusion

This chapter has demonstrated that African legal philosophy provides a compelling foundation for advancing disability justice on a global scale. While the field has traditionally centred on questions of existence, identity, and meaning, this chapter has argued for a necessary shift toward its practical applications. Drawing on my earlier research, I have illustrated how African legal philosophy offers a moral and legal framework that demands

99 Anke Graness, 'Is the debate on 'Global Justice' a Global One? Some Considerations in View of Modern Philosophy in Africa' (2015) 11(1) *Journal of Global Ethics* 126; Mogobe Ramose, 'Transcending Cosmopolitanism' (2014) 59(3) *Diogenes* 30; Michael Eze (2017) 'I am Because You Are: Cosmopolitanism in the Age of Xenophobia' (2017) 46(1) *Philosophical Papers* 85.

100 Martha Nussbaum, *For Love of Country?* (Beacon Press, 2002) 135.

101 Others have described this as 'rooted cosmopolitanism', see Bruce Ackerman, 'Rooted Cosmopolitanism' (1994) 104 *Ethics* 516.

the prioritisation of obligations toward people with disabilities — an urgent and long-overlooked necessity.

More specifically, this chapter has proposed a hypothecated global tax scheme as a viable mechanism for recognising and fulfilling obligations to people with disabilities worldwide. Expanding upon my previous work where taxation was presented as a means for people without disabilities to discharge obligations toward those with disabilities in a domestic context, this chapter has extended the discussion to the global sphere. The aim has been to explore how individuals across the world can support people with disabilities beyond their own nation-states. In this sense, taxation provides the most effective institutional mechanism for translating the obligations central to African communitarian philosophy into meaningful collective global action. Taxation can serve as a structured mechanism for transforming individual and societal collective obligations into an actionable global initiative. It provides individuals with a practical means of supporting people with disabilities, ensuring their well-being and addressing their needs. More than just a financial tool, taxation functions as a bridge between individual moral obligations and collective global commitments. It offers a direct and substantive pathway through which citizens — particularly those without disabilities — can actively contribute to improving the lives of people with disabilities worldwide.

To operationalise this idea, I have proposed a global hypothecated disability tax fund to work in collaboration with national hypothecated tax frameworks to ensure the allocation of resources to support people with disabilities worldwide. While such proposals may be ambitious, they represent a crucial starting point for broader conversations and further research. By reimagining taxation as a mechanism for global disability justice, this chapter has sought to inspire deeper inquiry into how African legal philosophy can be harnessed to address pressing global challenges, ultimately fostering a more just and inclusive world.

The Innocence of Crypto-Positivism: Dismantling Myths and Constructing Legal Fictions

Leonor Suárez Llanos[*]

1. Introduction: the problems of cryptology applied to law.

What possibilities does cryptopositivism have for understanding and directing law? To answer this question, I analyse whether it is possible to preach "objectivity" and "neutrality" of a social object such as law and what we know about it, or whether it encourages the entrenchment of power in force, depoliticisation and anomie, uncertainty and indeterminacy. I propose a coherent and critical positivism that favours representation, recognition and redistribution.

Cryptology —kryptós hidden and *lógos* knowledge— is the science of the hidden and develops in the tension between the concealment of information and the possibility of making it accessible under certain conditions[1].

The technique of encrypting information —cryptography— rests on the interaction between message, encryption key, and context. The cryptography of law shapes the "legal system" (a sequence of sets that integrate different results for similar issues, but maintain their unity as long as the rules of identification of the parent system do not change[2]) just like any cryptographic order, encoding its meaning, protecting it through rules and making it accessible only to those who master its languages and procedures. This explains the asymmetry of positions between those who know the significant structures and those who do not. Derrida and Kittler highlight this

* Catedrática of Philosophy of Law. Full Professor. University of Oviedo.

1 That is why it is a tool at the service of military, political, religious or economic power. In fact, cryptographic techniques from ancient Egypt were used in the 20th century, for example, to build the Enigma encryption machine, patented in 1918 and used by the German army from 1926 onwards.

2 Carlos E. Alchourrón, Eugenio Bulygin. *Análisis Lógico y Derecho*. Centro de Estudios Constitucionales, Madrid, 1991, pp. 395-397.

by postulating that writing as the creation and transmission of knowledge always has a reserve of meaning that cannot be fully translated[3] .

In this work, I address formalist, logicist, and nomotechnically hierarchical and closed legal cryptography through cryptanalysis, which investigates the methods that can decipher these systems of concealment.

I refer to the formalist and self-sufficient core of legal positivism as "crypto-positivism", which turns law into a closed, specialised language that uses its own codes and ciphers under the pretext of order, clarity and security, although what it largely promotes is uncertainty, indeterminacy, anomie and voluntarism.

2. What is known about law and how it is known: from myth to legal positivist fiction.

The key to knowledge lies in the method used to "identify" the object and to "access" its understanding. This has always been the Trojan horse with regard to knowing what is perceived of reality (or as reality). From myths to the generative algorithmic formatting of artificial intelligence, a long and varied path has been travelled, especially with regard to social objects. A journey in which "imagination" has always been present as a tool at the service of fundamental knowledge: whether in the form of myths, universal

3 Linguistic encryption, and even more so that of legal language, is developed around rules that create reality and are understandable to those who handle the encryption keys, but not in depth to others, to whom they inform and order practices. Plato's *Phaedrus* emphasised that the symbolism of writing (here, of the norm) lacks truth in comparison with *logos (Phaedrus* 274b et seq.) but is constitutive of reality (and even more so if it is a legal norm). Derrida emphasises that the secondary or subsidiary nature of writing with respect to language is not true; writing "affects all meaning in general, it has always affected it, that is to say, since the beginning of the game"; *De la gramatología.* Siglo XXI Editores, 1998, pp. 11-12. "The archive keeps, reserves, saves, in a more than natural way, that is, by making the law (*nomos)* or enforcing the law. It is nomological", *A Freudian Impression.* Siglo XXI Editores, 1994, pp. 5-6. (Cf. Javier Pavez. "Jacques Derrida: sobrevivir en la traducción, *Fenomenología, firma, traducción [en torno a Jacques Derrida]*", Pólvora, Santiago de Chile, 2015, pp. 511-ff). And Kittler emphasises, in his poststructuralist critique, that the modern hermeneutic conception of meaning is a form of discipline that has already died; to insist on its paradigm is to pay homage to an understanding of language processing that prevents us from understanding that "writing, as the creation and transmission of knowledge, always contains a reserve, a part of meaning that cannot be fully translated", *Redes de Discurso 1800/1900,* Siglo XXI, 1999, pp. 103-104; see Naím Garnica. "Friedrich Kittler. Romanticismo, medios y técnica en la filosofía alemana", *Revista de Ciencias Sociales y Humanidades*, n. 43, 2020, pp. 67-78.

or particular rational logos, or in the most versatile forms of pure fictional recreation.

2.1. From Myth to Rational Logos.

The transition from myth to logos marks the birth of philosophy: reason replaces mythological narrative as a way of understanding reality. Logos abandons cosmological explanation, ushering in universal rationality, thanks also to the power of fiction.

Before logos, knowledge was transmitted through stories that linked the will of the gods with the origin of the world, natural phenomena, and social order. Homer's Iliad and Odyssey, Hesiod's Theogony and Works and Days are good examples of how social norms and human experiences were transmitted through mythical narratives that gave meaning to power, justice and order, transmitting values, hierarchies and moral and practical guidance to the community. These were culturally foundational narratives, fundamentally symbolic and not subject to critical analysis or rational systematisation.

From the 6th century BC onwards, in the Ionian colonies, the search began for rational principles (archai) linking the knower with the known object, thus displacing the mythical model. Thales of Miletus postulated water as the principle; Anaximander, the apeiron; Anaximenes, air; Heraclitus, becoming and the unity of opposites as a universal rational order; Parmenides, the immutability of being and logic as the path to true knowledge; the Pythagoreans, number and mathematical harmony as the foundation of the cosmos, etc.

In the 5th and 4th centuries BC, human reason unfolded in the ethical, political and legal spheres. Socrates, in the face of Sophist relativism, proposed rational dialogue and maieutics as the path to moral truth and universal justice. Plato sought the logos in pure Ideas, systematising knowledge and demanding that law reflect the rational order of the cosmos. He criticised Protagoras and Gorgias, who reduced truth to human consensus, while Sophocles, in Antigone, highlighted the tension between physis (nature) and nomos (human law). And Aristotle, in Nicomachean Ethics and Politics, consolidated the transition to logos by linking ethics, politics, and rational deliberation; for him, law reflects the rational nature of man and his life in community (zoon logon echon).

In short, the evolution from myth to logos establishes an epistemological and ethical parameter of interest for this work: law, as rational mediation, transforms human experience into comprehensible and socially valid knowledge. This conversion laid the foundations for modern science and positivist legal theory: since the 19th century, law has aspired to organise and legitimise its object through rational structures, objective norms and a logical, rational and closed system. The aim is to achieve an objective knowledge of law that is certain, clear, secure and as objective as the positive social facts it regulates.

However, the complexity of social objects and their link to power, interest, and the "will to truth" shows that it is difficult to separate rational explanation from imaginative narrative. The "legal fictions" of modern logos secularly replace the ancient myths of Olympus and the justice of Zeus.

2.2. From Logos to Positivist Fiction.

In the legal sphere, the transformation of knowledge—what and how it is known—raises questions about the nature of law (positive fact, ideas, formal or material norms, beliefs) and how the observer of law can understand it without their act of knowledge ly altering what they are trying to know (the Cartesian doubt that opens up philosophical modernity: how to theorise about an object without the object being constituted by its theory).

The modern solution to these difficulties has been sought in "fiction". The word "fiction" comes from the latin verb fingere, which means to knead, to shape, to form with art. This fictio does not refer to lies or to the current pretending or deceiving, or to falsehood, but to modelling, to simulating the truth (Cicero[4]) of what we know[5]. Kant proposes "heuristic fiction" as an epistemological resource, in contrast to Hume's scepticism of fiction, in order to introduce rational hypotheses that guide experience[6] and enable knowledge. For his part, Nietzsche, in Beyond Good and Evil

4 Cicero, *De Oratore*, II, 62.

5 Cf. Jorge Volpi. *La Invención de Todas las Cosas. Una Historia de la Ficción.* Alfaguara, 2024.

6 In *Crítica de la Razón Pura*, in "La disciplina de la Razón Pura frente a la Hipótesis" and "La disciplina de la razón respecto de sus demostraciones", Taurus, 2005, pp. 442-ff.

(§34), reminds us that the world is a fiction that we have forgotten is such, and in On Truth, that "truths are illusions that have been forgotten, metaphors that have become worn out and without sensible force, coins that have lost their stamp and are now considered not as coins but as metal"[7].

Abandoning mythological narration, as I pointed out, the logos of law resorts to various fictions to give itself meaning. Crypto-positivism arises when this operation is taken to the extreme, and epistemological fingere becomes (a) fingir close to deception through technical pretence. Legal fiction, codified in formalised and self-sufficient languages, conceals its artifice and presents itself as a logical necessity, so that what began as a tool for understanding becomes a mechanism of opacity, as the law appropriates it, not as a search for rationality, but as if it "truly" embodied legal rationality.

Representative legal fiction, Vaihinger pointed out, revolves around the "as if" principle, which supports fundamental hypotheses about concepts constructed by the "legal imagination", favours construction and operates even in the absence of an objective and verifiable basis[8]. Thus, the notion of a "legal person" is a fiction that allows, for example, non-human entities to be treated "as if" they were subjects of rights and obligations, and it clearly shows that "fictions are conscious and useful, and even when admitted to be false, indispensable to life and science"[9].

Vaihinger's "legal fiction" also served Kelsen ("Reflections on the Theory of Legal Fictions") and Fuller ("What is a Legal Fiction?"). And Alf Ross, who, in "Legal Fictions", agrees with Vaihinger on the necessity of "as if" fictions, but warns of something important for the critique of cryptopositivism: that legal fictions run the risk of becoming opaque mechanisms that conceal their constructive, ideological, self-interested and contingent nature, presenting themselves as if they were objective and necessary realities[10].

---

7 Friedrich Nietzsche. *Sobre la Verdad y Mentira en Sentido Extramoral*, Tecnos, 2012, p. 6, *see* p. 12.

8 And that is because "we think and act as if the world were what our fictions represent" Vaihinger, *The Philosophy of "As If"*, Routledge, 2021, p. 13.

9 *Ibid.*, p. 14.

10 Because "theoretical legal fiction glorifies the image of law as an eternal and immutable order of divine authority. It invests the institution of judicial authority with a sanctity that conceals the person and influence of the judge", *Ficciones Jurídicas*, Fontamara, Mexico, 2003, p. 124.

I have nothing against legal and political fictions, nor do I consider them detestable ontological entities. In fact, I believe that legal imagination[11] has given birth to brilliant, fabulous and persuasive fictions that organise and sustain our understanding of the legal world and are useful for understanding, justifying and articulating actions, omissions and beliefs. Democracy, the rule of law and the welfare state, European legalism, stare decisis, marriage, property, responsibility, and the positive formalisation of individual rights as triumphs and shields against others are some of these fictions.

But fictions can be brilliant and at the same time problematic, intertwined with the "crises of law" and modern politics[12]: crises of law, jurisdiction (voluntarism), parliament (self-interested and electioneering), and crises of determination, security and legal certainty.

Fictions, crises and the consequence of general legal indeterminacy and that of specific concepts in particular, which multiply the ideological possibilities of domination, lack of control and abandonment of the practical basis of legal submission and "subordination discrimination" (Barrere). But let's take it one step at a time.

3. Cryptopositivism: the "fictions" of "legal imagination".

In law, fictions have been created around two "major central fictions": natural law and legal positivism. What legal positivism has come to is that there is an objective, closed and positive body of rules and sanctions that make up the legal system, positive law. What is known about this law is a corresponding description of an objective positive fact that is added to the fiction that yes, it does exist. A fiction of such magnitude, of course, gives rise to multiple formalist, normativist, historicist, sociological and realist variants, etc. For its part, natural law, in its variants, successively refines its set of fictions: that there is the order of positive law and that of natural law or objective justice, its first two fictions, and that between the two, a third fiction, there is a necessary relationship. There are variations on this, such as the Kantian fiction that justice or natural law must be positivised in order to be law, a variant with which modern legal logos insists on the

11 An essential reference here is *La Imaginación Jurídica* by Jesús Ignacio Martínez, Dykinson, 1999.

12 *See* Gunther Teubner. "Das regulatorische trilemma zur diskussion um post-instrumentales rechts modelle. *Quaderni Fiorentini per la Storia del Pensiero Giurudico Moderno*, n. 13, 1984, pp. 125-126.

harmonisation of the positive and the evaluative, as Aristotle, Plato and Thomas Aquinas had sought to do.

For modern logos, the logical victory is positivist, for obvious reasons: what "is" law is what "is positively" law. In reality, the scientific emergence of the methodology of knowledge affected law in the same way as other disciplines, establishing shared foundations of true knowledge, certainty and deductive reasoning within the framework of closed and complete systems of knowledge of "positive facts". But in the development of its proposal, almost everything becomes complicated for legal positivism.

The scientific assumptions of the time led, on the one hand, to the objectification of positive law and the method for understanding it (which, as in any other physical discipline, would be the description of the positive fact). And, on the other hand and correlatively, to the technification of its positive experience. In this way, nineteenth-century legal positivism was perfected around the perfect nomotechnics of codification and the exegetical method in its application. In accordance with this paradigm, a rigid separation between facts and values was imposed, and axiology and emotionality in knowledge and decision-making were renounced. All this was the seed of a cryptopositivism centred on procedural formalism, radicalised around neutrality and logic and akin to an exclusionary, monochromatic positivism at the service of efficiency, authority, order and security.

However, far from avoiding voluntarism, cryptopositivism risks an epistemology and practical development that are difficult for the non-expert to understand, tending towards anomie and naivety and which, far from avoiding voluntarism and interest, turns "cryptopositivised law" into an effective instrument for legitimising and neutralising injustice.

Therefore, in the face of cryptopositivism as a paradigm of legal knowledge and decision-making, I propose a reconstruction of legal knowledge and practice centred on coherence and factual and axiological reality as the core of legal knowledge.

In doing so, I am not returning to naive forms of natural law nor am I ultimately appealing to extra-legal moral criteria. Furthermore, I am appalled by the proposal to replace reason with emotion. But what I do emphasise is that the methodology of formalisation, objectivity and naive and partial description renders invisible the emotional and interest-based components that underlie normative will and institutional dynamics, which prevents them from being controlled. To address this, I systematise the critiques of cryptopositivist fiction on three levels (subject, object and method).

3.1. The fiction of the subject of law.

The accusation that modern individuals, unique and universally rational, free and autonomous, are alienated is not new. Marx already developed the theory of the psychological and ideological alienation[13] of individuals and society who succumb to the deception of private property and capitalist labour.

The modern subject, unconscious and insensitive to their own misery, is lost between consumerism and the banal mythology of a media that feeds this alienation. Their downfall begins with the loss of a sense of value, which is reduced to the act of consumption.

Jameson successfully coined the postmodern expression "pastiche" to describe the existence of the individual in a society bombarded by infinite symbols and media messages that instil a normative meaning into the market, bureaucracy and the social process[14] and immerse them in hedonism, utilitarianism, pragmatism... all certainty is nullified, even utopia. A "nonentity", "a nobody" has been born, "who does nothing, because having a project requires a commitment to a certain continuity over time"[15].

If the death of God made possible the birth of the powerful modern individual, today pastiche explains his slow agony. The bourgeois and enlightened model that gave meaning to liberal individualism is now dead or dying as a myth that never existed.

This "nonentity" is the ideal subject of cryptopositivism. Because his emptiness makes him ubiquitous in every decision, and his discipline legitimises the institutionalisation of coercion and order regardless of any substantive, evaluative or justice considerations. That is why it is urgent to

---

13 The notion of the alienation of the individual had already been used by Hegel, who had such an influence on Marx, although Marx transformed the positive character of Hegelian alienation into a negative concept. For Hegel, what becomes alienated is the idea in the historical and dialectical process of Universal Reason. However, for Marx, what becomes alienated is the individual who, due to his capacity to transform nature by creating his own market products, surrenders to the demands of the capitalist market (cf. notably, Marx's *Economic* and *Philosophical Manuscripts* of 1844, and cf. in relation to Hegel and Marx's concept of alienation, *Razón y Revolución,* Altaya, 1994, specifically on Marx, pp. 117-118 and 268-ff., by Marcuse).

14 "(W)e are impressed, bombarded, connected, inspected and (potentially) dissected by electronic media: TV, VCR, telephone, fax and computer" (Jameson, 1991, 19). Fredric Jameson. *Postmodernism, or the Cultural Logic of Late Capitalism.* Duke University Press, Durham, 1991, p. 19.

15 Cf. Fredric Jameson. "Postmodernism and Consumer Society", *La Posmodernidad.* Kairós. Barcelona. Jameson, 2002, p. 178, *see* pp. 170-175.

give meaning to the individual on the basis of what is fair and right, giving a voice to the victims of the cultural, economic and religious power system.

3.2. The fiction of the object of law: validity, legitimacy and force.

The second notable crypto-positivist fiction refers to the constitution of its object.

When a positive object is concrete and of measurable and decipherable consistency in demonstrative terms, the descriptive method naturally emerges as an instrument for understanding the object. However, when the object is doubtful in different senses, it is not the object that identifies the method, but rather the methodology and its agent that "constitute" the object. t law is doubtful and diffuse as a social object that dynamically relates intentions, wills, facts, beliefs, power, force, subordination, etc.

That is why legal positivism seeks scientific deductive rigour in the analysis of the language that refers to all those diffuse positive events in the form that specifies the already legally valid rules. Since what is identified as such is valid, the normativity that is "imposed" is legitimised, regardless of its social preponderance or the causes of its compliance. Specifically, the positivist mindset impeccably neutralised the "power" of invasive factual interests, turning it into a key to the legitimisation of law and a condition of its positive validity. In this framework, the trio of Kant, Weber and Kelsen illustrates the constitutive relationship between power, domination, legitimacy and legal validity.

In effect, the perfect and complete nineteenth-century certainty sought by legal positivism was feigned (moulded) as a normalisation of the factual reality of "power" and in favour of the reciprocal legitimisation of the State and the law. The aforementioned trio constitutively intertwines the concepts of freedom, power, legitimacy, and legal validity around a speculative process thanks to which the validity of state law is linked to a factual and voluntaristic format of power with apparent good intentions and "legitimacy"[16].

Kant offers an axiological foundation for power, and Weber achieves the sociological and economic neutralisation of the fact of power. The legal formulation of this power according to positive law is addressed

16 I analysed this carefully in "`Poder´, ¿nada nuevo?: Indeterminación, analítica y falacias", *Estudios sobre el Poder*, Dykinson, Madrid, in press.

paradigmatically by Kelsen, who perfects Kant's universalist rationalisation and Weber's sociological rationalisation of power thanks to the logic of description and the "purification" of his theory in the face of political and axiological claims[17].

In Kelsen, the relationship between law and power points to the connection between validity (legal) and efficacy (power)[18]. A theoretical (gnoseological) problem "of the most important and difficult of a positivist theory of law"[19] for him, which shows that power constitutes its object, politics, in the same way that the subject who knows takes possession of the object of knowledge and, reciprocally, this object that is believed to be known determines who knows it[20].

Faced with this difficulty, Kelsen opts for a middle way between idealism (false because an ineffective legal system is not law) and realism (false because there are valid legal norms that are not effective[21]). But in doing so, I believe he falls into certain contradictions in his assumptions and conclusions[22] that affect the promised purity of the separation between Sein and Sollen and that, on occasions, lead him to describe the law that is "as it should be" and, in others, to adapting his theory to the voluntaristic reality of a static normative order, which compromises the claim to lead "knowledge to the ideal of all science: objectivity and accuracy"[23].

As a legal science that seeks to describe positive law accurately cannot present it as a normative system of contradictions, since a scientific approach must determine true solutions that exclude incorrect alternatives, Kelsen emphasises that the object of description is not the particular contents of the norms, but the norms in the formal way in which science recomposes them around logical and epistemological principles. A legal norm is valid not because it is accepted or has legitimate content, but

---

17 *See* Ulises Schmill Ordóñez, "El concepto de Derecho en las teorías de Weber y de Kelsen", in *El Otro Kelsen*, UNAM, México, 1989, p. 173.

18 Cf. Patricia Cuenca, "La relación entre el Derecho y el poder en la Teoría Pura del Derecho de H. Kelsen", en *Revista Telemática de Filosofía del Derecho*, n. 13, 2010, pp. 273-296.

19 Hans Kelsen, *Teoría Pura del Derecho*, Porrúa, Mexico City, 1993, p. 219.

20 Hans Kelsen, *Esencia y Valor de la Democracia*, Editora Nacional, 980, p. 133.

21 Enrique Bocardo, *Tres Ensayos sobre Kelsen*, Universidad de Sevilla, 1993, pp. 66-69.

22 Explores these contradictions, among others, by José Delgado Pinto, "El voluntarismo de Hans Kelsen", *Estudios de Filosofía del Derecho*, Tecnos, Madrid, 2006, pp. 142-144.

23 *Ibid.*, p. 7.

because it belongs to a legal system that is valid because it is effective, regardless of the reasons for its effectiveness[24].

Kelsen ends up distancing himself from the mundane nature of power with the Fundamental Norm which, being an act of thought by someone who understands the factual order of coercion as a positive legal system, is alien to the moral quality of norms and limits itself to instituting "a power to produce norms... the power of norms". The point is that validity is resolved in effectiveness and the fictitious nature of the foundation "transforms power into law"[25]. It is true that power does not lie in the will of the norm but in the positive regulation that establishes who can create it, whether democratic or dictatorial, but the truth is that "the State will always be authoritarian... because... it determines the holder of authority and the way in which it is exercised; who should command and who should obey"[26].

At the end, with Kelsenian normative legal positivism, the fundamental fact of continuous effectiveness (which distinguishes the mandates of the band of thugs from those of the legal system) is the assumption that the Constitution and all its inferential developments must be complied with. Without the Fundamental Norm, legal power would be an exercise of force and naked power[27]. But with it, I fear, an expression of factual effectiveness, albeit rethought as a foundation. Something that holds true if and only if it "contradicts... the thesis assumed by pure theory about the impossibility of deriving statements of "ought to be" from statements of fact"[28].

In summary. The material rationalisation of positive law promoted by Kant around democracy and rights is materially circumvented because

24 "It is not a historical process that actually took place in the external world in which the state ceded its sovereignty to the legal order by submitting to it... it is a progress within knowledge itself, which, starting from the isolated consideration of the content of the power of domination, rises to the more general point that this content does not show its specific meaning except in the essential form of law, in indissoluble union with it", Hans Kelsen, *Teoría General del Estado*, Editora Nacional, Madrid, 1979, p. 142.

25 The rule of inference of legal validity is obvious at the expense of explaining little of that validity, since "it presupposes... what it sets out to prove" Enrique Bocardo. *Tres Ensayos...*, p. 65.

26 Hans Kelsen. *Teoría General del Estado*, Editora Nacional, Madrid, 1979, p. 142.

27 Patricia Cuenca, "La relación entre el Derecho y el poder en la Teoría Pura del Derecho de H. Kelsen", cit., pp. 284, 285, 288, 289 in relation to Mario Losano, "Validez y eficacia en la teoría pura del Derecho", *Teoría Pura del Derecho. Evolución y Puntos Cruciales*, Temis, 1992, pp. 143, p. 76.

28 Enrique Bocardo. *Tres Ensayos sobre Kelsen*, cit., p. 71.

there are large groups of the population who neither have the right to have rights nor participate in decision-making on the distribution of goods, rights and burdens. From that postulate of material rationalisation, Weber reduced political legitimacy, central to the justification of law, to the population's adherence to the maxims of action established by power and its economic model. And Kelsen culminated the epistemology of the constant transition between the material and the ideological with the idea that the effectiveness of compliance with the maxims of power is the premise of the conceived and founding concept of validity, so that legal positivism is concretised in the knowledge of the rules of the strongest, since these are the rules it considers to be law. And from there, he develops his systemic epistemic construction (technical analogy, logical institutions, alternative rule, empty legal space, exclusive general norm, etc.).

3.3. The "fiction" of legal knowledge.

Theory not only explains legal reality, it creates it. In the social sciences, theoretical categories have a constitutive—normative—character, and law is no exception. What we consider to be law depends, to a large extent, on how we conceptualise it. Even the term "law" ends up being integrated into the very constitution of its object. Methodological virtuosity and apparent scientific neutrality consolidated the conversion of law into an object that had to conform to the canons of its knowledge: a law as "scientific" and "objective" as the narrative that describes it.

This is neither new nor surprising; rather, it revives the old ideal of the Corpus Iuris (6th century), the Liber Iodiciorum (7th century) or Las Siete Partidas (12th-14th centuries). And 19th-century codification, with its desire for rationality and system, updated the ideal of normative unity, reinforcing the constitutive relationship between legal theory, concept and practice.

Well, the third crypto-positivist fiction is that of the method by which law is contemplated and produced. And on the path of logos, what follows from the assertion that understanding requires a responsible rational subject is to neutralise the object in order to reduce it to objective factual categories. As the first Copernican revolution demanded, we cease to seek immanent essences and s in what is known. The conditions of objectivity and neutrality would thus allow for scientific, descriptive and predictive knowledge of the object. Such are the foundations of nineteenth-century legal positivism that give us clues to its developments, obstacles and transformations.

Firstly, in its eagerness to detach itself both from the moralising pretensions of natural law and from the ideological commitments of legal realism, crypto-positivism affirms a strict separation between facts and values.

This separation has been widely discussed in contemporary epistemology, because if all norms are based on ideological, emotional, moral, and cultural assumptions, denying them does not eliminate them, but rather conceals them and shields them from criticism. Thus, the formalist legal positivist, who begins his analysis from the "description of the being" of law, ends up demanding that the judge apply a certain norm —the letter of the law or whatever he or she discreetly considers to be such— in the name of legal certainty or legality. Let us call this ideological positivism or state moralism: the name is irrelevant, but its prescriptive axiology is not.

Secondly, the condition that follows the previous search for logic and reason, for a law already reduced to fact, is to adopt a logically formalised language at the service of systematicity and legal technicians, specialists in doing things with words and preventing other words from the margins from altering the established fiction.

Thirdly, law submits to the ideal of a closed, hierarchical and formally coherent whole. In this way, it closes in on itself, defining by exclusion what is not law and rejecting the "impurities" derived from the indeterminacy or humanisation of its scientific criteria.

And fourthly, given the constitutive interweaving of practice and a crypto-positivist theory of law, the closed operational set of positive, coercive, nomotechnically perfect and legally secure rules must be the only law in each legal community (unit). This approach has been criticised from various fronts (free law, interest jurisprudence, CLS, principialism, critical theories of law in general, etc.) that censure compromises with established powers, the exclusion of critical and peripheral knowledge, and the perpetuation of the myth of the objectivity of pure knowledge and its neutrality where often there is only intuition, habit or covert power.

Andersen's "naked emperor" celebrates the technical trappings of legal scientificity, applauded by his court of experts. The scientific nature of the method conditions known reality, determining the consistency of law, previously isolated as a legitimate product of the state of force. As a result, the theory that categorically renounces the ontology of naturalism nevertheless reproduces the ontology of the powers that be as an inescapable, secure and orderly form of scientific truth.

But even that is not enough. Legal cryptography—its technification—far from guaranteeing security, produces opacity because the norm is understood as a self-sufficient formal system, not as a social instrument of intelligibility and agreement. In short, the problem with cryptopositivism is not only its artifice—its art of doing from theory—but also its artificial nature: a fictional art that, by hindering understanding and favouring indeterminacy, has far-reaching practical consequences.

3.4. Six dangerous fictions of the "legal imagination".

It is now time to review the three fictions (subject, object and method) of cryptopositivism in light of the risks posed by the five fictions that convincingly surround them.

The first two fictions are objectivity and neutrality. Simple and exclusive legal positivism conceives of law as a closed, autonomous, and self-sufficient system that articulates validity and application based on formal and procedural criteria. This view, resulting from the influence of the logical-empirical model of science in the legal sphere, privileges objectivity, neutrality in the description of legal facts, and positive law. In this way, simple legal positivism reduces legal knowledge to a primarily deductive, mechanical task, free from emotional overload and radically separated from the evaluative context.

However, I am convinced that if legal knowledge wishes to understand its object and not invent it in order to impose it, it must assume that law is made up of values, interests and emotions, and that interpretation cannot be reduced to a logical process or the automatic application of rules without conflict or ambiguity. Ignoring this conceals contingency behind the appearance of mathematical precision and perfect nomotechnics, and this crypto-positivist fiction favours (without embarrassment?) the "will to power" exercised through the norm.

These problems challenge the third crypto-positivist fiction, certainty, by generating opacity and legitimising indeterminacy. The certainty of law and its decisions, which Lyotard and Vattimo describe as a "myth"; a "meta-narrative" that has now become a "meta-story" for Derrida. The reality is that, as all normative claims implicitly involve controversy and dissent, foundational objectivity and certainty are impossible; there is always room for different and even contradictory interpretations, and we lack the objective criteria to select one of them. The realistic "thesis of indeterminacy" in the face of difficult cases, which is irrefutable, becomes radicalised because CLSs believe that every case is difficult[29]: "the radical indeterminacy of meaning... (is) inevitable"[30].

In fact, it is not difficult to find confirmation in case law, both minor and major, that crypto-positivism persists as a covert paradigm and produces effects contrary to the principle of intelligibility of the law. Thus, for example, the Spanish Constitutional Court's ruling 148/2021 on the limitation of rights, "suspension", "exception" or "general conditioning" of rights during the state of alarm during the pandemic "pretended" (modelled) scientificity, technical reasoning, doctrinal precision and neutrality, but greatly increased uncertainty and the image of complexity[31].

Consequently, the fourth dangerous fiction of crypto-positivist knowledge is that of discretion. The scientific approach was articulated around the fullness, coherence, unity, uniqueness, and exclusivity of the law in the face of moral impostures, gaps, and contradictions in content. In the event that there was occasionally some room for interpretation or doubts about factual classification, the decision of the authority's will "repeals" these circumstantial excrescences of the perfect legal system. The reasons for the authority's will and its effects will be of interest to other disciplines, but not to legal ones. What the judge must do is not 'overstep the mark' in his interpretation; and as long as he 'keeps himself in check', it is understood that he is making use of the discretion granted to him by the linguistic system of law.

The intrinsic indeterminacy of the language of law, however, not only radically restricts the possibilities of syllogism to demonstrate the truth of the conclusion, but also limits the prospect of self-controlled discretion. Every legal decision is a permanent evaluative and political choice that is transformed in the historical development of events and the victorious conceptions of what will be considered correct. Kelsen's paradigmatic normativism leaves little doubt in this regard; it is only possible to establish possible meanings of legal norms, and one must "avoid with the utmost

29 In the same vein, Lawrence B. Solum. "On the indeterminacy crisis: critiquing legal dogma", *University of Chicago Law Review*, n. 54, p. 496.

30 Mark Tushnet. *Red, White and Blue. A Critical Analysis.* Harvard University Press, 1988, p. 63.

31 Constitutional Court Ruling (TC) 148/2021, of 14 July 2021 on. Appeal of unconstitutionality 2054-2020 of various provisions of Royal Decree 463/2020, 14-03, declaring a state of alarm during the health crisis caused by COVID-19.

care the fiction that a legal norm always admits only one meaning, the "correct" meaning... a fiction that traditional jurisprudence uses to maintain the ideal of legal certainty[32].

In any case, uncertainty and indeterminacy are not the ultimate problem; ignoring or denying them is. Because in doing so, technification conceals something else, namely that the act of will of the legislator or the jurisdiction "should not be controlled". That is, control is deprived of content, when content is the essential part of law.

All of the above suggests that, fifthly, the supposed objectivity and crypto-positivist neutrality require the depoliticisation of law as one of the conditions of the classic separation between what is and what ought to be, between the positive world and moral reality. The so-called "exclusive reasons" —those of the second order which, according to Raz[33]— constitute precisely the core of legal reasons. This legal positivist approach is explicitly taken up by Schauer, who considers it the most useful for explaining the authority of rules[34]: in the process of normative formalisation, the "underlying reasons" —moral or political— are blurred and simplified in order to make the rules operational. From this perspective, the virtue of law lies in allowing legal operators not to continually re-evaluate the substantive reasons in each specific case[35].

The fiction, with regard to the depoliticisation of cryptopositivism, is twofold, as it consists of maintaining that politicisation neither reaches, first fiction, nor should it reach, second fiction, the decision in law. The effort to turn the will and interests of legal operators into a private matter is an alternative that, like the one that normatively kidnapped women into the chaos and oppression of domestic privacy, holds no more truth than its interest, its power, and its ability to exercise force in pursuit of its own sense of order. Therefore, the exclusion of value-based conflict from the realm of legal knowledge simply privileges the status quo served by technocratic rationality, hostage to a sophisticated model of hegemonic ideology with deep economic roots.

---

32 Hans Kelsen. *Pure Theory of Law*, Porrúa, 1993, p. 356.

33 *See* Joseph Raz. *The Authority of Law, Oxford University*, 1979, pp. 22–23, 27, 190–195 and 'Intention in interpretation', *Between Authority and Interpretation: On the Theory of Law and Practical Reason*, Oxford University, 2009, pp. 265–298.

34 Frederick Schauer. *Playing with Rules: A Philosophical Examination of Rule-Based Decision-Making in Law and in Life*. Oxford University, 1991, p. 69.

35 *Idem*. Schauer, pp. 25 and 51.

Law is politics. And it is so because, as Critical Legal Studies emphasise, neither the law nor casuistic review nor legal dogma or epistemology offer definitive answers to disputes. Gaps, contradictions, ambiguities, indeterminacy, mediation or legitimisation of the status quo are categories that permeate law with politics. Legal argumentation and legislation are permeated by political interests and decisions. And, although it is hidden under the rhetoric of neutrality, controversial legal epistemology participates in the same political disputes. Being aware of this prevents legal thinking from repressing[36] and dissolving substantive disputes into procedures that tend to favour the conservative dimension of the dispute. On the theses of "fundamental contradiction" and "strong indeterminacy", voluntarism conceals and legitimises objectivity[37] and encourages legal decisions to reproduce established social roles.

In short, the law and its decisions are political objects: they arise from and settle political disputes, especially in strong constitutional states that guarantee rights, where rules "must" conform to the substantive parameters of constitutional law, which is of a higher order. Herein lies the problem. If crypto-positivism denies the first, that rules and their applications are political, it hides the reality of the imposition of interests and de facto powers over rights and guarantees, which causes the collapse of the second condition of politicisation and prevents us from falling into a perfect state of power uncontrolled by legal anomie, the monitoring of substantive constitutional rules[38].

---

36 Clarifier Mark Kelman. *A Guide to Critical Legal Studies*, Harvard Univ. Press, 1987.

37 Cf. Stanley Fiss. "Going down the antiformalist road", *Doing What Comes Naturally: Change, Rhetoric, and the Practice of Theory in Literary & Legal Studies*, Duke University Press, 1989, p. 16.

38 Ferrajoli is clear: "A common idea in positivist doctrines is the non-evaluative nature of legal science and that laws cannot be criticised from within... On this basis, Kelsen configures the theory of law as 'pure'... and Bobbio criticises as natural law any subordination of judgements of validity to value judgements. It is clear that these theses are sacrosanct...: undoubtedly, jurists are not allowed, in scientific circles, to evaluate legal norms from outside and to condition judgements on validity to ethical-political or... extralegal assessments. However, in their usual formulation, they are misleading... By being confused with the thesis of the non-evaluative nature of legal science, they prevent... jurists from evaluating and criticising current law not only from the external or political point of view of justice, but also from the internal or legal point of view of validity. Precisely when it is the task of the jurist — not only civic and political, but even more so scientific — to assess the validity or invalidity of norms in accordance with both formal and substantive parameters of validity

In view of this, it is advisable not to deny the political substance of law, but to accept it in order to control it[39] and put it in favour of citizens' rights: listening to all parties, justifying the decision substantively and formally in public, listening to and recognising victims, addressing political demands, strengthening the function of guaranteeing rights and redistribution, etc.[40].

The sixth crypto-positivist fiction is to maintain that objectivity and systematisation favour legality and legal certainty. However, I insist that the disconnect between law, substance and experience generates anomie, loss of meaning, disaffection and delegitimisation. A self-referential conception of law absolutises the formal dimension of rules. The fact is that law must genuinely serve as a guide for action by providing certainty about consequences and how others will act, which promotes equality and freedom of planning and action. But to be a reliable guide for action, it should guarantee objectivity and certainty which, if not so certain and possible, only legitimise and ensure that the interests of the strongest will prevail. In other words, proceduralism does not depoliticise by ignoring the underlying controversy; it achieves the opposite by promoting the double "fetish" of the normative value of positive victorious practice and the epistemological legitimacy of social compliance with such a maxim.

For similar reasons, Ferrajoli accuses liberal democracies of totalitarian drifts in law and the state. These drifts point to Hegelian and utilitarian levels of primacy of security and order over the individual and their rights[41]. In my critique of the fiction of object legitimation (see supra), I already highlighted the problematic nature of the canonical criterion of legitimising those who hold power. The objection is weakened if the state is democratic, it is true (despite the difficulty, as Ferrajoli points out, that democracy is always imperfect[42]), but for this to be the case, crypto-positivism must renounce itself, incurring various contradictions.

A legal machinery that follows rules but lacks substantive guidance legitimises a void of justification that fosters uncertainty regarding action and

---

established by higher-ranking legal norms"; Luigi Ferrajoli. *Derecho y Razón,* Trotta, 2001, pp. 873-874.

39 *See* Peter Gabel. "The Spiritual Dimension of Social Justice", *Journal of Legal Education*, vol. 63, n. 4, 2014, pp. 680-684.

40 Cf., Juan Antonio Pérez Lledó. "Critical Legal Studies y el comunitarismo" *Doxa*, n. 17-18, 1995, pp. 142-143.

41 *See* Luigi Ferrajoli. *Derecho y Razón*, Trotta, 2001, p. 888.

42 *See idem*. p. 885.

its reasons, leading to arbitrariness, inconsistency and injustice in recognisable forms.

Anomie, then, is not an accidental defect but a structural consequence of the proceduralist and formalist model that limits the capacity of law to regenerate itself and adapt to emerging social demands.

In any case, just as Pintore's Law Without Truth did not renounce legal rationality by denying the truth of law, but rather sought to redefine it in a context of procedural transparency, democratic deliberation, and political and ethical consensus, my interest is to highlight that although descriptive, universal and predictive natural truth is far from law, it is possible to confront the insidious effects of anomie, uncertainty and indeterminacy, and the depoliticisation of law, first by recognising them and then by introducing approaches of coherence and dynamic legal validity and legitimacy, which I will refer to in a moment.

3.5. And what remains is "law without truth".

The deficits of objectivity and neutrality are the result of the lack of truth in law. That is why the assertions that rule X is true, that fact Y is truly legal, or that case Z will truly be judged are debatable.

Objectivity is linked to truth, and truth establishes a positive identification with the object, but with a negative capacity or exclusion of all assumptions that do not fit the description. This is what makes truth necessary, universalizable, and predictive. However, the law does not describe reality: it constitutes it. When it says "Madrid is the capital of Spain" or "you are married", it does not state facts, it creates them and transforms the will and legal position of individuals. That is why an "expropriation" is neither true nor false; what is true, for example, is that my car speeds along the motorway built on the (expropriated) land.

This issue of the truth of law and its propositions and consequences, as we can see, fascinates us jurists and gives rise to highly technical and delightfully debatable discussions.

In this context and paradigmatically, Anna Pintore draws out the consequences for positivism of the lack of truth by correspondence in law, including the restriction of critical thinking. She does so in Il diritto

Senza Verità, Giappichelli[43]. For her, if we consider that law is "true" by correspondence —as some naive legal positivists do— we turn the norm into an end in itself[44], deny the instrumental function of law and adopt an evaluative position that leads to norms being treated as moral or ethical principles that justify the voluntarism of the decision. This is something I previously developed in relation to legitimacy as validity in Kelsenian terms.

However, for Pintore, too, the absence of pre-existing "true" norms is an incentive, as it can open the way to deliberative choices, procedures, coherence, consensus, etc., which allow legal norms to be connected with democratic assessments; not as recognition of objective truth, but as collective agreement on normative procedures (with the ever-present risk that procedures will be captured by interests specific to power and instrumentalised through the law).

A requirement for justification which, as Ferrajoli[45] and Habermas[46] insist, serves to characterise that law is legitimate if it can be rationally accepted in a discursive process. The consequence of positivist formalism claiming that rules are valid simply because of their form is that criticism of their content or legitimacy is condoned.

4 Knowing in order to act: "maintaining the forms" and "retrointegrating" the substance.

With this last point, I return to the beginning, when I questioned the capacity of cryptopositivism to know and make social reality with the law.

---

43 "Directive discourses, such as legal discourse, cannot be classified as true or false"; only "metalinguistic discourses concerning law can be predicated, never law itself"; Anna Pintore. *El Derecho Sin Verdad (Law Without Truth)*, Dykinson, 2005, p. 17. Although I am convinced that the scope of this statement should be questioned in several ways, I cannot do so here.

44 "Associating law with truth makes it an end, or a principle, and leads to a misunderstanding of its instrumentality", *idem*. Pintore, p. 28.

45 With its constitutional principles and fundamental rights, e.g., Luigi Ferrajoli. *Derechos y Garantías*, Trotta, Madrid, 2004, pp. 15-ff.

46 Jürgen Habermas. *Facticidad y Validez. Sobre el Derecho y el Estado Democrático de Derecho en Términos de Teoría del Discurso*. Trotta, 1998, pp. 188-197. I analysed in depth the model of liberal political legitimacy centred on rights in *La Teoría Comunitarista y la Filosofía Política (Communitarian Theory and Political Philosophy)*. Dykinson, 2001, pp. 37-ff.

Legal practice is inevitably interpretative and evaluative. Lawyers are not mere operators of normative signs, but social interpreters, and their work is conditioned by ethical, emotional and political matrices. To ignore this in order to facilitate description distorts the object and the results. Law is without truth. And evaluative neutrality does not eliminate ideology, it simply hides it. That is why the scientific objective of a real positivism that knows and makes law should not be to "eliminate" values from legal reasoning, but to make them explicit, debatable and revisable according to rational and verifiable parameters.

In this latter sense, I propose formal legal coherence at the highest level, but also material and critical coherence and an "activation" of legal operators and iuspositivist theory in favour of rights, recognition and redistribution. The objective of incorporating substantive content is to control legislators and judges who play along with dictates, and responds to the formal "constitutional" condition of substantive adequacy and consistency as a condition of validity.

4.1. Critical coherence and "retrointegration of validity".

Realising the aspiration to correct the law —and articulating its legal utopia as legal positivist coherence— is no easy task, and requires the adoption of an "inclusive" legal positivism.

Principled moralism —paradigmatically represented by Dworkin— is appealing for various reasons[47]. However, it also risks falling into universalist conservatism, which can erode claims of liberation and justice and/or lead to counter-positivism. If, in addition, Judge Hercules grants moral authority to each judge to issue "the only" correct decision, this contributes to legitimising the lack of control of positive law.

In any case, the principled decision to shift the focus of the debate by emphasising that the separation between law and morality is no longer the crucial boundary of legal positivism is not insignificant for critical legal

47 I delved inclusionism in greater depth, as well as Dworkin's approach and the objections to it, in *El Posmodernismo Jurídico y la Filosofía del Derecho* (*Legal Postmodernism and the Philosophy of Law*), Tirant lo Blanch, 2018, pp. 177-199; and in "La coherencia jurídica pospositivista del posmodernismo jurídico", *Positività Giuridica. Studî ed Attualizzazioni di un concetto complesso,* Padova University Press, 2018, pp. 240-244.

positivism and forces us to reconsider the other two central theses of legal positivism: the social origin of law and judicial discretion.

The positivist coherence of the critical conception of law thus points to a theory that combines description, normativity and axiology; a critical and dynamic theory where justification and normativity are intertwined. Thanks to this, we can: adapt the continuum between regulating and deciding. Break the rigidity of "actually existing" law and open it up to internal criticism. Decentre the normative power of the rational legislator and recognise the legal creation of contracts and social practices that expand plurality. Replace the old autarchic validity with a heterarchical understanding, more attentive to the real fabric of social relations. And, above all, activate the instruments of material control required by a truly critical conception of politics, law, economics and culture.

Promoting the coherence of content from a legal positivist inclusionist perspective around the justice of dignity and rights should not exclude the use of formal parameters. On the contrary, it underlines the importance of previously defined and verifiable criteria of reasoning, such as the deductive reasoning of formal logic, although also at the service of the logic of the evaluative meaning of actions and their consequences for people and the world[48].

Thus, this substantive and descriptive coherence makes it clear that "the presumed need to choose between subsumption and weighing is an error that stems in large part from (confusing exclusive reason with absolute reason)[49]:... the fallacy of false opposition... We need both argumentative frameworks"[50].

Critical inclusionism faces the oxymoron of being both legal positivist and critical[51]. But by emphasising the political and social nature of the

48 Cf. Amalia Amaya, "Coherencia, justificación y Derecho", *Discusiones*, n. X, 2010, p. 234.

49 My parenthesis.

50 Manuel Atienza, "Ni positivismo jurídico ni neoconstitucionalismo: una defensa del constitucionalismo postpositivista". *Conceptos y Valores Constitucionales*, Plaza y Valdés, 2016, p. 21.

51 I addressed this in "Positivismo crítico comprehensivo (no incluyente, no exclusivo pero excluyente)", *Archiv für Rechts-und Sozialphilosophie, ARSP*, n. 106, 2007, pp. 80–93.

object it describes, given its lack of neutrality, it legitimately opens itself up to the critical perspective that orthodox objectivist positivism closes off[52].

These perspectives point to the "materialisation" of the relationship between the Constitution, the law and jurisdiction[53]. In this regard, I would highlight a double descriptive normative effect: that of "substantive retrointegration of the concept of validity" at the descriptive level, and that of "legal activation of guarantees" as a normative consequence of the description.

Identifying substantive criteria for consistency is very complicated and requires us to renounce many of the fictions that underpin our own constitutional fictions. "(D)iscovering conflicting policies and hidden possibilities in the expressions of legal texts". And also "deconstructing" interpretative methods[54] and objecting to those, such as textualism and originalism, that rely on a single, dogmatic and unjustified truth[55] .

---

52 A legal positivist theory cannot impose on the law what it should be. That is why the epistemological *approach* or metatheoretical character that serves the theorisation of 'critical legal positivism' is important. Because the *approach* does not decide, although it places us before the decision, 'it does not commit us to accepting the truth of any of the theses or conceptions that characterise legal positivism as a theory'; Genaro Carrio. "Dworkin y el Positivismo Jurídico", *Cuadernos Crítica*, n. 16, 1981, p. 11, neither the thesis of the "nature" of positive law, nor those of the rules, "sources" and properties of legal systems (completeness and consistency), nor that of the function of judges (*see* Norberto Bobbio, *El Problema del Positivismo Jurídico,* Fontamara. 1995, pp. 44-45, Genaro Carrió, G. "Dworkin y el Positivismo Jurídico", *Cuadernos Crítica,* n. 16, p. 10).

53 In which the legislative, executive and judicial branches interact, legal arguments are made, the law is tested, constitutional rights are developed and projected, norms are debated publicly and socially, and technological advances favour knowledge and control in their various facets (cf., Jack Balkin "What is a postmodern constitutionalism", *Michigan Law Review*, n. 90, 1992, p. 13).

54 For "none of the methods of interpretation with which we are familiar... offer a self-sufficient basis for legal interpretation... Rather... interpretation is a pragmatic enterprise that defines each method of interpretation through creative tension", in Jack M. Balkin. "Deconstruction's legal career". *Cardozo Law Review*, n. 27, 2005, p. 732. Cf. *Ibid.*, "What is a postmodern constitutionalism". *Michigan Law Review,* n. 90, 1992, pp. 1966-1988.

55 In other words, "the question is no longer so much how to interpret the text, but rather the legitimacy of legal discourse as a mechanism of power masked in the search for interpretive truth. Thus, the project of deconstructive criticism consists of accounting for a change in the legitimacy of the project of law considered as an instrument for characteristically generating legal truths", Alan Hunt, "The big fear: Law confronts Postmodernism", *McGill Law Journal.* n. 35, 1990, p. 514, cf. *idem,* pp. 512-ff.

To deconstruct interpretatively means to undo what has been asserted as true. And to understand that no interpretation —neither of the law, nor of the case, nor of justice —can claim to be the foundational, unique, true interpretation[56]. To rethink our model of rationality and reasonableness[57] and the function and procedures of legislation and judicial prosecution. And, of course, to thoroughly question the structure, nature and function of the Constitutional Court.

Critical coherence not only integrates principles and values, it puts them at the service of material and evaluative coherence, tracing the channels that dynamically give concrete form to their meaning.

This weakens the rigidity of objections such as that the law is a set of valid rules that may never be applied, or that there are "invalid rules that nevertheless display their full legal effectiveness"[58]. Validity, although static in its formal concept, adjusts its content to the concrete reality of each moment, and thus the legal system emerges as a living and dynamic chain of momentary systems in permanent transformation.

This vision facilitates understanding and managing the "practical revolution" that is already underway, questioning and reformulating the legal-dogmatic and factual categories and the mechanisms of formal and material oppression that still permeate our law.

Indeed, when the ontological metaphysics of the norm as a finished fact is abandoned and its dynamic and flexible conception is adopted, interpretation and meaning take centre stage, and formal validity is renewed thanks to the combination of the authority of the thesis of production with the critical (and mutable) determination of its meaning[59]. Because law is, above

---

56 Cf. Leonor Suárez Llanos, *El Posmodernismo...*, pp. 208-ff.

57 What is needed is "a transition from central logic to local logic of interdependencies. A doctrine... oriented towards a non-linear and dynamic model of equilibrium based on plural networks... Such a doctrine should, in relation to the network, structure interdependencies with respect to each case in a horizontal and decentralised manner", Karl-Heinz Ladeur. "Perspectives on a post-modern Theory of Law". *Autopoietic Law,* De Gruyter, Berlin 1988, 275. *See* Fernando Trazegnies Granda. *Postmodernidad y Derecho,* Ara, 1996, pp. 33-34.

58 Rafael Escudero Alday, *Los calificativos del positivismo jurídico*, Cívitas, Madrid 2004, p. 239.

59 The neo-institutionalist distinction between prima facie validity and validity considered in all circumstances, which I discussed in "El concepto dinámico de la validez jurídica neoinstitucionalista", *Anuario de Filosofía del Derecho (AFD),* vol. XXII, 2005, pp. 350-ff., is relevant here. Because formal validity is a *sine qua non* condition, but not a sufficient condition, *per qua,* of validity. Because legal rules are exclusive

all, a complex and living institution in constant dialogue with the world it orders.

Well, this "retrointegration of the concept of validity"[60] is, above all, a task of constantly defining the meaning of law that determines its concept of validity. An exercise in theoretical vigilance that must respond to a rigorous technique and a committed legal activation that highlights the link between legal theory, its method of application and the living reality of practice. In this way, validity ceases to be a fixed category and becomes the theoretical and practical key in whose dynamics legal knowledge and security are connected with social demands and critical justice as a programmatic horizon.

At this point, many of the most important tensions that critical and coherent positivism must face become evident, tensions that cryptopositivism manages on the edge of certain precipices from which it often ends up falling. The knots: does the Constitution of values already integrate the axiological content that should correct the rules? The answer is yes, as a regulative ideal and formal concept, and not as a practical reality of relevant significance that successively, critically and institutionally specifies the underlying reasons and content (political and evaluative reasons that are at the basis of the rule and "motivated" its creation) of the norms; I follow Schauer's distinction between reasons "underlying" and reasons "derived from" the rules[61]. There is also the question of whether the underlying reasons that justify that a case fits the generic specification of the general conditions of the rule should be those of the original will of the legislator or those of an identified morality. Perhaps the best answer is neither. Because it will have to be: justifiable in terms of correctness, and consistent in formal terms with the rule that can be applied to the range of cases to which the case under consideration belongs, and all of this

reasons (Raz) but are not absolute reasons (Atienza). And because an external point of view complementary to the internal one allows us to identify the critical arguments of positive law based on the inclusive mandate of constitutional justice. Cf. Luc Wintgens, "Creation and application of Law from a *legisprudential* perspective", *Justice, Morality and Society*, Juristförlaget, Lund, 1997, pp. 472-476.

60 Cf. Leonor Suárez Llanos. "El concepto dinámico de la validez jurídica neoinstitucionalista", *AFD*, vol. XXII, pp. 333-ff.

61 Frederik Schauer. *Playing with Rules: A Philosophical Examination of Rule-Based Decision-Making in Law and in Life*. Oxford University, 1991, pp. 51 and 59.

must be explicitly argued as justification for the decision[62]. In other words, any claim of material consistency must be supported by a powerful and contestable institutional justification that includes the prior determination of who judges, according to what criteria, and how that decision is justified in all its decisive, descriptive, probative, foundational, and justificatory dimensions[63].

From this perspective, theories of legislation and argumentation gain new momentum[64] in favour of a more correct and "coherent" law; not because of "cognitivist activism", but because of their ability to identify and inject reason into the cracks in justice, the legal and axiological gaps and the normative contradictions that legal positivism fosters[65] .

Because all theory, like all practice, is ideological, and recognising this requires us to decentrate law, to shift its axis towards a pluralism that is neither trivial nor ideologically biased, so that it can revolve around difference and freedom and offer a kaleidoscopic conception of political, social and vital diversity and plurality[66].

---

62 Cf. Juan Carlos Bayón. "El imperio de la ley y la interpretación y aplicación del Derecho: dos visiones", *Doxa*, n. 40, 2017, pp. 69-70.

63 I develop this neo-institutionalist proposal in "El concepto dinámico de validez jurídica neoinstitucionalista", *AFD*, n. 22, 2005, pp. 333-358.

64 There are various socio-cultural orders that rival each other in controlling the regulatory system, reflecting great social heterogeneity, and "legal theory cannot ignore this fact. This makes it necessary to promote a drastic change in the content of the philosophical-legal subdiscipline", Ana Julia Bozo de Carmona, "Toward a postmodern Theory of Law", 2013, p. 4) —*see* Ernesto Grün, "El Derecho postmoderno: un sistema lejos del equilibrio", *Doxa, n. 21-II,* 1998, pp. 174-175—.

65 *See* Robert Alexy, "El positivismo no inclusivo" (Non-inclusive positivism), *Doxa*, n. 36, 2013, 19. *See* Manuel Atienza, "Ni positivismo jurídico ni neoconstitucionalismo: una defensa del constitucionalismo postpositivista", *Conceptos y Valores Constitucionales,* Plaza y Valdés, Madrid 2016, pp. 21-23; Juan Pablo Alonso, "Principios jurídicos implícitos y coherencia", *Doxa,* n. 36, 2013, pp. 379-ff., Santiago Sastre Ariza, "Sobre la dificultad de los llamados casos fáciles, difíciles y trágicos", http://helvia .uco.es/bitstream/handle/10396/6982/dyo1_23.pdf?sequence=1&isAllowed, 1993, 299-305.

66 And "that it protects the original definitions of individuality by reasonably addressing the expectations of each particular interest group", Leonor Suárez Llanos. "La <<cultura jurídica>> y el <<pluralismo jurídico>>. Problemas de definición", *BFD*, n. 24, Madrid 2004, p. 48. *See* Roger Cotterrell, *Law's Community. Legal Theory in Sociological Perspective.* Clarendon Press. Oxford 1995, p. 310; Warwick Tie, *Legal Pluralism. Toward a Multicultural Conception of Law.* Aldershot, Dartmouth 1999, pp. 165-166.

Ultimately, a paradoxical conception of law[67] for which law is what it is plus its opposite. Not a scalpel that separates good from evil in a binary fashion, but a framework of (post)positive coherence that combines formal and narrative argumentative methods with an ethical conception of good and justice[68]. This allows for the material justification of ethical decisions—including legislative ones—by focusing (ethical foundation) on the "why" rather than the "what", while satisfying the logical conditions of the "how"[69].

4.2. The proposal for "coherent legal activation".

"Legal activism" fits into this context of legal positivism and must confront patterns of injustice, while guaranteeing the positivist commitment to legal certainty in the protection of rights and non-discrimination.

The terms "activation" and "activism" refer to different concepts. An "activist judge" causes concern due to their unchecked arbitrariness, evaluative subjectivity, legal uncertainty, systemic incoherence, and the violation of the democratic principle and the separation of powers that they represent[70] . I will not dwell on the figure of the activist judge (if he creates law, does he not distort the democratic principle[71]?), but suffice it to say here what I understand by "legal activation", as distinct from "activism", and why it is structurally relevant if linked to a rational and controlled judicial practice by those who execute it.

---

67 See François Ost, "Júpiter, Hércules, Hermes: tres modelos de juez", *Doxa*, n. 14, 1993, p. 187.

68 Cf. "La coherencia en el Derecho", *Doxa*, n. 35, 2012, p. 74.

69 For "the work of the jurist involves a theory about how the law should be. Deprived of that theory, what we today call 'legal positivism' becomes trivial and sterile", Fernando Atria, "La ironía del positivismo jurídico", *Doxa*, n. 27, 2004, p. 135.

70 *Judicial* activism originated in the United States in the 1940s and 1950s with reactionary activist judges who opposed legislation and social rights; *see* Manuel Atienza. *Una Apología del Derecho y Otros Ensayos*, (*Seven Theses on Judicial Activism*), Trotta, 2020, pp. 85-ff.

71 It suffices to warn certain crypto-positivist navigators, prone to conceiving of the judge as a mere executor, that: "The interpretation made by the body applying the law is always authentic. It creates law... But the interpretation made by the body that applies the law when it creates law for a specific case is also authentic, that is, it creates law...", Hans Kelsen. *Teoría Pura del Derecho*, Porrúa, 1993, p. 354.

Every normal legal positivist (and every democrat) recognises that judges have powers of interpretation and discretionary judgement within the framework of positive law. These powers are also exercised when legal facts are constructed from raw facts and legally classified in accordance with the authority emanating from the law. However, judicial discretion does not grant absolute power, but rather a competence structured by hierarchical rules that guarantee that the judgment is legally correctable and systematically justifiable[72].

The content of the "judicial activation" called for here touches on issues that legal positivism constantly questions[73] —the reasonable margins of discretion, consistency with the regulatory system, and the rationality of decision-making processes. And it is aware that the risk of "activating the law" is to exceed legality and promote arbitrariness and insecurity. Therefore, the proposal for legal activation implicitly assumes responsibility for the essential indeterminacy of the law and activates demanding conditions that favour legal predictability (coherent legislative subordination and institutionally legitimate creativity) in guaranteeing those rights.

Once this is guaranteed, "activation" makes it possible to confront the regulatory sclerosis that underpins and perpetuates injustices. Because formal equality cannot be understood as an empty or immobile formula, but rather as a flexible and operational legal concept that, by mandate of the positive law, requires material equality, substantive integration, argumentative reasoning, institutional loyalty, and structural application[74].

This approach is acceptable if "activism" is oriented, it is true, towards progressive, expansive conceptions of the meaning of rights and effective in their protection, but not towards other reactionary alternatives. But this is already enshrined in the constitutional text: the guarantee and development of fundamental rights is an essential part of a democratic model, a constitutional imperative (Articles 10 and 53 of the Spanish Constitution) that we must not erode in the name of anything, anyone, and least of all democratic pluralism.

---

72 *See* Neil MacCormick. *Legal Reasoning and Legal Theory*, 2003, Oxford University Press.

73 *See* Robert Alexy. *Teoría de los Derechos Fundamentales,* CEC, 1993, pp. 12-124, 376-385; Manuel Atienza. *Tras la Justicia,* Ariel, 1991, pp. 137-ff.

74 Luigi Ferrajoli. *Derecho y Razón*. Trotta, 2001, pp. 44-49, 574-ff, 871-872. Cf. Luigi Ferrajoli. *Contra el Creacionismo Judicial,* 2025, pp. 113-ff.

While the judge, the "lord of the law", affirms the clarity of the law and that it is not he but the syllogistic will of the law that passes judgement, the "activist" judiciary argues and decides, aware of its instrumental but central role in the development of the legal order[75], knowledgeable of the structural complexity of law in the constitutional state[76], and guarantor of "the necessary and flexible coexistence between law, rights and justice"[77].

That judges "create" law is neither new nor "surprising". However, the formula of "activation" requires and allows this to be done not intuitively, but by understanding what legal creationism consists of as opposed to cognitivism and dogmatism, inter alia, what its variants and limitations are, and when and how the "limited and guarantee-based judicial creation" of law is an expression of the application of the profound and substantive keys of the constitutional model of rights protection.

Within this framework, the Constitutional Court, like other legal bodies and operators, has been "activating" rights, freedoms and obligations, sometimes more successfully than others. Less successfully, when it postponed certain essential keys to equality, such as when it declared the constitutionality of segregation in the education of children and adolescents. It has been more successful, both formally and substantively, when it has "activated" the effective protection of rights in the face of legislative passivity (for example, when the legislature did not extend single-parent leave to the total amount of joint parental leave for the birth and care of a child), the inertia of the judiciary (inattentive to the structural determination of gender in evidentiary proceedings), or a reductionist political understanding (which presents gender as a reprehensible ideology, in the style of VOX). In these cases, the Constitutional Court acted with substantive rationality that justified extending its reasoning to the material and truly decisive aspects of the cases to be resolved. I addressed some of these issues in greater detail in previous works, which I refer to here[78].

75 *See* Manuel Atienza. *Filosofía del Derecho y Transformación Social*, Trotta, 2017, pp. 141-142.

76 *See* Jürgen Habermas. *Facticidad y Validez,* Trotta, 1998, pp. 302-308, 331-339.

77 Gustavo Zagrebelsky. *El Derecho Dúctil. Ley, Derechos, Justicia*, Trotta, 2003, p. 153.

78 In Leonor Suárez Llanos. "Activación jurídica por razón de género. Entre las razones poderosas y las otras ficciones jurídicas de la igualdad", *Género y Derecho,* Thomson-Reuters Aranzadi, 2025, in press; "El `truco o trato´ de la igualdad en la educación segregada por sexo y la ley 15/2022", *La Ley 15/2022, de 12 de julio, integral para la igualdad de trato y la no discriminación: Aportaciones multidisciplinares y teórico-*

5. Conclusions.

Being a legal positivist means, above all, being one in truth, and that requires a threefold condition: knowing in detail the law in force at any given time, not limiting oneself to its mere legitimising formula, and, in addition, attending to the intrinsic function of any legal system, differentiating it from that of other powers that be, thus acting in the name of social justice and the justified resolution of conflicts. Therefore, authentic legal positivism must remain alert to the risks of crypto-positivism, actively investigating the keys to the substantive coherence of the legal system and analysing the conditions of legal positivism within the "circular dynamics of its constant feedback between structure and substance" in the algorithms and languages with which humans constitute the law.

This is, of course, central to the development of artificial intelligence systems in general and, in particular, those related to law.

A substantive legal epistemology does not imply abandoning positive law, but rather deepening its normative and transformative meaning. Knowing the law inevitably means committing to it, because in its formal and institutional dimensions, as well as in its substantive dimension, the law decides and shapes the world we inhabit. Overcoming crypto-positivism does not mean renouncing rigour or reasonable procedures, but rather reformulating the way we conceive legal knowledge, moving towards a coherent epistemology that is conscious of its nature and the effects it produces.

críticas. pp. 227-254; "El derecho a la educación: sus brechas de justicia, conciencia y género", *Revista Telemática de Filosofía del Derecho*, n. 23, 2020, pp. 99-129.

Taking Stock: Philosophy of Law in the Age of the "Great Regression"

Eckardt Buchholz-Schuster

Abstract

The global situation in the 2020s gives rise to various great concerns: democratic constitutional states, human rights, international law and planetary health are increasingly under threat. This results in potentially new topics for an applied philosophy of law, which are outlined in this article from a German perspective. On a substantive level, these include extreme injustice through state and supranational omission, civil disobedience, the legitimation and defense of constitutional and international law, and on a methodological level, the need for clarification in terms of decision theory, argumentation theory and empirical research. Such an intensified legal philosophical treatment of current social and political issues requires an attitude that aims to project social and political impact and addresses relevant actors beyond its specialist community. This paper also argues for such an attitude within applied legal philosophy.

Introduction

Now, in the mid 2020s, we live in a nervous world that is characterized by a tension between unresolved problems of an international and sometimes global dimension, on the one hand, and a lack of political willingness or ability to attempt collective solutions on the other. Nationalist and populist centrifugal forces, which place national or personal claims on validity and interests above human rights and planetary health, are gaining increasing influence and importance in various countries. Agreements, international law, democratic constitutions and the rule of law are increasingly being politically relativized.

Against this backdrop, this paper will raise the question of how an applied philosophy of law, *i.e.* a philosophy of law that reaches social and political reality, can position itself in light of this challenging situation and how it could position itself in the future beyond the status quo. In particular, what are the challenges and potentials of an applied philosophy of law in a rapidly changing global environment? To what extent does it take note of threatening and dramatic international developments? Without claiming the ambivalent throne of a philosopher king, could and should it attempt to develop normative guiding concepts that aim to be recognized outside its professional community and try to generate social and political impact? Or should it rely instead on the self-healing powers of international law, politics and state and supranational institutions beyond legal-ethical analyses?

This article aims to approach these questions descriptively, normatively, methodologically and in terms of scientific theory, from a German perspective. Against this background, Section I outlines regressive manifestations of the present, but also, by way of contrast, the prevailing social and political restraint in German legal philosophy in the recent decades. Section II then examines examples of potential subject areas that have not yet been taken up by German legal philosophy, or only in isolated cases, and where the practical relevance results from current social and political significance. These topics are of both a substantive-normative and a methodological nature. Finally, Section III is dedicated to the question of future strengthening of the social and political or legal policy relevance of applied legal philosophy: Who are potential addressees outside the specialist community and how could we reach them?

I. Applied philosophy of law versus the great regression? A question of self-image

Since this article is concerned with the real and possible role of an application-oriented philosophy of law in the current age of regressive tendencies, it is necessary to clarify the relevant concepts and content in advance.

1. *Preliminary consideration: Manifestations of the 'Great Regression'*

What do I mean by great regression? The term 'Great regression' is used by Heinrich Geiselberger in the context of an anthology he published in 2017 dedicated to the contemporary intellectual situation.[1] The term ties in

1 Heinrich Geiselberger (ed), *The Great Regression* (Polity 2017) xiv.

with a study critical of globalization by sociologist Oliver Nachtwey, who speaks of 'regressive modernity'.[2] In my opinion, the developments that can be observed in the course of this regression can ideally be attributed to different levels, which in the complex reality, however, influence and overlap each other. With this caveat in mind, the following can be mentioned in particular:

- At an empirical level: Putative risks deriving from globalization that have become reality, including international terrorism, anthropogenic climate change, migration movements and the loss of statehood in various parts of the world.[3]
- At a political level: Associated symptoms such as ethnic, national and religious demarcations[4] with sometimes highly aggressive and authoritarian political shifts in emphasis, wars with the serious consequences for the civilian population (for example in the Middle East or in Eastern Europe), which can be politically reignited.
- At the legal level: Human rights violations[5], violations of international law[6], withdrawal from international agreements[7] (e.g. withdrawal from the International Criminal Court (ICC)), abandonment of constitutional principles and the rule of law.[8]

---

2 Oliver Nachtwey, *Die Abstiegsgesellschaft. Über das Aufbegehren in der regressiven Moderne* (Suhrkamp 2016).

3 Geiselberger (n 1) x.

4 ibid.

5 See Human Rights Watch, 'World Report 2023' < https://www.hrw.org/world-report/2023 > accessed 30 September 2025.

6 cf, eg, OSCE, 'Sixth Interim Report on reported violations of international humanitarian law and international human rights law in Ukraine' < https://www.osce.org/odihr/582835 > accessed 30 September 2025.

7 cf, eg, Presidential Actions, Putting America First in International Environmental Agreements, Executive Order January 20, 2025 < https://www.whitehouse.gov/presidential-actions/2025/01/putting-america-first-in-international-environmental-agreements/ > accessed 30 September 2025. See also < https://www.whitehouse.gov/presidential-actions/2025/02/withdrawing-the-united-states-from-and-ending-funding-to-certain-united-nations-organizations-and-reviewing-united-states-support-to-all-international-organizations/ > accessed 30 September 2025.

8 See, eg, European Commission, Directorate-General for Justice and Consumers, 2020 Rule of law report < https://commission.europa.eu/publications/2020-rule-law-report-communication-and-country-chapters_en > accessed 30 September 2025.

- On a communicative and participatory level: Post-factual simplifications or denials of facts[9], brutalization of social and political discourse[10], sometimes comparatively low voter turnout.[11]

In summary, the current situation is characterized by global risks that are increasingly being realized in conjunction with political, legal and communicative 'de-civilization processes'.[12]Added to this is the concern about loss of control through artificial intelligence.[13]

Ultimately, the great regression is a multi-layered phenomenon. It goes without saying that the negative developments outlined above at the non-immediate legal levels also have legal relevance. However, law and courts have apparently not yet had sufficient impact, either nationally or internationally, to curb these dangerous developments effectively. It remains to be seen whether the UN Pact for the Future adopted in September 2024[14], with its 56 actions will provide encouraging new impetus for the 'profound global transformation' it describes.[15] A certain degree of skepticism seems appropriate, as these actions are largely open to interpretation and there are no control mechanisms in place so far with regard to implementation or current and future violations.[16]

---

9 The phrase 'post-factual age' is sometimes used in this context. However, it is rightly pointed out that propaganda and disinformation are not new phenomena, see, eg, Wolfgang Frindte, Ina Frindte, 'In the Post-factual Age?' in Wolfgang Frindte, Ina Frindte (eds), *Support in Times of No Support* (Springer 2020).

10 cf, eg, Ruth Wodak, 'The boundaries of what can be said have shifted": An expert interview with Ruth Wodak (questions posed by Andreas Schulz)', (2020) Discourse & Society, 31(2) 235.

11 cf Lorenzo Macchi, 'Voter turnout in the European Parliament Elections in the European Union (EU) from 1979 to 2024' < https://www.statista.com/statistics/300427/eu-parlament-turnout-for-the-european-elections/ > accessed 30 September 2025.

12 Oliver Nachtwey, 'Decivilization: on regressive tendencies in Western societies' in Geiselberger (n 1).

13 Zoe Kleinman, 'World leaders set to vie for AI domination at Paris summit', *BBC* (6 February 2025) < https://www.bbc.com/news/articles/c17evw0k8g8o > accessed 30 September 2025.

14 Resolution A/RES/79/1 adopted by the General Assembly on 22 September 2024 < https://docs.un.org/en/A/RES/79/1 > accessed 30 September 2025.

15 ibid 1.

16 cf, eg, the reservations of the United States Mission to the United Nations 15 October 2024, Pact for the Future, Global Digital Compact and Declaration on Future Generations Key Deliverables and U.S. Explanation of Position:

> 6. In joining consensus on the adoption of these outcomes, the United States makes the following points of clarification:

2. *Applied philosophy of law: In search of a self-conception of legal philosophy with a social and political relevance to the present*

Practical relevance in the field of academic research is not a purely conceptual question, but also always a question of the focus of interest and the self-conception of researchers. Is there such a thing as an application-oriented self-conception in legal philosophy, and if so, what is its main focus? As already indicated, this article can at best provide a provisional answer to this question for the field of German jurisprudence. In this context, however, it is already disputed whether philosophy of law in general and legal ethics in particular should be regarded as part of philosophy[17] or as part of jurisprudence.[18]

Within the legal disciplines in Germany, the area of so-called *'Rechtsdogmatik'* (legal doctrine) is naturally characterized by a particularly high, but system-immanent and case-oriented practical application reference, which, however, goes too far for the legal sociologist Hubert Rottleuthner due to its lack of social scientific distance. Rottleuthner criticizes the fact that legal doctrine 'does not talk about practice in jurisdiction, legislation, etc., but like it and for it'.[19] In addition, Rottleuthner had already criticized the lack of distance from legal practice decades ago, not entirely without justi-

---

7. First, the United States understands that these instruments do not create or otherwise change any rights or obligations under international law. The United States further understands that these instruments do not accurately reflect existing international law in all respects and that the language regarding the Pact's alignment with international law reflects an intention that it be read consistently with international law.

8. The 'Right to Development': We note that the 'right to development' is not recognized in any of the core UN human rights conventions, does not have an agreed international meaning, and, unlike with human rights, is not recognized as a universal right held and enjoyed by individuals and which every individual may demand from his or her own government. We continue to be concerned that the 'right to development' identified protects States instead of individuals....

< https://usun.usmission.gov/pact-for-the-future-global-digital-compact-and-declaration-on-future-generations-key-deliverables-and-u-s-explanation-of-position/ > accessed 30 September 2025.

17 Arthur Kaufmann, 'Rechtsphilosophie, Rechtstheorie, Rechtsdogmatik' in Winfried Hassemer, Ulfried Neumann, Frank Saliger (eds), *Einführung in Rechtsphilosophie und Rechtstheorie der Gegenwart* (9th ed, C.F. Müller 2016).

18 Dietmar von der Pfordten, 'Rechtsethik in Eric Hilgendorf and Jan C. Joerden (eds), *Handbuch Rechtsphilosophie* (1st ed, J. B. Metzler 2017).

19 Hubert Rottleuthner, 'Rechtswissenschaft als Sozialwissenschaft', in Hilgendorf and Joerden (n 18), translation by myself.

fication, in relation to German legal philosophy. He consistently referred to this discipline, which in his opinion is primarily practiced by lawyers for lawyers and is questionable in qualitative terms, as '*Juristenphilosophie*' (philosophy of lawyers).[20]

One might be tempted to consider Rottleuthner's criticism of the symbiotic relationship between legal doctrine and legal practice, as well as his previous criticism of a philosophy of law / of lawyers practiced in Germany, predominantly within the legal community, to be somewhat overstated and possibly outdated in parts. After all, it is not the case that contemporary legal philosophy in Germany is closing its eyes to current social and political challenges such as globalization, interculturality or value pluralism.[21] Nevertheless, Rottleuthner's criticism describes both, the aspect of a lack of academic or social-scientific distance, and a personnel tendency, which is not inaccurately characterized by the phrase 'by academic lawyers for academic lawyers'. In the face of so much internal reference to legal application, a further practical relevance of jurisprudence and thus also legal philosophy may continue to be marginalized, the practical relevance with regard to societal, social and political realities.

However, in order to explore its practical relevance in the manner advocated here, it is not only necessary to ask which real, empirically verifiable challenges contemporary philosophy of law does and should deal with, and from which perspectives. It should also be asked for what purposes, by whom and with what communicative strategy or via which channels it would like to be heard with its assessments and concepts. The relevance of applications in this sense would not only be a thematic, possibly interdisciplinary, but also an addressee-related and communicative matter. For example, should the target audience of legal philosophy always be limited to those who are directly involved in the theory and practice of law, or do we also want to reach actors from politics and society with our analyses and evaluations? Against the background of the contemporary challenges outlined above, how far should practical relevance of legal philosophy go?

Significantly, a search for the term 'applied legal philosophy' in the German-speaking world in 2025 is not particularly fruitful, but instead leads back to a bygone era on the eve of the First World War, which in some respects resembles the nervous present. Rudolf Wassermann, a

20 Hubert Rottleuthner, 'Juristenphilosophie'[1970] Kritische Justiz 476.

21 See, eg, Brian Valerius, 'Globalisierung', Jan-Christoph Marschelke, 'Interkulturalität' and Stefan Seiterle, 'Wertepluralismus' in Hilgendorf and Joerden (n 18).

lawyer from Munich in an article published in 1914 under the title *'Angewandte Rechtsphilosophie'* (Applied Legal Philosophy)[22], wrote about contemporary writing by the German legal philosopher Fritz Berolzheimer. In 1907, Berolzheimer had characterized politics as the 'small change of legal philosophy' and legal philosophy, in contrast, as 'politics on the scale of the century'.[23]

Certainly, from today's perspective, especially in the age of self-confident political science, such overblown characterizations seem unrealistic and risky. The phrase 'applied philosophy of law' used by Wassermann was robbed of the opportunity to develop a wider impact with the outbreak of the First World War. The further course of the 20th century, with its numerous historical and ideological caesuras, also challenged an understanding of legal philosophy as 'politics on a century scale'. However, this does not mean that legal philosophy had no political points of contact in Germany in the first half of the 20th century. It certainly existed in those decades in various forms. Attempts to develop a doctrine of legal philosophy during the National Socialist era have been documented and partially analyzed.[24] Even immediately after 1945, discussions in Germany associated with the so-called *Naturrechtsrenaissance* (renaissance of natural law) not only had a legal, but also a legal policy component.[25] The same applies to Radbruch's formula. It is presumably no coincidence that normative orientation is sought precisely in times of noticeable political upheaval, and that the functional relationship between legal philosophy and politics in particular is quietly reconfigured.

---

22 Rudolf Wassermann, 'Angewandte Rechtsphilosophie' (1914) 7 Archiv für Rechts- und Wirtschaftsphilosophie 252.

23 Fritz Berolzheimer, 'Politik als Wissenschaft. Ihr Wesen und ihre Grenzen' (1907/1908) 1 Archiv für Rechts- und Wirtschaftsphilosophie (1907/1908) 210, 218, translation by myself.

24 See, eg, Kaveh Nassirin, 'Den Völkermördern entgegengearbeitet?' *FAZ* (Frankfurt, 11 July 2018) N 32; Hubert Rottleuthner, 'Rezension von Imke Schröder, Zur Legitimationsfunktion der Rechtsphilosophie im Nationalsozialismus. Kontinuität und Diskontinuität rechtsphilosophischer Lehren zwischen Weimarer Republik und NS-Zeit (2002); Maja Bleckmann, Barrieren gegen den Unrechtsstaat? Kontinuitäten und Brüche in den rechtsphilosophischen Lehren Alfred Manigks, Gustav Radbruchs und Felix Holldacks angesichts des Nationalsozialismus (2004)', [2007] ARSP 442, 448; Kenny Yang, 'The Rise of Legal Positivism in Germany: A Prelude to Nazi Arbitrariness?' (2012), 3 The Western Australian Jurist 245.

25 Eckardt Buchholz-Schuster, *Rechtsphilosophische Legitimation der Rechtspraxis nach Systemwechseln. Eine Untersuchung zur Funktion von „Juristenphilosophie"* (Berlin Verlag / Nomos 1998) 116-119.

In retrospect, however, the reticence of German legal philosophy towards society and politics or social and political reality is striking, at least since 1970 and the following decades. In Germany, despite some approaches to these issues since early 1970s, the focus of legal philosophy has not been on analyzing, legitimizing and, if necessary, criticizing legal practice, including legislative practice in their respective social and political contexts, thus striving for a social and political impact in appropriate cases. Instead, the aim is to perform, in normative terms, a neutral function in relation to legal practice. It is true, for example, that the question of gender and law has been explored in terms of its impact on society.[26] Similarly, professional philosophers are sometimes used to characterize the neighboring field of political philosophy[27], or the relationship between law and politics is analyzed descriptively from different perspectives.[28] Within one's own academic and professional community, one can and may do this observationally. However, attempts to use legal philosophical analyses that consider cultural, social, political or economic factors to contribute to influencing the underlying social attitudes, values and norms of law remain rare. Examples such as the field of feminist legal theories, which attempt to reduce negative social values such as prejudice and discrimination are exceptions.[29] A theoretical foundation for feminist foreign policy is anyway left to political science.[30]

Similarly, in Germany, the specific question of a possible social or political mission for legal philosophy is largely ignored in the face of the challenges and crises of the present. There are only a few exceptions.[31] While, for example, the relationship between law and ideology is discussed

---

26 Lisa Müller, 'Gender und Recht' in Hilgendorf and Joerden (n 18) with further references.

27 Norbert Campagna, 'Politische Philosophie' in Hilgendorf and Joerden (n 18) with further references.

28 Matthias Kaufmann, 'Politik und Recht' in Hilgendorf and Joerden (n 18) with further references.

29 Susanne Baer and Sarah Elsuni, 'Feministische Rechtstheorien' in Hilgendorf and Joerden (n 18) with further references.

30 cf Lyric Thompson and others, *Toward a Feminist Foreign Policy in the United States* (2020) International Center for Research on Women < https://www.icrw.org/wp-content/uploads/2020/05/FFP-USA_v11-spreads.pdf > accessed 30 September 2025.

31 cf Matthias Mahlmann, 'Der politische Moment der Rechtsphilosophie' (2017) 2 RW 181.

pragmatically and free of emotion in the Anglo-American field[32], in the German legal philosophy it almost seems as if the ideology-critical attitude in reaction to the renaissance of natural law of the late 1940s, which began in the early 1970s in parts of German legal-historical and legal-sociological research continues to the present. This attitude manifested itself, among other things, in clear and strong criticism of the supposed ideological bias and susceptibility to ideology of legitimization patterns shaped by natural law in German legal practice in the first post-war years.[33]

However, those who aim to keep the law and its philosophy as free as possible from normative influences in the sense of supposed rationality, are not acting as rationally and neutrally as claimed. A legal philosophy or legal theory with a more positivist orientation cannot be non-normative or non-ideological or judgmental, at least not without exception.[34] Even reference to the principle of the rule of law does not change this. Nowhere is this more evident than in the wake of political system changes, where the often-advocated submission to the normative standards of the factuality of a state that no longer exists is essentially to a decision in favor of the normative and possibly also criminal inviolability of that old system. As a result, it is certainly normatively characterized and by no means neutral or free of ideology.[35] A rationality postulate understood in this way therefore promises more than it is able to fulfil. Matthias Mahlmann describes this problem as follows:

> ... The problem lies in the fact that critique can become total, that it falls into self-contradictory scepticism, which loses the means of criti-

32 cf Christine Sypnowich, 'Law and Ideology', *The Stanford Encyclopedia of Philosophy* (Summer edn, 2024) < https://plato.stanford.edu/archives/sum2024/entries/law-ideology/ > accessed 30 September 2025.

33 Only a few of the many contributions that contained positions skeptical of ideology towards the German natural law renaissance after 1968 can be mentioned here: Wolf Rosenbaum, *Naturrecht und positives Recht. Rechtssoziologische Untersuchungen zum Einfluß der Naturrechtslehre auf die Rechtspraxis in Deutschland seit Beginn des 19. Jahrhunderts* (Luchterhand 1972) 125, 126, 190; Ingo Müller, *Furchtbare Juristen. Die unbewältigte Vergangenheit unserer Justiz,* (Kindler 1987) 226. See also Bernd Rüthers, *Entartetes Recht: Rechtslehren und Kronjuristen im Dritten Reich,* (C. H. Beck 1988) 180.

34 This is reminiscent of the classic communication theory analysis of Paul Watzlawick, Janet Beavin Bavelas, Don D. Jackson, *Pragmatics of Human Communication: A Study of Interactional Patterns, Pathologies, and Paradoxes* (W.W. Norton 1967), 49: one cannot *not* behave ... one cannot *not* communicate.

35 Buchholz-Schuster (n 25) 332-336.

> cising false claims, because these means themselves are captured and undermined by the totality of the negation of the possibility of truth and rightness. ...[36]

In particular, jurisprudence and its related philosophy cannot be expected to gain rationality by ignoring ideologies or real political and social developments that contribute or threaten to contribute (sometimes by omission) directly or indirectly to human rights violations, anti-democratic behavior and violations of international law. In this context, concerns about the ideological or political instrumentalization of the law and its legal-ethical foundations do not provide any convincing justification when viewed in the light of day.

In view of the contemporary developments and challenges noted above, it seems more than appropriate to abandon legal-philosophical restraint towards political and social realities, insofar as it results from skepticism towards the ideological susceptibility of legal and legal-ethical analyses. The legal-philosophical problem focus on 'law' should be expanded. In such a situation, an applied philosophy of law should not only analyze, legitimize and criticize national and international law and the attitudes and political views that underlie the law, but also its gaps and the partial, sometimes dramatic, disregard for the law. Applied legal philosophy should have the strength and courage to feed its red lines, which can be rationally justified on the level of legal-ethical theory, into sometimes irrational social, political, or populist discourses more proactively than before. The 'Science for Future' and 'World Lawyers' Pledge on Climate Action' initiatives, for example, provide examples of attempts to incorporate relevant scientific expertise into social and political discourse and thus strengthen practical relevance.[37]

In the following two sections, aspects associated with this proposed practical relevance of legal philosophy will be analyzed in more detail, in thematic terms (Section II) and then in terms of addressees and communication (Section III). What should we consider more intensively with regard to the manifestations of the great regression described at the beginning - and for whom? This outlines and illustrates the directions in which an

---

36 Mahlmann (n 31) 216, translation by myself.

37 cf < https://scientists4future.org/ > ; Saskia Stucki and others, 'World Lawyers' Pledge on Climate Action' (2021) < https://lawyersclimatepledge.org/wp-content/uploads/2021/08/Lawyers-Climate-Pledge_English.pdf > both accessed 30 September 2025.

applied philosophy of law that is orientated towards social and political realities could develop.

II. Exemplary topics of applied philosophy of law

Based on the regressive tendencies of the present and the classic fundamental questions of the philosophy of law, it is first necessary to identify some areas that could be addressed and which, in my opinion, deserve a stronger emphasis in legal philosophy. Naturally, legal philosophical thought will feel particularly challenged, in normative and thus legal-ethical terms, by developments and tendencies that violate human rights (see 1 below). However, there are also related methodological issues, which concern the question of the differentiation of well-founded normative concepts from theoretically unfounded ideology and the related question of a stronger consideration of empirical or social scientific perspectives (see 2 below). Normative and methodological questions are mutually dependent. In particular, the development of normative concepts would not only remain incomplete without quality and rationality criteria, but also without consideration of legally relevant social facts.

1. *Normative problem areas*

In the following exemplary suggestion of topics, the focus is less on issues of social and political relevance that have already been dealt with in the philosophy of law, but rather on current issues or existing gaps that have rarely been addressed.

1.1 Extreme injustice through state and supranational omission, e.g. in relation to climate change and the humanitarian challenges of migration

These are two current examples of intolerable conditions in the context of state and supranational omission. First, according to the German Federal Constitutional Court, it is a violation of constitutional law to expose younger generations to the consequences of anthropogenic climate change unchecked.[38] Secondly, it seems contrary to human rights to refrain from State or supranationally initiated rescue measures in the Mediterranean and other sea routes in relation to maritime emergencies involving migrants.[39] However, it appears that invoking national and international law alone has not yet been able to put an end to such intolerable developments and conditions. For courts in many countries, but also for a non-positivist legal philosophy based on legal ethics, this remains a normative challenge at present.[40]

The classic legal-ethical question of what right law should be in contrast to the wrong can be divided into the two basic questions of what right law should be and how it should be (methodically) recognized or realized.[41] This problem, which Gustav Radbruch had already expanded in 1946 for cases of statutory lawlessness[42], should be extended beyond established theories of justice with regard to the above-mentioned examples. Does extreme, intolerable injustice occur through state and supranational omission? With which legal-ethical concepts can such injustice be rationally and comprehensibly characterized as such? What minimum ethical requirements can we use to avoid such extreme injustice? How can institutional responsibility and attribution in relation to extreme injustice in supranational contexts be convincingly constructed and described?[43]

In my view, the ethical gaps in national and international law reflected in such issues contribute to exacerbating the existing problem of the difficult

38 BVerfG, Order of the First Senate of March 24, 2021 - 1 BvR 2656/18 -, para 249.

39 Eckardt Buchholz-Schuster, *Extreme Wrong Committed by National and Supranational Inactivity. Analyzing the Mediterranean Migrant Crisis and Climate Change from a Legal Philosophical Perspective* (2nd edn, Berliner Wissenschaftsverlag 2023) 37.

40 For an approximation of legal and philosophical perspectives in the context of the environmental crisis, see also Simone Zurbuchen, 'Introduction' in: Alain Papaux and Simone Zurbuchen (eds), *Philosophy, Law and Environmental Crisis / Philosophie, droit et crise environnementale. Workshop of the Swiss Society for Philosophy of Law and Social Philosophy, September 12–13, 2014, Swiss Institute of Comparative Law, Lausanne / Congrès de l'Association Suisse de Philosophie du Droit et de Philosophie Sociale, 12–13 septembre 2014*, (Franz Steiner Verlag 2016) 9 ff.

41 Arthur Kaufmann and Dietmar von der Pfordten 'Problemgeschichte der Rechtsphilosophie' in Hassemer, Neumann, Saliger (n 17) 23.

42 See Gustav Radbruch, 'Gesetzliches Unrecht und übergesetzliches Recht' (1946) 1 Süddeutsche Juristen-Zeitung 105; English version: Gustav Radbruch, Bonnie Litschewski Paulson and Stanley L. Paulson, 'Statutory Lawlessness and Supra-Statutory Law' (2006) 26 Oxford JLS 1.

43 Buchholz-Schuster, (n 39) 23, 25.

legal and political control of international developments such as anthropogenic climate change or maritime emergencies on migration routes. I argue that this unsatisfactory legal situation, which is difficult to resolve, contributes to a widespread lack of awareness of injustice and thus also to *laissez-faire* on the part of responsible actors in executive, legislative and supranational institutions. As a rule, a private individual will feel both legally and morally compelled to call for help for the victims of a serious traffic accident that they did not directly cause and that they witnessed. By contrast, when refugees have drowned in the Mediterranean and on other sea routes, in full view of the public, this has clearly worried political actors in state and supranational institutions within Europe far less.

However, there is no apparent reason in terms of democratic theory or norms to relativize the importance of human rights and the principle of universalization in such cases of institutionally tolerated human rights violations and inadequate protection of life.[44] Such a situation threatens to continue in the future unabated. An applied philosophy of law that addresses current global and international challenges should also focus on the complex of issues that relate to the normative assessment of state and supranational omissions, including the associated questions of responsibility and attribution. In this field, it is important to identify red lines of legal ethics precisely and then demand that they be observed by political actors. Even those within metaethics who are skeptical about a so-called moral realism of objectively existing or justifiable moral values[45] should acknowledge that there is a realism of the immoral, of objectively existing and cognitively graspable extreme injustice.[46]

1.2 Civil disobedience, legitimacy and defense of the democratic constitutional state

The democratic constitutional state, which seemed so secure a few decades ago, is currently struggling with numerous problems in its global manifestations and is increasingly threatened within and without. This is also

44 ibid n 25.

45 Moral realism is currently being advocated, for example, by Markus Gabriel, *Moral Progress in Dark Times: Universal Values for the Twenty-First Century*, Wieland Hoban (trans.) (Polity Press, 2022).

46 See n 55.

associated with normative legitimacy crises of various causes. The dismantling and destruction of democratic structures and institutions by elected governments with a tendency towards authoritarianism or patrimonialism, lawlessness combined with simple answers to complex challenges is only a symptom in this context.[47] The complexity of current challenges such as anthropogenic climate change or migration obviously pushes even the ideal-typical construct of the democratic constitutional state to its limits as long as its representatives are not able to account for these challenges in an ethically justifiable manner. In other words, democratic crises of legitimacy and an internal loss of confidence in the idea of the democratic constitutional state are also the result of the inability of democratic constitutional states to solve the existential problems of our time at national and international level in a mutually satisfactory manner.

What contributions could an applied philosophy of law make to counter these social and political losses of confidence in the democratic constitutional state? A not insignificant point in this context concerns the legitimacy of civil disobedience in a democratic constitutional state. As is well known, the philosophy of law also has conceptual approaches in this regard.[48] However, its positions are rarely visible in social and political debates, at least in Germany, and there is hardly a dominant opinion in terms of content in the legal philosophical debate on this normative problem. Public and political discussions about civil disobedience in Germany in recent years confirm this, with political and legal skepticism towards civil disobedience being predominant.[49]

47 cf Steven Levitsky and Lucan A. Way, 'The Path to American Authoritarianism. What Comes After Democratic Breakdown' *Foreign Affairs* (New York City, February 11 2025) < https://www.foreignaffairs.com/united-states/path-american-authoritarianism-trump > accessed 30 September 2025.

48 See Max-Emanuel Geis, 'Ziviler Ungehorsam', in Hilgendorf and Joerden (n. 18) 480 with further references; John Rawls, *A Theory of Justice* (10th impression, Oxford University Press 1990) 363.

49 cf, eg, Bennet Ribbeck, 'Amnesty condemns criminal association charges against climate activists in Germany' (*Clean Energy Wire*, 26 March 2025) < https://www.cleanenergywire.org/news/amnesty-condemns-criminal-association-charges-against-climate-activists-germany > accessed 30 September 2025. In many cases, the fact that the concept and role of civil disobedience in the rule of law has been the subject of well-founded analyses in recent decades has been ignored or was obviously unknown, especially outside of political theory. However, insufficient political, judicial and activist awareness of theoretical and legal-ethical concepts and rational criteria for the legitimacy of civil disobedience makes it difficult to have a socially,

John Rawls famously ascribes justified civil disobedience the role of introducing 'stability into a well-ordered society, or one that is nearly just.'[50] Ralf Dreier argues similarly in Germany in countering the objection that accepting a right to civil disobedience could undermine the the principle of representative democracy, stating that 'the change that is to be prevented has already occurred and the task is to channel it'.[51] However, unlike Rawls, Dreier argues on a purely constitutional and not on a legal-ethical or moral-philosophical level. This example makes it clear that there is still a need for discussion in legal philosophy with regard to the characterization or systematic positioning of civil disobedience as a supra-legal right, as a constitutionally legitimizable fundamental right or as a hybrid form.

The practical relevance of this systematic positioning arises from two points. On the one hand, it results from the fact that civil disobedience could be a format for bringing people arguing on different levels (morally, legally, politically, etc.) into conversation with each other on essential points in relation to existential issues such as anthropogenic climate change. This concerns the sometimes controversial question of extreme injustice (see also II. 1.1 above), and also the questions of the non-violence and proportionality of the disobedience directed against it. On the other hand, relevance results from the fact that civil disobedience, when serving the stabilizing function ascribed to it by Rawls and Dreier in relation to democratic constitutional states, represents an alternative to the political system changes demanded by parts of the climate protection movement ('system change not climate change'). In this context, it should be considered that democratic states endanger their own political stability in the medium and long term and thus indirectly also their protection of human rights and fundamental rights through hesitant action on climate protection due to diminishing resources as a result of climate change.[52]

---

legally and politically rational debate - not only with regard to the legitimacy of civil disobedience, but above all with regard to the triggers of civil disobedience.

50 Rawls (n 48) 383.

51 Ralf Dreier, 'Widerstandsrecht im Rechtsstaat? Bemerkungen zum zivilen Ungehorsam' in Ralf Dreier (ed), *Recht – Staat – Vernunft. Studien zur Rechtstheorie*, (2nd edn, Suhrkamp 2016) 70. See also Samira Akbarian, *Ziviler Ungehorsam als Verfassungsinterpretation* (Mohr Siebeck 2023).

52 See Felix Ekardt, Fraziska Heß 'Intertemporaler Freiheitsschutz, Existenzminimum und Gewal-tenteilung nach dem BVerfG-Klima-Beschluss. Freiheitsgefährdung durch Klimawandel oder durch Klimapolitik?' (2021) 11 ZUR 579, 583 with further references.

The place of civil disobedience in the democratic constitutional state is closely linked to its core legitimacy. Here too, an applied philosophy of law could make an important contribution, especially with regard to elected governments that have tendencies towards authoritarianism or patrimonialism as well as lawlessness, in relation to their own national constitutional law. This core of legitimacy is formed, among other things, from instrumental rationality and efficiency, but above all from the normative principles of human autonomy and dignity.[53] However, more recent events such as in the Mediterranean or at Guantanamo Bay raise doubts as to whether human dignity is still respected and treated as a supreme value, at least in democratic constitutional states. And in this context, Radbruch's well-known relativism argument does not exactly seem like a legal philosophical legitimization of the value of human dignity:

> Propositions of Ought can be based only on other propositions of Ought and can be proved only by them. Exactly for this reason ultimate propositions of Ought cannot be proved, are axiomatic, capable not of cognition but only of confession. Wherever there meet in dispute antagonistic contentions about the ultimate propositions of Ought ... decision between them cannot be made with scientific clearness ...[54]

However, these three problems mentioned regarding relation to the principle of human dignity should not be a reason to abandon legal philosophical attempts to sharpen and legitimize the concept of human dignity in the direction of political responsibility. Today, in particular, the exact opposite is true: even if Radbruch's statement quoted above is correct, rationality criteria could still be developed for normative commitments, which could be based not least on empiricism and historical experiences of injustice.[55]

---

53 See Mahlmann (n 31) 184.

54 Gustav Radbruch, *Rechtsphilosophie* (3rd edn., Quelle & Meyer 1932) 8; translation according to Arnold Brecht, 'The Rise of Relativism in Political and Legal Philosophy' (1939) 6 Social Research 393, 400 fn 3.

55 cf on the relativism argument Robert Alexy, 'Zur Verteidigung eines nichtpositivistischen Rechtsbegriffs' in Werner Krawietz and Georg Henrik v. Wright (eds), *Öffentliche oder private Moral? Vom Geltungsgrunde und der Legitimität des Rechts. Festschrift für Ernesto Garzón Valdés* (Duncker & Humblot 1992) 102 (translation by myself):

> In order to dispel this skeptical objection, it must be shown that a sentence such as:
> (1) The physical and material annihilation of a minority of the population for racial reasons is extreme injustice,
> is capable of rational justification, while a sentence such as:

On this basis, it would then be possible to formulate a sharp but also differentiated critique of the philosophy of law against political attitudes that reject a democratic core of legitimacy based on human dignity and threaten democratic constitutional states from within or without.[56]

1.3 Legitimation and defense of international law

The omnipresent internal and external threats to democratic constitutional states bring us to another potential subject area for reflection on the content of applied legal philosophy in the 21st century. In the last two decades, there has been an increasing convergence of legal philosophy and international law, especially in the Anglo-American field with a focus on customary international law or the international rule of law.[57] German legal philosophy was also comparatively restrained in this respect during the same period.[58] However, just as with regard to the democratic constitutional state, the question arises as to what contribution an applied philosophy of law would like to make to the increasingly urgent legitimization and defense of international law as we enter the second quarter of the 21st century. There are increasing signs that basic rules of international law, such as the prohibition

(2) The physical and material annihilation of a minority of the population for racial reasons is not extreme injustice,
can be rationally refuted.

56 cf Mahlmann (n. 31) 200. In my opinion, current considerations in legal philosophy to replace the anthropocentric understanding of law of our time with a 'post-human' concept of law appear questionable with regard to their potential impact on the recognition of human dignity as the highest value; cf 33. Tagung des Jungen Forums Rechtsphilosophie, 24. und 25. September 2025, Universität Münster, Person – Subjekt – Individuum, Call for Papers < https://www.jungesforumrechtsphilosophie.com/media/call-for-abstracts_jfr_2025.pdf > accessed 30 September 2025.

57 An overview can be found, for example, in Andreas Follesdal and Steven R. Ratner, 'Introducing David Lefkowitz's Philosophy and International Law' (*EJIL: Talk!*, November 4 2021) < https://www.ejiltalk.org/introducing-david-lefkowitzs-philosophy-and-international-law/ >accessed 30 September 2025. See also the article by Veronica Rodriguez-Blanco, 'What Makes a Transnational Rule of Law? Understanding the Logos and Values of Human Action in Transnational Law' in section V. of this anthology.

58 One of the few exceptions: Günther Kreuzbauer, *Die Norm im Völkerrecht: Eine rechtsphilosophische und rechtstheoretische Untersuchung* (Lit 2006); for France, cf. an older contribution from a more political-philosophical perspective by Agnès Lejbowicz, *Philosophie du droit international : L'impossible capture de l'humanité* (Presses Universitaires de France - PUF 1999).

of the use of force (Art. 2(4) UN Charter) or the right to self-determination, could increasingly lose their post-1945 status established in future.[59] In addition, the binding effect of free trade agreements, the alliance obligation under Art. 5 of the North Atlantic Treaty and the functioning of the International Criminal Court, as well as the principle of *pacta sunt servanda* as a fundamental norm of the rules-based international order, also appear to be under threat at present.[60]

While Gustav Radbruch's 1946 formula still focused on the question of statutory lawlessness[61], we are currently increasingly encountering a phenomenon that could also be described as governmental lawlessness at the international level. This manifests itself, on the one hand, through the aforementioned ethical loopholes not covered by law, which contribute to extreme injustice through state or supranational *laissez-faire* or omission[62], and, on the other hand, through deliberate or condoned active violations of relevant international law.[63]

Legal philosophical positions on governmental lawlessness are likely to face similar issues as in relation to the legitimation and defense of the democratic constitutional state outlined above. Once again, it would be a matter of shedding new light on and revitalizing the relevant core of legitimacy, which is closely related to that of the democratic constitutional state. From my point of view, it would be helpful to develop rationality criteria for normative commitments underlying international law in relation to its broader defense against cynical power-political calculations and an overemphasis on the relativity argument, in particular to human dignity.[64] In this context, too, empiricism and extreme experiences of injustice by the State should be taken into consideration as the basis for such rationality criteria. As a result, one would need to rationally refute political or philosophical attitudes that amount to relativizing or even denying the significance

---

59 Franz C. Mayer, 'Eine transatlantische Verfassungskrise?' (2025) LTO < https://www.lto.de/recht/hintergruende/h/der-amerikanische-albtraum-teil-2 > accessed 30 September 2025.

60 ibid.

61 Radbruch (n 42).

62 See II. 1.1.

63 eg, John B. Bellinger III, 'How Russia's Invasion of Ukraine Violates International Law' (*CFR*, 28 February 2022) < https://www.cfr.org/article/how-russias-invasion-ukraine-violates-international-law > accessed 30 September 2025.

64 See Fabiana Oliveira Pinho, *Menschenwürde als Topos im Völkerrecht. Eine Untersuchung zur juristischen Argumentation auf supranationaler Ebene aus rhetorisch-empirischer Perspektive* (Duncker & Humblot 2023).

of central principles of international law such as respect for fundamental human rights and the principle of equality of states.[65] The current example of the Russian war against Ukraine shows that aggressive war within Europe, which was long thought to have become unlikely, can once again be waged politically and legitimized with no small degree of success. It also drastically illustrates that disregarding the concept of Sovereign Equality of States in international law threatens to thwart the protection of democratic self-determination and autonomy. This also underlines the close substantive relationship between the core legitimacies of international law and the democratic constitutional state. However, it also underlines the urgent need for a current legal-philosophical defense of those cores of legitimacy based on human dignity, especially in times of current and imminent wars with the most serious consequences for the civilian population.

2. *Problematic areas of methodology*

In my view, legal-ethical red lines in terms of precisely identified extreme injustice and legitimation approaches in relation to democratic constitutional states and international law need to be methodologically supplemented by rational criteria in the form of approaches based on decision-making or argumentation theory, as well as empirical reviews in order to be able to evaluate them and protect them from possibly unfounded criticism of ideology or relativism in legal policy discourses.

2.1 Theory formation on legal-ethical decision-making and argumentation

Prescriptive or normative theories of legal decision-making and, in particular, legal argumentation theories have been established branches of German legal theory for decades.[66] However, differentiated theories of legal-ethical decision-making and legal-ethical argumentation have, as far as can be

---

65 cf, eg, UN Charter: preamble; art 1 ff CFR; art 2 TEU.

66 See, eg, Jochen Schneider, 'Theorie juristischen Entscheidens' in Hassemer, Neumann, Saliger (n 17); Ulfried Neumann, *Juristische Argumentationstheorie* (Nomos 2023).

seen, not yet been realized.[67] Yet they could provide important contributions and impulses for the promotion of applied legal-ethical evaluation and legitimation of concepts, especially in today's world.

The criteria for assessing legal-ethical rationality, approaches and models of legal-ethical argumentation, and distinguishing between legal-ethical argumentation and pure rhetoric or sham argumentation should be examined or classified in terms of argumentation theory. Argumentation-theoretical criteria for assessing the legal-ethical rationality of legitimation concepts could include, for example, the existence of a transparent justification for the necessity of legal-ethical argumentation in individual cases (for example, the existence of a legal-ethical loophole), a clear demarcation or positional determination vis-à-vis the legal level of argumentation, conceptual quality (i.e. conclusive reference to a classical concept of justice with clear terminology, functionality and limited relativism, for example, in the sense of the Radbruch formula[68]), or retention of the conceptually anchored terminology in one's own argumentation context, etc.[69] Furthermore, possibilities for dealing with postmodern irrationalism and populism in legal ethics should be demonstrated within the framework of differentiated theories of legal-ethical decision-making and argumentation.

2.2 Empirical examination of positions relevant to legal ethics and legal policy as well as constitutional and international law principles

Insofar as legal philosophy deals with the methodology and science of law beyond normative or legal ethical issues, it should be noted that since the 1970s, German legal theory has occasionally advocated the program of legal science as social science, albeit with little resonance to date.[70] This refers to the supplementation of conventional jurisprudence by a theoretically distanced social science aimed at empirical testing.[71] Such empirical testing could, for example, relate to questions of the origin, effectiveness and effects

67 See, however, corresponding efforts with a socio-ethical focus in Julian Nida-Rümelin, *Entscheidungstheorie und Ethik. Decision Theory and Ethics* (2nd, Extended ed, Herbert Utz 2004).

68 cf Stanley L. Paulson, 'Radbruch on Unjust Laws: Competing Earlier and Later Views?' (1995) 15 OJLS 489.

69 cf Buchholz-Schuster (n. 25) 32-34, 334-336.

70 Rottleuthner (n 19) 251-254 with further references.

71 ibid 253.

of laws, attitudes and opinions towards the law within society and the role of the law in everyday life.[72] Even if such empirical perspectives on the law continue to be largely ignored within contemporary German jurisprudence, the approach of supplementing legal perspectives from a social science perspective, aiming to increase rationality in legal ethics and legal policy discourses seems worth considering.

There are empirical, rather than speculative, questions to be answered concerning trends in the course of the great regression and the role of constitutional law and international law in this context. What role do given legal frameworks play in relation to the *laissez-faire* attitude of political actors and institutions towards climate change or maritime emergencies in connection with migration? What attitudes prevail within Western societies and their political representatives today regarding the value of democratic constitutional states and human dignity? What are the results of methodologically sophisticated empirical content analyses of court decisions and political statements on anthropogenic climate change or related cases of civil disobedience? How has international law developed as a social fact beyond legal-historical perspectives since the Second World War, and how might it continue to develop as a social fact? Where do political actors seek further normative guidance? The list could go on. It is clear that such questions, which should be examined from a social science or sociology of law perspective, go far beyond the rationality criteria for normative commitments based on empiricism and historical experiences of injustice advocated in Sections II. 1.2 and 1.3 above.

III. On the future strengthening of the social and political relevance of applied legal philosophy

In this context, two questions arise: Should the social and political relevance of applied legal philosophy be strengthened in light of the numerous thematic points of reference outlined above in relation to the regressive realities of the present. If so, how could this be achieved? In the following, I will outline some considerations on this theme.

With regard to the first question, I would like to begin by quoting Matthias Mahlmann again, who speaks in this context of the 'civilizing business of the philosophy of law':

72 ibid.

> Democracy, the constitutional state and an international order based on fundamental rights are products of a philosophy of law that has reached people politically. The constitutional state and democracy were political demands that ... became reality ... because people were captured by the persuasive power of these ideas. Reflection on the philosophy of law is only one of many voices in a civilizing process, not the most audible, nor the most politically important. But it should be one of the voices that - especially in the current crisis situation - raises its voice to defend a certain form of human coexistence - that is the core of its business. This formulates a requirement for reflection in this area: not to become comfortable in political irrelevance ...[73]

Basically, the political relevance of legal-philosophical thinking and the development of target groups outside of one's own academic community (actors from politics and society) is convincingly justified in historical terms. This justification, similar to the defense of human dignity against relativistic skepticism or political disregard outlined above, relies on empiricism and historical experiences of injustice. Moreover, the inner ethical attitude or constitution of social and political actors is also taken into consideration.[74]

Would democratic constitutional states then also have to fear a group of self-proclaimed legal philosopher kings? There is no cause for concern in this respect, neither prognostically nor conceptually. Within the polyphonic democratic constitutional states of the 21st century, even applied legal-ethical reflection with social and political references would, in all likelihood, be just one of many voices, albeit perhaps an occasionally newly perceptible one. Conceptually, it should be pointed out that the project of applied legal philosophy outlined here is not about overplaying democratic decision-making processes in terms of legal philosophy. Rather, the aim would be to defend the place of legal-ethical reason in the sometimes irrational world of politics and thus to identify a space and a terrain for genuine human judgment.[75] This would mean defining red lines of legal ethics that should not be crossed with regard to the preservation of human dignity, but also with regard to the protection of democratic constitutional states and international law.

---

73 Mahlmann (n. 31) 219, translation by myself.

74 ibid 199.

75 Haig Patapan, *Modern Philosopher Kings. Wisdom and Power in Politics* (Edinburgh University Press 2023) 186, 187.

But how could the social and political relevance of applied legal philosophy be strengthened? How do we come together with stakeholders from the legislative, judicial, political and social spheres? The Covid-19 pandemic has shown in Germany and other countries that politicians in particular are more or less open to expert knowledge in times of crisis.[76] However, whether this also applies in the same way to expert knowledge on legal ethics, outside the natural sciences, remains to be seen. Clarity with regard to the potential addressees would be important in any case. If contributions from legal philosophy are also aimed at society and politics, then actors from civil society such as NGOs, but also governments, legislatures, international organizations etc., become potential addressees. Incidentally, a proactive role of legal-philosophical actors would be required in the communication of normative guidance. Consideration should also be given to breaking new ground:

- Consideration could be given, for example, to seeking a stronger advisory and impulse-giving function vis-à-vis politics at various levels, following the example of, or in cooperation with, Councils on Foreign Relations, and to providing normative orientation or argumentation aids.[77] What is the general state of the voice of legal philosophy in legislative and reform practice? In this context, it would be enlightening if an applied philosophy of law were to clarify not only its functional relationship with politics, but also political science.
- Social media platforms could also be increasingly used for ethically sound contributions on current political developments. Nowadays, social media platforms have a major influence on the formation of public opinion.[78]
- Efforts could be made to strengthen the networking of those legal-philosophical actors who publish on topics of social and political relevance.

76 cf, eg, Paul Cairney and Federico Toth, 'The politics of COVID-19 experts: comparing winners and losers in Italy and the UK' (2023) 42(3) Policy and Society 392.

77 eg, European Council on Foreign Relations < https://ecfr.eu/london/ >, German Council on Foreign Relations < https://dgap.org/en/research/programs/think-tank-lab > accessed 30 September 2025.

78 cf Ruprecht Polenz, *Tu was! Kurze Anleitung zur Verteidigung der Demokratie* (C.H. Beck 2024).

- An attempt could be made to contact political institutions or public officials directly and draw attention to their own contributions to legal ethics with corresponding practical relevance.[79]
- Where this appears necessary at a national level, professional and legal policy should also work to ensure that reflection on legal philosophical questions in legal training and practice is institutionally secured through appropriate reforms to training and professional law.[80]

IV. Conclusion

Having said all this, what can an applied philosophy of law achieve in the face of social and political trends in our crisis-ridden, sometimes regressive times? The list of topics presented in this article was merely exemplary. The challenges for contemporary law and legal ethics are too manifold to be fully explored here.[81] In my view, the first step would be to clarify one's own functional relationship to the great regression and its manifestations, which are becoming more noticeable from year to year.

Ultimately, this means deciding between potential social and political relevance or actual irrelevance. In an article a few years ago, I referred to this as a 'legal-philosophical self-diagnosis'[82], which should be combined

79 In March 2023, the author contacted various public officials and institutions at national and European level with responsibilities in the area of migration and climate protection in order to draw attention to the legal and ethical issue of possibly inadequate rescue and climate protection measures (see n 38). Feedback was received in one case. See letter from author to European Commission, Directorate-General for Climate Action (CLIMA), Executive Vice-President Frans Timmermans (16 March 2023) and Email from European Commission, Directorate-Generale Climate Action, Directorate A – Strategy to author (27 April 2023).

80 For an example from the Netherlands, see the contribution by Derk Venema, 'Philosophy of Law in Professional Ethics Training for Judges', in section VI. of this anthology. See also the current MCT-based research study on this issue by Ewa Nowak Nowak, Renetta Bos and others, 'Conceptualizing Extended Jurisprudential Competence of Legal Professionals to Uphold the Democratic Rule of Law. Recent Study on Law Students' Moral Competence Development from Six European Countries' in Ana Margarida Gaudêncio (ed), *Exploring the Boundaries of Law* (Springer 2025).

81 Consider, eg, questions of intercultural justice or the inconsistent application of human rights, which are not dealt with in depth here.

82 Eckardt Buchholz-Schuster, 'Rechtsphilosophische Horizonte und die Globalisierung' in Bärbel Frischmann and Christian Holtorf (eds), *Über den Horizont. Standorte, Grenzen und Perspektiven* (de Gruyter 2019).

with an even stronger consideration of the political and social realities of the present. The normative restraint that has characterized at least parts of German legal philosophy and legal theory in recent decades, out of concern about ideological appropriation of jurisprudence, should be reconsidered and, if possible, overcome in the face of the challenges of the 21st century. The normative taking sides in favour of human dignity, democratic constitutional states and international law should not be confused with arbitrary ideology or the arrogance of philosopher kings, but should be rationally justified, especially in the face of such objections or reservations in these times. The same would apply to corresponding initiatives to achieve a stronger social and political impact with contributions to legal ethics by using normative evaluations also to reflect the inner ethical stance of social and political actors.

One possible thematic consequence of these functional considerations on the role of applied philosophy of law would be a normative philosophy of law that is both rationally and empirically orientated and which marks red lines of legal ethics for politics where ethically incomplete law has so far reached its limits at various levels. A second thematic branch can be seen in the legitimization and defense of the democratic constitutional state, including its inherent civil disobedience, and of international law.

In this context, the identification of red lines of legal ethics requires a consensual, metaethical realism of the objectively existing extreme injustice[83], together with reliable criteria or concepts of legal ethics for its cognitive understanding. What is also required, however, is the clarification of questions of institutional responsibility and attribution, all of this in a form that can also be translated into the everyday language of social and political discourse. The legitimation and defense of democracy and international law demand a legal-ethical return to their respective cores of legitimacy as well as empirically or historically based rational criteria to support them. Finally, both areas require suitable rational criteria, in terms of argumentation and decision-making theory, as well as legal facts that have been seriously established by a social science perspective. In this regard, it would be particularly important to expose overt or covert attempts to relativize the humanistic significance of human dignity, democratic constitutional

83 Whether the idea of a procedural theory of avoiding extreme injustice developed following John Rawls in the 21st century, which aims in a similar direction, would run counter to a corresponding metaethical realism must be left open at this point. Cf Rawls (n 48).

states or international law from an epistemological, ethical or political perspective, as clearly as possible, as sham arguments.

Admittedly, the bottom line is that this is a very comprehensive and demanding specification for applied legal philosophy in the 21st century. But what would be the alternative? Mere appeals to the common sense of moral realism do not fulfil our own scientific requirements, nor do they prevent political irrationality. The value of human dignity, in its state, institutional and legal manifestations, is once again under threat in our time, and must be defended, even in terms of legal philosophy. Stating the facts of the great regression is no longer enough. One should also pass legal ethical judgment where judgment is due.

II.
Legality and the Rule of Law

Legality vs. Extreme Injustice by Omission: Normative-Legal Aspects of Local Authorities' Disobedience

Adela Gąsiorowska

Abstract

In the absence of appropriate responses from the national and international authorities, local authorities (LAs) frequently contribute to reception policies on their own initiative. Moreover, they do not always act in line with the national policies, and sometimes even overstep their competence to support asylum seekers. This raises the question of whether, in certain circumstances, such actions taken by LAs can be legitimised from a legal-ethical perspective.

The chapter analyses the normative-legal aspects of LAs' actions that exceed their competence, in cases where national and supranational authorities fail to act within their own. In particular, it answers two questions, (1) can LAs' actions that exceed their competence be legitimised in such cases, and (2) should LAs be obliged to take these actions, when they have the necessary resources and factual ability to act?

The research problem is analysed on the basis of LAs' actions within reception policy. The answers to the research questions are based on a literature review across four areas: empirical studies on local turn in migration policies, literature on the principle of legality, Radbruch Formula and further studies of the extreme injustice by omission, and literature on civil and judicial disobedience.

1. Introduction

Modern crises, such as climate change, emerging armed conflicts, and the growing scale of migration create new challenges for public authorities, including in the field of human rights protection. These challenges also concern LAs, whose role in this field seem vital. First, local communities are often the most impacted actors by such crises. Second, according to the rules of decentralisation and subsidiarity, LAs — being closer to citizens

— are better able to address their needs (Hepburn & Zapata-Barrero 2014, Scholten and Penninx 2016, Anisiewicz et al. 2024).

At the same time, the legal status of LAs is specific compared to other levels of government. On the one hand, LAs should have full discretion in dealing with local matters. On the other hand, their discretion is restricted. It has to be performed within the limits of the law, and it is limited to only these matters, which are not excluded from their competence, while the legal framework of LAs' functioning is usually established by the central legislature (Ziller 2012). Consequently, there might exist national public policies, within which the competence of LAs is marginal.

One such policy used to be migration policy, especially in the field of asylum seekers' reception, in which the LAs have been traditionally involved only to a limited extent (Scholten and Penninx 2016). At the same time, there is often a lack of systematic migration policies at the national level (Campomori & Caponio 2014). Consequently, LAs contribute to migration policies on their own initiative, including in reception activities (Bazurli 2019, Dimitradis & Ambrosini 2023, Alagna 2023). Importantly, facing insufficient action on the part of national authorities, LAs do not always act in line with the national policies. Indeed, some of them even exceed their competence to support asylum seekers, driven by the need to answer the humanitarian emergency (Bazurli & Kaufmann 2022).

Such activity seems to be contrary to the principle of legality, according to which the public authorities can exercise only these powers which are granted to them by law (Ziller 2012). It raises the question of whether LAs exceeding their competences — in cases where national and international authorities fail to act within their competences — can be legitimised from a legal-ethical perspective. And if so, how?

The studies on migration policies provide a broad empirical evidence concerning various types of relationships between LAs and national authorities within migration policies, as well as the drivers of these relationships (for example, Scholten & Penninx 2016, Schammann et al. 2021, Bazurli, Caponio & de Graauw 2022). However, there is a lack of research investigating the normative-legal aspects of behaviour of LAs, including situations where they resist national policies and exceed their competence. Also, the literature on the principle of legality does not focus on this subject.

Thus, it seems helpful to refer to the legal-philosophical concepts addressing situations in which resisting statutory law is permitted, or even expected. Unfortunately, the existing literature on these issues concentrates on the national and supranational level and it does not address the problem of LAs exceeding their competence in cases of extreme injustice. Therefore, the chapter focuses on this issue.

In particular, this chapter aims to answer the following questions:

1) Can LAs' actions that exceed their competence be legitimised in cases where national and supranational authorities fail to act within their competence?
2) Should, in such cases, LAs be obliged to take actions exceeding their competence when they have the necessary resources and factual ability to act?

The abovementioned problem will be analysed on the basis of LAs' actions within reception policy. By the term "reception", I understand a set of measures that a certain level of government provides to asylum seekers, including providing housing, food and clothing — simultaneous to submission of the asylum application by the asylum seekers, and registration of these applications by the relevant authorities.[1]

The analysis of the described research problem seems crucial. First, the migration crisis and the need to receive asylum seekers constitute a challenge of great importance and urgency, particularly from the perspective of human rights protection. Additionally, as empirical studies show, reception policy is in practice an area in which LAs exceed their competence in order to provide humanitarian aid, due to the insufficient action on the part of higher-level authorities. Finally, the problem of national and international authorities' inaction has already been noted in the legal-philosophical literature, which points out that modern threats to human rights protection, including in the field of asylum seekers' reception, result to a large extent not from actions taken, but from governments' *laissez-faire* attitude (Buchholz-Schuster 2023).

The paper was prepared on the basis of the literature review, which concerned four areas:

1) empirical studies on local turn in migration policies — to illustrate how LAs in practice respond to the need of asylum-seekers' reception,
2) literature on principle of legality — to explain how it should be applied to LAs' actions,

1 Council Directive 2003/9/EC of 27 January 2003 laying down minimum standards for the reception of asylum seekers.

3) Radbruch Formula and further studies of the extreme injustice by omission — to consider under what conditions it can be applied to the lack relevant authorities' action, and
4) literature on the concepts of civil and judicial disobedience (mainly in Rawls's and Graver's formulation, respectively) — to analyse if these concepts can be analogously applied to LAs' actions.

The findings of the literature review were next used to answer both research questions. Thus, in the following parts of the chapter, I will describe the findings of the literature review in each of the four aforementioned areas (Sections 2–5) and then provide the answers to the research questions (Section 6).

2. LAs Within Migration Policies

2.1. Types of LAs' responses in migration policies

Following so-called "local turn" in migration policies, migration studies have been recently analysed with the use of the multi-level governance framework (Zapata-Barrero, Caponio & Scholten 2017). The framework was introduced by Marks (1992), who described through it how "supranational, national, regional, and local governments are enmeshed in territorially overarching policy networks" (Marks 1993). Besides the vertical dimension of MLG, studying interdependence between various levels of government, the framework is also used in its horizontal dimension to analyse interdependence between governmental and non-governmental actors (Bache & Flinders 2004). Thus, implementing the framework, the migration studies investigated how LAs interact with different levels of government and non-state actors, including exploring how and why LAs respond differently to similar challenges (Bousiou 2021).

With regard to the vertical dimension, various distinctions of interactions between sub-state and national governments have been created based on possible divisions of competences and level of policy coordination between these governments (Scholten and Penninx 2016, Zapata-Barrero & Barker 2014). Most importantly, Scholten and Penninx (2016) distinguished four types of relations between sub-state and national government within migration policies: centralist, localist, multi-level governance, and decoupled.

In the context of this chapter, the decoupled type of relationship seems to be significant in particular, characterised by the absence of meaningful coordination between different levels of government and by divergence or contradiction between their policies. As Scholten and Penninx (2016) argue, the lack of cross-level policy coordination can lead to conflicts between governments of different levels, and consequently, their policies may differ — in particular sub-state policies can diverge from or contradict national policies. Cases of LAs who contradict actions of national authorities have been broadly described in the empirical literature (i.a. Bazurli 2019, Agustín & Jørgensen 2019, and Sabchev 2021). Some of the LAs exceeded their competence to provide help for asylum seekers (Bazurli & Kaufmann 2022).

Although the horizontal dimension of LAs' actions is less relevant in the context of this chapter, it is worth mentioning numerous studies that have identified cases of cooperation between LAs and civil society. What is important, in the analysed cases, is that they often jointly opposed national policies in order to support asylum seekers during humanitarian emergencies (Bazurli 2019, Agustín & Jørgensen 2019, Dimitriadis et al. 2021, Alagna 2023).

So called "solidarity" or "welcome" cities (for example, Agustín & Jørgensen 2019, Sabchev 2022) — showing inclusive and solidarity attitudes towards asylum seekers and defending their human rights — seem to constitute the prevailing majority of cases analysed in the literature. It has to be noted, however, that there are also cases manifesting opposite attitudes. First, many of LAs remain inactive within migration policies (Schammann et al. 2021). Second, some of the studies identified anti-asylum-seekers' attitudes among LAs, manifested through crackdowns toward asylum seekers, or their exclusion from local services (Bazurli, Caponio & de Graauw 2022). Importantly, some of the LAs also protested against inclusive elements of national policies (Sabchev 2021).

2.2. Drivers of LAs responses

The empirical studies also provide evidence on diversified drivers of LAs' response. In particular, various responses are claimed to depend on the institutional framework in which LAs operate, including institutional system in a certain state, level of its decentralisation, legal and structural discretion of LAs, or institutional rules governing interactions at the local level (Schammann et al. 2021; Bazurli, Caponio & de Graauw 2022; Bazurli & Kaufmann 2023). Another factor that seems to play an important role in determining LAs' responses is the level of convergence with national government, including ideological match across governments and the level of the risk of intergovernmental antagonism (de Graauw 2021; Bazurli & Kaufmann 2023). Sabchev (2022), in turn, underlines the significance of the level of financial and operational support to LAs from a national government. Moreover, LAs' responses can vary depending on the differing effectiveness of national policy and on the level of humanitarian emergency (Bazurli 2019; Bazurli & Kaufmann 2023; Bazurli, Caponio & de Graauw 2022).

LAs' responses are also driven by various horizontal factors, such as the capacity of a municipality, including its size, economic situation, location, and level of urbanisation (Schammann et al. 2021, Bazurli, Caponio & de Graauw 2022, Sabchev 2022). Active responses are, in turn, additionally enhanced by the engagement of civil society and existence of networks or coalitions of local actors (Bazurli 2019, Schammann et al. 2021, Bazurli & Kaufmann 2023, Bazurli, Caponio & de Graauw 2022, Alagna 2023). Finally individual factors can also play an important role, including political ideology, partisanship, or the leadership skills of the person holding position in an LA (Bazurli & Kaufmann 2023, Sabchev 2021, Schammann et al. et al. 2021, Sabchev 2022).

3. Principle of legality as a standard of LAs actions

3.1. Principle of legality as the element of the legal state

As mentioned above, a situation in which LAs exceed the competence prescribed to them in law is questionable from the perspective of principle of legality, holding that public authorities can only exercise those powers that are granted to them by law (Ziller 2012). The principle is claimed to be one of the fundamental elements of the concept of legal state (Ali 2024, Neuman 1986). The concept was introduced in the nineteenth century in Germany and became one of the key elements of the German doctrine of administrative law, represented by Otto Mayer and his followers (Bitner, Kulesza 2009). Contrary to the concept of police state, it assumes that the authorities are bound by the legal rules, which should be applied in equal manners to individuals (Ziller 2012).

Within this framework, the principle of legality was aimed to limit the state's power and secure the individuals' freedom against the state's arbitrariness, in particular in the sphere of their liberty and property (Ali 2024, Kuta 1969). Consequently, the German doctrine of administrative law initially concentrated only on the coercive acts of public administration, which interfered with the liberty or property of individuals (Bitner, Kulesza 2009). Nevertheless, since over time public administration began to perform more organisational function and undertake noncoercive activities, aimed at improving well-being of citizens, such activities have also become the objects of interest of the German legal science (Kuta 1963). Also, French administrative science placed great emphasis on the organisational role of the state (Kuta 1969). Therefore, shaped in this way, the principle of legality became part of the administrative tradition of the whole of continental Western Europe (Ziller 2012), not only as an element of the national laws, but also of the EU law (Ali 2024).

3.2. Principle of legality - key assumptions

As Neumann (1986) explains, the essence of the principle of legality is that "the state is bound by its own laws, and that every interference of the state must be reducible to such laws". Consequently, in order to take a decision with legally binding consequences, public authorities must be vested with competence to do so, on the basis of the general law (Neumann 1986, Ziller 2012). The main aim of the principle is to safeguard individuals' liberty and property against the State's coercion. It defines an area in which the individuals are free from State interference and it makes such an interference predictable (Bitner, Kulesza 2009, Ali 2012). Moreover, the principle also safeguards other values, such as the State's budget (Ziller 2012).

Broadly understood, legality includes two elements, the requirement to have a statutory provision authorising a public authority to perform a certain action and the requirement that this action complies with the higher-level statutory law (Bitner, Kulesza 2009). Consequently, since the principle is applicable to both general law-making and individual decision-making, public authorities' acts are governed by a specific hierarchy: Individual decisions have to comply with general regulations, which have to comply with statutory law, which, in turn, has to comply with a constitution (Ziller 2012).

3.3. Scope of LAs' discretion in the light of principle of legality

Since the principle of legality concerns both central and local administration (Ziller 2012) to take any action, LAs need to have an appropriate legal basis. Therefore, the question is, how the legal basis should be formulated, in particular, how detailed it has to be, and how much discretion it should grant to public authorities. It seems that scope of such a discretion can vary among different legal systems. However, there are three general factors that seem to differentiate it.

First, as Bitner and Kulesza (2009) argue, the scope of discretion depends on the function performed by the administration. According to the authors, both coercive and noncoercive actions performed by the LAs need to have a statutory authorisation. However, the degree of specificity of legal basis, and consequently the scope of LAs' discretion is different in these two cases. As for coercive actions, where LAs act in the sphere of citizens rights, the authorising provisions have to be more specific and should cover a scope, a form, and procedures of the action. As mentioned above, however, LAs undertake many noncoercive activities aimed at fulfilling the collective needs of local communities and the management of local development (Kulesza 2009). In this case, an LAs should have some freedom to decide what exact action, and in what time and order, should it take to fulfil its legally defined aims. Thus, the requirement for a legal basis for noncoercive activities is much less strict and the legal basis can have a framework nature (Bitner, Kulesza 2009).

With regard to the noncoercive actions, the scope of LAs' discretion can be further differentiated by the general level of independence of local government in a certain state. The international rules concerning local government independence are in particular established by the European Charter of Local Self-Government (ECLSG). According to Articles 4.2. and 4.5 of the ECLSG, LAs should, within the limits of the law, have full discretion to exercise their initiative with regard to local matters; and where powers are delegated to them by a central or regional authority, they should be allowed discretion in adapting their exercise to local conditions. At the same time, the basic powers and responsibilities of LAs should be prescribed by the constitution or by statute (Art. 4.1. of the ECLSG), while the law limiting their discretion is usually established by the central legislature (Ziller 2012). Thus, the level of LAs' discretion in performing their powers can be different among various states — it depends on the adopted model of local government, in particular on how independent from central administration LAs are (Ostrowska 2016). Importantly, the model adopted in a certain state results not only from the literal wording of provisions of constitution or statutory law, but also from the interpretation adopted by the courts or authorities who supervise LAs (Kulesza 2009).

Finally, the scope of LAs' discretion depends on the LAs' independence within certain public policy. According to the Article 4.2 of the ECLSG, the LA's discretion is limited only to matters which are not excluded from their competence nor assigned to any other authority, while the decision about such exclusion or assignment lies with the central legislature. The literature on MLG assumes that within certain policies national authorities provide ground rules for lower levels of governments and have some control over transfers of power to other levels (Bache & Flinders 2004). Therefore, the scope of LAs' discretion can vary among different public policies; in some of them the scope of LAs action can be very broad, while in others there might be very little room for LAs' activity.

Presented considerations can be shifted to the ground of reception policies. First, it should be noted that the vast majority of reception activities have a noncoercive character, since they centre around provision of services such as housing, food, or clothing. However, it seems that during the provision of these services, LAs might also make some decisions of coercive character. The general level of LAs' independence and the scope of actions not excluded from LAs within the reception policy vary among different countries. As abovementioned empirical findings indicate, there exist different models of relationships between local and central administration. In some of these models, the LAs' actions are planned and controlled in a top-down manner by central administration, while in other models LAs independently formulate their own policies.

Thus, for LAs' actions within reception policies, which are taken:

(1) without any legal basis, or
(2) on the basis of a framework character and:
    a) have a coercive character, or
    b) are taken in a legal system, where the level of LAs' independence is not high enough to conclude that the legal basis for LAs' noncoercive action can have a framework character, or
    c) are excluded from LAs competence or assigned to other authorities in statutory law.

There arises a question: Can these actions be legitimised if they are taken in order to defend asylum-seekers' human rights, while national and supranational authorities fail to act within their competence?

4. Extreme injustice by omission

4.1. Extreme injustice in Radbruch Formula

In this context, it seems useful to refer to the Radbruch Formula, whose further elaborations can help explain under what conditions the absence of relevant authorities' action can be considered extreme injustice. The Formula, which in its shortest form states that extreme injustice is no law (Alexy 2010), was introduced and developed by Radbruch as a response to the cases of extremely unjust laws of the Third Reich (Radbruch 1945, Radbruch 1946). It was based on the assumption that "there are principles of law that are weightier than any legal enactment, so that a law in conflict with them is devoid of validity" (Radbruch 1945, translated by Alexy 2019). Consequently, in the post-war period, the Formula was applied by the courts of the Federal Republic of Germany to deny validity of the Nazi regime's laws, which were so clearly unjust that their application would lead to ruling against, rather than on behalf of, the law. (Paulson 2006). Next, it was also applied in the cases of East German border guards involved in the Berlin Wall shootings (ibid).

The Formula includes two formulations:

> *"(I.) The conflict between justice and legal certainty may well be resolved in this way: The positive law, secured by legislation and power, takes precedence even when its content is unjust and fails to benefit the people, unless the conflict between statute and justice reaches such an intolerable degree that the statute, as 'flawed law', must yield to justice.*
> *(II.) It is impossible to draw a sharper line between cases of statutory lawlessness and statutes that are valid despite their flaws. One line of distinction, however, can be drawn with utmost clarity: Where there is not even an attempt at justice, where equality, the core of justice, is deliberately betrayed in the issuance of positive law, then the statute is not merely 'flawed law', it lacks completely the very nature of law. [...]"* (Radbruch 1946).

Therefore, the Formula reflects the conflict between justice and legal certainty, where the latter requires legal norms to be "as determinate as possible" (Alexy 2015). Both of the rules, along with the legal purposiveness, constitute the idea of law. According to the Formula, however, the rules can be ranked, with justice being the rule of primary importance (Paulson 2006).

Thus, contrary to the positivist theory, the Formula is based on the assumption that there is a connection between morality and legal validity. The Formula does not, however, require an exact overlap between law and morality and claims that the unjust law is, generally speaking, valid (Alexy 2008). Only when the injustice of the law reaches an intolerable degree, the law must be seen as statutory lawlessness, lacking the nature of law.

Radbruch elaborates also how in this context justice should be understood, defining it as "the equal treatment of equals" (Radbruch 1946). He also points out exemplary cases of extremely unjust law, which are those who denied people human rights or imposed the same punishment for crimes with very different gravity. Defining the content of justice, Radbruch also appeals to the importance of human rights and their absolute nature (Alexy 2019, Paulson 2006).

4.2. Extreme injustice by omission

Although in its classical form, the Radbruch Formula referred to law (effect of a legislative action), Herbert (2017) applied it also to legislative omission. Such omission takes place "when the legislature has omitted to make a regulation which is necessary." (ibid, translated by Buchholz-Schuster 2023). As with the original form of the Formula, it refers to only those cases of legislative omissions that cause intolerable and extreme threats to justice. Moreover, there have to be some minimum requirements recognisable regarding the lacking regulation, which allow one to detect extreme injustice and which indicate a direction of lacking regulation (Buchholz-Schuster 2023). When such an omission occurs, an "ethical statutory gap" arises, creating an obligation for the legislature to close it.

The concept of extreme injustice by omission was further developed by Buchholz-Schuster (2023). In particular, he expanded the applicability of the Formula to the cases of omission committed by national executive authorities and supranational organisations. First, he shifted the concept of extreme injustice by omission to the supranational level, pointing out that the supranational legislature can also create ethical regulatory gaps. Second, he claimed that governments are responsible to close ethical regulatory gaps created by the legislature. Consequently, all branches of power — legislative, judicial, and executive — are obliged to correct the extremely unjust state of affairs, resulting from the authorities' omission, using means that fall within their legal competence and are factually possible. And if executive authorities of any level do not make such an effort, the additional "executive action gap" arises.

It seems that the described concept of extreme injustice by omission can be easily shifted to the local level. In such cases, the legislative authorities of local government may create ethical regulatory gaps, which would lead to an obligation of all local government authorities to close these gaps within a framework of their competence and factual possibilities. A similar situation would take place if the gaps resulted from the omission of higher-level authorities. However, the situation becomes more complicated when the higher-level authorities create an ethical regulatory gap, while LAs are not granted adequate competence to close it. Therefore, to explain this situation, it seems useful to refer to concepts related to disobedience to the law.

5. Disobedience to the law

5.1. Civil disobedience

According to the literature on extreme injustice by omission, if the legislative authority creates the ethical statutory gap, it can be closed by other entities, even contrary to the statutory law. In particular, it can be closed through civil disobedience or by a judge, even if it would be contrary to the principle of separation of powers (Herbert 2017, Buchholz-Schuster 2023).

Civil disobedience is defined by Rawls (1996) as "public, nonviolent, and conscientious act contrary to law, usually done with the intent to bring about a change in the policies or laws of the government." According to Rawls, civil disobedience should rest on political conviction and be justified by moral principles instead of self-interest. Since it is public and nonviolent, the person who performs it accepts the possibility of being arrested and punished. Similarly, Bielefeldt (2011), based on Rawls and other authors, points out four features of civil disobedience: purposeful violation of law, public character, nonviolent character, and readiness to accept punishment for the violation. However, the nonviolent character, and readiness to accept the punishment are the matter of dispute in the literature (ibid).

Similar to the legal-philosophical concepts described in the previous section, the concept of civil disobedience is tightly connected with the idea of justice. Rawls (1996), refers in this context to the contract theory, claiming that certain arrangements are unjust if they do not "accord with the principles for assigning and securing fundamental rights and liberties which would be chosen in the original position". Consequently, Rawls accepts a situation when the unjust law is not obeyed. Nevertheless, similar to Radbruch and his followers, he restricts this possibility only to laws that "exceed certain bounds of justice" and violate it substantially and clearly.

Additionally, Rawls imposes another restriction: Civil disobedience should be used only as a last resort. He points out that civil disobedience is not a regular political action, but can be used only when all regular legal and democratic means have been exhausted and the authorities refuse to correct an unjust state of affairs (Rawls 1996, Bielefeldt 2011). It is claimed that the lack of such restriction would pose a risk to maintaining legal and democratic order (Bielefeldt 2011).

In this context a broader question arises, whether civil disobedience can be performed in democratic legal states, considering that politically motivated violations of law can raise a risk of weakening a legal culture and consequently threaten the rule of law (ibid). There are strong arguments supporting this possibility. In particular, Rawls (1996) explains that within democratic legal state, acts of civil disobedience are aimed to appeal to the sense of justice of the majority and show that in the opinion of the protesters, the contested law does not honour the conditions of social cooperation. Also, Bielefeldt (2011) argues that civil disobedience is consistent with democratic principles and is a part of civic engagement. In support of this view are the public character of civil disobedience and the fact that the right to perform it is granted to everyone, regardless of their views.

5.2. Judicial disobedience

Besides civil disobedience, the literature on disobedience to the law distinguishes the concept of judicial disobedience, also referred to as judicial resistance (Graver 2016, Zajadło 2011). There are, however, some important differences between these concepts. First, while a citizen performing civil disobedience deliberately breaches law, a judge performing judicial disobedience executes it — either properly interpreting statutory law, or appealing directly to the higher-level norms (Zajadło 2011, Piekarczyk 2017). Second, it is claimed that judicial disobedience has even more extraordinary character than civil disobedience and should be used only in very rare and extreme cases (Zajadło 2011).

In practice, cases of judicial disobedience were studied in various countries, including Nazi Germany, USA, Republic of South Africa, and some countries of South America (Graver 2016). Importantly, similar to civil disobedience, it is accepted to be performed also in democratic legal state. Indeed, taking into account the possible sanctions which can be imposed on judges, it is even more rational to expect judges to be disobedient to extremely unjust law in a democratic state than in an authoritarian regime (Zajadło 2011).

At the same time, however, judges who did not perform the judicial disobedience and therefore applied extremely unjust law, were generally not brought to justice in most of the cases (Graver 2016). This situation raises a question, if judges are obliged to perform judicial disobedience and resist extremely unjust law.

Although there exist arguments against such an obligation, appealing in particular to legality and separation of powers, Graver provides argumentation in favour of it. First, he advocates the assumption that while civil disobedience against law that breaches human rights is a right of citizens, in the case of public authorities it is an obligation. What is more, some authors claim that disobedience on the part of authorities' disobedience is even more expected when citizens engage in civil disobedience (Zajadło 2011). Second, Graver refers to the states' international human rights obligations to prosecute authorities that breach human rights, which should also concern judges. Replying to the legality argument, he argues that it is justified to expect that judges will interpret law in the light of human rights and principles of justice, and therefore, judges who enforce law grossly infringing on human rights should be held responsible. As the author expresses it, "one can never commit gross violations of human rights with the legitimate expectation that one will not be punished, and the law should not protect such an expectation" (Graver 2016). When there is a question of separation of powers, in turn, Graver points out that democratic legitimacy of judges' actions is a secondary issue in case of law "so contrary to any conception of justice that they may be deemed unacceptable under any setting".

6. LAs' legitimacy and responsibility for exceeding their competences

6.1. Legitimacy of LAs to overstep their competences

In the following section I will provide answers to the research questions, on the basis of the considerations described in previous parts of the chapter.

The first question was formulated in the following way: Can LAs' actions that exceed their competence be legitimised in cases where national and supranational authorities fail to act within their competence?

The answer to this question should be affirmative. In such cases, a conflict arises between the principle of justice and principle of legality (as well as with legal certainty). Thus, based on the concepts analysed above, it should be assumed that there are cases, when the principle of justice must take precedence over the other two. Therefore, in order to satisfy the requirement of justice, exceeding the competence may be legitimised. Being more specific: analogous to the assumptions expressed regarding extreme injustice by omission —that an ethical regulatory gap can be closed by a judge, even contrary to the principle of separation of powers — it should be assumed that a similar gap may also be closed by an LA, even contrary to the principle of legality. Moreover, since citizens and judges can, under specific conditions, disobey an extremely unjust law, it should be acknowledged that LAs are also entitled to perform "local disobedience" to counteract an extreme injustice (even though, in such a case, LAs do not counteract an "active" law, but extreme injustice by omission). Additionally, it should be assumed that, similarly to civil and judicial disobedience, a "local disobedience" should be acceptable or even more expected in democratic legal states.

Nevertheless, on the basis of the abovementioned concepts, the following conditions have to be fulfilled to consider certain action as legitimised:

1) the action can be taken only when there exists a corresponding ethical regulatory gap on the side of relevant higher-level authorities, which leads to an extreme injustice by omission; and the action must be taken to counteract this extreme injustice;
2) extreme injustice should be defined in this context through the reference to equality and protection of human rights — analogously to the understanding of justice adopted within Radbruch Formula and concepts of civil and judicial disobedience;
3) the action should be taken only as a last resort, in particular when an LA exhausted all means lying within its competence to convince competent authorities to take appropriate actions and yet there is refusal from their side to close the regulatory gap (analogously to the condition imposed by Rawls on civil disobedience). This condition seems to be justified in the context of "local disobedience" all the more so given that, in practice, LAs influence higher-level authorities and participate

in national decision-making in various ways (Trucco 2021, Caponio & Borket 2020).

Considering the remarks provided in Section 3. it should be noted that the legitimacy of LAs action can be explained in two different forms:

1) If the action has coercive character, is excluded from LAs' competence or assigned to other authorities in statutory law, or is undertaken without any legal basis; an LA's action should be legitimised, provided that principle of legality must yield to justice. Thus, the LA can undertake such an action to counteract extreme injustice, even though it is contrary to the principle of legality.
2) If the action is undertaken on the framework legal basis in the legal system, where the level of LAs' independence is not high enough to conclude that the legal basis can have a framework character, an LA's action can be legitimised through proper interpretation of the existing law (performed by the LA, its supervising authorities, or judge). In that case, the LA does not act against the principle of legality. Instead, the existing legal basis is interpreted in the light of justice and human rights. Consequently, in order to satisfy the demands of justice, the LA becomes competent to take given action, even if under regular circumstances it would need a specific legal basis (similarly to the explanation of judicial disobedience provided by Graver, 2016).

6.2. Obligation to exceed competence

The research Question 2 was as follows: Should (in cases where national and supranational authorities fail to act within their competence) LAs be obliged to take actions exceeding their competence when they have the necessary resources and factual ability to act?

The answer to this question also seems to be affirmative. In addition to the arguments presented in the answer to the first question, it has to be justified, why LAs are not only entitled but also obliged to take such action. It appears that the arguments supporting the imposition of such an obligation to judges can be applied to local authorities as well. In particular, as mentioned above, the obligation to protect human rights is claimed to concern all public authorities. Additionally, it appears that the argument applied to judges — that they are obliged to resist extremely unjust law, even if it contradicts the principle of separation of powers — can analogously be applied to LAs acting contrary to the division of competences established by statutory law. Since judges are obliged to resist extremely unjust law, it should be also acknowledged that LAs are obliged to resist an extreme injustice by omission, that is to take actions aimed at restoring justice. The difference between these situations lies in the fact that, if LAs fail to fulfil this obligation, they do not apply the extremely unjust law, but rather commit omission that deepens the state of extreme injustice.

In this case there are some conditions which should be met in order to acknowledge that LAs are obliged to take an action (besides the condition mentioned in the question, requiring LAs to have the necessary resources and factual ability to act):

1) analogously to the answer to the first research question, it considers only situations when there exists a corresponding ethical regulatory gap on the side of relevant higher-level authorities, which leads to an extreme injustice by omission, and there is a need to take an action which can counteract the extreme injustice;
2) extreme injustice should be defined in the same way as in the first question — through the reference to equality and protection of human rights;
3) there must be at least minimum requirements recognisable considering the action that should be taken in the given circumstances (similarly to the condition formulated by Herbert, 2017, in reference to ethical regulatory gap);
4) finally, it seems that, analogously to judicial disobedience, the LA's resistance should be even more expected in cases where citizens engage in civil disobedience. Interestingly, existing empirical literature on disobedient LAs shows that their activity is indeed enhanced when civil society actively supports asylum seekers (see, sub-section 2.2).

7. Conclusion

The study presented in this chapter allowed for the formulation of the concept of LAs' legitimacy to exceed their competence, in cases where national and supranational authorities fail to act within their competence, as well as their obligation to take such action. Therefore, the study fills a research gap in migration studies, by providing a normative-legal analysis of LAs' disobedience. Consequently, it contributes to theoretical-legal scholarship by integrating, in this context, existing research on the principle of legality with studies on extreme injustice by omission, civil disobedience, and judicial disobedience.

At the same time, the study formulates rather abstract conditions for both research questions. Thus, its main limitation is that it does not formulate detailed standards of LAs' behaviour which, under specific circumstances, should be met. Consequently, it does not define specific conditions under which the LAs should be held responsible for failing to fulfil an obligation to take action exceeding their competence.

The problems outlined above can be a subject to further studies. Although it might be challenging to precisely define the standard of LAs' behaviour and conditions of their responsibility, it seems that their normative direction can be reconstructed on the basis of the existing research on extreme injustice by omission and judicial disobedience (including Gaver 2016 and Buchholz-Schuster 2023).

Specific conceptualisation of both issues would have to be, in turn, prepared on the basis of empirical evidence (Buchholz-Schuster 2023). Fortunately, there exists extensive empirical studies which not only show how differently LAs respond to the need of asylum-seekers' reception, but also explain the reasons for these differences. The findings of these studies, or preferably their more systemised developments, might provide appropriate data needed to precisely conceptualise the outlined problems. In particular, they can help explain how exactly extreme injustice should be defined and what is the standard of justice and human rights protection in the context of asylum-seekers' reception. Additionally, the standard of LAs' behaviour may be reconstructed based on the studies that show a variety of LAs' responses and identify factors that, in practice, enhance or constrain their ability to act.

Findings from such studies would provide a specific standard of LAs' behaviour, which could be used by the LAs themselves, their supervisory authorities and courts, as well as legislative bodies responsible for creating the legal framework for local governments. Therefore, these findings could not only benefit legal science but also contribute somehow to the protection of asylum seekers' human rights.

8. References

Agustín, O.A., Jørgensen, M.B. (2019). Solidarity cities and cosmopolitanism from below: Barcelona as a refugee city. Social Inclusion, 7(2), 198-207.

Alagna, F. (2023). Civil Society and Municipal Activism Around Migration in the EU: A Multi-Scalar AllianceMaking. Geopolitics, 29(4), 1245–1271. https://doi.org/10.1080/14650045.2023.2230902.

Alexy, R. (2008). On the Concept and the Nature of Law. Ratio juris, 21(3), 281-299.

Alexy, R. (2010). The dual nature of law. Ratio juris, 23(2), 167-182.

Alexy, R. (2019), Gustav Radbruchs Rechtsbegriff. In: Borowski, M. (ed., 2019), Modern German Non-Positivism, Tübingen: Mohr Siebeck, pp. 7-18.

Alì, A. (2024). The Principle of Legality as a Pillar of the EU's Rule of Law: Bridging the Gap between International and National Law. In The Rule of Law in the EU: Challenges, Actors and Strategies (pp. 225-243). Cham: Springer International Publishing.

Bache, I., Flinders, M. (2004). Multi-level Governance. Oxford: Oxford University Press.

Bazurli, R. (2019). Local Governments and Social Movements in the 'Refugee Crisis': Milan and Barcelona as 'Cities of Welcome'. South European Society and Politics, 24(3), 343–370. https://doi.org/10.1080/13608746.2019.1637598.

Bazurli, R., Caponio, T., de Graauw, E. (2022). Between a rock and a hard place: mayors, migration challenges and multilevel political dynamics. Territory, Politics, Governance, 10(3), 297–305. https://doi.org/10.1080/21622671.2022.2046633.

Bazurli, R., Kaufmann, D. (2023). Insurgent Asylum Policies in European Cities: A Multi-Level Governance Perspective. Urban Affairs Review 59(4), 1129-1159. https://doi.org/10.1177/10780874221091594.

Bielefeldt, H. (2011). Widerstandsrecht, In Internationales Handbuch der Gewaltforschung, Wiesbaden.

Bitner, M., Kulesza, M. (2009). Zasada legalizmu a zdolność kontraktowa jednostek samorządu terytorialnego. Samorząd Terytorialny 6, 5-19.

Bousiou, A. (2021). Solidarity and Contestation: Local Refugee Reception Practices at the South-Eastern EU Border Islands. Journal of Immigrant & Refugee Studies 22(1), 84–97. https://doi.org/10.1080/15562948.2021.2001614.

Buchholz-Schuster, E. (2023). Extreme Wrong Committed by National and Supranational Inactivity: Analyzing the Mediterranean Migrant Crisis and Climate Change from a Legal Philosophical Perspective. Berliner Wissenschafts-Verlag. 2. Edition.

Campomori, F., Ambrosini, M. (2020). Multilevel governance in trouble: The implementation of asylum seekers' reception in Italy as a battleground. Comparative Migration Studies 8(1), 22.

Caponio, T., Borkert, M. (2010). The local dimension of migration policymaking. Amsterdam: Amsterdam University Press.

Dimitriadis, I., Ambrosini, M. (2024). Framing Asylum at the Local Level: Experts' Narratives of Conflictual Dynamics in the Post-Reception Period in Italy. Migration & Integration 25, 257–279. https://doi.org/10.1007/s12134-023-01075-z.

Graver, H.P. (2016). Judges against justice. Springer-Verlag Berlin An.

Hepburn, E., Zapata-Barrero, R. (2014). The politics of immigration in multi-level states: Governance and political parties. Basingstoke: Palgrave Macmillan.

Herbert, M. (2017), Radbruch'sche Formel und gesetzgeberisches Unterlassen. Eine philosophische und methodologische Untersuchung. Baden-Baden: Nomos Verlagsgesellschaft.

Kulesza, M. (2009). O tym, ile jest decentralizacji w centralizacji, a także o osobliwych nawykach uczonych administratywistów. Samorząd Terytorialny 12, 7-22.

Marks, G. (1992). Structural Policy in the European Community'. Euro-politics, Institutions and Policy-making in the 'New' European Community. The Brookings Institution.

Marks, G. (1993). Structural policy and multilevel governance in the EC. The state of the European Community 2, 391-410.

Neumann, F. (1986). The rule of law: political theory and the legal system in modern society.

Ostrowska, A. (2016). Zasada legalizmu a kompetencja do udzielenia dotacji z budżetu jednostki samorządu terytorialnego. Samorząd Terytorialny 3, 47-57.

Paulson, S.L. (2006). On the Background and Significance of Gustav Radbruch's Post-War Papers, Oxford Journal of Legal Studies 1(26), 17–40, https://doi.org/10.1093/ojls/gqi043.

Piekarczyk, S. (2017). Nieposłuszeństwo obywatelskie i sędziowskie w obliczu kryzysu konstytucyjnego. Forum Prawnicze 4(42), 80-96.

Radbruch, G. (1946). Gesetzliches Unrecht und übergesetzliches Recht. Süddeutsche Juristen-Zeitung 5, 105-108.

Rawls, J. (1969). The Justification of Civil Disobedience. In Civil Disobedience, New York: Pegasus.

Sabchev, T. (2021). The role of local political leadership in the reception of forced migrants: evidence from Greece. Territory, Politics, Governance, 10(3), 306–326. https://doi.org/10.1080/21622671.2021.1927815.

Sabchev, T. (2022). Potential and Limits of Municipal Solidarity with Refugees: A Case Study of the Greek Island of Tilos. Journal of Immigrant & Refugee Studies, 22(3), 614–631. https://doi.org/10.1080/15562948.2022.2077502.

Schammann, H., Gluns, D., Heimann, Ch, Müller, S. Wittchen, T., Younso, Ch., Ziegler, F. (2021). Defining and transforming local migration policies: A conceptual approach backed by evidence from Germany. Journal of Ethnic and Migration Studies, 47(13), 2897-2915.

Scholten, P., Penninx R. (2016). The multilevel governance of migration and integration. [in:] GarcésMascareñas, B., Penninx, R. (eds.). Integration processes and policies in Europe: Contexts, levels and actors. Springer.

Trucco, D. (2021). Border town authorities and the multilevel politics of the 'transit migrant' emergency. Territory, Politics, Governance, 10(3), 465–484. DOI: https://doi.org/10.1080/21622671.2021.1954989.

Zajadło, J. (2016). Nieposłuszeństwo sędziowskie, Państwo i Prawo 1, 18–39

Zapata Barrero, R., Barker, F. (2014). In The politics of immigration in multi-level states: Governance and political parties. Basingstoke: Palgrave Macmillan, 2014.

Zapata-Barrero, R., Caponio, T., Scholten, P. (2017). Theorizing the 'local turn' in a multi-level governance framework of analysis: a case study in immigrant policies. International Review of Administrative Sciences, 83(2), 241-246. https://doi.org/10.1177/0020852316688426.

Ziller, J., Peters, B.G., Pierre, J. (2012). The continental system of administrative legality. The SAGE Handbook of Public Administration, 323-32.

Thinking about Law and its Rule at our Time

John Murungi

The above topic is problematic in multiple ways. What law is is not clear and consequently, what its rule is is not clear. Also, what is meant by our time is not clear. I anticipate that the investigation of this state of affairs will highlight the problematicity of these ways and contribute to the search for their clarity and for possible solutions to the noted problems. The search is a matter of thinking and also a matter of translating the products of this thinking into practice.

What appears to be self-evidently the case is that the rule of law is unintelligible if one does not know what law is. To know what law is is to know how it rules. Ultimately, how it rules defines it. These claims reminds me of a question some of us have heard: "What comes first: chicken or egg ?" How should one think about the rule of law in a way that avoids the perplexity that is entailed by this question? How is one to think about law and its rule fruitfully? Is thinking about it more than conceptual gymnastics, more than what is referred to as scholasticism in the Euro-West? It appears that in thinking about the rule of law, thinking critically about thinking must be undertaken if it is to contribute to our understanding of this rule.

Friedrich Nietzsche, a 19th Century German philosopher, who is not conventionally read as legal philosopher, makes an observation that is relevant to thinking about law and its rule at our time. He says,

> All modern philosophizing is political, policed by governments, churches, academies, customs, fashion, and human cowardice, all of which limit it to fake learnedness.[1]

Fake learnedness is not worn on the face. To understand what it is, one has to remove the make-up which, in some cases, is very difficult to do, especially when it has been in place for a long time. At times, make-up becomes reality and reality becomes make-up. Appearance becomes reality

1 Friedrich Nietzsche, Philosophy in the Tragic translated by Marianne Cowan, Washington, DC: Regnery Gateway, Inc., 1962, pp 37-38.

and the two become indistinguishable. Thinking about law and its rule is not immunized from this transubstantiation, from this simulacrum. If the immunity of this thinking is compromised, it is the duty and obligation of those in the service of truth to unmask this compromise, declare the truth, and to reverse this transubstantiation both in theory and in practice. Law is law not as it is thought but also as practiced.

What Nietzsche says about modern philosophizing applies to modern thinking about law and its rule. Our thinking about this rule is policed and so is law as it is practiced. How it is policed is not self-evident. It should also be evident that Nietzsche is not solely interested in informing us how thinking is policed or in unmaking it; he is also interested in having it de-policed and in having it unmasked. He is interested in freeing it so that we can freely think or engage in liberating thinking -the kind of thinking that is appropriate and necessary today for truthful thinking about law and its rule.

For the most part, today, our thinking about law and its rule is policed not only in the academy but also in the practice of law, in the way that law rules. It is in the academy where formal thinking about law and its rule takes place. This thinking is conceptualized and referred to as discipline. It takes place as a discipline among other academic disciplines. All disciplines in the academy are policed. When one enters a law school as a student, one is disciplined to think like a lawyer. Should, one end up practicing law, the practice embodies and expresses this discipline. The disciplining continues under the aegis of legal profession societies or legal profession associations, and of course, by the state in which law is practiced. It is the duty and the responsibility of law Professors to discipline law students into thinking like a lawyer. They meet this responsibility because they too have been disciplined to think like a lawyer. They are police officers in law school. If they are successful in police work, they are rewarded in multiple ways -having the products of their legal research published in scholarly journals or law books, granted tenure, promoted, awarded salary raise, etc.

What Nietzsche says about modern thinking applies not only to the Euro-Western world but also extends to the rest of the world. The rest of the world has been and is under pressure to modernize in the Euro-Western way since the Euro-Westerners project themselves as having the monopoly of the paradigm or the monopoly of the blueprint of modernity. Legal education and legal practice are among the agents of modernization, at least, in the eyes of Euro-Westerners. As Edmund Husserl, a European thinker has pointed out in reference to Europeans,

> Therein lies something unique, which all other human groups, too, feel in regard to us, something that apart from all considerations of expediency, becomes a motivation for them -despite their designation to retain their spiritual autonomy constantly to Europeanize themselves, whereas we, if we understand ourselves properly, will never, for example, Indianize ourselves. I mean we feel (and in all its vagueness this feeling is correct) that in our humanity there is an innate entelechy that thoroughly controls the changes in the European image and gives to the sense of development in the direction of an ideal image of life and of being, as moving to an eternal pole.[2]

Husserl is not conventionally understood as a jurist, a law professor or as a lawyer. However, what he says has a bearing on our understanding of what constitutes modern thinking -thinking that is largely Euro-centric. What he says is not solely a personal opinion. He expresses a common European opinion. For the most part, debates about law and its rule take place in the Euro-Western world and marginalizes the rest of the world.

Since the birth of modernity, Euro-Westerners have set out to modernize the non-European world. As understood in the Euro-West, thinking about law and its rule is one of the means of accomplishing this project. Euro-Westerners have constituted themselves as the missionaries of modernity. They send missionaries of law and its rule to non-Euro western world. They police the non-European thinkers of law and its rule and have reduced these thinkers to dependents of Euro-Western thinkers of law and its rule. In liberal and critical jurisprudence, radical thinking about this situation is yet to gain traction in the Euro-West world and in the rest of the world To the extent that they are not deaf to what Nietzsche says, non-European thinkers of law and its rule ought to de-police that hitherto guided and that continues to guide their thinking about law and its rule. Unfortunately, there is little truly liberating incentive to do so. Dependency on the modern Euro-Western thinking about law and its rule is deeply rooted. The danger posed by this thinking is barely recognized.

Today, we face a global crisis in thinking about law and its rule. Our thinking requires a radical critique of a deeply rooted conventional modern thinking. Successful resistance to the prevailing global imperialist thinking about law and its rule is beneficial to humankind. Resistance cannot succeed if it is fuelled by prevailing Euro-Westen modern thinking. Genuine

2 Edmund Husserl Phenomenology and the Crisis of Philosophy Quentin Lauer, New York: Harper Rowe Publishers, Inc. 1965, p. 157.

success in resisting thinking calls for an anti-modern radical re-thinking. One must know what one is waging war against if one expects victory.

Inattentive thinking about the topic of this essay can overlook the necessity of thinking about the component of this tile: "thinking" and the "rule of law." If attention is not paid to these components, the title will not be thought out adequately and so will the connection between the two. I have in mind thinking about thinking and about thinking about law and its rule and thinking about how the two types of thinkings relate to each other. Often, we are in hurry or preoccupied in thinking about this or that without thinking about the thinking that is in the background. There is, to be sure, the possibility of careless thinking that ignores or that is estranged from specific subjects of thinking. This possible danger is to be kept in mind and avoided as one thinks about thinking. Thinking about the nature of law has direct bearing on how it rules and necessarily thinking how it rule has a direct bearing on what it is.

As we enter the Twenty First century how law and its rule is thought and understood matters in shaping this Century. How it was thought and understood in previous centuries may have been proper in those centuries, but it should not be assumed that it is proper for our century. It behooves the inhabitants of every century to think for themselves how the rule of law is to be thought of and how it is to be understood if its mummification is to be avoided. As Frantz Fanon pointed out in his classic study of colonialism, "Each generation must discover its mission, fulfil it of betray it. In relative opacity."[3]

Fanon, although often thought of as a psychiatrist, has something significant to contribute to the understanding of modern discussion of law and its rule. In the Wretched of the Earth, Fanon's focus was on colonialism. In thinking about modern conception of law and its rule. Including colonialism is not a diversion. It is a central idea that must be taken into consideration. Evidently, modern Euro-Western thinkers about law and its rule did not take the colonial context law and its rule seriously. They ignored or were oblivious of the fact that in colonial world, law and its rule was in the service of the colonizers. They belonged to the colonizing nations of the Euro-West which shaped their understanding of law and its rule. Even Karl Marx – a major critic of modern liberal jurisprudence, was mostly blind to about this factor. The class analysis of law and its rule subordinate the

3 Fantz Fanon, The Wretched of the Earth, translated by Richard Philcox New York: Grove Press, 2004, p. 145

colonial factor to the evolution of capitalism. He and Engels declared that Communism was a spectre that haunted Europe but not anti-colonialism.

Another important aspect of Frantz Fanon thinking is calling attention to the elemental role that racism played in the colonized world. In part, colonialism was driven by racism and modern law would be not fully intelligible if racism is not considered. What is often forgotten in the reigning discussion of law and its rule is how law and its rule was exhibited in the colonial world. European thinkers in this area were silent or ignored how law and its rule as understood in colonizing Europe. From the colonized view, law and its rule not only ignored colonialism but was not only compatible with it but also was a staunch support and justifier of colonialism. Law and its rule as understood in colonizing Europe legitimized dehumanizing the colonized. Fanon was quite clear that from the standpoint of the colonized, anti-colonialism called for a different and oppositional concept of law and its attendant rule. Euro-Western thinkers of law and its rule were in complicity with the colonizer's version of law and its rule.

Today, the situation that Fanon talked about in the colonial period pertained to that period of history. What law and its rule meant then is not what it means today. We are living in a post-colonial period. Out time calls for a different conception of law and its rule. How the law ruled yesterday should not be assumed to be how it rules today or how it will rule tomorrow or the day after tomorrow. Thinking is inescapably historical. Accordingly, thinking about how law rules ought to be appropriately placed in the context of philosophy of history. Generally, legal education ignores this context. It is not a part of the curriculum in legal education. What constitutes appropriateness is yet to be fully thought out, and most likely, it will remain as such partly because the notion of philosophy of history is yet to be fully thought out. In what follows, what is said about thinking about the rule of law at our time should be understood in the spirit of lived open-mindedness. Tomorrow and the day after tomorrow, a part of what we think about law and its rule will be outdated.

There are those in in the Euro-West and in the Middle East who have spoken about God or about Nature as the source of our understanding of law and its rule. The implication is that there is an eternal and unchanging nature of law and by implication, believe its rules is consequently, ahistorical. In spite the belief otherwise, God and Nature are historical constructions that reflect a particular culture's imagination of what God is or what Nature is. In either case, the rule of law is essentially a human rule of law that is disguised as Divine rule or as the rule of Nature. For the ultra-religious conservatives, this claim is viewed as the evidence of the greatest blasphemy -the blasphemy of blasphemies, or as an anathema that deserves extreme torture or death. Indeed, for millions of believers, it is not recognized that the rule of law is nothing more than human rule disguised as Divine rule of law or as the rule of Nature. It must not be forgotten that, at least, in Christianity, Nature is God's Nature. For some believers, the true knowledge of Nature necessarily leads to the knowledge of God. Ultimately, the rule of Nature is Divine rule and Divine the rule is the rule of Nature. Apparently, it is absurd to separate the two. Divine rule and the rule of Nature are expressions of each other. Law and its rule in the Euro-West is largely a Christian idea. This is the case despite the avowed secularism in the modern Euro-West. The secular and the sacred are two sides of the same coin.

If it is conceded that the rule of law in the Euro-West is a Christian idea, what is implied in this claim is not self-evident. One must consider the anthropology it presupposes; ultimately, the world view it presupposes. To fully appreciate what is being claimed here, one can imagine about an idea of the rule of law based on Taoism, Buddhism, or the religions of the so-called Indigenous peoples (usually deemed uncivilized peoples by Euro-Westerners) their anthropologies and their cosmologies. Without thinking about all these anthropologies and cosmologies, there is a possibility of mistaking what is parochial with what is universal or vice versa. As we think about law and its rule in the international arena or in a global arena, it is important to bear in mind the multiplicity of the sense of law and its rule. For the most part, at our time, this perspective is unrecognized or ignored in legal education.

What is theological or religious varies from culture to culture and from one historical phase to other historical phases. Ultimately, the ideas of neutrality and impartiality of the rule of law that is venerated in modern Euro-West is a cover up of theological or religious ideas or at least, parochial ideas in disguise. Not to be forgotten is the fact that in the Euro-West, God is a Euro-Western God and Nature is a Euro-Western Nature. In the world there exists multiple conceptions of God and multiple conceptions of Nature. Evidently, this is unacceptable to monotheists and to those who believe that there is only one true conception of nature. This is reflected in the conceptions of law and its rule as it is generally understood in the Euro-West and in other God-centered territories.

In spite of possible disagreements, the idea of God and the idea of Nature are culture specific. We live in a polytheistic world, in a poly-religious world, and in a poly-cultural world. Thinking about thinking about law and its rule, this context ought to be considered. Islamic jurisprudence deserves credit for not disguising its theological and religious background and so is Judaic jurisprudence. Because of the conflicts in beliefs about God and Nature, there is likelihood that the rule of law based on God or on Nature harbours internal conflict that negatively impact the thinking about law and its rule but also how the rule of law rules.

Hidden in the concept of God and in the concept of Nature is the concept of Man. Both Theology and Naturelogy are Anthropologies. Nietzsche's thinking is to be credited for reminding us of this truth.[4] It is also Nietzsche who reminds us that, "One should not go to church if one wants to breathe pure air."[5] What he says about the church applies to any other religious edifices such as the temple or the mosque. The edifices provide evidence of man evasion from himself. A conception of law that is based thereby exemplifies man's flight from himself. It is this flight that was exported to or imposed on millions of non-European peoples in the name of law and its rule.

Despite the noteworthy controversy surrounding his thinking, I credit Martin Heidegger, a major German philosopher, for problematizing thinking. He reminds us that what thinking is should not be taken for granted as it appears to be the case since the apparent birth of European's modernity[6] (for Euro-Westerners, this modernity appears to be the exclusive measure of modernity). René Descartes claimed that man is a thinking thing what he meant by thinking and by man and about the connection between the two is or ought to be contentious. If thinking has an essential bearing on the being that thinks; that is, on man, then, there cannot thinking about thinking without thinking about man. Man is not only the subject that thinks but in, thinking, he expresses what and who he or she is. The implication here is that logic, as understood in the academy (an area in the Euro-West that is thought to be the home of thinking), does not exhaust what thinking is unless it is thought of as an expression of what it is to be a human being, unless the science of logic, is the science of man (anthropology in the strictest sense). That is, if indeed, man is a thinking being, it is not clear

4 Friedrich Nietzsche, Joyful Science, translated by Thomas Common, New York: Fredrick Ungar Publishing Co. 1960, p. 165.

5 Friedrich Nietzsche, Beyond Good & Evil, translated by Walter Kaufmann, New York: Random House, Inc. 1989, p. 43.

6 See Martin Heidegger, What is Called Thinking, translated by J Glenn Gray, New York: Harper & Row Publishers, 1968.

what Descartes fully understood what is meant by man. His thinking of thinking and his thinking about man was Christo-centric.

To the extent that Descartes has influenced modern European concept of thinking, and the modern European thinking about man, there remains an issue in and about what passes as thinking in Europe and in the way that Europe thinks about what a human being is. It could be the case that that what Europeans have in mind is European man as is evidenced in modern European history. There is a European version of humanism that is radically subject to contestation to the extent that it excludes non-Europeans. If it does not appear contentious, it may be due to the fact that the truth of being human remains radically and broadly unexamined. It appears that Europeans, for centuries, Europeans have been deaf to the Delphian oracle, "Know thyself." This is ironic for Europeans have projected themselves as the heirs of Ancient Greek philosophy. Descartes is not the first man to concern himself with what a human being is and to the extent that law and its rule bears on what a human being, Cartesian understand of man is not definitive. The Euro-Western man does not have a monopoly on the understanding of what a human being is.

How man is understood is radically reflected in his thinking about nature and its rule, and in thinking about the phase of human history in which we live. The rule of law is what it is by the way or in the way it is thought. The current phase of history is what it is in and how it is thought. This phase is the face of what law is and consequently, the face of the version of how the law rules. Each phase of history generates its version of the nature of law and a version of how law rules. It is indeed historically true that phases of history are not mechanically related and are not monads in the Leibnizian sense.[7] They overlap each other in yet to be fully examined ways. Like every other time, our time is dynamic and transitory. As its inhabitants and its creatures, we too are dynamic, transitory, and so is our thinking about law and its rule. Petrified or mummified thinking distorts thinking and also what is thought.

The fact that today's thinking is problematic and that how we think about what or who we are is equally problematic is gradually being recognized not only in the Euro-West but also in the rest of the world. In the Euro-West, Martin Heidegger informs us that,

7 See Monadology, Gottfried Wilhelm Leibniz, edited by Paul Lodge and Lloyd Strickland, Oxford: Oxford University Press, 2020.

> Let us not fool ourselves. All of us, including those who think professionally, as it were, are often thought poor; we are far too easily thought-less. Thoughtlessness is an uncanny visitor who comes and goes everywhere in today's world. For nowadays we take everything in the quickest and cheapest way, only to forget it just as quickly, instantly.[8]

He then adds,

> ... man today is in flight from thinking. This flight from thought is the ground of thoughtlessness. But apart from this flight is that man will neither see nor admit it. Man today will even flatly deny this flight from thinking. He will assert the opposite. He will say -and quite rightly- that there were no time such far reaching plans, so many inquiries in so many areas, research carried on as passionately as today.[9]

In addition to what Heidegger says, Friedrich Nietzsche , fellow German, has lamented the plight of modern European man. He points out,

> Among Europeans of today there are not lacking those who may call themselves homeless ones in a way that at once a distinction and an honor; it is by them that my secret wisdom and *gaya scienza* is especially to be laid to heart! For their lot is hard, their hope uncertain: it is clever feat to devise consolation for them. But what good does it do! We children of the future how could we be at home in the present? We are unfavorable to all ideals which could make us feel at home in this frail, broken-down, transition period, and as regards the 'realities" thereof, we do not believe in their *endurance.* The ice which still carries has become very thin: the thawing wind blows; we ourselves, the homeless ones are the agency that breaks the ice, and the other too thin "realties."[10]

The thinking of both Heidegger and Nietzsche reach only a few academics and does not register with most people even in the Euro-West. If what they say bears on our thinking about law and its rule and the phase of history in which we live, it should be clear that what we think about the rule of law and about the phase of history we live in calls for a radical re-thinking of the thinking that prevails today. Moreover, to the extent that thinking bears

8 Martin Heidegger, Discourse on Thinking, translated by John M. Anderson and E. Hans Freund, New York: Harper & Row Publishers, 1976 , pp 44-45.

9 Ibid..

10 Friedrich Nietzsche, Joyful Wisdom, translated by Thomas Common, New York: Fredrick Ungar Publishing Co. ,1973, pp. 342-3.

on what and who we are, what we are is not what it ought to be. Given the prevailing flight from thinking that plagues us, what is said is likely to be ignored. It is unfortunate that the deafness that plagues Euro-Westerners has been exported by them to non-Europeans and, unfortunately, Some non-Europeans import it. Consequently, thinking about the nature of law and its rule, and consequently, the version of being human that is at stake, non-Europeans cannot be outsiders to what is said about the nature of law and its rule and cannot avoid thinking about their own sense of law and its rule. Both Euro-Westerners and non-Westerners are plagued by the issue that plagues thinking. They cannot avoid re-thinking their thinking or re-thinking of what and who they are as they think about the nature of law and its rule. It is not enough to list the features principles or elements of the rule as of the rule of law without re-thinking the nature of law and its rule as H.LA Hart or Joseph Raz do.[11] These thinkers ignore or are oblivious of the sense of being human that is at stake in law and its rule.

The flight from thinking that Heidegger speaks about and the homelessness that Nietzsche speaks about have become planetary. Even in the midst of their otherness or in the midst of their differences, the human community is indivisible. However, in the phase of human history we live in, sections of the human community are oblivious or ignore the intrinsic connection they have with one another. This status of the human community has an essential bearing on what we think about law and its rule. Thinking about law and its rule that prevails today does not faithfully reflect this fact, this truth.

Before Heidegger and Nietzsche, GWF Hegel, another prominent German philosopher, made a claim on being human that is relevant to what is said above. The claim is a challenge in the way we think about ourselves, and consequently the way we construe the nature of law and its rule as it applies to us. Hegel said,

> The Negro, as already observed exhibits the natural man in his completely wild and untamed state. We must lay aside all thought of reverence and morality- all that we call feeling - if we would rightly comprehend him;

11 See H.L. A Hart, The Concept of Law, Oxford: Oxford University Press, 1972 , and his article 'Positivism and the Separation of Law and Morals" in in Harvard Law Review, Vol. 71, N. 4, (1958). The Authority of Law by Joseph Raz, Oxford university Press, 2009.

> there is nothing harmonious with humanity to be found in this type of character.[12]

He adds,

> In Negro life the characteristic point is the fact that consciousness has not yet attained to the realization of any objective existence, -as for example God or Law, -in which the interest of man's volition is involved and in which he realizes his own being.[13]

Hegel and fellow Europeans who share his opinion affirm the humanity of the European at the expense of the humanity of the African. By Negro, he has in mind Africans. What he has in mind is nonsensical. It is nonsensical because an African is not a Negro. An African is an African. A Negro is a European invention -an invention that Hegel and millions of fellow Euro-Westerners embrace today. Unfortunately, millions of Africans have been misled and have embraced this false self-identity. If there is nothing harmonious with humanity in the Negro, evidently, the Negro is not a human being and is not able to think of himself as such. Moreover, as far as the rule of law pertains to a human being, it does not pertain to a Negro since he is not a human being. Hegel reinforces this belief when he claims that the Negro has not attained consciousness of law.[14] According to him. the Negro has yet to realize the consciousness of being human is a mode of consciousness that has apparently been attained by a European. It appears that it is proper and natural to treat a Negro as a non-human since it is only a human being who can be treated as a human being. Human rights do not apply to him since they apply only to those who are human.

Walter Mignolo has raised an important question regarding the humanity of man. He asks, "Who speaks for the human in Human Rights?[15] Speaking and writing about human rights has become fashionable, especially after the end of the Second World War. Indeed, it has become fashionable to include human rights as an important ingredient in thinking about the rule of law as exemplified in the crafting of current constitutions. For example, this is evidenced in the post-Apartheid South African Constitution. The

12 Georg Wilhelm Friedrich Hegel, Lectures on Philosophy of history translated by J. Sirbree London" 1861, p. 97.

13 Ibid. p, 97.

14 WGF Hegel Lectures on the Philosophy of History.

15 Walter D. Mignolo, Who Speaks for the „Human" in Human Rights? hiol_05_01_mignolo_who_speaks_for_the_22human22_in_22human_rights22.pdf (139.87 KB) retrieved, december 6. 2025

human to which these rights bear appears to be passed over by speakers and writers of human rights, unless it is assumed that what human rights are intended to humanize those who hitherto have been excluded from the community of men. Humanization without a radical re-thinking of the community into which one is humanized calls for radical re-thinking if one is to avoid being humanized in a way into what one ought not to be humanized. The humanization that is taking place should remind us of the deceptive nature of assimilation and integration that was fashionable after the Second World War as evidenced in the crusade for civil rights. Civil rights ought not to be mistaken for human rights. Having civil rights is not identical to having human rights. Civil rights can violate human rights. There are those who resisted and who today resist being assimilated or integrated because they understand that the community into which they were assimilated or integrated covers up the de-humanizing aspect of what they were pressured to assimilate or to integrate into. Genuine humanization that recognizes the worth of *every* human being calls for a radically oppositional and different human community. The paradigm of what the human is appears to have been construed by those who have excluded fellow human beings from the elemental community of the human. What constitutes and who constitutes such a community ought to be subjected to dialectical critical thinking on what such a community is and on what our perception and conception of law and its rule ought to be.

Our phase of history calls for a human community that recognizes and affirms the worth of every human being who constitutes the human community -a community that has to be radically thought for we are heirs of false or erroneous conception of humanism. In his book, *Humanism and Terror*, Maurice Merleau-Ponty,

> In its own eyes Western humanism appears as the love humanity, but for the rest of men it is only the custom and institution of a group of men, their password, and an occasion of their battle cry. [16]

In his preface to Frantz Fanon's book *The Wretched of the Earth*, Jean-Paul Sartre, a Twentieth Century French thinker calls for the striptease of Euro-Western humanism to reveal the version of humanism that it services.[17] In

16 Maurice-Merleau-Ponty, Humanism and Terror, translated by John O'Neil, Boston: Beacon Press, 1969, p 179.

17 Frantz Fanon, Th Wretched of the Earth, translated by Richard Philcox, New York: Grove Press, 2004, p. lvii

his book, Fanon indicates that violence was a central feature of colonialism. Indeed, one would have hoped that at the end of the Second World War, European colonizing powers would forego the dehumanization to which the colonized were subjected. For the most part, these powers resisted the recovery of the full humanity of the colonized. The dishonest and superficial granting of formal independence by the colonizing powers was not intended to restore the full humanity of the colonized. For the colonizers, law and its rule was compatible with the colonization of the colonized just previously it was compatible with slavery. It was a major weapon in the war of colonization. After the formal end of colonialism, neo-colonialism emerged, and it continued to be a major weapon in legitimizing neo-colonialism. Colonizers became neo-colonizers and continued to enjoy the fruits of colonialism.

There prevailed a thinking of law and its rule during the colonial period that legitimized colonialism. For the colonizers colonizing the colonized was not a violation of the rule of law. Dehumanizing the colonized was legal. From the standpoint of the colonized, it was illegal because it robbed them of their humanity. Their sense of law and its rule conflicted with the idea of law and its rule that was embraced by the colonizers. Thus, the declaration of the rights of Man and Citizen did not apply to French colonial subjects because they were not included in the community of men as understood by the French colonizers. Thus, the Declaration of the Rights of Man and of the Citizen (1789) by the French Assembly did not only not have a place for the French colonial subjects in Africa, Asia or elsewhere but was silent on the dehumanization of these subjects. This was also the case with other European imperialist nations. In the United States, the Declaration of Independence had no place for Native Americans or for the enslaved African.

One incompletely understands the nature of law and its rule in the modern world if one does not consider modern colonialism. One of the distinctive features of modern colonialism is that it is deeply and broadly racist. In the Nineteenth Century Karl Marx noted that the specter of Communism haunted Europe. One of the points he failed to see or to bring up is that there other spectres that haunted Europe: Anti-racism, and Anti-patriarchy. What should be evident is that European modernity was distinctively and unabashedly dehumanizing and racist. It legitimized the enslavement and colonization of Africans and other people who were non-Europeans. Thinking about law and its rule in the world of slavery and in the world of colonialism legitimized dehumanization of Africans and legitimized the plunder and the pillage of their resources. This is a historic thinking about law and its rule that, for the most part, today, has confined this criminality to the underground landscape of legal thinking. It is criminality that is not taught in law schools. It is not a part of the reigning legal education or legal history. It is excluded from the history of the rule of law. It is a historic Tort that is buried under modern European Tort Law literature. Euro-centric Criminal Law radically ignores or erases it. Law and its rule has been weaponized in the war against Africans and on other non-European peoples. What is called for in the phase of history in which we live is weaponization of law and its rule to counter the opposing weaponization of law and its rule-to counter the current dehumanizing and the degrading of conception of law and its rule.

The historic covering up of the unseemly side of nature of law and its rule was supported in the early phase of legal positivism by John Austin, one of the n English architects of Legal Positivism. He claimed that,

> The existence of law is one thing; its merit or demerit is another whether it be or not is one inquiry; whether it be or not be conformable to an assumed standard; is a different inquiry. A law that exists is a law, though we happen to dislike it or though it vary from the text, by which we regulate our approbation and disapprobation.[18]

This claim was proposed in pursuit of the clarity of the idea of law and consequently in the pursuit of the clarity of the law's rule. Law was to be sharply distinguished from non-law and its rule was to be sharply distinguished from other non-law rules -such as moral rule or religious rule. Consequently, introducing racial or gender aspects would dirty up law and its rule. Logical and formal purification of law and its rule from these contaminations apparently would make the study of law and its rule a scientific study among other scientific studies. Joseph Raz -a major contributor to Legal Positivism, claims that,

> Rule of law is not to be confused with democracy, justice, equality (before the law or otherwise), human rights or any kins of respect for persons or for dignity of man. A non-democratic legal system a promote democracy, of human rights or extensive poverty or racial segregation, sexual inequalities and religious persecution may in principle conform to

18 John Austin, The Province of Jurisprudence Determined, Indianapolis: Hackett Publishing Company, Inc., 1998, p. 184.

> the requirements of the rule of flaw better than any of the legal system of more enlightened Western democracies.[19]

It does not take a genius to see how what is said could legitimize racism and oppression as was the case in Apartheid South Africa or in misogynist or fascist society. How could one be critical of the Nazi regime if one accepted this idea of law and its rule? How could one be critical of the South African Apartheid conception of law and its rule or think of the racist conception of law and its rule anywhere? Ultimately, what John Austin, Joseph Raz and their followers wanted to do is to purify law and its rule logically and formally and thereby make law and its rule what it is not and what it would never be.

The Frankfurt School of Social Research embarked on critical theory within the Marxist jurisprudence intending to sharpen the distinction between what law and its rule is from what it ought to be, It was largely silent on critical feminist jurisprudence and on critical would only be liberalized to make room in a Euro-centric thinking about law and its rule. It could be argued that even if these omissions were recognized as major contributions in thinking about law and its rule, it would have negligible effect in radically transforming Euro-centric jurisprudential hegemony that reigns globally. What ought to be recognized and affirmed is a global plurality of jurisprudence.

The pressure to scientize thinking about law and its rule seeks to deprive thinking about law and its rule of its appropriate grounding. Professor Lawrence Rosen, a professor of cultural anthropology, has a quote in his book on law that says,

> If you think you can think about a thing, inextricably attached to something else, without thinking of the thing it is attached to, then you have a legal mind.[20]

Pluralism in our world is an inescapable reality. Today, in thinking about law and its rule how do we think about law and its rule in a way that preserves healthy heterogeneity and differences in the human community? More specifically how do we find a way of living that affirms heterogeneity and differences in the human community? How do we create such a community?

---

19 Joseph Raz, The Authority of Law, New York: University of Oxford Press Inc., 2009, p. 211.

20 Lawrence Rosen, Law as Culture, Princeton: Princeton University Press, 2006, p xi.

What Austin and Raz and their followers say cannot be fully understood if one does not recognize the ideological objective in what they say. The critics of Legal positivism did an inadequate job for the failed to bring up the comprehensive sense of law and its rule. Law and its rule does not exist outside the various societal, cultural, and political aspects that constitute the human world and that fails to point out how these forces constitute law and its rule. They failed to call attention to what is falsely done in the name of law and its rule. They sought to make us blind to what is done in the name of law and its rule. There are cultural, moral, ethical, political, racial, and gender prejudices that are passed on as inoperative in the conception of law and its rule. They impose these pre-judices as if they were not pre-judices, thereby making them objective features of law.

I may be radically wrong, but it seems to me that underlying the Euro-Western version of law and its rule law is fundamentally Christian.[21] One must think about European society and about European culture. If it is borne in mind that Christianity has been and is still formative of Euro-Western self-consciousness, non-Europeans are subject to Euro-Western missionary activity in matters that relate to thinking about law and its rule. Realization of oneself is a result of Christian evangelical activity, among non-Europeans, thinking about law and its rule is a Christian thinking that is produced in non-Europeans by Europeans. In other words, the rule of law amounts to the domestication of African cleansing him from the wilderness that he harbours. The rule of law must be exported to the Negro land (to African and to Africans in diaspora. Africa is not Negro land or Black land. It is African land. The upsurge of the Christian Europe has had global or plenary consequences. Modernity is a European phase of history that is global in scope.

A Euro-West that is not decolonized in its thinking about the nature of law and its rule cannot enter into an honest and truthful conversation with non-Europeans about the nature of law and its rule. It is also the case that non-Europeans who were colonized by Europeans cannot engage in such conversation if their thinking about law and its rule is not de-colonized. Those who were neither the colonized nor the decolorizer cannot truthfully engage in thinking about law and its rule if their thinking does not arise from or exhibit decolonized thinking about law and its rule. What is at stake in thinking about law and its rule affects all members of the human community. Colonization has affected and affect the entire human commu-

21 See Carl Schmitt, Political Theology, Chicago: university of Chicago Press, 2005

nity. What is at stake is the architecture of this community. Law and its rule ought to be the architecture and the blueprint of the human community.

It is equally important to bear in mind that thinking about law and its rule is not reserved exclusively for legal scholars or for the practitioners of law. It encompasses all human beings. No human being is an outsider when what is human is a stake. Current professionalization of law keeps us estranged from ourselves. Law and its rule is about human beings ruling themselves in a way that affirms their common humanity. The entire human community is the guardian of law and its rule. In guarding they guard their common sense of being. If one is critical of Eurocentric law and its rule, it is because so far it has failed to do so. Non-European thinking about law and its rule will consequently fail if it does not affirm our communal mode of being.

One wrongly thinks about what is said in this essay if one believes that what is said is based on a dichotomy where on one side you there is a radically Evil section of humanity and on the other side there is a radically Good section of the human community. This Manichaeism ought to be confined to a museum of human antiquity as a reminder to human beings on how they should think about the human community that befits them. It is a radically faulty perception of the world in which we ought to be living. If this community appears ridiculously utopian, it is a counter to the prevailing real dehumanization that is today. Our is an obscene time of human history. There prevails a denial of the dignity of the human community. The current architecture of the human community calls for a radical transformation under the proper guidance of a rule or law that fuels the desire to establish and affirm our common humanity. The current thinking about law and its rule – thinking that is grounded on parochial nation-state patriotism is a major obstacle on the path to the realization of the kind of human community that we ought to have.

Rule of law is more than a species or rulism. It is more than a statement of how human beings ought to conduct their affairs among themselves or a statement of the consequences of failing to do so. It is more than an expression of humanism. It is a weltanschauung – an expression of the world that is both human and non-human -a cosmic expression. In this expression it is not an object of or for human knowledge because, to be as such, a human being has to be separate from it. He or she has to exist as a subject for which it is an object. Separation has to be set aside. It is to be lived. Poetry, perhaps, which appears to be furthest from conventional legal education, has the potential to open up to us what the world of law is.

As Hermann Hesse, the German-Swiss poetic thinker reminds in his poem titled " Stages" reminds us,

> As every flower fades and as all youth
> Departs, so life at every stage,
> So every virtue, so our grasp of truth,
> Blooms in its day and may not last forever.
> Since life may summon us at every age
> Be ready, heart, for parting, new endeavor,
> Be ready bravely and without remorse
> To find new light that old ties cannot give.[22]

To be educated about how we ought to think about law and its rule, poetry and other artistic expressions have much to offer us provided we are open to what they express. As Bob Marley, a prominent Reggae musician, says, "One love one heart, let's together and feel all right." Essential thinking about law and its rule affirms love among all of us. Evidently, this is not the driving force in legal education or in legal practice. It is about sharing oneness and feeling all right. To understand it, feeling matters -not the feeling that conventional psychologists speak about, but the cosmic feeling. It is more than cognition. Being together is not limited to human beings. It encompasses everything that is. Hence, its cosmic aspect.

As we become more and more globalized, this process implicates our thinking about law and its rule. How law and its rule was previously construed should not be placed in the museum of history of legal thinking. It is time for us to indulge in imagining a conception of law and its rule that is appropriate for our still emerging time. Given the unfolding process of globalization, perhaps thinking about law and its rule without borders is in order. Must there not be such a thinking? For those who doubt the possibility of such a law and its rule, ought they also to doubt the possibility of human rights -rights that appear fashionable today? Should believers in human rights at the same time be believers in a universal foundation of law and its rule? Neither what has been nor what is ought to be decisive in the determination of law and its rule. Being human is at stake. In human beings there is a teleology of being human. This teleology is not a monopoly of this or that individual or this or that sector of the human community. One cannot be fully human in isolation from all other human beings, and no

22 Hermann Hesse, Stages poem.

sector of the human community is human at the expense of or in isolation from any pr all other sectors of the human community.

At our time, the way we think about law and its rule plays a major role in the creation of the world in which we seek to live. In the formation of this role and in the creation of the world to come, all individual human beings and all sectors of the human communities ought to work together. Law and its rule is more than an affair of law scholars, law practitioners, or legislators. Ultimately, it is a affair of all human beings working together. Law and its rule matters to all of us. It is about all of us, not as outsiders but as ones who make it what it ought to be, for our communal good. Communally we ought to define what this good ought to be. This may come across as unrealistic given the weight of Euro-modernity that is pervaded by Leibnizian metaphysics that reduces us to a collection of monads whereby individuals have only external relations with one another and where the human community is nothing more than a collection of monadic communities. The conception of law and its rule is similarly construed. What I am calling for is the abandonment of this metaphysics and for institution a radically different and oppositional metaphysics. As I envisage it, law and its rule ought to be an agent of this new metaphysics -a new world outlook. If this comes across as anachronistic, it is so in the light of the current de-humanized or dehumanizing world. What is anachronistic or untimely is the current conception of law and its rule.

III.
Human Rights and Social Contexts

Universal Human Rights and the Ethics of Cultural Diversity. Toward an Intercultural Legitimacy of Human Rights

Hyungjoon Jun

Abstract

This article examines how human rights can gain legitimate authority across cultural boundaries. I argue that three conditions must converge: fair procedures, psychological empathy, and material equality. Existing scholarship typically treats these as competing concerns, but the evidence suggests they actually depend on each other. Drawing on Rawls and Habermas on fair procedures, Smith on moral imagination, and Fraser on material conditions, the analysis shows how these elements work together in practice. Unlike previous approaches that balance these concerns externally, this synthesis reveals their internal connections - each dimension enables and requires the others for legitimate norm-formation. Extending Sen's distinction between closed and open impartiality, the analysis shows how domestic theories of justice can address global challenges of intercultural legitimacy. Through examination of cases including South Africa's Truth and Reconciliation Commission and European Court decisions on cultural diversity, the article demonstrates how institutional designs either facilitate or obstruct intercultural dialogue. The framework challenges traditional state-consent models while avoiding cultural relativism. It presents capabilities-based approaches as promising foundations for reconciling universal human rights with cultural diversity, conceptualizing rights as spaces of freedom that accommodate variation while maintaining core protections. Justice emerges through ongoing democratic iterations requiring institutions that cultivate both constitutional stability and cultural adaptability.

Keywords: Universal human rights, Cultural diversity, Discourse ethics, Participatory parity, Capabilities approach, Intercultural legitimacy

1. Introduction

Universal human rights face a persistent challenge: How can norms claim authority across cultures with fundamentally different conceptions of human flourishing? This tension has sharpened as populist and authoritarian movements challenge liberal international order.[1] The universality of rights is increasingly questioned when ethical systems diverge across cultures, from China's promotion of "development rights" over civil liberties to regional human rights systems that emphasize cultural relativism over universal standards.[2] What one society may hold as essential for a flourishing life might contradict the foundational values of another. Recent scholarship in the Global South critically challenges the presumed universality of human rights frameworks often grounded in Western liberal traditions. For instance, Makau Mutua (2002)[3] critiques the human rights project as embodying a Western "savior" narrative, while Bhuta (2012)[4] highlights how universality claims risk masking power imbalances between North and South. Abdullahi An-Na'im (1992)[5] calls for "intercultural legitimacy" grounded in dialogue with local traditions rather than mere transplantation of Western norms. Similarly, Daniel Bell (2006)[6] and Joseph Chan (2006)[7] discuss Asian communitarian perspectives that emphasize duties and communal values as coequal to individual rights. Despite this diversity, there remains a need to identify a basis for ethical communication across cultural boundaries. Without such a basis, mutual understanding diminishes and social cohesion becomes compromised. As this article shows, justice in

1 Mounk, Y. (2018). *The people vs. democracy: Why our freedom is in danger and how to save it* (pp. 15-34). Harvard University Press.

2 Hopgood, S. (2013). *The endtimes of human rights* (pp. 158-179). Cornell University Press.; Davies, M. (2014). An agreement to disagree: The ASEAN Human Rights Declaration and the absence of regional identity in Southeast Asia. *Journal of Contemporary Asia*, 44(3), 456–478.

3 Mutua, M. (2002). *Human rights: A political and cultural critique*. University of Pennsylvania Press.

4 Bhuta, N. (2012). Rethinking the universality of human rights: A comparative historical proposal. In A. Emon (Ed.), *Islamic law and international human rights law: Searching for common ground?* Oxford University Press.

5 An-Na'im, A. A. (1992). *Human rights in intercultural perspectives: A quest for consensus*. University of Pennsylvania Press.

6 Bell, D. (2006). Asian Values and Human Rights. In Pellegrini, A. et al. (Eds.), Human Rights in East Asia: With Special Reference to China. Hong Kong: Hong Kong University Press.

7 Chan, J. (2006). Community, Harmony and Rights in East Asian Contexts. Critical Review of International Social and Political Philosophy, 9(4), 667–688.

culturally plural societies requires the integration of multiple normative frameworks that account for universal principles.[8]

Cultural differences manifest in moral norms, social practices, and visions of a good life. However, these different ethical environments do not necessarily imply antagonism or moral relativism.[9] They require a structure of communication that allows individuals to recognize one another as moral agents despite their differences. Such mutual recognition forms the groundwork for intercultural dialogue, not by demanding consensus on substantive moral doctrines but by creating a willingness to listen, respond, and participate in a shared public space. At the core of this communicative process is the relational self, an individual formed through emotional and cognitive relations with others. This reflects how human identity emerges not in isolation but within a web of intersubjective interactions that reflect shared meanings, values, and hopes.[10] A good life becomes not a solitary pursuit but a social achievement rooted in mutual recognition and public participation. This understanding aligns with Habermas's discourse ethics, which grounds legitimacy in communicative procedures that respect each participant as a co-author of shared norms.[11]

The relationship between justice and the good life is constitutive rather than secondary. Structures of injustice distort self-understanding, inhibit participation, and perpetuate domination.[12] Therefore, securing universal human rights must attend to the ethical foundations of justice and the dialogical capacities that sustain it. Mutual recognition affirms the dignity of others as co-participants in shaping the social world[13], - an active valuing that engages with the other's unique perspective while acknowledging their agency within a shared normative space. The denial of recognition excludes

8 Benhabib, S. (2002). *The claims of culture: Equality and diversity in the global era* (p. 8). Princeton University Press.

9 On cultural differences and moral communication, see Taylor, C. (1994). Multiculturalism: Examining the politics of recognition (p. 25). Princeton University Press; Parekh, B. (2006). Rethinking multiculturalism: Cultural diversity and political theory (2nd ed., p. 111). Palgrave Macmillan; Ricoeur, P. (2005). The course of recognition (D. Pellauer, Trans., p. 213). Harvard University Press.

10 Nussbaum, M. C. (2001). *Upheavals of thought: The intelligence of emotions* (p. 305). Cambridge University Press.

11 Habermas, J. (1996). *Between facts and norms: Contributions to a discourse theory of law and democracy* (W. Rehg, Trans., p. 305). MIT Press.

12 Sen, A. (2009). *The idea of justice* (p. 72). Harvard University Press.

13 Honneth, A. (1995). *The struggle for recognition: The moral grammar of social conflicts* (J. Anderson, Trans., p. 129). Polity Press.

individuals from discourse and harms their self-relations, producing feelings of invisibility, humiliation, or marginalization.[14] Without dialogical capacity for mutual recognition, rights claims risk appearing as externally imposed doctrines rather than genuinely shared commitments.

Before proceeding, it is essential to clarify key terms. "Intercultural legitimacy" refers to norms that can claim validity across cultural boundaries through deliberative processes that meaningfully include affected voices while respecting difference. The "integrated approach" developed here integrates three co-constitutive dimensions: procedural impartiality, psychological readiness for perspective-taking, and material sufficiency for effective participation.

This paper argues that existing approaches to intercultural human rights legitimacy fail because they address only one dimension of the problem while neglecting others. Existing approaches suffer from different blind spots. Rawlsian proceduralism emphasizes fair institutions but says little about the psychological and material conditions that make genuine participation possible.[15] Communitarian approaches rightly stress cultural recognition, yet struggle when different cultural claims conflict. Critical theorists like Fraser effectively diagnose structural inequalities but offer limited guidance for justifying norms across cultural boundaries. I argue that legitimate human rights norms require three elements working together: procedural fairness, psychological empathy, and material equality. Rather than treating these as separate concerns to be balanced, this analysis shows how they depend on each other. Previous approaches typically treat these as competing priorities.[16] But examining cases like South Africa's Truth and Reconciliation Commission reveals how they actually reinforce each other in practice. This integration yields concrete institutional implications for designing international legal processes that can generate genuinely intercultural consensus on human rights norms.

---

14 Fraser, N. (2003). Social justice in the age of identity politics: Redistribution, recognition, and participation. In N. Fraser & A. Honneth, *Redistribution or recognition? A political-philosophical exchange* (p. 36). Verso.

15 See generally Rawls, J. (1999). The law of peoples (pp. 65--88). Harvard University Press (procedural limitations); Taylor, C. (1992). Multiculturalism and the politics of recognition (pp. 25-73). Princeton University Press (communitarian critiques).

16 Fraser, N. (2009). *Scales of justice* (pp. 12-29). Columbia University Press.

2. Foundations of Intercultural Justice

2.1. The Original Position and the Impartial Spectator

John Rawls's *A Theory of Justice* famously begins with a thought-experiment that makes visible the structural determinants of fairness. In the "original position," the parties' epistemic resources are radically curtailed by a veil of ignorance. They know the general facts of social life but remain ignorant of their own class, race, talents, or conception of the good. From this vantage they must choose principles for regulating the basic structure, which includes institutions that fix rights, duties, and the distribution of primary goods. Rawls devotes an extended discussion to specifying the cognitive and motivational restraints that make the choice situation compelling. The parties are risk-averse but not indifferent, rational but not benevolent, and aware that whatever they decide will bind them irrevocably. The procedural constraints explain why only two principles survive reflective equilibrium. These are the priority of equal basic liberties and the difference principle, which requires that allowable inequalities work to the maximal benefit of those least advantaged, subject to fair equality of opportunity.[17] The derivation of these principles demonstrates that impartiality is not an abstract moral intuition but the product of a decision procedure that neutralizes positional bias. This methodological innovation represents a constructivist alternative to intuitionism and utilitarianism.[18] The original position serves as a heuristic device intended to model our considered judgments about justice while removing the distorting influence of arbitrary social advantage. Critics like Michael Sandel have argued that this approach presupposes an implausibly "unencumbered self" detached from constitutive attachments.[19] However, this misreads Rawls's project, which aims not to describe actual persons but to construct a choice situation that yields principles we can reflectively endorse from our situated positions. As Joshua Cohen observes, the original position models an idea of impartiality, not a metaphysical conception of the person.[20]

---

17 Rawls, J. (1971). A Theory of Justice (pp. 7-12, 60-65, 118-130). Harvard University Press. For analysis, see Freeman, S. (2007). Rawls (p. 36). Routledge.

18 Freeman, S. (2007). *Rawls* (p. 36). Routledge.

19 Sandel, M. (1982). *Liberalism and the Limits of Justice* (p. 179). Cambridge: Cambridge University Press.

20 Cohen, J. (1989). Democratic Equality, Ethics 99(4), 731.

Critics argue that Rawls's original position inadequately explains how real citizens develop the psychological capacities needed for such impartial reasoning. Rawls pre-empts part of this worry in his later chapters on the sense of justice, arguing that democratic institutions must cultivate two moral powers in citizens, namely a capacity for a conception of the good and a capacity to act from principles of justice.[21] However, this raises the question of how such moral psychology develops in real historical contexts. Here, Adam Smith's analysis of sympathy complements Rawls in crucial ways. Smith maintains that moral judgment is mediated by an "impartial spectator," an imagined figure whose disinterested gaze we internalize through a lifelong process of social interaction.[22] By repeatedly assessing our conduct against what any well-informed onlooker could approve, we learn to restrain self-love and align our passions with a shared moral order. Smith's "man within the breast" fills the motivational gap Rawls leaves open. Citizens habituated to spectator-approval are psychologically prepared to look past personal advantage when constitutional controversies press them to adopt an original-position attitude.

Martha Nussbaum's work significantly develops the intersection between Adam Smith's concept of sympathy and John Rawls's notion of public deliberation. She accentuates that the imaginative capacity to comprehend the circumstances of others is not merely a beneficial trait but a crucial precondition for individuals to engage in reasoned civic discourse. Consequently, Nussbaum posits this imaginative empathy as a constitutive element of robust civic education, indispensable for fostering meaningful participation in democratic life.[23] Smith's understanding of sympathy provides a psychological and affective foundation for the kind of impartial reasoning later central to Rawls's theory of justice. His account of human emotional capacities anticipates the conditions for objective judgment that are formalized in the concepts of the original position and public reason.[24] Already within the context of eighteenth-century commercial society, Smith confronted the problem of how individuals might transcend their particular perspectives

21 Rawls, J. (1971). *A theory of justice* (pp. 453-462). Harvard University Press.

22 Smith, A. (1976). The theory of moral sentiments (pp. 110, 134-135). Oxford University Press.

23 Nussbaum, M. C. (1995). Poets as judges: Judicial rhetoric and the literary imagination. *University of Chicago Law Review*, 62(4), 1486.

24 Griswold, C. (1999). Adam Smith and the virtues of enlightenment (p. 259). Cambridge University Press. See also Rothschild, E. (2001). Economic sentiments: Adam Smith, Condorcet, and the Enlightenment (p. 52). Harvard University Press.

to arrive at judgments capable of achieving wide moral acceptance. The underlying concern in both frameworks is the possibility of establishing shared normative agreement despite the diversity of individual interests and experiences.

Smith's and Rawls's theories share deeper conceptual alignment beyond their individual contributions. Rawls's political liberalism requires "free-standing" reasons that all reasonable citizens could accept despite their divergent comprehensive doctrines. This crucial requirement finds a compelling parallel in Smith's dictum that genuine moral approbation must possess inter-subjective intelligibility. For Smith, idiosyncratic preferences or unexamined sentiments cannot form the binding moral claims. Instead, such claims must be testable and confirmable through shared human experience and the judgment of others. A critical distinction, yet ultimately a point of synthesis, lies in their respective approaches to securing impartiality. Rawls structurally achieves impartiality *ex ante* through the hypothetical veil of ignorance in the original position, which strips parties of particularizing information. In contrast, Smith cultivates impartiality *ex post*, through the dialogical testing of sentiments within a dynamic "social marketplace of judgment," where individuals refine their moral responses through interaction with actual and imagined spectators. Synthesizing these two perspectives yields a richer, more comprehensive understanding of how public norms achieve legitimacy. It suggests that institutions can successfully encode impartial principles when citizens, whose moral psychology has been refined through the imaginative exercise of "spectator-reasoning," are already predisposed to affirm these norms as legitimate.

This combined framework illuminates Rawls's concept of the "reasonable," which defines the boundaries of public reason. While Rawls defines the reasonable primarily as a willingness to propose and abide by fair terms of cooperation and to recognize the burdens of judgment (acknowledging the inherent difficulties in reaching shared conclusions), Smith's account provides a compelling psychological and affective genesis for this very capacity. The internal cultivation of the impartial spectator, a process demanding imaginative projection into the perspectives of others, furnishes a plausible mechanism through which individuals learn to transcend their particular biases and recognize the legitimacy of differing, yet reasonable, perspectives. This implies that the "reasonable" is not merely a cognitive disposition or a purely rational choice, but rather a socially cultivated moral virtue, continuously honed through ongoing imaginative engagement with diverse others. This insight offers a more robust and empirically grounded understanding of how reasonable pluralism can be genuinely sustained within democratic societies, moving beyond abstract principles to the lived experiences of moral formation.

This synthesis of Smith's and Rawls's framework carries significant implications for our understanding of judicial review. As Cass Sunstein cogently argues, judges engaged in constitutional interpretation are compelled to adopt a position of "second-order impartiality." This demands a transcendence of their first-order personal preferences to arrive at judgments grounded in broadly acceptable reasons.[25] The deliberative constraints that Rawls imposes on parties within the hypothetical original position find the striking institutional parallel in the self-imposed limitations of courts. These limitations are evident in established doctrines such as justiciability, *stare decisis*, and adherence to canonical methods of interpretation. Such practices, instantiate what Frederick Schauer calls rule-based decision-making, which systematically sacrifices particularized judgment to achieve the benefits of predictability and constraint on official discretion.[26] Within this context, Smith's impartial spectator provides a psychological model for how judges might internalize such constraints as professionally appropriate despite their inevitable situatedness.

Finally, Rawls and Smith together illuminate the dynamic nature of impartiality. Rawls stresses stability and argues that principles must garner citizens' reflective endorsement over time, while Smith emphasizes adaptability. The impartial spectator is sensitive to changing social knowledge and thus able to revise moral verdicts. A justice theory adequate to pluralist democracies must exhibit both qualities. It must provide constitutional fixity sufficient to secure basic liberties and distributive fairness, and cultural plasticity sufficient to integrate new perspectives generated by social evolution and migration. Seyla Benhabib captures this dual requirement in her concept of democratic iterations, which refers to the ongoing processes through which universal principles are contested and reappropriated in particular contexts.[27] Similarly, Rainer Forst describes impartiality as a

---

25 Sunstein, C. (1996). *Legal reasoning and political conflict* (p. 44). Oxford University Press.

26 Schauer, F. (1988). Formalism. *Yale Law Journal*, 97(4), 535.

27 Benhabib, S. (2004). *The rights of others* (p. 19). Cambridge University Press.

recursive practice that continuously reexamines its own premises in light of excluded perspectives.[28]

The practical convergence of Rawlsian procedural design and Smithian psychological readiness finds compelling illustration in South Africa's Truth and Reconciliation Commission (TRC), which demonstrates how these apparently distinct theoretical frameworks operate as mutually reinforcing mechanisms in practice. The Commission's institutional design created what can be understood as a real-world approximation of Rawls's original position through its "impartial truth" standard that applied equally to all parties regardless of their political status.[29] By ensuring that "no side was exempt from appearing before the commission," the TRC prevented the emergence of "victor's justice" that might privilege the testimony of the newly empowered majority.[30] However, this Rawlsian procedural equality would have remained merely formal without the psychological transformation that Smith's theory anticipates. Crucially, the TRC's effectiveness depended on participants' developing capacity for what Smith calls sympathetic imagination. Commissioners and participants were repeatedly called upon to transcend their particular allegiances and imagine how their judgments would appear to a disinterested observer concerned with the moral foundations of the new democracy.[31] This Smithian psychological work was not merely supplementary to the Rawlsian procedures but constitutive of their success. The procedural impartiality created space for moral imagination, while the cultivation of sympathetic perspective-taking gave substance to formal equality. Gibson's empirical research reveals this theoretical synthesis in practice: the truth and reconciliation process contributed to democratization precisely by helping create "a more reconciled society" where former enemies could participate together in democratic institutions. [32] This outcome required both, the institutional design that prevented domination and psychological development that enabled genuine recognition across difference. The TRC thus illustrates how procedural

28 Forst, R. (2012). *The right to justification* (J. Flynn, Trans., p. 213). Columbia University Press.

29 Gibson, J. L. (2006). The contributions of truth to reconciliation: Lessons from South Africa. *Journal of Conflict Resolution*, 50(3), 409-432.

30 Truth and Reconciliation Commission of South Africa. (1998). *Truth and Reconciliation Commission of South Africa report* (Vol. 1, Chapter 1, para. 35). Juta.

31 Gibson, J. L. (2004). *Overcoming apartheid: Can truth reconcile a divided nation?* (pp. 15-34). Russell Sage Foundation.

32 Gibson, J. L. (2006). The contributions of truth to reconciliation (pp. 428-430). *Journal of Conflict Resolution*, 50(3), 409-432.

impartiality and sympathetic imagination function as co-constitutive rather than merely complementary elements of legitimate norm-formation.

2.2. Intercultural Legitimacy, Discursive Recognition, and Material Redistribution

If Rawls and Smith map the micro-foundations of impartiality, Amartya Sen interrogates its macro-political reach. Sen distinguishes closed from open impartiality. Closed impartiality models the viewpoints of co-citizens who share an institutional habitat. This is exactly the scenario Rawls presupposes.[33] Open impartiality, by contrast, requires that deliberators admit the standpoints of "distant strangers," whose reasons may not be rooted in the same legal-cultural soil.[34] In a global order marked by deep pluralism and cross-border externalities, justificatory adequacy depends on this expanded audience. Smith's impartial spectator already anticipates open impartiality, for nothing in his account limits the imagined observer's provenance. Indeed, Smith explicitly invokes "distant and unknown persons" when explaining the corrective force of sympathy.[35] This means that impartiality cannot remain limited to domestic contexts. It must evolve into an inter-cultural practice of reason-giving that respects diversity while resisting relativism. The distinction between closed and open impartiality carries significant implications for international law. The traditional model of legal obligation based on state consent appears increasingly insufficient in a global context where state actions routinely impact individuals beyond their own citizenry individuals who lack any meaningful participation in those decisions.[36] At the same time, the existing global order maintains structural conditions that contribute to severe poverty, while insulating those in affluent societies from moral and legal accountability.[37] Addressing this asymmetry requires a more inclusive justificatory framework, one that extends moral consideration across national boundaries. While such a cosmopolitan orientation challenges legal systems still grounded in territorial

33 Sen, A. (2009). *The idea of justice* (p. 125). Harvard University Press.
34 Ibid., 129-130.
35 Smith, A. (1976). *The theory of moral sentiments* (p. 140). Oxford University Press.
36 Buchanan, A. (2004). *Justice, legitimacy, and self-determination: Moral foundations for international law* (p. 303). Oxford University Press.
37 Pogge, T. (2008). *World poverty and human rights* (2nd ed., pp. 25-26). Polity.

sovereignty, emerging practices of transnational judicial dialogue suggest a growing openness to intercultural forms of reason-giving aligned with open impartiality.[38]

The tension between closed and open impartiality emerges clearly in the European Court of Human Rights' treatment of cultural diversity claims. In *S.A.S. v. France*, the Grand Chamber upheld France's ban on face-covering garments by a vote of fifteen to two, accepting the novel justification of "living together" as a legitimate aim under the European Convention.[39] The majority reasoned that concealing one's face in public undermined social interaction essential for democratic life, even though this concept had no prior basis in the Court's jurisprudence. However, the UN Human Rights Committee reached the opposite conclusion when considering identical French legislation, finding that the ban violated religious freedom under the International Covenant on Civil and Political Rights.[40]

This divergence illustrates the practical significance of Sen's distinction between closed and open impartiality. The European Court explicitly deferred to France's democratic decision-making processes through the margin of appreciation doctrine, reflecting the closed impartiality characteristic of regional human rights systems. By contrast, the UN Committee applied universal standards across a more diverse constituency, embodying the open impartiality that Sen argues is necessary for legitimate global norms. The dissenting judges in S.A.S. criticized the majority's acceptance of the vague "living together" concept as overly broad and undefined.

Habermas operationalizes that practice through his discourse theory of law. A norm is valid only if all affected can accept it in a rational discourse free from domination. Legitimacy arises procedurally from the communicative presuppositions of argumentation, including equal participation rights, absence of coercion, and the possibility of challenge and revision.[41] Such procedures instantiate recognition in two dimensions. First, they acknowledge every participant as a competent co-author of norms. Second, they presuppose symmetrical respect, for reasons directed at another implicitly affirm her status as an equal moral person. Recognition, therefore, functions as the constitutive grammar of impartial justification.

38 Slaughter, A.-M. (2004). *A new world order* (pp. 65-71). Princeton University Press.

39 S.A.S. v. France [GC], no. 43835/11, ECHR 2014, Judgment of 1 July 2014.

40 Human Rights Committee. (2018). *Hebbadj v. France*, Communication No. 2807/2016; *Yaker v. France*, Communication No. 2747/2016.

41 Habermas, J. (1996). *Between facts and norms* (W. Rehg, Trans., pp. 107-108). MIT Press.

This insight has been extended to constitutional law through interpretations of the First Amendment as safeguarding the communicative processes essential for democratic legitimation. Likewise, the equal protection clause has been read as requiring a form of recognition that affirms each citizen's status as a full participant in collective self-determination.[42] The legal doctrines emerging from these constitutional provisions thus institutionalize the discursive conditions that Habermas identifies as prerequisites for legitimate lawmaking. In this view, law is understood not merely as a system of rules but as a framework of social meanings that shape and regulate relations through practices of mutual recognition.[43] These legal doctrines provide essential frameworks, institutionalizing the discursive conditions for legitimacy. However, their formal promise of recognition remains incomplete and fragile where background injustices distort communicative power. Without addressing these underlying inequalities, even the most well-designed procedures can fail to achieve genuine democratic legitimation. Nancy Fraser famously argues that mal-distribution of resources and mal-recognition of status are "co-original" injustices that reinforce each other.[44] Severe economic inequality erodes self-respect and public voice, undermining discourse conditions. Conversely, status hierarchies rationalize unequal resource shares. A justice theory that prizes impartial justification must therefore integrate redistribution into its core. Rawls's difference principle offers a distributive baseline robust enough to secure the material independence necessary for effective participation, while Fraser's critique cautions that formal-egalitarian procedures cannot compensate for the silent exclusions generated by poverty and stigmatization.

A prominent line of critique highlights the role of cognitive schemas that systematically obscure particular forms of domination. Under conditions of racial subordination, for instance, what appears as impartial reasoning to privileged participants may in fact reproduce blind spots that render some injustices invisible. Addressing this challenge calls for deliberative practices oriented toward differentiated forms of solidarity, which actively

42 Michelman, F. (1986). The Supreme Court 1985 term - Foreword: Traces of self-government. *Harvard Law Review*, 100(1), 33.

43 Balkin, J. (1998). The declaration and the promise of a democratic culture. *Widener Law Review*, 4, 168.

44 Fraser, N. (2003). Social justice in the age of identity politics. In N. Fraser & A. Honneth (Eds.), *Redistribution or recognition?* (p. 19). Verso. On structural exclusions, see Mills, C. (1997). The racial contract (pp. 18-19). Cornell University Press; Young, I. M. (2000). Inclusion and democracy (p. 41). Oxford University Press.

seek to counteract structural barriers to equal participation. Legal scholars Kimberlé Crenshaw's theory of intersectionality shows how conventional antidiscrimination doctrines overlook the mutually constitutive effects of race, gender, and class, thereby misrecognizing many experiences of oppression.[45] Crucially, the integrated approach advanced here offers concrete pathways for actively challenging the epistemologies of ignorance and their resultant blind spots.

(1) Procedural impartiality, by requiring that all affected voices are genuinely heard and taken seriously, helps create public spaces in which marginalized experiences are no longer overlooked by dominant narratives. For example, the specific harms experienced by women of color in low-wage sectors must be brought to light. This procedural safeguard increases the likelihood that systemic biases will be revealed.
(2) However, being heard alone is insufficient. The psychological readiness described by Adam Smith ensures these voices are met with *empathy*. Developing the ability to consider the situation of others fosters the internal motivation to look beyond one's own privilege and recognize the legitimacy of different claims, thus piercing through cognitive frameworks built on ignorance.
(3) In addition, the notion of material sufficiency, drawing from the work of Rawls and Fraser, provides the social and economic conditions that enable effective participation. When individuals have access to resources, education, and personal security, they are better positioned to engage in public life, question dominant norms with confidence, and help shape a shared conception of justice.

Taken together, procedural inclusion, psychological receptiveness, and material support shift the recognition of injustice from a passive observation to a sustained effort to address the underlying conditions that obscure or distort public understanding. This approach enables more inclusive collective deliberation that accurately identifies and addresses injustice.

Putting the strands together, an interculturally legitimate human-rights regime would meet three cumulative tests. (1) Procedural impartiality: Norms must be justifiable to all affected persons under conditions approximating Habermasian ideal discourse. (2) Psychological readiness: Citizens must possess Smithian sympathetic capacities that enable them to imagine

45 Crenshaw, K. (1989). Demarginalizing the intersection of race and sex. *University of Chicago Legal Forum*, 1989, 139-167.

and care about how rules impact others, including foreigners. (3) Material sufficiency: Background institutions must satisfy a Rawlsian-Fraserian criterion of distributive fairness so that no group is structurally silenced. When these conditions converge, universal rights such as the prohibition of torture or protections for expressive freedom cease to appear as Western "exports" and instead emerge as co-authored conclusions of a norm-generating conversation that is both locally rooted and globally open.

This convergence is visible in the development of international human rights law, which increasingly relies on the idea of overlapping consensus. This refers to a substantive agreement reached through diverse justificatory paths.[46] The Universal Declaration of Human Rights reflects this approach, having been shaped by a drafting process that deliberately included representatives from various cultural and philosophical backgrounds. As Mary Ann Glendon documents, figures like Charles Malik, P.C. Chang, and Eleanor Roosevelt worked to articulate principles that could be affirmed from multiple worldviews.[47] The resulting document reflects what Joshua Cohen calls "justificatory minimalism," a framework that secures essential protections while remaining open to diverse interpretations of their foundations.[48]

This analysis suggests that recognition and redistribution are not competing agendas but mutually enabling dimensions of the same emancipatory project. Adequately resourced agents are more likely to exercise the empathic perspective-taking that Smith describes, and societies animated by such moral imagination are more inclined to ratify Rawlsian principles that insulate the vulnerable. This integration has implications for pressing questions in international law. Consider the debate over economic and social rights, which some dismiss as aspirational rather than justiciable. Elizabeth Anderson challenges this division, arguing that capabilities necessary for democratic citizenship, including material subsistence, education, and healthcare, are preconditions for the meaningful exercise of civil-political rights.[49] Martha Nussbaum similarly contends that the distinction between "negative" and "positive" rights obscures their shared purpose.

46 Held, D. (2002). Law of states, law of peoples: Three models of sovereignty. *Legal Theory*, 8(1), 26.

47 Glendon, M. A. (2001). *A world made new: Eleanor Roosevelt and the Universal Declaration of Human Rights* (pp. 143-144). Random House.

48 Cohen, J. (2004). Minimalism about human rights: The most we can hope for? *Journal of Political Philosophy*, 12(2), 193.

49 Anderson, E. (1999). What is the point of equality? *Ethics*, 109(2), 317-318.

That purpose is to enable human flourishing across diverse life plans.[50] The practical implication is that courts enforcing constitutional or human rights provisions should adopt what Katharine Young calls a "typology of review" that calibrates judicial intervention based on institutional capacity and the severity of the deprivation at issue.[51] This approach preserves democratic discretion while ensuring that no right is categorically excluded from meaningful protection.

Recent developments in critical theory have decisively demonstrated that the concepts of recognition and redistribution, far from being competing frameworks, represent a "false antithesis," as articulated by theorists such as Nancy Fraser. Contemporary conceptions of justice, therefore, necessitate the simultaneous pursuit of both these dimensions, as they are inextricably linked and mutually reinforcing. Building upon this foundational insight, a comprehensive integrated approach emerges, which endeavors to systematically connect the politics of recognition with tangible redistributive guarantees, and further, with the crucial psychological dispositions essential for their sustained efficacy. This approach offers a more holistic understanding of justice, moving beyond one-dimensional approaches and integrating the various facets required for genuine societal transformation. It posits that a truly just society must address both the symbolic and material aspects of inequality, while also fostering the individual and collective mindsets that facilitate such change.

3. Recognition, Redistribution, and Deliberative Democracy: Habermas's Critical Dialogue with Fraser

3.1. Fraser's Theory of Recognition and Participatory Parity

Fraser defines participatory parity as the normative standard requiring that social arrangements should ensure that every individual can participate equally in all domains of social interaction.[52] This principle serves as Fraser's alternative to both liberal individualism and communitarian identity politics, focusing on the institutional conditions that enable or prevent equal participation rather than on cultural recognition *per se*. For Fraser,

50 Nussbaum, M. C. (2011). *Creating capabilities* (pp. 65-67). Harvard University Press.

51 Young, K. (2012). *Constituting economic and social rights* (pp. 142-143). Oxford University Press.

52 Fraser, N. (2009). *Scales of justice* (p. 16). Columbia University Press.

misrecognition is not a psychological injury to identity but a condition of status subordination when institutionalized hierarchies of cultural value deny certain groups standing as full partners in social life. Injustice occurs when cultural disrespect or stereotyping excludes people from forums of debate or decision-making, even without formal legal barriers.[53] Fraser insists that economic redistribution and cultural recognition address different obstacles to parity. Lack of resources and lack of equal respect are distinct injustices that are causally intertwined yet analytically separate. Later, Fraser adds a third political dimension concerning representation and voice in democratic processes, reflecting that who counts as a participant is itself a matter of justice.[54] This integrated approach offers legal scholars a robust analytical tool for understanding how laws and legal institutions might perpetuate or ameliorate different forms of injustice.

By elevating participation as justice's measure, Fraser's framework shares affinities with Habermas's emphasis on inclusive deliberation while raising questions that his theory can address. Fraser's principle underscores that formal inclusion is insufficient, as inequalities persist even when all individuals are formally permitted to participate. This insight emerged in her critique of Habermas's early public sphere model, which showed that the bourgeois public's openness was undermined by gender, race, and class exclusions. In response, Fraser argued for "subaltern counterpublics" where subordinated groups formulate oppositional interpretations of their needs. Though they approach normative justification differently, both agree that democracy must attend to who speaks and on what terms. For legal theorists, this convergence highlights the inadequacy of purely procedural accounts of legal legitimacy that do not interrogate the substantive conditions of participation in legal discourse. Fraser's argument necessitates consideration of how legal systems might need to be reformed to address both formal and informal barriers to participation, particularly for historically marginalized groups whose perspectives have been systematically excluded from legal reasoning and jurisprudence.

The practical significance of Fraser's participatory parity framework becomes evident when examining international human rights processes that systematically exclude affected voices. The drafting of the ASEAN Human Rights Declaration in 2012 exemplifies how procedural exclusions

53 Fraser, N. (2000). Rethinking recognition. *New Left Review*, 3, 107, 114.
54 Fraser, N. (2005). Reframing justice in a globalizing world. *New Left Review*, 36, 69, 73.

undermine the legitimacy of normative outcomes. Despite civil society organizations' sustained advocacy for meaningful participation, the ASEAN Intergovernmental Commission on Human Rights excluded them from substantive engagement, limiting consultation to what Mathew Davies describes as "carefully managed consultations" held only toward the end of the process.[55] The Commission refused to publish drafts or allow public access to deliberations, with civil society organizations noting the lack of transparency and failure to consult meaningfully during the drafting process.

This exclusionary approach produced a declaration that civil society organizations widely rejected as failing to meet international human rights standards. Human Rights Watch characterized the resulting document as a declaration of government powers disguised as a declaration of human rights, while sixty-five grassroots and international organizations condemned its adoption. The process violated Fraser's participatory parity framework by denying civil society meaningful voice in norm-formation while privileging state interests over affected communities. This case demonstrates how formal institutional processes can systematically exclude the very voices most essential for legitimate human rights norm-making, producing declarations that lack both moral authority and practical effectiveness in protecting human dignity.

3.2. Discourse Ethics and the Moral Basis of Parity

At first glance, Nancy Fraser's participatory parity and Habermas's discourse ethics appear to diverge in their foundational orientations. Fraser adopts a pragmatic, outcome-focused approach that evaluates social arrangements based on whether they enable equal participation, while Habermas emphasizes the procedural conditions of argumentation itself.[56] Fraser's theory emerges from her critique of recognition politics and redistribution debates, whereas Habermas grounds his approach in the universal

55 Davies, M. (2014). An agreement to disagree: The ASEAN Human Rights Declaration and the absence of regional identity in Southeast Asia. Journal of Contemporary Asia, 44(3), 456-478. For civil society criticism, see Human Rights Watch (2012). Civil Society Denounces Adoption of Flawed ASEAN Human Rights Declaration; FORUM-ASIA statement by 65 civil society organizations (2012).

56 Habermas, J. (1990). *Moral consciousness and communicative action* (p. 43). MIT Press.

pragmatics of communication. However, this apparent divergence masks a deeper convergence around the principle of universal moral respect. Both thinkers ultimately underscore the fundamental principle that all human beings deserve equal consideration in the formation of norms that govern collective life. In discourse ethics, a norm is considered valid only if all those affected could reasonably accept its foreseeable consequences and side effects in terms of how it serves the interests of everyone involved. Such norms must therefore be capable of gaining recognition from all affected parties, a requirement that assumes relations of symmetrical respect in which each participant is treated as an equal co-author of the norms. This discourse-ethical perspective offers crucial insights for legal theory, especially in constitutional adjudication, where the legitimacy of fundamental norms hinges on their acceptability to all members of the political community.

Fraser's principle of parity elaborates this procedural insight substantively, translating equal respect into concrete social conditions for actual peer participation. From a Habermasian perspective, Fraser's theory effectively operationalizes the discourse-ethical principle institutionally. Justice, in this view. is conceived as both an outcome (parity) and a process designed to prevent exclusion or silencing due to power asymmetries during deliberation. This dual conception has significant implications for legal institutions, suggesting that courts must be concerned not only with the substantive content of rights but also with ensuring that legal processes themselves do not reproduce patterns of domination and subordination.[57]

However, Habermas might ask on what basis participatory parity is justified as the guiding norm of justice. Fraser appeals to equal moral worth as self-evident. A Habermasian reconstruction would ground this rationally in the pragmatic presuppositions of communication. That is, in any argument disregarded due to the speaker's status. Habermas elucidates the idealized conditions of uncoerced discourse, where the better argument alone prevails. Although never fully realized, the ideal speech situation serves as a regulative ideal approximated in dialogue,[58] demanding egalitarian reciprocity. Each participant is granted an equal right to initiate speech acts, question assertions, and express attitudes without fear. This concep-

57 see Young, I. M. (1997). Asymmetrical reciprocity: On moral respect, wonder, and enlarged thought. *Constellations*, 3(3), 340-363.

58 Habermas, J. (1984). *The theory of communicative action, Vol. 1: Reason and the rationalization of society* (T. McCarthy, Trans., p. 42). Beacon Press.

tion strongly resonates with legal thought that emphasizes the centrality of rational argumentation and mutual justification to legal legitimacy.

Fraser's formulation is outcome-oriented, focusing on the capacity to participate as a peer, whereas discourse ethics is predominantly procedure-oriented, emphasizing the deliberative process itself. In any policy debates, Fraser would ask whether the proposal will promote participatory parity. Her perspective is that of a critical theorist evaluating social arrangements against a normative benchmark. Habermas, by contrast, emphasizes who gets to set and evaluate the norms, namely, the participants themselves through communicative will-formation. From his standpoint, the legitimacy of an outcome is secured if and only if it emerges from a discourse in which all those affected have had an equal opportunity to contribute reasons.[59] This does not necessarily conflict with Fraser's principle. In fact, a law or policy that perpetuates severe inequality would likely fail Habermas's discourse principle, as the disadvantaged could not freely consent to it. But Habermas would stress that the only reliable way to determine whether an arrangement truly permits all to participate as peers is to subject it to inclusive public deliberation under conditions approximating parity. In other words, parity itself must be tested and achieved through discourse. Here, Habermas might be seen as adding a reflexive twist to Fraser's account. The critical theorist's role is not to impose a standard of parity from above, but to ensure the communicative processes by which society defines and realizes justice are themselves parity-promoting.[60] This highlights the importance of democratic procedure in Habermas's reconstruction of Fraser's norm. This productive synthesis of Fraser's substantive vision of participatory parity and Habermas's procedural discourse ethics carries significant implications for the design and reform of international legal institutions. To genuinely address global injustices, such institutions must move beyond purely formal legal processes to actively cultivate conditions of communicative freedom and material equity. This means not only ensuring formal access to international tribunals and deliberative bodies but also recognizing and dismantling the ingrained status hierarchies that silence marginalized voices on the global stage. Furthermore, it necessitates addressing the systemic maldistribution of resources that often prefigures these communicative disadvantages, ensuring that all affected parties, re-

59 Habermas, J. (1996). *Between facts and norms* (W. Rehg, Trans., p. 107). MIT Press.

60 Habermas, J. (1990). *Moral consciousness and communicative action* (p. 89). MIT Press.

gardless of their geopolitical or economic standing, possess the material independence necessary for authentic participation in global norm-setting. Only by embedding both recognition and redistribution into the very fabric of international law can a truly legitimate and universally accepted human rights regime be realized

3.3. Recognition, Identity, and Democratic Law

Fraser's conception of recognition deliberately eschews a "politics of identity" that valorizes group identities for their own sake. She critiques recognition politics that "reify" group identities or encourage separatism within minority groups. Instead, she focuses on equalizing group members' status in society at large. Habermas considers this approach consistent with his understanding of multicultural recognition in constitutional democracies. He maintains that no inherent tension exists between individual rights and the acknowledgment of group-specific identities. A properly understood, individual-based theory of rights, in his view, entails the need to recognize collective identities.[61] Respecting persons requires promoting the viability of cultural forms of life in which they form identities. Individuals can be truly free and equal only if their cultural contexts enjoy public respect and protection. This insight has profound implications for legal systems faced with claims from cultural minorities seeking legal protections or accommodations.

Both thinkers shift the focus from esteem for cultural content to equal respect for persons who bear that culture. The core idea is not that every cultural practice is beyond criticism, but that members of minority groups must not be structurally subordinated because of cultural affiliation. This approach allows for a critique of cultural practices that may impede the equal participation of some group members while still acknowledging the importance of cultural belonging to individual identity and well-being. Such a nuanced perspective is particularly valuable in legal contexts where

61 Habermas, J. (1994). Struggles for recognition in the democratic constitutional state. In A. Gutmann (Ed.), *Multiculturalism: Examining the politics of recognition* (p. 113). Princeton University Press.

courts must balance respect for cultural difference with commitment to fundamental rights and democratic principles.[62]

Habermas diverges from Fraser in his emphasis on law and democratic institutions as mediators of recognition claims. While Fraser speaks of recognition as cultural and societal transformation, Habermas, as a legal theorist, emphasizes translating recognition demands into justiciable rights and policies. He contends that liberal rule of law, properly adapted, can secure cultural recognition in a generalizable way through laws (anti-discrimination statutes, minority language rights, religious accommodations) that guarantee equal respect for different identities while upholding the universalist core of citizenship.[63] For Habermas, a pluralist society's constitution must express an "internal connection between public and private autonomy". Citizens must have both private freedom to pursue cultural life and public freedom to participate in politics as equals ; these freedoms are co-original and mutually supporting.[64] He endorses extensive protections for nondominant cultural groups based not on intrinsic cultural merit but on securing individual autonomy conditions for all citizens.[65]

A Habermasian critique might press Fraser to elaborate on how recognition can avoid devolving into fragmented identity politics. Fraser warns against misrecognition struggles that "freeze" identities or privilege group authenticity over individual autonomy. Habermas strengthens this by insisting on constitutional principles and discursive justification for any recognition claim. Claims for cultural recognition must be tested for compatibility with universalizable norms. They must not infringe upon others' rights or equal liberties. Legitimate recognition politics will seek generalizable accommodations, not exemptions undermining social cohesion or basic rights.[66]

If group-specific rights were to be asserted in a way that shields a cultural group from public criticism, for example, by appealing to the authority of tradition, such a move could be seen as conflicting with the communicative openness that the public sphere requires. In this regard, Fraser's

---

62 For a judicial application of these principles, see Justice McLachlin's opinion in Syndicat Northcrest v. Amselem, [2004] 2 S.C.R. 551, 2004 SCC 47 (Can.).

63 ibid 128.

64 Habermas, J. (1996). *Between facts and norms* (W. Rehg, Trans., p. 104). MIT Press.

65 Habermas, J. (1998). *The inclusion of the other* (p. 203). MIT Press.

66 Habermas, J. (1994). Struggles for recognition in the democratic constitutional state (p. 131). In A. Gutmann (Ed.), *Multiculturalism: Examining the politics of recognition.* Princeton University Press.

position is in fact consistent with that of Habermas. She does not support unconditional protections for group-specific traits, particularly when such protections come at the expense of dissenting voices within the group or infringe upon the rights of others. Instead, she commends recognition claims that foster interaction and cooperation across deep cultural divides and that serve as genuinely emancipatory responses to serious forms of injustice. Both Fraser and Habermas, then, favor a status egalitarian model of recognition aimed at integrating diverse citizens as equals, rather than a self-esteem model aimed at validating each group's identity *per se*.[67] By anchoring recognition in the language of legal rights and public reason, Habermas provides tools to ensure that recognition struggles enhance democratic unity in diversity. His discourse theory would encourage members of various cultures to enter dialogue, address mutual concerns, and arrive at arrangements that all can accept as just. This process itself exemplifies participatory parity.

3.4. Law, Democracy, and Participatory Parity

Habermas complements Fraser's project by explaining how participatory parity can be institutionalized. Fraser identifies the moral imperative of parity and diagnoses three key obstacles: economic exploitation, cultural domination, and political exclusion. Habermas adds a theory of the democratic constitutional state as the vehicle for realizing justice under plural conditions. In *Between Facts and Norms*, he argues that modern law mediates between factual social realities and normative demands through democratic discourse. Legitimate laws result from deliberative processes where citizens exercise communicative freedom and public autonomy. Laws are legitimate when citizens' contributions in the informal public sphere filter into formal lawmaking, influencing outcomes so that citizens see laws as expressing their collective will.[68] This vision rests on institutionalized participatory parity. All citizens should have equal rights and effective opportunities to participate in public discourse. Habermas recognizes that formal rights can be empty if social inequality or private power concentrations skew the public sphere. In a Habermasian reconstruction, socioeconomic redistribution is not only about fairness but democratic legitimacy. Material

67 Fraser, N., & Honneth, A. (2003). *Redistribution or recognition?* (p. 29). Verso.
68 Habermas, J. (1996). *Between facts and norms* (W. Rehg, Trans., p. 110). MIT Press.

inequalities that prevent full participation undermine the moral-political validity of democratic outcomes. Habermas's earlier work diagnosed how uncontrolled markets and bureaucratic power can "colonize the lifeworld", corroding social bonds and communicative freedoms that democracy requires.[69] By securing individuals' basic resources and independence, society empowers them to participate in public life as equals.

Where Habermas adds nuance is in describing how these changes occur and are validated. Fraser emphasizes social movements and contestation as driving forces behind justice expansions. Habermas agrees that movements push new issues into public debate but also posits a more formal mechanism. The public sphere and deliberative politics serve as rational conduits for transforming demands into legitimate laws. Movements succeed when they articulate claims appealing to generalizable interests and convince a broad public through reasons. The result should be institutional innovation justified to everyone, not just a particular group.

Habermas's theory helps extend Fraser's insights while preserving the fundamental idea that justice and democracy demand inclusive and uncoerced deliberation. Interpreted through Habermas's theoretical framework, Fraser's project of integrating recognition with redistribution emerges as a powerful account of justice. Habermas would support her central thesis that participatory parity serves as an appropriate measure of justice. At the same time, his critical reconstruction suggests that parity must be secured via discursive and legal means that Fraser sometimes leaves implicit. By rooting the parity principle in communicative reason's universality, Habermas provides it with firmer normative justification. It is not only a moral intuition but also a presupposition of any argument about justice. This enriches Fraser's vision, ensuring that recognition politics complement rather than compete with redistribution, yielding a comprehensive vision of democratic justice that neither ignores differences nor lets them undermine democratic community.[70]

4. Conclusion

This article has developed a comprehensive framework for understanding justice in culturally plural societies by systematically integrating insights

---

69 Habermas, J. (1987). *The theory of communicative action, Vol. 2: Lifeworld and system: A critique of functionalist reason* (T. McCarthy, Trans., p. 327). Beacon Press.

70 Fraser, N. (2005). Reframing justice in a globalizing world. *New Left Review*, 36, 75.

from procedural, psychological, and material approaches to intercultural legitimacy. The central theoretical contribution lies in demonstrating that apparently competing approaches - Rawlsian procedural impartiality, Smithian sympathetic imagination, Habermasian discourse ethics, and Fraser's participatory parity - address complementary rather than contradictory dimensions of a complex normative challenge. The integrated approach reveals that legitimate human rights norms must emerge from deliberative processes that simultaneously ensure procedural fairness, cultivate psychological readiness for perspective-taking, and address material inequalities that distort communicative power. This synthesis moves beyond previous approaches that treat recognition and redistribution as competing political strategies, instead showing their conceptual interdependence for generating norms capable of claiming validity across cultural boundaries. The framework's innovation consists in revealing how Sen's distinction between closed and open impartiality provides the bridge between domestic theories of justice and global challenges of intercultural legitimacy, enabling evaluation of institutional designs capable of fostering intercultural dialogue under contemporary conditions of legal and normative pluralism. The analysis suggests that current international human rights institutions inadequately address these tripartite conditions, with regional systems risking legitimization of exclusions that cannot survive broader moral scrutiny, while global institutions often lack the local knowledge necessary for effective implementation.

The framework draws primarily on Western philosophical traditions and institutional examples from liberal democratic contexts, though the theoretical synthesis aspires to intercultural validity. Future research should examine how concepts like sympathetic imagination, participatory parity, and communicative freedom translate across different cultural and political systems, while developing concrete institutional mechanisms and evaluation criteria for assessing whether particular institutions successfully embody the tripartite requirements. Justice in culturally plural societies emerges as a fundamentally relational and dialogical project requiring institutional arrangements that facilitate genuine intercultural dialogue under conditions of substantive equality. The theoretical synthesis demonstrates that achieving intercultural legitimacy for human rights norms requires simultaneous attention to procedural design, psychological development, and material conditions rather than focus on any single dimension of institutional reform. Universal human rights and cultural diversity prove to be mutually constitutive rather than inherently conflicting, with universal rights establishing conditions for diverse cultural expressions to flourish while cultural diversity enriches understanding of human flourishing and dignity. The project of intercultural human rights legitimacy emerges as an ongoing process of democratic iteration through which universal principles are continuously contested, interpreted, and reappropriated in particular contexts while maintaining their claim to intercultural validity. This requires institutional designs that can balance constitutional fixity with cultural plasticity, providing stable protection for basic liberties while remaining open to new perspectives generated by social evolution, migration, and intercultural encounter.

References

Anderson, E. (1999). What is the point of equality? *Ethics, 109*(2), 287-337.

An-Na'im, A. A. (1992). Human Rights in Intercultural Perspectives: A Quest for Consensus. Philadelphia, PA: University of Pennsylvania Press.

Appiah, K. A. (2006). *Cosmopolitanism: Ethics in a world of strangers*. W. W. Norton.

Balkin, J. (1998). The declaration and the promise of a democratic culture. *Widener Law Review, 4*, 167-180.

Bell, D. (2006). Asian Values and Human Rights. In Pellegrini, A. et al. (Eds.), Human Rights in East Asia: With Special Reference to China. Hong Kong: Hong Kong University Press.

Benhabib, S. (2002). *The claims of culture: Equality and diversity in the global era*. Princeton University Press.

Benhabib, S. (2004). *The rights of others*. Cambridge University Press.

Bhuta, N. (2012). "Rethinking the Universality of Human Rights: A Comparative Historical Proposal." In A. Emon (Ed.), Islamic Law and International Human Rights Law: Searching for Common Ground? Oxford University Press.

Buchanan, A. (2004). *Justice, legitimacy, and self-determination: Moral foundations for international law*. Oxford University Press.

Chan, J. (2006). Community, Harmony and Rights in East Asian Contexts. Critical Review of International Social and Political Philosophy, 9(4), 667-688.

Cohen, J. (1989). Democratic equality. *Ethics, 99*(4), 727-751.

Cohen, J. (2004). Minimalism about human rights: The most we can hope for? *Journal of Political Philosophy, 12*(2), 190-213.

Crenshaw, K. (1989). Demarginalizing the intersection of race and sex. *University of Chicago Legal Forum, 1989*, 139-167.

Davies, M. (2014). An Agreement to Disagree: The ASEAN Human Rights Declaration and the Absence of Regional Identity in Southeast Asia. *Journal of Contemporary Asia*, 44(3), 456-478.

Forst, R. (2012). *The right to justification* (J. Flynn, Trans.). Columbia University Press.

Fraser, N. (1990). Rethinking the public sphere: A contribution to the critique of actually existing democracy. *Social Text, 25/26*, 56-80.

Fraser, N. (1995). From redistribution to recognition? Dilemmas of justice in a 'post-socialist' age. *New Left Review, 212*, 68-93.

Fraser, N. (2000). Rethinking recognition. *New Left Review, 3*, 107-120.

Fraser, N. (2001). Recognition without ethics? *Theory, Culture & Society, 18*(2–3), 21-42.

Fraser, N. (2003). Social justice in the age of identity politics. In N. Fraser & A. Honneth (Eds.), *Redistribution or recognition?* (pp. 7-109). Verso.

Fraser, N. (2007). Identity, exclusion, and critique: A response to four critics. *European Journal of Political Theory, 6*(3), 305-338.

Fraser, N. (2009). *Scales of justice: Reimagining political space in a globalizing world.* Columbia University Press.

Fraser, N., & Honneth, A. (2003). *Redistribution or recognition? A political-philosophical exchange.* Verso.

Freeman, S. (2007). *Rawls.* Routledge.

Gibson, J.L. (2004). *Overcoming Apartheid: Can Truth Reconcile a Divided Nation?* (New York: Russell Sage Foundation), 15-34.

Gibson, J.L. (2006). The Contributions of Truth to Reconciliation: Lessons from South Africa. *Journal of Conflict Resolution*, 50(3).

Glendon, M. A. (2001). *A world made new: Eleanor Roosevelt and the Universal Declaration of Human Rights.* Random House.

Griswold, C. (1999). *Adam Smith and the virtues of enlightenment.* Cambridge University Press.

Habermas, J. (1984). *The theory of communicative action, Vol. 1: Reason and the rationalization of society* (T. McCarthy, Trans.). Beacon Press.

Habermas, J. (1987). *The theory of communicative action, Vol. 2: Lifeworld and system: A critique of functionalist reason* (T. McCarthy, Trans.). Beacon Press.

Habermas, J. (1990). *Moral consciousness and communicative action* (C. Lenhardt & S. W. Nicholsen, Trans.). MIT Press.

Habermas, J. (1996). *Between facts and norms: Contributions to a discourse theory of law and democracy* (W. Rehg, Trans.). MIT Press.

Habermas, J. (1998). Struggles for recognition in the democratic constitutional state. In C. Cronin & P. De Greiff (Eds.), *The inclusion of the other: Studies in political theory* (pp. 203-236). MIT Press.

Habermas, J. (2010). The concept of human dignity and the realistic utopia of human rights. *Metaphilosophy, 41*(4), 464-480.

Held, D. (2002). Law of states, law of peoples: Three models of sovereignty. *Legal Theory, 8*(1), 1-44.

Hopgood, S. (2013). *The Endtimes of Human Rights* (Cornell University Press) 158-179.

Human Rights Committee, *Hebbadj v. France*, Communication No. 2807/2016 (2018); Yaker v. France, Communication No. 2747/2016 (2018).

Markell, P. (2003). *Bound by recognition.* Princeton University Press.

Michelman, F. (1986). The Supreme Court 1985 term - Foreword: Traces of self-government. *Harvard Law Review, 100*(1), 4-77.

Mills, C. (1997). *The racial contract.* Cornell University Press.

Mounk, Y. (2018). *The People vs. Democracy: Why Our Freedom Is in Danger and How to Save It* (Harvard University Press) 15-34.

Mutua, M. (2002). Human Rights: A Political and Cultural Critique. Philadelphia, PA: University of Pennsylvania Press.

Nussbaum, M. C. (1995). Poets as judges: Judicial rhetoric and the literary imagination. *University of Chicago Law Review, 62*(4), 1477-1519.

Nussbaum, M. C. (2001). *Upheavals of thought: The intelligence of emotions.* Cambridge University Press.

Nussbaum, M. C. (2011). *Creating capabilities.* Harvard University Press.

Parekh, B. (2006). *Rethinking multiculturalism: Cultural diversity and political theory* (2nd ed.). Palgrave Macmillan.

Pogge, T. (2008). *World poverty and human rights* (2nd ed.). Polity.

Post, R. (2000). Reconciling theory and doctrine in First Amendment jurisprudence. *California Law Review, 88*(6), 2353-2374.

Rawls, J. (1971). *A theory of justice.* Harvard University Press.

Rawls, J. (1993). *Political liberalism.* Columbia University Press.

Rawls, J. (1999). *The law of peoples.* Harvard University Press.

Renteln, A. D. (1990). *International human rights: Universalism versus relativism.* Sage Publications.

Ricoeur, P. (2005). *The course of recognition* (D. Pellauer, Trans.). Harvard University Press.

Rothschild, E. (2001). *Economic sentiments: Adam Smith, Condorcet, and the Enlightenment.* Harvard University Press.

Sandel, M. (1982). *Liberalism and the limits of justice.* Cambridge University Press.

Schauer, F. (1988). Formalism. *Yale Law Journal, 97*(4), 509-548.

Sen, A. (2009). *The idea of justice.* Harvard University Press.

Slaughter, A.-M. (2004). *A new world order.* Princeton University Press.

Smith, A. (1976). *The theory of moral sentiments* (D. D. Raphael & A. L. Macfie, Eds.). Oxford University Press.

Sunstein, C. (1996). *Legal reasoning and political conflict.* Oxford University Press.

Taylor, C. (1992). *Multiculturalism and the politics of recognition.* Princeton University Press.

Truth and Reconciliation Commission of South Africa (1998). *Truth and Reconciliation Commission of South Africa Report,* Volume 1 (Cape Town: Juta)

Young, I. M. (1997). Asymmetrical reciprocity: On moral respect, wonder, and enlarged thought. *Constellations, 3*(3), 340-363.

Young, I. M. (2000). *Inclusion and democracy.* Oxford University Press.

Young, K. (2012). *Constituting economic and social rights.* Oxford University Press.

Reconsidering Age Discrimination: Intersectional, Contextual, and Comparative Perspectives

Hyun Jung Lee[1]

Abstract

This article critically examines the European Court of Human Rights' (the ECtHR, the Court) evolving approach to age discrimination, employing intersectionality theory to expose persistent gaps in human rights protections. Although the ECtHR has gradually recognized age as a protected ground under Article 14 of the European Convention on Human Rights (the ECHR), its jurisprudence remains limited by single-axis frameworks, deferential standards of review, and inadequate remedies. Drawing upon critical race theory and comparative constitutional analysis, this article demonstrates that the Court's reliance on rigid comparator approaches and the margin of appreciation doctrine systematically undermines the rights of individuals facing compounded disadvantage at the intersection of age and other identity categories. The analysis identifies a pronounced hierarchy among discrimination grounds, with age consistently afforded less sufficient protection than race, gender, or sexual orientation. Through detailed examination of important ECtHR cases, including *Carvalho Pinto de Sousa Morais v. Portugal* (2017) and *Stec and Others v. United Kingdom* (2006), this article argues that the ECtHR's current approach fails to address the structural and intersectional dimensions of ageism, leaving older persons exposed to overlapping forms of disadvantage with reparation challenges. This article concludes by advocating for a contextual and intersectional framework, drawing on South African Constitutional Court and Inter-American Court of Human Rights (IACtHR) jurisprudence, as a pathway toward more effective protection of age-related rights within the European Human Rights System.

1 Dr. Jur. Friedrich Alexander University Erlangen-Nuremberg, Germany. hyun.jung.lee@fau.de.

Keywords: Ageism, Intersectionality, European Court of Human Rights, Discrimination, Human Rights Law, Reparations, Comparative Jurisprudence

1. Introduction

Ageism arises when "age" is used as a basis to categorize individuals and establish social hierarchies, producing injustice, harm, and lack of solidarity.[2] Unlike immutable traits such as race or sex, age is a universal and temporal characteristic: Every individual, given time, transitions through social categories of age, challenging the static insider-outsider paradigm that traditionally grounds anti-discrimination law. This temporal and universal aspect renders the boundaries between privileged and marginalized groups uniquely permeable in the context of age, with individuals potentially moving from privileged to stigmatized positions over their life course. Moreover, age is not merely biological, but it is also culturally constructed, with norms that vary widely across societies and historical periods. This doctrinal and conceptual ambiguity has contributed to the relative invisibility of ageism as a form of discrimination within legal frameworks. As the Council of Europe has recently observed, age remains the only protected characteristic for which states frequently succeed in objectively justifying differential treatment.[3] The persistence of such justifications in law effectively devalues age as a ground of protection and perpetuates the normalization of age-based disadvantage.[4] Despite its pervasiveness and profound social impact, age discrimination remains significantly less theorized and institutionally recognized in human rights jurisprudence than other grounds of discrimination.

Within the European human rights system, the absence of explicit recognition of age as a protected ground has led to the development of various international and regional legal and policy instruments since the 1990s, including the UN Principles for Older Persons (1991)[5], the EU Employment

2 World Health Organization 2021, *Global Report on Ageism*, Geneva: WHO.

3 Eder-Gitschthaler, A. (Rapporteur) (2024), *Overcoming Age-based Discrimination against Older Persons*, Council of Europe Parliamentary Assembly, Doc. 15735, 5 December 2024.

4 Ibid.

5 United Nations General Assembly, *United Nations Principles for Older Persons*, General Assembly resolution 46/91, 16 December 1991.

Equality Directive (2000/78/EC)[6], and a series of Council of Europe action plans aimed at promoting the rights of older persons[7]. Notably, Article 14 of the ECHR does not explicitly include age, instead subsumes it under "other status".[8] As reflected in a recent Council of Europe report, most international human rights instruments, including the ECHR, do not expressly prohibit age discrimination.[9] This legal ambiguity perpetuates a situation in which policies subject to strict scrutiny, when justified by gender or race, are often tolerated if premised on age-based on distinctions.

In light of these challenges, intersectionality theory has become an important analytical tool for addressing these doctrinal and practical gaps. Originating with Kimberlé Crenshaw's analysis of Black women's experiences, intersectionality highlights the unique and compounded forms of disadvantage that emerge at the intersection of multiple identity dimensions. Crenshaw's insight - that "the intersectional experience is greater than the sum of racism and sexism"[10] - applies with particular relevance to age. Stereotypes and institutional biases related to age and gender can reinforce each other, producing forms of compounded discrimination not adequately addressed by traditional legal analysis. Empirical studies reinforce this view: Research on workplace discrimination demonstrates that gender stereotypes persist and are often intensified by assumptions about frailty, asexuality, or dependence in later life, imposing a distinctive double burden on older women.[11] Recent Council of Europe reports note that older women face discrimination arising from the intersection of gender and age, resulting in heightened exclusion and vulnerability.[12]

---

6 Council Directive 2000/78/EC of 27 November 2000 establishing a general framework for equal treatment in employment and occupation, OJ L 303, 2.12.2000.

7 For example, Council of Europe, *Council of Europe Action Plan to promote the rights and full participation of people with disabilities in society: improving the quality of life of people with disabilities in Europe 2006–2015*, adopted by the Committee of Ministers, Recommendation Rec (2006)5.

8 Eder-Gitschthaler, A. (Rapporteur) (2024), *Overcoming Age-based Discrimination against Older Persons*, Council of Europe Parliamentary Assembly, Doc. 15735, 29 Nov. 2024.

9 Ibid.

10 Crenshaw, K. (1989), *Demarginalizing the Intersection of Race and Sex: A Black Feminist Critique of Antidiscrimination Doctrine, Feminist Theory and Antiracist Politics*, University of Chicago Legal Forum 1989, 139-167.

11 Eder-Gitschthaler, A. (Rapporteur) (2024), *Overcoming Age-based Discrimination against Older Persons*, Council of Europe Parliamentary Assembly, Doc. 15735, 29 Nov. 2024.

12 Ibid.

The ECtHR or the Court has been slow to acknowledge intersectional discrimination explicitly. While the Court has interpreted Article 14 to include age within the meaning of "other status"[13], its reasoning typically relies on "vulnerability" framing rather than a developed intersectional analysis. In cases like *N.B. v. Slovakia* (2012)[14] and *B.S. v. Spain* (2017)[15], the Court recognized the vulnerability of Roma women and a Nigerian sex worker, respectively, without addressing these as instances of intersectional discrimination.[16] This tendency to obscure the distinctiveness of compound disadvantage highlights the ongoing doctrinal limitations of the ECtHR's approach.

This article critically examines the ECtHR's evolving doctrine on age discrimination through an intersectional perspective. It maps the Court's jurisprudence on ageism, evaluates its treatment of intersecting grounds of discrimination, and identifies both areas of progress and persistent hesitation. Ultimately, the analysis aims to clarify how Strasbourg doctrine could more effectively address the structural and intersectional dimensions of age-based inequality.

13 Wladasch, K. (2024), *Is there any room for vulnerability in Article 14 cases? The case law of the European Court of Human Rights*, LBI für Grund- und Menschenrechte.

14 In this case, a Romani woman was sterilized without her informed consent during a C-section while still a minor (17 years old). The ECtHR held that sterilizing the applicant without valid consent violated Article 3 (inhuman and degrading treatment) and Article 8 (private and family life), noting her particular vulnerability as a young Roma woman. Although the Court recognized her vulnerability, it did not frame the sterilization as intersectional discrimination under Article 14 (ECtHR, *N.B. v. Slovakia*, Application No. 29518/10, 12 June 2012).

15 In B.S. v. Spain, a Nigerian sex worker in Spain was stopped, beaten, and racially abused by police officers on multiple occasions, with domestic courts failing to investigate possible discriminatory motives. The ECtHR found violations of Article 3 and Article 14 in conjunction with Article 3. Crucially, the Court acknowledged the applicant's "particular vulnerability inherent in her position as a African woman working as a sex worker, which could be implicitly applied an intersectional interpretation (ECtHR, *B.S. v. Spain*, Application No. 47159/08, 24 July 2012).

16 Wladasch, K. (2024), *Is there any room for vulnerability in Article 14 cases? The case law of the European Court of Human Rights*, LBI für Grund- und Menschenrechte.

2. The Legal Dynamics of Age Discrimination: Intersectionality and Social Construction

2.1. Intersectionality: Challenge to Single-Axis Legal Frameworks

Intersectionality theory emerged from Black feminist scholarship, most notably the work of Kimberlé Crenshaw, who demonstrated that anti-discrimination law frequently fails individuals who belong to multiple marginalized groups. Crenshaw's analysis revealed that traditional legal frameworks, organized around discrete categories such as race and gender, systematically exclude Black women from effective protection by compelling them to frame their claims as either racial or gender-based discrimination. Neither approach adequately reflects their lived experiences of compounded disadvantage.[17] Her seminal observation that "the intersectional experience is greater than the sum of racism and sexism" fundamentally challenges the prevailing assumption in anti-discrimination law that multiple forms of discrimination are simply additive, rather than producing qualitatively distinct forms of marginalization.[18]

This theoretical insight has profound implications for the analysis of age discrimination, which often intersects with other social identities in ways that produce unique forms of disadvantage that cannot be reduced to isolated analyses of age, gender, race, disability, or socioeconomic status. Intersectionality exposes the analytical limitations of legal regimes that address disadvantage through compartmentalized categories, showing how such approaches frequently render invisible those individuals whose experiences of discrimination occur at the intersection of multiple axes of identity. Single-axis frameworks, which typically rely on formal-equality models emphasizing identical treatment and similarly situated comparator groups, prove particularly inadequate for addressing the complex, contextual, and cumulative realities of intersectional discrimination.[19] This critique is echoed in European equality law scholarship, which highlights how the

17 Crenshaw, K. (1989). "Demarginalizing the Intersection of Race and Sex," *University of Chicago Legal Forum* 1989(1), 139-167, at 140.

18 Crenshaw, K. (1991). "Mapping the Margins: Intersectionality, Identity Politics, and Violence against Women of Color," *Stanford Law Review*, 43(6), 1241-1299, at 1244.

19 Fredman, S. (2010). *Discrimination Law*, 2nd ed., Oxford University Press, pp. 94-96.

Court of Justice of the European Union's adherence to a single-ground logic has left intersectional harms largely unaddressed.[20]

The application of intersectionality to age discrimination is a relatively recent development within legal scholarship, yet it has generated important insights regarding the social construction of age and its interaction with other identity categories. Israel Doron argues that, whereas race and gender are now widely understood as social constructs, age is still commonly conceptualized as an objective, biological fact, rather than as a culturally mediated category subject to social interpretation.[21] Cultural-gerontology research makes the same point: Stephen Katz demonstrates how chronological age acquires significance only through culturally specific regimes of productivity and normality.[22] Recent EU policy analysis further confirms that age-related norms are deeply intertwined with broader equality agendas, influencing access to resources and civic participation across the life course.[23]

The shortcomings of single-axis approaches become particularly evident when examining the intersection of age discrimination and gender, which can generate distinct forms of disadvantage for older women. Cultural studies have long identified a "double standard of aging," whereby physical changes considered acceptable - or even valued - for men are stigmatized in women.[24] Gerontological and feminist research documents gendered ageism: Stereotypes concerning sexuality, productivity, and social worth that differ fundamentally from those applied to either younger women or older men.[25] Large-scale social psychology studies also reveal that percep-

20 Schiek, D. (2018). "On Uses, Mis-Uses and Non-Uses of Intersectionality before the Court of Justice (EU)." *International Journal of Discrimination and the Law*, 18(2-3), 82-103, at pp. 85-86.

21 Doron, I. (2018). "Re-thinking old age: Time for AGEIVISM." *Human Rights Defender*, 27, 33-40, at pp. 34-35.

22 Katz, S. (2005). *Cultural Aging: Life Course, Lifestyle, and Senior Worlds*, University of Toronto Press, pp. 11-13.

23 Georgantzi, N. (2018). "The European Union's Approach Towards Ageism." In Ayalon, L & Tesch-Römer, C. (eds.), *Contemporary Perspectives on Ageism. International Perspectives on Aging*, Springer, 341-368, at p. 346.

24 Sontag, S. (1972). "The Double Standard of Aging." *The Saturday Review*, 55(39), 29-38, at p. 32.

25 Calasanti, T. M., & Slevin, K. F. (eds.). (2006). *Age Matters: Re-Aligning Feminist Thinking*, ch. 9 "Gendered Ageism/Age(ed) Sexism," pp. 203-205.

tions of competence and warmth in older adults are shaped by both gender and age, highlighting the compounded nature of bias.[26]

Recent phenomenological studies exploring the intersection of ageism and racism further illustrate how older adults from racial minority backgrounds experience distinctive patterns of discrimination, with age-based stereotypes interacting with racial prejudice to create forms of disadvantage that cannot be explained by reference to either ground in isolation.[27] These empirical findings reinforce intersectionality theory's core claim: that legal frameworks premised on single-axis understanding of identity are systematically inadequate for capturing the complexity of discrimination as actually experienced by individuals with multiple marginalized identities. The continued reliance on such frameworks within European human rights law thus constitutes not merely a technical limitation, but a significant barrier to achieving substantive equality for those who face intersectional forms of age discrimination.

2.2. The Social Construction of Age: Legal Doctrines and Structural Implications

Within contemporary legal and policy frameworks, age functions not simply as a biological or chronological fact but as a socially constructed category that carries significant normative weight. This construction shapes access to opportunities, social recognition, and fundamental rights across all domains of social life.[28] Legal systems routinely use age to determine eligibility, entitlement, or exclusion in areas such as political participation, legal capacity, employment, retirement benefits, and access to public services. Yet these distinctions often rely on deeply embedded cultural assumptions

26 Hummert, M. L., Garstka, T. A., Shaner, J. L., & Strahm, S. (1994). "Stereotypes of the Elderly Held by Young, Middle-Aged, and Elderly Adults." *Journal of Gerontology: Psychological Sciences*, 49(5), 240-249, at p. 244.

27 Steward, A. T., De Fries, C. M., Dunbar, A. Z., *et al.* (2023). "A Phenomenological Understanding of the Intersection ality of Ageism and Racism Among Older Adults: Individual-Level Experiences." *Journals of Gerontology: Series B*, 78(5), 880-890, at pp. 880-882.

28 Fredman, S. & Spencer, S. (eds.) (2003). *Age as an Equality Issue: Legal and Policy Perspectives*. Hart, pp. 12-14.

about individual capacities, needs, and social value at different stages of life, rather than on objective or universally valid criteria.[29]

The naturalization of age-based classifications masks their social and historical contingency, presenting negotiated boundaries as if they were biologically determined and therefore immutable. This tendency becomes especially problematic when legal rules reinforce societal inequalities by excluding older persons from economic, political, or social life based on stereotypes of decline, dependence, or irrelevance. Empirical research substantiates the harms produced by institutional and structural ageism: according to the World Health Organization's Global Report on Ageism, such forms of ageism are associated with poorer physical and mental health, reduced social participation, and even diminished life expectancy for older adults.[30] Furthermore, a comprehensive systematic review of 422 studies involving seven million participants across 45 countries found that ageism negatively affected health outcomes in 96 percent of cases reviewed.[31]

In legal doctrine, age-based classifications often receive a markedly lower degree of judicial scrutiny compared to other protected characteristics. While distinctions based on race, gender, or sexual orientation are generally subject to strict or heightened judicial review, age is typically examined under a more deferential rational-basis standard. This is exemplified by the U.S. Supreme Court's decision in *Massachusetts Board of Retirement v. Murgia,* where mandatory retirement for police officers at age 50 was upheld under rational-basis analysis.[32] European jurisprudence reflects a similar hierarchy; in *Schwizgebel v. Switzerland,* the ECtHR upheld an upper age limit for adoptive parents on broad welfare grounds, deferring to the state's wide margin of appreciation.[33] Similarly, in *Palacios de la Villa v. Cortefiel*

---

29 Baars, J. (2012). *Ageing and the Art of Living.* Johns Hopkins University Press, pp. 52-54.

30 World Health Organization (2021). *Global Report on Ageism.* Geneva: WHO, p. 30.

31 Chang, E-Shien, et al (2020). "Global Reach of Ageism on Older Persons' Health: A Systematic Review." *PLOS ONE* 15 (1): e0220857, p. 9.

32 This tendency is exemplified by the U.S. Supreme Court's decision in *Massachusetts Board of Retirement v. Murgia,* where a mandatory retirement policy for police officers at age 50 was upheld under rational-basis review, reflecting age's status as a non-suspect classification. (*Massachusetts Bd. of Retirement v. Murgia,* 427 U.S. 307, 312 (1976)).

33 ECtHR, *Schwizgebel v. Switzerland,* No. 25762/07, 10 June 2010 (upholding an age-based adoption limit under Article 14 in conjunction with Article 8, according a wide margin of appreciation to the State due to non-uniformity of national age thresholds and the best interests of the child).

Servicios SA, the Court of Justice of the European Union upheld mandatory retirement at age 65 as objectively justified under Directive 2000/78/EC, applying a deferential proportionality assessment to the Member State's legitimate employment policy aim.[34]

These hierarchical review standards have significant implications for intersectional claims. When age is treated as a "less serious" ground of discrimination, the compounded harms suffered by older women of color or older persons with disabilities are likely to remain invisible within doctrinal structures designed for single-axis analysis. As a result, European human rights law continues to struggle to provide substantive equality for individuals facing intersecting forms of marginalization, highlighting the urgent need for legal doctrines that are structurally attentive, context-sensitive, and fully responsive to the socially constructed nature of age.

3. The European Court of Human Rights' Approach to Age Discrimination

3.1. The Gradual Recognition of Age as a Protected Ground

The ECtHR has proceeded incrementally and cautiously in its development of an approach to age discrimination, reflecting broader European uncertainties concerning the circumstances under which age-based distinctions are permissible. In contrast to more established grounds such as race or gender, age is not expressly enumerated in Article 14 of the ECHR, but instead falls within the residual category of "other status". The Court has interpreted this category expansively, yet its jurisprudence reveals persistent doctrinal hesitancy.[35]

The Court first confirmed that age could count as an "other status" in *Schwizgebel v. Switzerland (2010)*, a case concerning statutory age limits for adoption. Here, the Court recognized that differential treatment on the basis of age could potentially give rise to an issue under Article 14, even

34 The Court of Justice of the European Union (Grand Chamber), *Félix Palacios de la Villa v Cortefiel Servicios SA* (Case C-411/05) EU:C:2007:604 (16 October 2007) (finding automatic retirement at 65 objectively justified under Directive 2000/78/EC as pursuing legitimate employment-policy objectives and constituting proportionate means).

35 Council of Europe (2025). *Guide on Article 14 of the European Convention on Human Rights and on Article 1 of Protocol No. 12 to the Convention - Prohibition of Discrimination*, §§ 168-170.

though it ultimately found no violation in the specific circumstances.[36] Commentators regard this interpretive development as a significant conceptual shift. Nonetheless, it simultaneously underscored the Court's reluctance to elevate age to the status of a suspect ground comparable to race or gender.[37]

Subsequent judgments have expanded this recognition while simultaneously highlighting its limitations. For instance, in *Andrle v. Czech Republic (2011),* the Court reaffirmed that age constitutes a relevant ground within the ambit of Article 14, thereby extending the Convention's equality guarantees to differential treatment on the basis of age.[38] However, in adjudicating the contested pension scheme, the Court applied a deferential standard of review, invoking the wide margin of appreciation traditionally afforded to States in matters of economic and social policy. This approach stands in marked contrast to the Court's practice in cases involving suspect classifications such as race or gender, where "very weighty reasons" are typically required to justify differential treatment and a more rigorous standard of scrutiny is applied. Critical analysis of *Andrle* suggests that, notwithstanding the Court's doctrinal recognition of age as a protected status, the practical application of Article 14 in age discrimination cases reveals a judicial reluctance to extend the Conventions' strongest equality protections to claims grounded in age.[39]

The classification of age solely as "other status" continues to generate doctrinal ambiguity. Because this category is inherently residual, the Court must determine on a case-by-case basis both the boundaries of protection and the appropriate level of scrutiny.[40] This interpretive flexibility grants the Court substantial discretion, which, in practice, often leads to narrow-

36 "the applicant may consider herself to have been treated differently from a younger single woman who, in the same circumstances, would be likely to obtain authorisation to receive a second child with a view to its adoption. Accordingly, the applicant may claim to be a victim of a difference in treatment between persons in analogous situations." (ECtHR, *Schwizgebel v. Switzerland,* No 25762/07, 10 June 2010, para. 85. - recognizing that differential treatment based on age may trigger Article 14 in conjunction with Article 8, while upholding an age limit for adoption under a broad margin of appreciation).

37 O'Cinneide, C. (2010). "Age Discrimination and the European Court of Justice: EU Equality Law Comes of Age," ERA conference paper, pp. 3-5.

38 ECtHR, *Andrle v. Czech Republic*, no. 6268/08, 17 February 2011, §§ 46-50, 56-61.

39 Blackham, A. (2022). *Reforming Age Discrimination Law: Beyond Individual Enforcement*, OUP, pp. 98-101.

40 Council of Europe (2025), §§ 168-170.

er rather than broader protection against age-based discrimination. Such doctrinal flexibility has fostered an implicit hierarchy, with age persistently subject to lighter scrutiny than grounds such as race, gender, or sexual orientation. This dynamic is particularly detrimental to intersectional claims, in which age interacts with other forms of disadvantage and thus demands more rigorous judicial analysis.

3.2. The Margin of Appreciation and Age Discrimination in Socioeconomic Contexts

The ECtHR has consistently relied on the margin of appreciation doctrine to defer to national authorities in matters of socioeconomic policies. When such deference is combined with age-based classifications, it results in a notably lenient standard of review, leaving many structural forms of ageism beyond the effective reach of the Convention's equality guarantee. In the Grand Chamber's foundational judgment in *Stec and Others v. United Kingdom (2006)*, the Court affirmed that States enjoy a "wide margin of appreciation in the complex arena of social and economic policy", intervening only where a measure is "manifestly without reasonable foundation."[41] This standard, initially articulated in the context of social security jurisprudence under Article 1 of Protocol No. 1[42], has since become the touch-stone for assessing age-related pension rules, mandatory-retirement clauses, and benefit eligibility - even though ageism, like sexism or racism, often embeds stereotypes concerning capacity, productivity and social value.

Following *Stec*, the Court indicated its willingness to extend the manifestly-without-reasonable-foundation (MWRF) standard to a range of age-based welfare disputes. In *Carson and Others v. United Kingdom*, expatriate pensioners challenged that the "freezing" of UK State pensions in certain countries, contending that the policy unfairly penalized them on the basis of residence (and, indirectly, age). The Grand Chamber nonetheless found that "questions of economic strategy" fell within the State's broad discretion, concluding that the contested policy was neither arbitrary nor

---

41 ECtHR (GC), *Stec and Others v. United Kingdom*, nos 65731/01 & 65900/01, 12 Apr 2006, §§ 51-55.

42 Ibid. §§ 53-66.

disproportionate.[43] The same deferential logic reoccurred in *Runkee and White v. United Kingdom (2007)*, where the Court upheld gender-differentiated survivor benefits on grounds that the impugned rules formed part of a complex pension scheme aimed at "balancing competing priorities."[44] Even beyond classic pension disputes, the Court has invoked the margin to uphold occupational exclusion schemes; for example, in *Stummer v. Austria (2011)*, it accepted the State's exclusion of working prisoners from the public old-age insurance system, emphasizing the State's wide discretion in organizing social security, and finding that fiscal and administrative reasons for the exclusion were not "manifestly without reasonable foundation".[45]

While the Court maintains that the margin of appreciation is "not unlimited," it rarely scrutinizes how age-specific rules interact with gender, disability or race to amplify vulnerability. In *Carson*, the applicants - UK pensioners living abroad - raised issues that disproportionately affected older women, many of whom had moved abroad for family-related reasons, though the Court did not specifically address these gendered dimensions. In *Runkee*, widowers challenged the denial of benefits historically reserved for widows, highlighting the gendered legacy of the policy. Nevertheless, in both judgments, the Court failed to engage substantively with these gendered dynamics, instead deferring to fiscal justifications presented at a highly abstract level. The MWRF test has been criticized for reducing complex empirical controversies to deferential rational-basis review, which allows potentially outdated stereotypes to persist unchallenged by the judiciary.[46]

The Court's approach treats age as an inherently fluid or "natural" characteristic, thereby neglecting the reality that chronological thresholds are systematically deployed to structure legal entitlements across social and economic domains. The ECtHR's broad adoption of *Stec*-style deference imposes a substantial evidentiary burden on applicants, who must prove that facially neutral welfare measures produce discriminatory effects on the

43 ECtHR (GC), *Carson and Others v. United Kingdom*, no 42184/05, 16 Mar 2010, §§ 61-67.

44 ECtHR, *Runkee and White v. United Kingdom*, Judgment of 10 May 2007, nos. 42949/98 and 53134/99, §§ 40-42.

45 ECtHR (GC), *Stummer v. Austria*, no 37452/02, 7 Jul 2011, §§ 98-110.

46 Meers, J., (2020) "Problems with the 'Manifestly Without Reasonable Foundation' Test," *Journal of Social Security Law* 27 (1) 12-22, at 14-17.

basis of age.[47] If analogous justifications were advanced in cases concerning gender-based or race-based classifications, the Court would almost certainly demand closer empirical support and more structured proportionality analysis.[48] Yet, in the context of age, the Court is often willing to accept general, unquantified appeals to fiscal prudence or administrative convenience.

3.3. Hierarchies of Protection in ECtHR Jurisprudence

A persistent and problematic feature of the ECtHR's anti-discrimination jurisprudence is the emergence of an implicit hierarchy among protected grounds, with age consistently relegated to secondary importance behind race, gender, or sexual orientation. While differential treatment based on suspect grounds such as gender or sexual orientation generally triggers an "enhanced" scrutiny requiring states to present "very weighty reasons" supported by compelling evidence, age-based distinctions are typically reviewed under a far less structured stringent proportionality test or, in welfare disputes, the manifestly-without-reasonable-foundation ("MWRF") threshold developed in the Court's social-security case law.[49] Nothing in the text of Article 14 suggests that some forms of discrimination are inherently more serious than others; this hierarchy instead appears to rest on unexamined judicial assumptions that age categories are "natural" or inherently neutral in ways that race or gender classifications are not.

These assumptions are particularly evident in the Court's approach to stereotypes. In *Konstantin Markin v. Russia (2012)* the Grand Chamber struck down a refusal of parental leave to a divorced father, holding that "references to traditions, general assumptions or prevailing social attitudes" about gender roles can never justify differential treatment.[50] When the ground is age, however, similarly broad generalizations often go unchallenged. In *Schwizgebel v. Switzerland (2010)* the Court accepted, without empirical evidence, the State's assertion that significant age differences

47 Blackham, Alysia (2022) *Reforming Age Discrimination Law: Beyond Individual Enforcement* (OUP) 118-120.

48 O'Cinneide, C. (2010) "Age Discrimination and the European Court of Justice: EU Equality Law Comes of Age," ERA Conference Paper, 9-12.

49 Gerards, J. (2012). "The Prism of Fundamental Rights," *European Constitutional Law Review 8*; no. 2: 173-202; Fredman, S. (2016). "Substantive Equality Revisited," *International Journal of Constitutional Law*, 14(3), 712-738, at 727.

50 ECtHR (GC), *Konstantin Markin v. Russia*, no 30078/06, 22 Mar 2012, §§ 127-129.

between adoptive parent and child could justify restricting adoption, deferring to concerns about the burdens facing older single adopters. In Stec (2006), the ECtHR found that linking benefit eligibility to state pensionable age - effectively limiting benefits for older persons - was "reasonably and objectively justified," and did not amount to unjustified discrimination. The Court accepted broad policy justifications regarding working life and retirement, without scrutinizing the underlying assumptions about age as rigorously as it would with sex-based distinctions. As a result, a double standard emerges: while gender stereotypes in social policy attract vigorous judicial scrutiny, age-based policies are frequently accepted as legitimate considerations within the State's wide margin of appreciation.[51]

This hierarchy has significant implications for intersectional claims. In *Carvalho Pinto de Sousa Morais v. Portugal (2017),* the applicant was an older woman who suffered disabling gynecological injuries; the domestic court's inadequate damages award was based on assumptions that an older woman's sexuality and social life were of little significance. Although the ECtHR acknowledged the sexist element, it largely marginalized the age dimension, framing the violation almost exclusively as gender discrimination.[52] A similar limitation in the scope of judicial reasoning is evident in *Stummer v. Austria (2011)*, where the exclusion of prison labor from the old-age insurance scheme implicated both prisoner status and age; yet the Court focused primarily on the former and deferred to the State on the latter.[53] This reasoning produces a ceiling effect: When age is at issue, the overall standard of review drops to that reserved for age, even where other suspect classifications are also engaged.

The Court's approach to ranking discrimination grounds is both conceptually flawed and detrimental in practice. Shreya Atrey shows that intersectional harms are systematically under-protected because courts disaggregate multi-axis claims and resolve them on the "favored" ground alone, leaving the age-related component unaddressed.[54] Alexandra Timmer likewise argues that the Court's promising anti-stereotyping turn will remain incomplete so long as ageist assumptions escape rigorous evidentiary test-

51 ECtHR (GC), *Stec and Others v. United Kingdom* [GC], nos. 65731/01 and 65900/01, Judgment of 12 April 2006, §§ 52, 59-66.

52 ECtHR, *Carvalho Pinto de Sousa Morais v. Portugal*, no 17484/15, 25 Jul 2017, §§ 53-54.

53 ECtHR (GC), *Stummer v. Austria*, no 37452/02, 7 Jul 2011, §§ 94-102.

54 Atrey, S. (2019). *Intersectional Discrimination.* Oxford University Press, 105-108.

ing.[55] Rectifying the inconsistency would not require textual amendment but rather an even-handed application of existing principles: the Court should demand empirical support for age-based generalizations just as it does for claims grounded in sex or race, and where multiple grounds coincide it should apply the highest level of scrutiny applicable to any one of them. Until such adjustments are made, the implicit hierarchy embedded in the Court's case-law will continue to dilute the Convention's promise of equal protection, leaving older persons, especially older women, migrants and disabled people - structurally under-protected within the European human-rights system.

4. Intersectional Age Discrimination: Doctrinal and Methodological Challenges

4.1. Doctrinal Challenges in Recognizing Compound Disadvantage

As Crenshaw and other scholars have shown, people with multiple marginalized identities don't just face more discrimination, they face different kinds of discrimination that emerge from how these identities interact.[56] When this lens is applied to the overlap of age and gender, it becomes apparent that older women confront unique stereotypes about sexuality, productivity and social relevance that cannot be captured by analyzing either age or gender in isolation. Empirical gerontological research confirms that older women are judged more harshly than both younger women and older men with respect to attractiveness, competence and economic value, illustrating what scholars call "gendered ageism," a bias that "exceeds the sum" of its parts.[57]

55 Timmer, A. (2011). "Toward an Anti-Stereotyping Approach for the European Court of Human Rights," *Human Rights Law Review*, 11(4), 707-738, at 720-722.

56 Crenshaw, K. (1989). "Demarginalizing the Intersection of Race and Sex," *University of Chicago Legal Forum* 1989(1), 139-167, at 149-150; Crenshaw, K. (1991). "Mapping the Margins: Intersectionality, Identity Politics, and Violence against Women of Color," *Stanford Law Review*, 43(6), 1241-1299, at 1244-1245.

57 Calasanti, T. M., & Slevin, K. F. (eds.) (2006). Calasanti, T. M., & Slevin, K. F. (eds.). (2006). *Age Matters: Re-Aligning Feminist Thinking*. Routledge, 203-206; Hummert, M. L., Garstka, T. A., Shaner, J. L., & Strahm, S. (1994). "Stereotypes of the Elderly Held by Young, Middle-Aged, and Elderly Adults." *Journal of Gerontology: Psychological Sciences*, 49(5), 240249, at 244-245.

Yet, despite the theoretical clarity of intersectionality and its growing empirical foundation, the ECtHR has shown a persistent reluctance to acknowledge intersectional harm explicitly. Its judgments frequently privilege single-axis reasoning, "demoting" the age component of claims whenever a more established ground - typically gender - is present. In *Moraru and Marin v. Romania*[58], the imposition of different compulsory retirement ages for male and female civil servants necessarily implicated both age and sex as grounds of potential discrimination. However, the Court confined its analysis strictly to gender-based discrimination, assessing the applicants' claims exclusively through the lens of gender. The dimension of age, and the compounded disadvantage faced by women required to leave the workforce earlier solely by virtue of their gender, remained unexamined. This narrow framing not only fails to capture the full complexity of the applicants' lived experience but also perpetuates a doctrinal pattern in which age is effectively subordinated as a "secondary" ground, thereby evading the rigorous scrutiny mandated by Article 14 of the Convention, and Article 1 of Protocol No. 12. Notably, neither provision establishes a hierarchy among protected grounds; yet, in practice, the Court's reasoning privileges gender discrimination while leaving intersectional harms unaddressed.

The same analytical pattern characterizes a wide range of cases in which age intersects with other protected characteristics. Mandatory-retirement litigation, for example, routinely raises both sex and age issues because female employees have historically faced earlier exit ages and lower accrued benefits. Nevertheless, the Court tends to resolve these disputes by focusing on the gender dimension alone, thereby implicitly validating ageist assumptions about productivity and dependency.[59] Such reasoning disregards intersectionality's central insight that the resulting disadvantage cannot be disaggregated into neat, severable parts but must instead be viewed as a "unique, composite" harm generated by the interaction of both grounds.

A notable, if isolated, departure from this single-axis model is *Carvalho Pinto de Sousa Morais v. Portugal (2017)*, in which the domestic courts reduced damages for a 50-year-old woman rendered incontinent and unable to have sexual relations, reasoning that sexual life "is not as important" for a woman of her age. The Strasbourg Court unanimously condemned

58 ECtHR, *Moraru and Marin v. Romania*, Fourth Section, Applications nos. 53282/18 and 31428/20, Judgment of 20 December 2022, final 20 March 2023, paras. 107-111.

59 Blackham, A. (2022). *Reforming Age Discrimination Law: Beyond Individual Enforcement*, Oxford University Press, 118-121.

this as impermissible stereotyping, emphasizing that the applicant's age and gender together were decisive in the discriminatory award and that both "prejudiced assumptions about female sexuality and age" violated Article 14.[60] Crucially, the Court refused to separate the two dimensions, recognizing that the injury flowed from their interaction - an authentic, if rare, embrace of intersectional reasoning. Nevertheless, subsequent judgments have not generalized the methodology deployed in *Sousa Morais*; age-related elements continue to be marginalized whenever another better-established ground is present, indicating an absence of sustained doctrinal commitment to intersectionality.

Comparative analysis highlights the practical implications of this gap. In jurisdictions such as Canada and South Africa, courts regularly employ an "additive-plus" or "composite-ground" approach, which requires a thorough examination of the cumulative effects of multiple grounds of discrimination and mandates the application of the highest standard of scrutiny prompted by any of the intersecting grounds.[61] By contrast, the ECtHR's fragmented approach perpetuates protection gaps for older women, racial-minority elders and older persons with disabilities, whose compound disadvantage remains largely unacknowledged within European human rights law. Unless the Court develops coherent doctrinal tools - such as a principled presumption that compound claims trigger the highest level of scrutiny applicable to any intersecting ground - intersectional age discrimination will continue to evade meaningful judicial redress.

4.2. Methodological Challenges: The Limits of Comparator Analysis and Evidentiary Gaps

A persistent barrier to the effective recognition of intersectional age discrimination in ECtHR case law is the Court's adherence to a conventional comparator model. This framework requires applicants to demonstrate less favorable treatment relative to a "similarly situated" group, a method that may suffice for single-axis discrimination but fundamentally fails in cases involving intersecting identities. As Kimberlé Crenshaw argued over thirty years ago, obliging Black women to compare themselves either to Black

60 ECtHR, *Carvalho Pinto de Sousa Morais v. Portugal*, no 17484/15, 25 Jul 2017, §§ 52-55.

61 Atrey, S. (2019). *Intersectional Discrimination*. Oxford University Press, 105-109.

men or to white women "obliterates" the compound dimension of their disadvantage and compels the artificial separation of mutually constitutive identities, thereby misrepresenting the reality of intersectional harm.[62] Gerontological research similarly demonstrates that the same dynamic for older women, whose social positioning cannot be captured by looking separately at younger women or at older men.[63] Yet the comparator requirement compels litigants to disaggregate their identities, thereby obscuring the very harm they seek to expose.

The ECtHR's fidelity to comparator analysis has led to significant analytical distortions. In *Moraru and Marin v. Romania* (2022), while the impugned rule clearly implicated both age and sex, the Court framed the discrimination solely in terms of sex, neglecting to address the intersectional disadvantage faced by women required to exit the labor market at an earlier age.[64] Similar misfires are evident well beyond age; critics of the Court's sexual-orientation cases - most famously *Schalk and Kopf v. Austria (2010)* - note that the use of married heterosexual couples as the "comparator" for same-sex partners masked structural exclusion instead of revealing it.[65] Critics have highlighted that using married heterosexual couples as the reference group for same-sex couples concealed the structural exclusion underlying the case, a methodological move that failed to recognize the substantive inequality at issue.[66]

The limitations of comparator analysis are not only conceptual but also evidentiary. EU and the Council of Europe agencies repeatedly record the statistical invisibility of older minority women, older disabled people and other multiple marginalized groups: Labor-market, health and social-service datasets rarely present disaggregated figures that would let courts see compounded disparities.[67] Without numbers, applicants struggle to shoulder the evidentiary burden that formal equality frameworks impose. The

---

62 Crenshaw, K. (1989). "Demarginalizing the Intersection of Race and Sex," *University of Chicago Legal Forum* 1989(1), 139-167: 149-150.

63 Calasanti, T. M., & Slevin, K. F. (eds.) (2006). Calasanti, T. M., & Slevin, K. F. (eds.). (2006). *Age Matters: Re-Aligning Feminist Thinking*. Routledge, 203-206.

64 ECtHR, *Moraru and Marin v. Romania*, nos. 53282/18 and 31428/20, 20 December 2022, §§ 107-124.

65 ECtHR. *Schalk and Kopf v. Austria*, no 30141/04, 24 June 2010, §§ 102-113.

66 Fredman, Sandra (2016). "Substantive Equality Revisited." *International Journal of Constitutional Law* 14 (3): 727.

67 European Union Agency for Fundamental Rights. *Second European Union Minorities and Discrimination Survey - Main Results* (FRA, 2017), 56-58.

Grand Chamber's judgment in *D.H. and Others v. Czech Republic (2007)* showed that robust statistics can prove indirect discrimination even where no tidy comparator exists, yet the Court has never systematized that data-sensitive approach for intersectional age claims.[68] In practice, the absence of disaggregated data begets legal invisibility, perpetuating a feedback loop in which those who are unseen in statistics remain unseen in law.

These methodological and evidentiary shortcomings have prompted leading equality scholars to urge a paradigm shift away from strict comparator tests. Sandra Fredman advocates a "central capabilities and dignitary harm" model that asks whether a contested rule entrenches pre-existing disadvantage rather than whether two groups are identically placed.[69] Shreya Atrey proposes an "intersectional lens" that obliges courts to examine how multiple grounds combine to produce distinctive subordination, dispensing with false symmetries.[70] Alexandra Timmer and Dagmar Schiek similarly call for contextual, history-sensitive analyses that look to structures of power, not mirror images.[71] Adopting such frameworks would allow Strasbourg to acknowledge compound age discrimination without forcing applicants into misleading comparisons, and to draw on qualitative testimony, social-science research and structural indicators - exactly the kind of material the Court already relied upon in *Sousa Morais* when it condemned intersecting sexist and ageist stereotypes.[72]

Transitioning toward comparator-light or comparator-free approaches is thus essential for European equality jurisprudence to confront the complex realities of intersectional disadvantage in the twenty-first century. Without such a paradigm shift, individuals such as older women of color with disabilities - and countless others at the intersection of multiple marginalizations - will remain trapped between evidentiary blind spots and doctrinal constraints, their injuries largely invisible in the very forum tasked with protecting their rights.

---

68 ECtHR. *D.H. and Others v. Czech Republic* [GC], no 57325/00, 13 Nov 2007, §§ 188-189.

69 Fredman, Sandra (2011). *Discrimination Law*. 2nd ed., Oxford University Press, 136-142.

70 Atrey, Shreya (2019). *Intersectional Discrimination*. Oxford University Press, 66-68.

71 Timmer, Alexandra (2018). "Toward an Anti-Stereotyping Approach for the ECtHR." *Human Rights Law Review* 11 (4) (2011): 720-722; Schiek, Dagmar. "On Uses, Mis-Uses and Non-Uses of Intersectionality before the CJEU." *International Journal of Discrimination & Law* 18 (2-3) (2018): 86-88.

72 European Court of Human Rights. *Carvalho Pinto de Sousa Morais v. Portugal*, no 17484/15, 25 July 2017, §§ 53-55.

4.3. Remedial Challenges: Learning from Comparative Jurisprudence

The remedial framework presently employed by the ECtHR in age-discrimination litigation has proven systematically inadequate for capturing the full spectrum of harm inflicted on victims of intersectional discrimination, largely because the Court confines itself to declaratory findings and pecuniary awards aimed at restoring the *status quo ante*. Such backward-looking, individualized relief is ill-suited to violations whose roots lie in systemic exclusions, institutional cultures and entrenched stereotypes. In *Stec and Others v. United Kingdom* (2006), the Grand Chamber limited redress to compensation, without ordering the United Kingdom to amend the pension rules that had generated the discrimination, leaving the impugned policies intact and available to affect future cohorts of older people. In *Carson and Others v. United Kingdom* (2008), the Grand Chamber found no violation and thus awarded neither compensation nor any changes to the challenged pension rules, allowing the policy to continue unchanged.[73] Even in *Carvalho Pinto de Sousa Morais v. Portugal (2017)*, where the Court explicitly criticized the national court's reliance on both ageist and sexist stereotypes, the remedy was limited to an award of just satisfaction (damages) under Article 41. The Court did not direct Portugal to undertake any broader structural reforms, such as mandatory judicial training or measures targeting the underlying discriminatory reasoning.[74]

From an intersectional perspective these compensatory remedies mask, rather than mend, the dignitary injuries, social exclusion and structural marginalization suffered by older women, minority elders and disabled seniors. Contemporary remedial scholarship therefore calls for transformative or integral reparation capable of tackling root causes rather than merely monetizing effects. Sandra Fredman argues that effective equality demands remedies "designed to change the underlying structures of disadvantage," not merely to pay for their consequences.[75] Dinah Shelton similarly contends that monetary payments alone "rarely achieve deterrence or guarantee non-repetition," urging courts to craft *forward-looking* measures

73 ECtHR (GC). *Carson and Others v. United Kingdom*, no 42184/05, 16 March 2010, §§ 89-91; *Stec and Others v. United Kingdom*, nos 65731/01 & 65900/01, 12 April 2006, § 72.

74 ECtHR. *Carvalho Pinto de Sousa Morais v. Portugal*, no 17484/15, 25 July 2017, §§ 46-62.

75 Fredman, Sandra (2011). *Discrimination Law*, 2nd ed., Oxford University Press, pp. 214-219.

such as guarantees of legislative reform, public apologies and training programmes.[76]

The IACtHR offers a compelling comparative example. Applying the principle of "reparación integral" (comprehensive reparation), the Court regularly combines pecuniary compensation with symbolic, institutional, and structural measures. In *Gomes Lund et al. ("Guerrilha do Araguaia") v. Brazil* (2010), for instance, the IACtHR ordered the State not only to pay damages to the victims' families but also to conduct a public act of acknowledgment of responsibility, establish a search and identification program for the disappeared, create a dedicated archive, and adopt legislative and administrative reforms - including measures to remove amnesty obstacles to criminal prosecution of those responsible for enforced disappearances.[77] Similarly, in the case of the *Workers of the Fireworks Factory in Santo Antônio de Jesus v. Brazil* (2020), the IACtHR required the State not only to provide pecuniary compensation to the victims' families, but also to guarantee access to health care and psychological assistance, implement regulatory reforms for workplace safety, and adopt educational and awareness-raising measures to prevent similar tragedies.[78] These remedies addressed both the individual harms suffered and the structural deficiencies - such as inadequate regulation and social vulnerability, that had enabled the violations. Such orders exemplify what Shreya Atrey describes as a "dignity-centred, structural" approach to compound harms, extending reparation to the broader community affected and seeking to dismantle the systemic conditions that perpetuate discrimination and risk.[79]

Adopting comparable integral reparation within the European system would allow the ECtHR to acknowledge the multidimensional nature of intersectional age discrimination. Possible orders include (i) public apologies recognizing the equal worth of older persons, (ii) mandatory training for judges and civil servants to dispel ageist stereotypes, (iii) repeal or amend-

---

76 Shelton, Dinah (2015). *butler in International Human Rights Law*, 3rd ed., Oxford University Press, pp. 352-356.

77 Inter-American Court of Human Rights. *Gomes Lund et al. ("Guerrilha do Araguaia") v. Brazil*, Judgment (Merits, Reparations and Costs), 24 November 2010, §§ 249-319.

78 Inter-American Court of Human Rights. *Workers of the Fireworks Factory in Santo Antônio de Jesus v. Brazil*, Judgment (Preliminary Objections, Merits, Reparations and Costs), 15 July 2020, §§ 382-425.

79 Atrey, Shreya. *Intersectional Discrimination*, Oxford University Press, 2019, pp. 146-149.

ment of discriminatory statutes, (iv) institutional monitoring to guarantee non-repetition, and (v) positive-action schemes promoting the participation of older adults in public life. Such an evolution would require the Court to reconceive its role from a primarily compensatory adjudicator to an agent of structural change. In *D.H. and Others v. Czech Republic* (2007), for example, the Grand Chamber went beyond awarding compensation by directly linking statistical evidence of systemic Roma exclusion from mainstream education to a violation of Article 14, and, in accordance with Article 46 of the Convention, called upon the respondent State to implement general measures capable of eliminating discriminatory practices in school placements.[80] Although the Court did not prescribe a specific desegregation plan, it required the government to adopt appropriate reforms to prevent similar violations in the future, thus embracing an incipient structural approach to remedies. Aligning Strasbourg's remedial practice with these transformative principles would furnish more meaningful justice to individuals who experience *compound* disadvantage at the intersection of age and other protected characteristics, while advancing the Convention's broader aim of real and effective equality across Europe.

5. Conclusion

The ECtHR has recognized age as an "other status" under Article 14, marking a notable advance in the protection of older persons' rights. Nevertheless, its approach to equality remains anchored in single-axis reasoning, rigid comparator frameworks, and predominantly compensatory remedies. While these doctrinal tools may suffice for discrimination claims that track a single, clearly defined ground, they systematically falter when age discrimination intersects with other identities such as sex, race, or disability. In such cases, compound harms cannot be adequately disaggregated or redressed by existing methods. The Grand Chamber's judgments in *Carson* (2010) and and *Stec* (2006) demonstrate that although age claims are formally recognized, they are frequently subject to weak scrutiny and limited remedies[81]. The recent judgment in *Moraru and Marin (2022)* is

80 ECtHR (GC). *D.H. and Others v. Czech Republic*, no 57325/00, 13 November 2007, §§ 207, 209, 216-217.

81 ECtHR (GC), *Carson and Others v. United Kingdom*, no 42184/05, 16 Mar 2010; ECtHR (GC), *Stec and Others v. United Kingdom*, nos 65731/01 & 65900/01, 12 Apr 2006.

emblematic; despite the clear involvement of both age and sex, the Court's reasoning effectively allowed the age dimension to recede once a "stronger" ground, i.e. gender, was identified, leaving the compounded disadvantage unaddressed.[82]

This persistent gap between doctrinal analysis and the lived realities of older women, minority elders, and disabled seniors means that protection against intersectional age discrimination remains largely nominal. Comparative constitutional jurisprudence points to workable alternatives. The South African Constitutional Court, for example, has developed a contextual equality test - articulated in *Harksen v. Lane* (1997) and further refined in *Minister of Finance v. Van Heerden* (2004) - that interrogates whether a contested measure, assessed in its full historical and social context, serves to advance or undermine substantive equality.[83] This approach eschews artificial comparator groups and directly engages with the structures that generate overlapping forms of exclusion. Equality theorists such as Sandra Fredman and Shreya Atrey have emphasized the necessity of such context-sensitive, structurally aware analysis for capturing the full range of intersectional disadvantage.[84]

Real transformation, however, requires not only doctrinal innovation but also a remedial shift. In *Gomes Lund et al. v. Brazil (Guerrilha do Araguaia, 2010)*, the IACtHR required not only damages but also a public act of acknowledgment, the creation of archives, and legislative reforms to address the systemic roots of enforced disappearance[85]. Similarly, in case of *the Workers of the Fireworks Factory in Santo Antônio de Jesus v. Brazil* (2020), the IACtHR ordered healthcare guarantees, psychosocial support, strengthened workplace safety, and educational initiatives - measures designed to address both the immediate injuries and the broader conditions that enabled the harm.[86] Shreya Atrey has described this model

82 ECtHR, Moraru and Marin v. Romania, nos. 53282/18 and 31428/20, 20 December 2022, §§ 107-123.

83 South African Constitutional Court, Harksen v. Lane [1997] ZACC 12; Minister of Finance v. Van Heerden [2004] ZACC 3.

84 Fredman, Sandra. *Discrimination Law*, 2nd ed., Oxford University Press, 2011, pp. 136-142; Atrey, Shreya. *Intersectional Discrimination*, Oxford University Press, 2019, pp. 66-68.

85 IACtHR, *Gomes Lund et al. v. Brazil* (Guerrilha do Araguaia), Judgment (Merits, Reparations and Costs), 24 Nov 2010, paras 278-304.

86 IACtHR, *Workers of the Fireworks Factory in Santo Antônio de Jesus v. Brazil*, Judgment, 15 Jul 2020, paras 330-343.

as "dignity-centered" and "structural," aiming to secure reparations not just for individual applicants, but for all those affected by the violation.[87]

Importing such a paradigm into the Strasbourg system would permit the ECtHR to order, for example, mandatory anti-ageism training for judges and civil servants, systematic review and repeal of discriminatory retirement practices, or the adoption of monitoring frameworks for institutional bias - steps that transcend "cheque-book" remedies and engage with the underlying social dynamics of exclusion. This contextual and transformative approach would not only close the persistent gap between recognition and protection but would also fulfill the Convention's promise of equal dignity for Europe's ageing populations by meaningfully addressing the realities of intersectional discrimination.

Bibliography

Books

Atrey, Shreya, *Intersectional Discrimination* (Oxford University Press, 2019)

Baars, Jan, *Ageing and the Art of Living* (Johns Hopkins University Press, 2012)

Blackham, Alysia, *Reforming Age Discrimination Law: Beyond Individual Enforcement* (Oxford University Press, 2022)

Calasanti, Toni M and Kathleen F Slevin (eds), *Age Matters: Realigning Feminist Thinking* (Routledge, 2006)

Fredman, Sandra, *Discrimination Law* (2nd edn, Oxford University Press, 2011)

Fredman, Sandra and Sarah Spencer (eds), *Age as an Equality Issue: Legal and Policy Perspectives* (Hart, 2003)

Katz, Stephen, *Cultural Aging: Life Course, Lifestyle, and Senior Worlds* (University of Toronto Press, 2005)

Shelton, Dinah, *Remedies in International Human Rights Law* (3rd edn, Oxford University Press, 2015)

Journal Articles

Butler, R N, 'Age-Ism: Another Form of Bigotry' (1969) 9(4) *The Gerontologist* 243

Chang, E-Shien and others, 'Global Reach of Ageism on Older Persons' Health: A Systematic Review' (2020) 15(1) *PLOS ONE* e0220857

Crenshaw, Kimberlé, 'Demarginalizing the Intersection of Race and Sex' (1989) *University of Chicago Legal Forum* 139

Crenshaw, Kimberlé, 'Mapping the Margins: Intersectionality, Identity Politics, and Violence against Women of Color' (1991) 43(6) *Stanford Law Review* 1241

---

87 Atrey, Shreya. *Intersectional Discrimination*, Oxford University Press, 2019, pp. 66-68.

Cuddy, A J C, S T Fiske and P Glick, 'The BIAS Map: Behaviors from Intergroup Affect and Stereotypes' (2007) 92(4) *Journal of Personality and Social Psychology* 631

Doron, Issi, 'Re-Thinking Old Age: Time for Ageivism' (2018) 27(2) *Human Rights Defender* 33

Fredman, Sandra, 'Substantive Equality Revisited' (2016) 14(3) *International Journal of Constitutional Law* 712

Georgantzi, Narina, 'The European Union's Approach Towards Ageism' in L Ayalon and C Tesch-Römer (eds), *Contemporary Perspectives on Ageism* (Springer, 2018)

Gerards, Janneke, 'The Prism of Fundamental Rights: The ECtHR's Ground-by-Ground Approach under Article 14' (2021) 21(3) *Human Rights Law Review* 576

Hummert, Mary L and others, 'Stereotypes of the Elderly Held by Young, Middle-Aged, and Elderly Adults' (1994) 49(5) *Journal of Gerontology: Psychological Sciences* P240

Meers, Jed, 'Problems with the "Manifestly Without Reasonable Foundation" Test' (2020) 27(1) *Journal of Social Security Law* 12

Payne, S and L Doyal, 'Older Women, Work and Health' (2010) 60(3) *Occupational Medicine* 172

Schiek, Dagmar, 'On Uses, Mis-Uses and Non-Uses of Intersectionality before the Court of Justice (EU)' (2018) 18(2-3) *International Journal of Discrimination and the Law* 82

Sontag, Susan, 'The Double Standard of Aging' (1972) 55(39) *Saturday Review* 29

Steward, Andrew T and others, 'A Phenomenological Understanding of the Intersectionality of Ageism and Racism Among Older Adults: Individual-Level Experiences' (2023) 78(5) *Journals of Gerontology: Series B* 880

Timmer, Alexandra, 'Toward an Anti-Stereotyping Approach for the European Court of Human Rights' (2011) 11(4) *Human Rights Law Review* 707

Cases

European Court of Human Rights

Andrle v Czech Republic, no 6268/08, 17 February 2011

Carvalho Pinto de Sousa Morais v Portugal, no 17484/15, 25 July 2017

Carson and Others v United Kingdom (Grand Chamber), no 42184/05, 16 March 2010

D.H. and Others v Czech Republic (Grand Chamber), no 57325/00, 13 November 2007

Konstantin Markin v Russia, no 30078/06, 22 March 2012

Moraru and Marin v Romania, nos 50550/06 and 1765/08, 16 July 2015

Runkee and White v United Kingdom, nos 42949/98 and 53134/99, 25 October 2007

Schalk and Kopf v Austria, no 30141/04, 24 June 2010

Schwizgebel v Switzerland, no 25762/07, 10 June 2010

Stec and Others v United Kingdom (Grand Chamber), nos 65731/01 and 65900/01, 12 April 2006

Stummer v Austria (Grand Chamber), no 37452/02, 7 July 2011

Court of Justice of the European Union

Palacios de la Villa v Cortefiel Servicios SA, C-411/05, 16 October 2007

Inter-American Court of Human Rights

Gomes Lund et al. (Guerrilha do Araguaia) v Brazil, Judgment (Merits, Reparations and Costs), 24 November 2010

Workers of the Fireworks Factory in Santo Antônio de Jesus v Brazil, Judgment (Preliminary Objections, Merits, Reparations and Costs), 15 July 2020

South African Constitutional Court

Harksen v Lane NO 1998 (1) SA 300 (CC)

Minister of Finance v Van Heerden 2004 (6) SA 121 (CC)

US Supreme Court

Massachusetts Board of Retirement v Murgia, 427 US 307 (1976)

Official Documents and Reports

Council of Europe, *Guide on Article 14 of the Convention - Prohibition of Discrimination* (updated 2025)

Eder-Gitschthaler, Andrea (Rapporteur), *Overcoming Age-based Discrimination against Older Persons* (Council of Europe Parliamentary Assembly, Doc 15497, 29 November 2024)

European Institute for Gender Equality, *Gender & Ageing Report* (EIGE, 2020)

European Union Agency for Fundamental Rights, *Second European Union Minorities and Discrimination Survey - Main Results* (FRA, 2017)

O'Cinneide, Colm, *Age Discrimination and the European Court of Justice* (ERA Conference Paper, Trier, 2010)

United Nations General Assembly, *United Nations Principles for Older Persons*, Resolution 46/91, 16 December 1991

Wladasch, Katrin, *Is There Any Room for Vulnerability in Article 14 Cases? The Case Law of the European Court of Human Rights* (LBI for Human Rights, 22 January 2024)

World Health Organization, *Global Report on Ageism* (WHO, 2021)

Legal Instruments

Council Directive 2000/78/EC of 27 November 2000 establishing a general framework for equal treatment in employment and occupation [2000] OJ L303/16

The Significance of Legal Philosophy for German Social Law

Daniel Herbe

Abstract

Social law plays a special role in the German legal system and in citizens' lives. It governs the legal relationship between citizens and the state as a social state from birth to the end of life. Because, by force of the Constitution, social law is oriented toward a value order and toward ideas rooted in legal philosophy such as human dignity, autonomy, and the free, just, and equal development of the individual's personality, examining this field of law promises valuable insights for applied social policy. This paper investigates the constitution-immanent social constitution as expressed in social law, with a view to laying the foundations for a new legal-philosophically grounded policy based on the liberal-democratic basic order.

I. Introduction

German social law, grounded in human dignity (Art. 1 Basic Law, Grundgesetz, "GG") and in the idea of the social state (Art. 20 GG), as a constitutional principle and objective of state policy within a "social democracy in the form of a constitutional state"- prima facie translates foundational concepts and theories of legal philosophy into real social and public policy.

According to the Federal Constitutional Court (Bundesverfassungsgericht, BVerfG), these provisions of the Basic Law secure an entitlement to physical and socio-cultural existence as well as a minimum level of participation in social, cultural, and political life for every person.[1] They define the fundamental legal relationship between the individual and the state within its territory. The Basic Law demands respect for the autonomous self-determination of individuals without abandoning helpless persons.

1 See BVerfG, order 18 June 1975 in: BVerfGE 40, 121, 133; BVerfG order 5 November 2019 (sanctions in social law) file reference number: - 1 BvL 7/16 -; guiding principle 1, m.n. 117 ff.

Article 1(1) GG protects human dignity as the individual understands and is conscious of themself[2]. Pursuant to Art. 1(2) GG, the German people therefore commit themselves, through their Basic Law, to inviolable and inalienable human rights as the basis of every human community, of peace, and of justice in the world[3].

The aim of this paper is to ask whether, and what, normative concepts the legislature and courts have developed and implemented from these foundational concepts and theories, and where these concepts shape this field of law. Insofar as the social law in force (de lege lata) has become part of an applied social and political reality, and thus affected law and policy. This contribution also seeks to show whether and how a transferrable methodology can be derived from the dogmatics of social law, a toolbox for states that, especially in times of crisis, seeks not only to assert but practically to realize legitimacy, the rule of law, justice, human rights, and a life in dignity.

II. German Social Law de lege lata

1. Emergence and Foundations

In 1949 the Federal Republic of Germany (FRG) committed through its Constitution, the Basic Law (GG),[4] to the protection and guarantee of human dignity (Art. 1(1) GG) as an objective constitutional principle[5] and supreme constitutional value[6]. Added to this is Art. 20 GG as a "fundamen-

2 Vgl. BVerfGE 142, 313, 338 f. m.n. 73.

3 To the philosophical foundations of human rights see Paul Tiedemann: *Philosophische Grundlagen der Menschenrechte*, 1st ed. 2023; critical of the substantive content and universality of human rights: Stefanie Schmahl: *Universeller Menschenrechtsschutz* (2025).

4 Basic Law for the Federal Republic of Germany (FRG) 23 May 1949; Federal Law Gazette Part III, section number 100-1.

5 BVerfGE 45, 187 (227); 72, 105 (115); 109, 279 (311); 117, 71 (89); Stern, *Das Staatsrecht der BRD*, Part III/1, 23; Hufen, *Staatsrecht* II, § 1 m.n. 12; On the history of social law before 1949 see also Michael Stolleis, *Geschichte des Sozialrechts*, 2003 and On the history of social law after 1945 see Eberhard Eichenhofer, *Deutsches Sozialrecht nach 1945*, 1st ed. 2023.

6 E.g., in established case law: BVerfGE 6, 32 (41); 30, 173 (193); 72, 105 (115); 96, 375 (399); 115, 118 (152); 117, 71 (89); BVerfG in: new legal weekly (NJW) 2017, 611 (619); BVerfG, 2 BvR 916/11, 2 BvR 636/12, resolution 1 December 2020, m.n. 189. See also from case law of LVerfG eg RhPfVerfGH in: NVwZ-RR 2007, 721 (724). Similar from

tal norm of the state," which, alongside the state objectives of democracy, the rule of law, republicanism, and federalism, also enshrines social statehood (see Art. 20(1) "a social federal state" and Art. 28(1) GG "a social constitutional state"). The constituent power shielded these principles from legislative amendment through the so-called eternity clause, see Art. 79(3) GG.

An important vehicle for the development of social law in Germany, initially in view of legislative restraint, was case law, above all that of the Federal Constitutional Court (BVerfG, established in Karlsruhe in 1951[7], the Federal Administrative Court (Bundesverwaltungsgericht, BVerwG, established in Leipzig in 1952)[8], and the Federal Social Court (Bundessozialgericht, BSG, established in Kassel in 1954)[9]. On the basis of this case law, for example, the Federal Social Assistance Act (BSHG) was enacted, which entered into force in 1962 and was reformed and transformed by the legislature in 2005 into basic income support for jobseekers (Book II of the Social Code - SGB II) and social assistance (SGB XII) as comprehensive regimes ensuring subsistence.

The constitutional terms "social state" and "principle of the social state" are indeterminate legal concepts not further defined in the Basic Law. The BVerfG interpreted these terms conclusively and derived from the social state principle mandates for social security and social justice.[10] The social state mandate to the legislature encompasses numerous duties of state regulation and design[11]. Specifically, it concerns the promotion of social balance as well as measures to ensure internal and external security as fundamental tasks of the state. The mandate is, however, limited to social state tasks and

---

the literature instead of many: Nipperdey, in: Neumann/Nipperdey/Scheuner (Hrsg.), *Die Grundrechte*, Part 2, 1 (9) "At the top of the legal system stands the highest value: human dignity.

7 BVerfG order 17 May 1961: "The principle of the welfare state does not empower the state to engage in arbitrary social engineering".

8 BVerwGE 1, 195; order 25 June 1954, Az: V C 78.54: "Under the German Constitution, those affected have a subjective public right to social benefits if they are in need of assistance, i.e., a legal entitlement to social benefits—in this case, specifically an entitlement to welfare benefits."

9 BSGE 6, 213 ff, 219: "The welfare state principle of Article 20 I does not constitute a suitable basis for deriving specific, enforceable legal claims".

10 BVerfGE 45, S. 376, 387.

11 BVerfGE order 23 September 2024, file reference number 1 BvL 9/21, m.n. 45.

by itself lacks subjective-rights content[12]. The BVerfG' s case law fills this gap by combining guarantees of fundamental rights, the equality principle, and the social state principle[13]. The social state principle entitles and obliges the legislature to pursue social policy and thus the comprehensive legal shaping of society[14]. According to the Court, the most important aims of the social state are: to assign the legislature a social regulatory mandate, to achieve domain-specific concretizations in the service of effective freedom and (factual) equality in conjunction with fundamental rights, to set limits for the legislature through core social-state content and, in particular, to secure a subsistence minimum in line with human dignity[15].

The term "social law" is defined in neither the Constitution nor in ordinary legislation (e.g., in the Social Code). It only came to be used uniformly in professional and public discourse in the FRG between the 1960s and 1980s[16]. The guiding motif of the field is the protection of the weak and the unfolding of the idea of justice[17]. In an intentional sense, social law is the sum of all legal rules that provide for the granting of public services in kind or cash, and services to private parties, on the basis of social insurance or provision, that offset a disadvantage, promote vocational training or entry into employment, or aid in situations of need[18].

The fundamental rights of the Basic Law have both an immediate effect in social law, for example in the prohibition of discrimination against persons with disabilities (Art. 3(3) sentence 2 GG), in the mandate to promote women (Art. 3(2) sentence 2 GG), and in the protection of the family (Art. 6 GG), but also mediate those effects by limiting and framing the legislature's design of social-law provisions. In interpretation, the value judgments and directives of the legislature must be observed, according to which the law of the Social Code is to implement mandates through social rights (see §§ 1, 2 SGB I).

---

12 BVerfG order 19 December 1951 in: BVerfGE 1, 97; Eichenhofer, *Sozialstaat, Sozialrecht und soziale Rechte,* in: Miriam Meßling/Thomas Voelzke (Hrsg.), *Die Zukunft des Rechts- und Sozialstaats,* Festschrift für Rainer Schlegel (München 2024), S. 117 ff.

13 Wapler, in: Dreier, GG-Comment (4th ed. 2023), Art. 1 GG m.n. 69, 157 ff.

14 Eichenhofer, *Sozialrecht,* § 5, S. 69, m.n. 120.

15 See: Andreas Voßkuhle: "Der Sozialstaat in der Rechtsprechung des Bundesverfassungsgerichts", in: SGb 4 / 2011, S. 181 – 186.

16 See Michael Stolleis, *Geschichte des Sozialrechts in Deutschland* (2003), S. 307.

17 Wannagat, *Lehrbuch des Sozialversicherungsrechts,* Part 1, (1965), S. 170; quoted from Eichenhofer, *Sozialrecht* (13th ed. 2024) § 1 m.n . 4.

18 Eichenhofer, *Sozialrecht,* § 11 m.n. 13.

Social law also contains, in § 2(2) SGB I, a specific rule of interpretation for the application and interpretation of the Social Code, which modifies classical interpretive methods[19]. The modification lies in the different weighting of the interpretive and balancing processes that are required to be undertaken. Pursuant to § 2(2) SGB I, social rights are to be taken into account in interpreting the provisions of this Code and in exercising discretion, and it must be ensured that these social rights are realized as fully as possible. This means that greater force is accorded to the social aims and tasks of social law[20]. The stronger weighting of social rights manifests itself in that, when interpreting indeterminate legal concepts in social law, the interpretive outcome that best realizes social rights is to be prioritized among multiple legally plausible outcomes. Following these statutory interpretive rules, case law has highlighted and developed, inter alia, the mandate of citizen-friendly interpretation of statutes[21], the principle of favorability in application filing[22], the mandate of insurance-friendly interpretation of social benefit obligations,[23] the strict standard for limiting social-law claims[24], as well as the supervisory and support duties of benefit-granting bodies[25].

19 So truly Hannes Berger, "Die Gesetzesauslegung im Sozialrecht", in: New journal for social law (NZS) 1/2020 S. 11 f; The classification of the social law interpretation method in classical legal methodology is controversial, See also and for the current state of opinion: BSG 30 September 1992, file reference number: 11 Ar 73/91; Krahmer/Trenk-Hinterberger, Comment to SGB I, 3rd ed. 2013, § 2 m.n. 10; Mrozynski, SGB I, 4th ed. 2010, § 2 m.n. 16.

20 Hannes Berger, "Die Gesetzesauslegung im Sozialrecht" in: New journal for social law (NZS) 1/2020, S. 12.

21 BSG 8 February 2012, File reference number: B 5 R 38/11 R, in: new legal weekly (NJW) 2012, S. 2139, 2141: "This principle of social law dictates that whenever individual bases for entitlement allow room for interpretation, this room must be filled with the normative content of the social rights set out in Sections 3-10 of SGB I".

22 BSG 29 November 2007, file reference number: B 13 R 44/07 R: "Social security agencies may not adhere strictly to the wording of an applicant's declaration when considering their claim for benefits but must always assume that the beneficiary wishes to claim the type of benefit that is most favorable to them".

23 BSG 21 November 2002, file reference number: B KR 13/02 R in: new journal for social law (NZS) 2003, S. 657, 659.

24 BSG 28 September 1993, file reference number: 1 RK 37/92 m.n. 21.

25 BSG 17 April 1986, file reference number: 7 Rar 81/84, m.n. 22, 29: "Special notification obligations of the social security provider if there is scope for maneuver in the administrative procedure for the benefit claim. If, during the examination of an application, other options for the beneficiary come to light that are obviously more appropriate and would probably be taken up by the applicant, the benefit provider must inform the applicant of this option".

From its regulatory subject matter, the legislature conceives social law as the law of public benefit administration, as both a special branch of administrative law[26], and as part of public law[27]. Intense scholarly discourse and doctrinal research revealed an internal structure specific to the field: it is complex[28] and, as a "cross-sectional matter," encompasses and touches numerous areas of law, such as administrative, tax, criminal, family, and obligations law.

"Social law in the formal sense"[29] is understood as the law governing the subject matters of the Social Code (plus those statutes listed in § 68 SGB I), while "social law in the material sense" extends to additional subject matters found in other statutes[30].

2. Concretization through the Social Code (SGB)

In 1970 the legislature began to consolidate all legal norms in the material social-law context and existing and future social benefit entitlements into a single codification, combining its parts into an overall system, and to presenting them as a systematic unity[31]. This comprehensively captured the regulatory subject matter of social law and made it more accessible and transparent, simplifying it for practitioners. In the Brandt I Cabinet (1969–1972) of the 8th Federal Government under Federal Chancellor Willy Brandt, the SPD/FDP coalition agreement ("We want to dare more democracy") had already agreed in 1969 that the social-law statutes, until

26 According to § 1 SGG, social jurisdiction is exercised by independent special administrative courts that are separate from the administrative authorities; See also other overviews: Waltermann/Schmidt, a.o., *Sozialrecht*, 2022; Kokemoor, *Sozialrecht*, 2018; Igl/Welti, a.o., *Sozialrecht*, 2007; Muckel, a.o., *Sozialrecht*, 2019.

27 According to a dogmatically unconvincing opinion, social law, alongside private law and public law, is a separate area of law that regulates social benefits and is thus a sub-area of social law, which in turn is a sub-area of law, see: Eichenhofer, *Sozialrecht*, 13th ed. 2024, § 1 m.n. 1f, 4.

28 Hans Zacher, "Sozialrecht und Gerechtigkeit" in: Kaufmann (1988), S. 673: "The complexity of social law and the complexity of justice correspond to each other".

29 On the formal concept of social law see: Zacher, "Was ist Sozialrecht?" in: Zacher (publisher) *Abhandlungen zum Sozialrecht* (1993), S. 249 ff.

30 Waltermann/Schmidt, a.o., *Sozialrecht* (15th ed. 2022), § 2 m.n. 32 ff, S. 16 ff.

31 German parliamentary document VI/3764; For more information on the codification of the SGB, see Eichenhofer, *Sozialrecht* (13th ed. 2024), m.n. 167 ff.

then dispersed across individual acts, should be consolidated in a unified codification, the Social Code[32].

In implementation, the legislature decided against a sin codifying it all at once and instead adopted a "step-by-step approach with limited subject-matter reform"[33]. The General Part of the Social Code ‚SGB I, entered into force on 1 January 1976. Thereafter, the legislature discussed, drafted, deliberated, and enacted further parts and books of the SGB successively (most recently by 2019, updated 2024). At present there are SGB I – XII and XIV.[34] Under the legal fiction in § 68 SGB I, statutes belonging to material social law (e.g., the Federal Training Assistance Act - BAföG, the Advance Maintenance Payments Act, UVG, the Federal Child Benefit Act, BKGG, and the Housing Benefit Act, WoGG) have, "until their incorporation into this Code". been deemed, since 1976, to be its special parts, with the (privileging) consequence that the procedural provisions of SGB I and SGB X (and not the stricter, more formal Administrative Procedure Act) apply.

The books of the SGB are numbered and cited with Roman numerals (SGB I, SGB II, etc.). Because the books entered into force successively, their sections are not numbered sequentially across the entire Code (as in the Civil Code, BGB) but restart at § 1 within each book.

3. Structure and the Social-Law Relationship

Under § 1(1) sentence 2 SGB I, the law of the Social Code is an important instrument for safeguarding the fundamental rights of the Basic Law. Through social benefits and social and educational assistance, it shapes the realization of social justice and social security (see § 1(1) SGB I).

---

32 See government statement Willy Brandt 28 Oktober 1969, in: Bavarian State Library, S. 39.

33 See Article I of the law from 11 December 1975, Federal Law Gazette I S. 3015.

34 SGB IV - Common rules for social security (1 July 1977); SGB X - Administrative procedures, protection of social data, cooperation between service providers and their relationships with third parties (1 January 1981); SGB V - Statutory health insurance (1 January 1989): SGB VIII - Child and youth welfare services (1 January 1991); SGB VI- Statutory pension insurance (1 January 1992); SGB XI - Social care insurance (1 January 1995); SGB VII - Statutory accident insurance (1 January 1997); SGB III- employment promotion (1 January 1998); SGB IX - Rehabilitation and participation of people with disabilities 1 July 2001); SGB II - Basic income support for job seekers (1 January 2005); SGB XII - welfare (1 January 2005); SGB XIV - Social compensation (1 January 2024).

The social benefits provided under the reservation of statute in the relevant books of the SGB (cf. § 31 SGB I) are the object of social rights, and are formulated as legal entitlements. The legislature defines their content in the various books of the SGB. Pursuant to § 11 sentence 1 SGB I, they exist uniformly and nationwide in the form of cash benefits, in-kind benefits, services, and mixed forms thereof. Under § 11 sentence 2 SGB I, personal and educational assistance is included among services. The binding force of social benefits is differentiated between mandatory benefits (§ 38 SGB I) and discretionary benefits (§ 39 SGB I). Mandatory benefits arise upon fulfillment of the statutory requirements (see § 40(1) SGB I), whereas discretionary benefits arise only upon the responsible body's decision and its notification (see § 40(2) SGB I).

In a social-benefit procedure characterized by citizen friendliness, simplicity, dispatch, and low thresholds, as regulated in SGB I and SGB X,- the existence of claims is examined in a constitutionally sound and transparent manner. By filing an application pursuant to § 16 SGB I or § 9 SGB X, or through official initiation ex officio upon becoming aware of a need (e.g., in social assistance under § 18 SGB XII), a public-law social-law relationship arises between persons within the meaning of § 30(1), (3) SGB I who have their domicile or habitual residence within the territorial scope of the statute and the respective competent public benefit providers, i.e., the corporations, institutions, and authorities listed in §§ 18–29 SGB I (cf. § 1(2) SGB X). The requirement of an application is intended to prevent imposing a legal advantage on beneficiaries against their will and to respect and secure the constitutionally guaranteed autonomy and free will of citizens under Art. 2 GG.

Beneficiaries do not only receive advantages but also bear statutory duties to cooperate (see §§ 60–67 SGB I) in establishing, realizing, or limiting claims to social benefits. This expectation of an activating social state is founded in mutual solidarity[35]. Duties to cooperate exist only insofar as they are proportionate (see § 65 SGB I) and only after beneficiaries have been informed of the consequences of non-cooperation (§ 66(3) SGB I). The social-law relationship and benefit claim terminate through fulfillment (for monetary payments: disbursement, § 47 SGB I), set-off and netting

35 Muckel, a.o., *Sozialrecht*, 2019, § 8 m.n. 69.

(§§ 51 f. SGB I), waiver (§ 46 SGB I), forfeiture[36], the well-founded assertion of the statute of limitations defense (§ 45 SGB I), or the beneficiary's death.

At the level of substantive benefits, different structures and mixed forms are evident in the way the SGB regulates their financing, with there being contribution-financed insurance benefits (SGB III, V, VI, VII, XI), tax-financed state benefits (SGB II, XII), and state-financed municipal benefits (SGB II, VIII, XII). A hallmark of more recent developments in social law is internationalization, through embedding in European law[37] and international treaties[38].

4. The Impact of Legal Philosophy on German Social Law: The Social-State Constitution

1. Legal Philosophy and Social Law

Ideas and concepts from legal philosophy have exerted a decisive and important influence on the emergence and development of social law from the outset.

The subject and task of legal philosophy is the normative aspect of reflection on law: how law ought to be, the fundamental values of legal order, and the grounds of its validity[39]. The central theme of legal philosophy is justice[40]. Legal philosophy addresses legal order as a whole; it is a sub-discipline of both practical philosophy and legal scholarship.

Legal scholarship is likewise concerned with the normative force of legal norms in relation to the social and economic conditions of life they are meant to regulate[41]. Legal application is therefore always about realizing the intended shaping of social life that motivated the norm.

---

36 A claim is forfeited if the entitled parties have not asserted it for a longer period of time and, in addition, have given the service provider the justified impression through their behavior that they will not assert the claim in the future either.

37 See Regulation (EC) No. 883/2004 of the European Parliament and of the Council of April 29, 2004, on the coordination of social security systems; EU Charter of Fundamental (2000/2009).

38 E.g., Convention on the Rights of the Child (CRC) November 20, 1989, Convention on the Rights of Persons with Disabilities (UN CRPD) 3 December 2006.

39 Rüthers, a.o., *Rechtstheorie* (13th ed. 2025) § 1 m.n. 22.

40 Neumann, Ulfrid, *Einführung in die Rechtsphilosophie und Rechtswissenschaft*, (1st ed. 2025) § 4 m.n. 6.

41 Neumann, *Einführung*, § 13 m.n. 1, 14.

Social law is a relatively young field of law, arising from a philosophically grounded critique of law, and it contributes decisively to the social and legal ordering of life. Through the development of social law, the traditional opposition of private and public law was overcome. Autonomous social groups were enabled to create norms beyond state legislation, and securing human existence in dignity was moved to the center of legal regulation, with repercussions across the entire legal system[42].

2. The Social-State Constitution

On the basis of the general suffrage achieved in the so-called Weimar Constitution of the German Reich of 1918/19, the economically weak were able to make their social concerns the subject of state policy for the first time [43]. Democracy, founded on electoral equality, thus became a social state[44].

By enshrining human dignity and the social-state principle, the constituent power embedded in the Constitutio,–incidentally, a social constitution reflecting its utopian ideal of a dignified, solidaristic, and just society. Through subsequent concretization in the SGB and elaboration by case law, the philosophically grounded tesserae of this social constitution become visible and applicable. The following presents those individual tesserae and describes their interrelations within the overall system.

3. The Concept/Idea of Human Dignity

The idea of human dignity underpins the foundations and runs throughout the framework of the social constitution. The guarantee of human dignity in Art. 1(1) GG is an objective constitutional principle[45] and also a

42 See, in more detail, Eichenhofer, "Soziales Recht" in: social law (SR) 5/2022, S. 187-189.

43 Mahlmann, *Konkrete Gerechtigkeit. Eine Einführung in Recht und Rechtswissenschaft der Gegenwart*, 3rd Ed. Baden-Baden 2017, m.n.176.

44 Vogel, in: Bsirske/Kocsis/Traub (publisher),`Gegen den schleichenden Abbau des Sozialstaats`, Hamburg 2012, S. 13.

45 BVerfGE 45, 187 (227); 72, 105 (115); 109, 279 (311); 117, 71 (89); Stern, *Das Staatsrecht der BRD*, Part III/1, 23; Hufen, *Staatsrecht II*, § 1 m.n. 12.

fundamental right[46]. It is the human being's right to have rights[47]. Art. 1(1) GG presents itself as "the ultimate root and source of all subsequently formulated fundamental rights" and is, against this background, "itself the material principal fundamental right"[48]. Human dignity is of fundamental importance[49]. According to the BVerfG, the principle of the rule of law "more precisely shapes" the guarantee of human dignity in Art. 1(1) GG.[50]

This constitutional provision exerts significant normative force and a radiating effect on the understanding of the Basic Law's fundamental rights.

46 As here, affirming the fundamental nature of human dignity, e.g. already BVerfGE 109, 133 (151); 125, 175 (222); BerlVerfGH, New legal weekly (NJW) 1993, 515 (517); Karsten Nowrot, "Der Menschenwürde Werk und des Republikprinzips Beitrag - Gedanken und Anmerkungen zu Verbindungslinien zwischen zwei Konstitutionsprinzipien und ihren normativen Prägeeffekten auf das Verständnis der Grundrechte des GG" Heft 50, Mai 2022, S. 9; Starck, in: von Mangoldt/Klein/Starck a.o. (publisher) GG-Comment, Part. 1, Art. 1, m.n. 28 ff.; Hufen, Staatsrecht II, § 1 m.n. 9 ff.; Kirste, in: Kirste/De Souza/Sarlet (publisher), Menschenwürde im 21. Jahrhundert, 117 (127); Poscher, in: Herdegen/Masing/Poscher/Gärditz (publisher), *Handbuch des Verfassungsrechts*, § 17, m.n. 49 ff.; Michael/Morlok, *Grundrechte*, m.n. 132; Dederer, yearbook of public law (JöR) NF 57 (2009), 89 ff.; Herdegen, in: Dürig/Herzog/Scholz (publisher), GG-Comment, Part 1, Art. 1 I (stand Mai 2009), m.n. 29; However, this qualification is known to be controversial, with some expressing criticism or rejection of it e.g., Dürig, public law archive (AöR) 81 (1956), 117 (118 ff.); Dreier, in: the same (publisher) GG-Comment, Part I, Art. 1 section 1, m.n. 121 ff.; Gröschner, in: Siegetsleitner/Knoepffler (publisher), *Menschenwürde im interkulturellen Dialog*, 17 (21 f.); Isensee, public law archiv (AöR) 131 (2006), 173 (191); the same in: Merten/Papier (publisher), *Handbuch der Grundrechte*, Part IV, § 87, m.n. 103 ff.; Geddert-Steinacher, *Menschenwürde als Verfassungsbegriff*, 164 ff.

47 Hannah Arendt, *Elemente und Ursprünge totaler Herrschaft. Antisemitismus, Imperialismus, totale Herrschaft*, 9th ed. 2003, S. 614.

48 Nipperdey, in: Neumann/Nipperdey/Scheuner (publisher), *Die Grundrechte*, Part 2, 1 (12).

49 Schmidt-Aßmann, in: Isensee/Kirchhof (publisher), *Handbuch des Staatsrechts, Part. II*, § 26, m.n. 30 ("The rule of law is based on the recognition of a predetermined human dignity (Art. 1 I GG), which in turn gives substance and direction to the state's tasks of guaranteeing security, freedom, and social equality. Art. 1 I GG in particular highlights the fundamental structures of the rule of law. "); Volkmann, in: Herdegen/Masing/Poscher/Gärditz (publisher), *Handbuch des Verfassungsrechts*, § 16, m.n. 15 ("Menschenwürde [...] als materielle Grundnorm der Rechtsstaatlichkeit"); see also Kirste, in: ders./Sprenger (publisher), *Menschliche Existenz und Würde im Rechtsstaat*, 103 ff.; von Arnauld, in: Depenheuer/Grabenwarter (publisher), *Verfassungstheorie*, § 21, m.n. 28 ff.

50 See BVerfG in: New legal weekly (NJW) 2017, S. 611, 618.

The doctrinal approach, ultimately tracing back to Immanuel Kant[51] and, as regards the normative meaning of Art. 1(1) GG, developed especially by Günter Dürig[52], derives from the guarantee of dignity a prohibition on treating the individual as a mere object. This is surely the best-known and, especially in judicial practice, most influential approach to concretizing this constitutive decision of the Constitution[53]. In the "object formula," a kind of negative definition[54], a doctrinal method is manifested that approaches the meaning of Art. 1(1) GG by starting from possible modes of violation. In terms of fundamental-rights doctrine, it determines the scope of protection by proceeding from the interference[55].

Because of its normative force and consequential interactions, the fundamental right in Art. 2(1) GG has likewise undergone domain-specific elaborations in BVerfG case law. In its seminal "Elfes" judgment of 1957, for example, by expressly invoking the dignity guarantee and its significance for Art. 2(1) GG, the Court concluded that "a sphere of private life design is constitutionally reserved to the individual citizen, that is to say there exists a final inviolable realm of human freedom withdrawn from the influence of all public authority"[56]. Another important, domain-specific elaboration is the right to informational self-determination, which guarantees the individual the authority, in principle, to determine for themself the disclosure and use of their personal data[57]. In its decision on the constitutionality of the Air Security Act, the Court, especially relied on the - individual-rights position of crew and passengers affected by the downing of an aircraft (Art. 2(2) sentence 1 in conjunction with Art. 1(1) GG), through explicit reference to human dignity made absolute. The court attributed insufficient weight to the implications for the parts of the population and the political

51 Kant, *Die Metaphysik der Sitten*, 1797, S. 354 "for human beings cannot be used by anyone (neither by others nor even by themselves) merely as a means, but must always be used as an end at the same time, and therein lies their dignity. [...]" .

52 Dürig, public law archiv (AöR) 81 (1956), 117 (127) "Human dignity as such is affected when a specific human being is degraded to an object, a mere means, a replaceable entity" .

53 See only BVerfGE 27, 1 (6) (It is contrary to human dignity to make people mere objects in the state. [...]."); BVerfGE 115, 118 (153); 122, 248 (271); BVerfG, in: new legal weekly (NJW) 2017, 611 (619).

54 Dreier, in: Härle/Preul (publisher) *Menschenwürde*, 167,182 f.

55 Kirste, in: Kirste/De Souza/Sarlet (publisher), "im 21. Jahrhundert", 117, 121.

56 BVerfGE 6, 32 (41).

57 BVerfGE 65, 1, 41 ff (census 1983), see Article 1 II of the EU GDPR of May 15, 2018, and Article 8 of the Charter of Fundamental Rights of the EU.

community also affected by a terrorist attack[58]. Against the backdrop of these exemplary decisions, much speaks in favor of the proposition that the Art. 1(1) GG dignity guarantee, alongside its distinctive normative force for understanding and applying the Basic Law's other fundamental rights, presents itself as primarily individual-oriented[59], especially in the BVerfG' s jurisprudence.

4. Social Justice and Social Security

In the early years of the FRG after 1949, public debate on social justice initially played a subordinate role. A prospering, seemingly unstoppable economy allowed for a largely unquestioned expansion of the social state that is best summarized by the maxim "Prosperity and social benefits for all"[60]. In the 1970s, a socio-economic paradigm shift gradually took place as a response to the end of sustained growth[61]. The realization gained ground that social achievements were not necessarily permanent, and that cuts in social law would be necessary. Roughly at the same time, John Rawls's "A Theory of Justice"[62] sparked a renaissance of discourse on social justice that continues today, not only in academia but especially in political debate. With the entry into force of SGB I in 1976, legal-philosophical discourse over interpreting the term "social justice" deepened anew.

Under § 1(1) sentence 1 SGB I, the law of the Social Code is to shape social benefits, including social and educational assistance, for the realization of social justice and social security. In doing so, the legislature "highlighted the two main concerns of the social constitutional state - social justice and social security - as binding foundations of social law"[63]. The term social

58 BVerfGE 115, 118, 153 (Aviation security Act).

59 Karsten Nowrot, "Der Menschenwürde Werk und des Republikprinzips Beitrag", Heft 50, May 2022, S. 16; Schaefer, Public law archive (AöR) 135 (2010), 404 (416) ("Rather, the concept of dignity in Article 1 I GG consolidates all aspects of individual freedom that are only imperfectly covered in Articles 2–19 GG [...]."

60 Erhard 1957, S. 253.

61 See Becker/Hauser 2004, S. 7.

62 John Rawls, *Eine Theorie der Gerechtigkeit*, 1971: He establishes the following two principles of justice in particular: Firstly, all citizens must be granted equal fundamental political freedoms and rights; secondly, social and economic inequalities may only exist if there is equal opportunity for all citizens to attain social positions and if the least advantaged gain the greatest advantage from this.

63 German parliamentary Document 7/868, S. 22.

justice is an indeterminate legal concept. It is neither defined by statute nor found elsewhere in the SGB. There is, however, a shared point of reference to which all theories appeal and on which they can agree: all claims to (social) justice aim at the question of how rights, opportunities, and material and immaterial goods ought to be distributed in a society[64]. In attempting to answer this question, most authors revert to Aristotle's Nicomachean Ethics, which distinguishes various forms of justice, above all geometric and arithmetic justice, from which, following Thomas Aquinas, the legal-philosophical tradition derives the distinction between distributive justice (iustitia distributiva) and corrective/commutative justice (iustitia commutativa).[65]

Discourse on social justice focuses on evaluating distributive justice and thus the question of the criteria according to which a society's resources are s should be distributed among its members in order to create a socially just and common-good oriented order[66].

Social justice primarily targets social inclusion and thus qualitative baseline variables such as access to opportunities and participation. If distributive justice is viewed as the central element of a public-law-regulated (social) state, the question must be taken up anew by what criteria the "wealth of nations" is to be apportioned among members of society. It must be borne in mind that the allocation or, better, redistribution of resources may not be undertaken arbitrarily under the legal order. It must rest on as concrete a rules for distribution as possible, because Art. 3(1) GG at least excludes arbitrariness in state allocation procedures.

Distribution according to the principle of equality is probably the most cogent of the available rules: each person is assigned an identical share of income and wealth, opportunities and rights, social assistance and state benefits: "to each the same." Allocation by the principle "to each what is needed", by contrast, requires the operationalization of a generally accepted legitimate level of need. Agreement must be reached on how those needs which are to be covered by state benefits can be distinguished from purely

64 See only: Becker/Hauser 2009, 13.

65 Aristotle, *Nikomachische Ethik* 1130b30 until 1131a9 (quoted from Röhl/Röhl 2008, 339): "Justice (...) has two basic forms: one is effective in the distribution of public recognition, money, and other values to which the citizens of an orderly community are entitled. Here, it is possible that one person receives the same as another or not the same. A second basic form is that which ensures that the exchange relationships between people are lawful. ".

66 Kostorz, *Sozialrecht und soziale Gerechtigkeit*, 2004, S. 77.

subjective desires and wants. In essence, this is the question of what is necessary and required in the individual case.

Reflexivity and self-referentiality are also to be added to the subjectivity and plurality of these concepts of justice. In all disputes over (social) justice, we are not only arguing about the evaluation of a state of affairs perceived as (un)just, but also about the meaning of the very concept of justice[67]. Complete justice is unattainable in human communities; it naturally stands in tension with the democratic majority principle. In a liberal - and thus pluralistic - constitutional state, only a defensible compromise between opposing conceptions of justice can yield system-conforming solutions.[68]

Social law presents itself "as a heterogeneous conglomerate of different principles of justice". It rests both on elements of commutative justice and on the three criteria of distributive justice, namely the principles of equality, merit, and need[69].

The social state, by virtue of its democracy-functional legitimacy, appears as a strategy of political justice[70]. In such a social state, the community bears co-responsibility for those economic, social, cultural, and political framework conditions without which participatory rights can only be realized to a limited extent and with great difficulty, or even not at all. In this sense, it is only in the democratic and social constitutional state that the positivization of justice is completed[71].

The legal-philosophical content of social justice in § 1(1) sentence 2 SGB I is the legal and moral command of fraternity and solidarity as an expression of mutual connectedness among people and reciprocal responsibility in standing by one another. The mandate of social statehood (Arts. 20, 28 GG) is intended to empower and impel the state to active social shaping the realization of social security means that the state becomes the guarantor of securing subsistence, which is the basis of freedom and inclusion[72].

---

67 Peter Kostorz, *Sozialrecht und soziale Gerechtigkeit*, 2004, S. 73.

68 Bernd Rüthers, *Das Ungerechte an der Gerechtigkeit*, 3rd ed. 2009, S. 172, 179.

69 Peter Kostorz, *Sozialrecht und soziale Gerechtigkeit*, 2004, S. 93.

70 See also already Hans Zacher, "Sozialrecht und Gerechtigkeit", S. 690, in: *Rechtsstaat und Menschenwürde: Festschrift für Werner Maihofer zum 70. Geburtstag* /hrsg. von Arthur Kaufmann, Frankfurt am Main 1988.

71 Otfried Höffe, Politische Gerechtigkeit, Grundlegung einer kritischen Philosophie von Recht und Staat, 1987, S. 471 f.

72 Eberhard Eichenhofer, Sozialrecht, 13th ed. 2024, § 1 m.n. 9.

Social security therefore primarily safeguards the freedom to lead a self-determined life grounded in work rather than social equality[73].

5. Social Law as Theory/Social Rights

The theory of social law explains the emergence and unfolding of social law[74]. It also touches on fundamental questions of law, for it has always embodied a critique of deficits and/or injustices in the individualistic legal order. As early as the late 19th century, Anton Menger, in his study on the product of labor, "The Right to the Whole Produce of Labour", postulated a right to existence, shaped individually according to life circumstances: for young people aimed at education, at maintenance for adults and provision for the elderly and infirm [75]. He thereby raised the question whether, in the industrial age, a right to existence ought to be recognized.

Gustav Radbruch developed a theory of social rights arising from the inadequacies of the bourgeois legal order inherited from the 19th century[76]. In overcoming this legal order through legislation he perceived a new guiding image of law. Social rights, in his view, rest on a structural transformation of legal cognition and a new concept of the human being. Social law is not a law tailored to the depersonalized, de-individualized, isolated human being abstracted from socialization, but the concrete and socialized person[77]. From this emerged social rights, which apply to concrete life situations, shapes them, and derives a critique of prevailing law from them. These social rights appear as a victory of equity over ossified justice.[78] Whereas individualistic law is grounded in equality, social law is founded on the idea of redress. In the former, commutative justice prevails;, while in the latter distributive justice, toward which social right is oriented[79]. Law faces the fundamental task of basing its regulations on a juridical

73 Ulrich Becker, in SRH § 1 m.n. 1, 3 ff.

74 See also the treatise by Eichenhofer, "Soziales Recht" in: social right (SR) 5/2022, S. 170-192 with a presentation of historical developments and European references.

75 Menger, *Das Recht auf den vollen Arbeitsertrag in geschichtlicher Darstellung*, Stuttgart 1886, § 1 b.

76 Radbruch, *Der Innere Weg, Aufriß meines Lebens*, 2nd ed. Stuttgart 1961.

77 Radbruch, *Der Mensch im Recht*, 3rd ed. Göttingen 1957, S. 35-37.

78 Radbruch, *Der Innere Weg*, S. 163.

79 Radbruch, *Rechtsphilosophie*, Stuttgart 1970, S. 159.

type of person appropriate to social reality[80]. Against this background, the socially embedded, the collective person, is to be considered the foundation of social rights[81]. The basic idea of social rights is no longer the idea of persons but that of redress between unequal persons[82]. Social rights are thus characterized by four features. Behind the leveling abstraction of its conceptualization of a person, it first reveals individual distinctiveness and social positions of power or powerlessness. Instead of equality, redress prevails, while even the most private legal relationship appears as a "social relation". Social rights thus restore harmony between legal form and legal reality[83]. The idea of social rights does not merely mean special law for the less affluent but a different stylistic form of law. Social rights are the result of a new conception of the human being in law[84].

The Basic Law of the FRG does not contain fundamental social rights or other differentiated social programmatic clauses; however, the BVerfG has derived a subjective right to the provision of benefits necessary for subsistence from the guarantee of human dignity in Art. 1 GG[85].

Already in 1976, with the General Part of the SGB (SGB I), the legislature implemented, corresponding to the rights set out in the 1961 European Social Charter[86], the social rights listed in §§ 3 – 10 SGB I in order to shape[87] per § 1 SGB I, social justice and social security. They serve as interpretive standards for the provisions of the SGB and must be observed in the exercise of discretion (§ 2(2) SGB I), and it must be ensured that social rights are realized as fully as possible (§ 2(2) second half-sentence SGB I). Because they apply as programmatic clauses addressed to the legislature,

80 Radbruch, *Der Mensch im Recht*, S. 3.

81 Radbruch, *Vorschule der Rechtsphilosophie*, 2nd Ed. Göttingen 1959, § 33 V.

82 Radbruch, *Der Mensch im Recht*, S. 3.

83 Radbruch, *Rechtsphilosophie*, S. 102.

84 Radbruch, *Der Mensch im Recht*, § 33 I.

85 BVerfG 18 June 1975 in: BVerfGE 40, S 121, 133: "Social welfare is one of the "obvious" duties of a welfare state; a "dignified existence must be guaranteed for everyone."

86 The Federal Republic of Germany signed the European Social Charter (ESC) on October 18, 1961, and ratified it on January 27, 1965. It thus entered into force for Germany on February 26, 1965. The ESC contains fundamental social, economic, and cultural rights. It was expanded and modernized in the revised version of 1996. The revised ESC came into force on July 1, 1999, but not for the Federal Republic of Germany: Germany signed the revised version but has not ratified it to date. In 2017, the EU adopted the "Pillar of Social Rights," comprising 20 rights.

87 Promotion of education and employment; social insurance, social compensation; reduction of family expenses; subsidies for adequate housing; child and youth welfare; social assistance; participation of persons with disabilities.

they are not themselves actionable rights. Rather, rights may be asserted only when, the elements of a claim, with their requirements and content, have been implemented and specified in the provisions of the special parts of the SGB (see § 2(1) sentence 2 SGB I).

6. The Social Obligation of Property

Under Art. 14(2) sentence 2 GG, the use of property shall also serve the public good. The social obligation of property under Art. 14(2) GG delineates the duties and constraints attached to property. In constitutional terms, the social obligation restricts the scope of protection under Art. 14(1) GG by permitting, under Art. 14(2) GG, content- and limit-determining statutes as constitutionally justified interferences[88]. Legislative materials show that the constituent power primarily had land policy in mind. The mandate of socially just use is not only a directive for the owner's concrete behavior but primarily a guideline for the legislature to consider the public good when regulating the content of property[89]. It rejects a property order in which individual interests enjoy unconditional priority those of the community. With the principle that property entails obligations, a legal and social-philosophical ideal, rooted in Christian social teaching[90], has likewise found constitutional anchorage.

According to the BVerfG, while reaffirming property as an elemental fundamental right within a liberal order, the social obligation has been concretized in various ways, including that not every property is subject to

88 Englbert Niebler, "Die Sozialbindung des Eigentums nach der Rechtsprechung des Bundesverfassungsgerichts", S. 230, : Lecture by the Federal Constitutional Court judge on October 30, 1981, at the Forestry University Week in Munich: "Every statutory provision governing content and restrictions must both respect the fundamental value judgment of the Basic Law in favor of private property and be consistent with all other constitutional norms, in particular the principle of equality, the fundamental right to free development of personality, and the principles of the rule of law and the social state".

89 BVerfG order 10 March 1981, in: BVerfGE 56, 249, 260 (Bad Dürkheim gondola lift accident).

90 Thomas von Aquin quoted after: Andreas Rohner, *Das Eigentumsrecht nach dem heiligen Thomas von Aquin:* S. 69 in: Divus Thomas (1930) Jahrbuch für Philosophie und spekulative Theologie Band III: "People should regard and treat external things not as their property, but as common goods, insofar as they should readily agree to share them with those in need."

such an obligation, but only property with social relevance and function[91]. The social obligation is especially comprehensive for real property used as rental housing. Since a large portion of the population depends on the use of rental housing, and thus on others' property, far-reaching restrictions on property guarantees are justified[92].

Moreover, the Constitutional Court has established that regulations under Art. 14(2) GG may not rest solely on administrative acts or case law; they require legislative action[93].

Scholarship views the constitutional social obligation of property as part of the Constitution's general social reservations[94].

7. Subsidiarity, Personal Responsibility, and Solidarity

Exercising its constitutionally guaranteed power of design[95], the SGB legislature has bound the possibility and scope of drawing on subsistence-securing social benefits to the principle of subsidiarity. Thus, existing possibilities for self-provision take precedence over public assistance. In adopting the subsidiarity principle, the legislature concretizes the social-state principle in Art. 20(1) GG. The constitutional objective obliges all state organs directly, but especially requires, for its realization, far-reaching concretization, particularly by the legislature[96]. Within its broad margin of appreciation and design, it decides by what means and along which path the social state objective is to be pursued. A limit lies in the obligation to secure for every person a subsistence minimum compatible with human dignity[97].

91 BVerfGE 37, 132, 140; 38, 348, 370; 42, 263, 294 and BVerfG order 6 December 2016 - 1 BvR 2821/11, m.n. 297 (Social commitment to rental housing); However, property owners and developers are not obligated to offer social housing as such indefinitely, see order BGH 8 February 2019.

92 BVerfGE 37, 132, 142 (Limitation of rent to the local comparative rent); BVerfGE 87, 114 (146), in: New legal weekly (NJW) 1993, 2523 (rental price controls).

93 BVerfG, order 10 March1981, file reference number 1 BvR 92/71; BVerfGE 56, 249, (260).

94 Walter Leisner, `Sozialbindung des Eigentums", in: *Schriften zum Öffentlichen Recht*, Band 196 (Berlin 1972) S. 62.

95 See order BVerfG 5 November 2019, (Sanktionen im Sozialrecht) file reference number: - 1 BvL 7/16 -, guiding principles 1, 2.

96 See BVerfGE 65, 182, 193; 71, 66, 80.

97 BVerfGE 125, 175, 222.

Tax-financed social benefits are thus available only when people cannot primarily secure their own subsistence . Even the social constitutional state depends on ensuring that public funds intended to assist needy members are used only in cases of genuine need[98]. This includes a duty to use currently available means from income, assets, or third-party support before claiming public benefits. The associated conservation of the state's finite financial resources preserves its future capacity to shape policy, precisely realizing the social state objective.

Accordingly, under § 1(1) sentence 2 SGB I, the law of the Social Code is to help secure a life in human dignity, create equal preconditions for the free development of personality, especially for young people, protect and promote the family, enable the earning of a livelihood through freely chosen work, and to avert or offset particular burdens of life, including through help toward self-help.

The legislature may also impose proportionate duties on needy beneficiaries so that they actively and reasonably contribute to overcoming their own need. The legitimate aim of such duties is not, however, to promote the development of one's personality. The Basic Law is unfamiliar with such paternalism; there is no "sovereignty of reason" of state organs over rights-holders[99]. Rather, the Constitution demands respect for individuals' autonomous self-determination without simply abandoning helpless persons.

Responsible self-action presupposes, first, the possibility of determining one's own courses of action and goals. This requires an "infrastructure of self-responsibility," which the state must guarantee[100]. Art. 1(1) GG protects human dignity as the person understands and is conscious of themself in their individuality[101]. This excludes duties to cooperate that aim at state tutelage or attempts at "improvement". Thus, the subsidiarity of social benefits links duties to cooperate in social law in a legitimate and constitutional manner, by respecting human autonomy and by demanding the self-responsible action presumed of legally competent adults[102]. This is

98 BVerfGE 142, 353, 371, m.n. 39.

99 BVerfGE 142, 313, 339, m.n. 74 with further evidence.

100 Lamia Amhaouach-Lares, a.o.: Sabine Knickrehm in: "Tagungsbericht zur Zweiten Jungen Tagung Sozialrecht (17 - 19 March 2025) – Solidarität und Eigenverantwortung", in: new journal for sozial law (NZS) 13/2025, S. 498.

101 BVerfGE 49, 286, 298.

102 So eg § 1 I SGB V: Health insurance, as a solidarity-based community, has the task of maintaining, restoring, or improving the health of the insured. This also

evident especially in the principle of wishes and choices permeating all of social law[103].

Solidarity and self-responsibility are mutually conditioning: solidarity finds its limit in self-responsibility, whose exercise, in turn, is impossible without solidarity. Accordingly, for example, basic income support for job-seekers concretizes subsidiarity through the Fördern und Fordern principle in § 2(1) sentence 1 SGB II: that employable persons in need must exhaust all possibilities to end or reduce their need. This also serves the legitimate aim of conserving public (financial) resources. Employable beneficiaries must also fulfill the duties to cooperate in §§ 31, 32 SGB II to avoid benefit reductions under §§ 31a, 31b SGB II.

Through the objective of "social justice," social law and its concretizing special parts of the SGB have also, incidentally, implemented solidarity as an expression of mutual connectedness and reciprocal responsibility in standing by one another[104]. In the Charter of Fundamental Rights of the European Union (CFR), which entered into force with the Treaty of Lisbon on 1 December 2009, solidarity is recognized as an indivisible and universal value.

In essence, the matter is a sense of belonging and empathy among individuals. Social law thus unfolds as solidarity in social market-economy systems on three levels: social insurance, provision, and assistance. It encompasses all legal norms that serve to hedge social risks. For example, by force of statute, the statutory health insurance system conceives of itself as a solidarity community (§ 1(1) sentence 1 SGB V).

includes promoting the health literacy and personal responsibility of the insured. Insured persons are jointly responsible for their health; they should contribute to preventing illness and disability or overcoming their consequences by leading a health-conscious lifestyle, participating in preventive health measures at an early stage, and actively cooperating in medical treatment and rehabilitation.

103 See § 33 S. 2 SGB I, § 15 SGB VI, § 5 SGB VIII, § 8 SGB IX, § 13 SGB XII.

104 Piazolo, "*Solidarität. Deutungen zu einem Leitprinzip der EU*` (2004), quoted after: Eichenhofer, *Sozialrecht* (13th ed. 2024), § 1 m.n. 7.; critical of this: Nikolaus Dimmel,`Entsolidarisierung im Sozialrecht?`, in: Streifzüge 2020, S. 78: "Social law has nothing to do with solidarity. It is about abstract risk compensation among strangers as a risk community."

III. Conclusion and Implications for Social Law de lege ferenda

This investigation of the structures and foundations of German social law has shown that this field is the practical grammar of legal philosophy. It translates human dignity and solidarity into actionable claims, procedures, and institutions that make citizens bearers of effective freedom. By securing the material preconditions of political participation, by inculcating parity in decision-making, and by curbing administrative power through procedure, social law functions as democracy's infrastructure.

New social law, as needed in Germany, Europe, and worldwide, would be required on two levels: first, material universal law with binding and enforceable social rights.

A European social-law order, and in the long term a worldwide social-law order, must be created. In this, the social constitution of the Basic Law presented above, the case law[105], and the social rights already established in European and international law, such as the EU Charter of Fundamental Rights (2000), the European Convention on Human Rights (1951), the International Covenant on Economic, Social and Cultural Rights (UN Social Covenant, 1966), and the European Pillar of Social Rights (2017)[106] can and must serve as models. The BSG already participates in judicial networks such as the Network of European Superior Courts (SCN) and the European Union's Judicial Network (JNEU).

Second, the transformation and development of new social law requires a different, and transformed, legal consciousness among people alongside additional procedural and institutional structures. To cultivate this new consciousness, the envisaged world social-law order should, at all civil-society and state levels and in all institutions (e.g., schools, training and educational establishments, apprenticeships, universities), in line with existing international agreements (e.g., UN-CRC, UN-CRPD), at minimum implement a central provision with the following content:

105 See eg., conclusion BVerfG 24 March 2021, file reference number: - 1 BvR 2656/18 – (climate protection) "The state's duty to protect also includes the obligation to protect life and health from the dangers of climate change. It can also establish an objective legal obligation to protect future generations. ".

106 Entschließung des Europäischen Parlaments vom 19 January 2017 zu einer europäischen Säule sozialer Rechte (2016/2095(INI)); Eichenhofer, *Sozialrecht der EU* (9th ed. 2025), § 3 m.n. 28: "With the European Pillar, the EU reaffirms and renews its promise of prosperity and well-being".

Article 3 – Raising Awareness

(1) The States Parties undertake to take immediate, effective, and appropriate measures to
    a) raise awareness throughout society, including at the family level, regarding social rights and to promote respect for those rights and for dignity;
    b) combat stereotypes, prejudices, and harmful practices against persons with disabilities, including on grounds of gender or age, in all areas of life;
    c) promote awareness of individuals' capabilities and contributions to the creation of a world social-law order.

(2) Measures to this end include:
    a) initiating and permanently conducting effective public awareness campaigns with the aim of
        i) increasing openness to individuals' social rights,
        ii) fostering positive perceptions of people and greater social awareness toward them,
        iii) promoting recognition of individuals' skills, merits, and abilities and of their contribution to working life and the labor market;
    b) promoting a respectful attitude toward individuals' social rights at all levels of the education system, including all children from early childhood;
    c) calling upon all media to portray people in a way consistent with the purpose of this Convention;
    d) promoting training programs to sharpen awareness of people and their social rights.

For enforcement, alongside national social courts, the creation of a European Social Court in the medium term and, subsequently, a World Social Court is necessary. There, judges decide who have studied legal history, legal philosophy, and social law extensively and in depth as compulsory subjects[107]. In the panels, such judges cooperate with lay judges and decide

107 See on judicial and scientific policy reform and the current state of discourse Item 2 of the resolution of the 95th Conference of Ministers of Justice on full legal training on June 5–6, 2024, in Hanover: "In order to continue to stimulate interest and enthusiasm for a career in law, to encourage critical thinking and reflection on the special position of lawyers in society, and to continue to prepare graduates as

on the basis of a World Social Court Statute agreed upon by all states of the world according to the majority principle.

For national implementation of such a world social-law order, analogous to the UN-CRPD, a governmental focal point should be established at a Federal Ministry for Social Rights. As an independent body (monitoring mechanism) for legal questions or disagreements or conflicts, a low-threshold German Institute for Universal Social Rights should be created. This independent body would promote compliance with individuals' social rights and monitor the implementation of the world social-law order in Germany. To this end, a monitoring body would issue opinions and recommendations on political, administrative, or judicial decisions and call for compliance with the world social-law order where necessary.

A governmental coordination office should be established with the Federal Government Commissioner for Social-Law Matters. It would facilitate implementation of the world social-law order and actively involve civil society in the implementation process. The coordination office would thus form the interface between civil society and the state level. It would fulfill its role in particular through public outreach and awareness-raising measures. In this way, the "invisible hand"[108] of legal philosophy would work within social law and guides people and social policy toward the creation and realization of a dignified, just, solidaristic, and peaceful world.

The (new) social law of the world social-law order could then radiate powerfully, as an applied and living legal philosophy and as a transformative new consciousness in a time of crisis and regression, against undemocratic and rule-of-law-violating social and political tendencies, thereby strengthening and defending human dignity and the democratic constitutional state.

---

well as possible for the challenges of professional practice, the Ministers of Justice consider it appropriate to use the recommendations presented in the report as food for thought for further improvements in legal education."*in:* https://netzwerk-sozialrecht.net/wp-content/uploads/2024/08/beschluss-jumiko_zukunft_der_volljuristischen_ausbildung.pdf; (accessed 4 October 2025); see also from scientific discourse: Robert Horn/Julia Pfeffer: "Sozialrecht gehört in die juristische Ausbildung", see Interview in Publicus 18 April 2024.

108 Based on Adam Smith, *An Inquiry into the Nature and Causes of the Wealth of Nations* (1776).

IV.
Environmental and Technological Challenges

Competing Conceptions of Sustainability

Heidi M. Hurd[1]

Abstract

This paper explores four theories of sustainability in an effort to identify and assess the strength of their philosophical presuppositions, and thus the moral strength of their constraints on present practices that have long-term environmental consequences. As I argue, "weak" theories of sustainability are most at home with the preference utilitarianism that undergirds modern welfare economics, but as a result, they presuppose that nature's treasure is valuable only if, and only to the extent that, it is valued by humans. While the community of those whose preferences count might be expanded beyond that of humans so as to make theories of weak sustainability less anthropocentric, and thus far less vulnerable to charges that they will permit the continued decimation of the environment in the name of satisfying human greed, such accounts will still be unable to capture the intuitions of those who take natural resources, systems, spaces, and places to be valuable in their own right, rather than merely as instruments of welfare. Yet "strong" theories of sustainability predicated on an alternative, deontological moral theory are likely to prove equally disappointing. Deontology has a number of scope limitations that will make it indifferent to a wide array of environmentally exploitative practices and that will thus render its use impotent, even by those who would happily wield claims of right on behalf of nonautonomous, and even nonsentient, entities. Could we leave deontic ethics altogether and instead ground a theory of strong

1 Ross and Helen Workman Chair in Law and Professor of Philosophy, University of Illinois. I am grateful to the University of Hawaii Press for granting me permission to reprint, in part, and otherwise draw on sections of a previous article entitled, Heidi M. Hurd, 'Fouling Our Nest: Is (Environmental) Ethics Impotent against (Bad) Economics?' in Roger T. Ames & Peter D. Hershock, Value and Values: Economics and Justice in an Age of Global Interdependence. Honolulu: University of Hawaii Press. pp. 82-108 (2017). The arguments advanced in that previous piece proved illuminating when examining the presuppositions and implications of the competing conceptions of sustainability that are the focus of this contribution.

sustainability in aretaic ethics? This piece closes by outlining the promise and perils of such a strategy.

Key Words

Sustainability; market failures; utilitarianism; welfare economics; deontology; interest theory (of rights); precautionary principle; moral considerability; aretaic duties; virtues; vices

Introduction

Why are we seemingly impotent to make changes that will reverse the devastating effects of our own actions on the ecological health of the planet? Environmental economists who concede that our present environmental practices are "uneconomical" will trace Pareto inefficient practices to market failures--externalities, open access resources, non-rival and non-excludable public goods, and information asymmetries (to name only a few). They will thus seek the elimination of "dirty subsidies" that encourage, rather than discourage, environmentally wasteful practices, and they will strategize about the effective use of command and control regulations, pollution quotas, trading regimes, taxes, tariffs, and better-defined property rights as means of correcting market imperfections.

My project in this paper is not to find fault with these strategies. While I cannot help but wonder whether calling on committed capitalists to cure the ills of capitalism is not like seeking veterinary care from a taxidermist, I shall resist the temptation to suggest that there are some things that cannot be commodified, and there are some things that ought not to be, even if they can be. Instead, I want to suggest that our environmentally destructive practices may reflect a philosophical failure that is far more serious than the failure of market mechanisms. As I shall discuss, our leading schools of ethical thought are deeply anthropocentric. As such, they appear to license the exploitation of "natural capital" so long as that exploitation does not violate the aggregated preferences, personal interests, or individual rights by which leading utilitarian and rights theories specify the parameters of permissible action. It is no surprise, then, that efforts to employ their precepts as a means of defending accounts of weak sustainability against charges of illicit anthropocentrism are bound to disappoint. And efforts to invoke them in the service of bolstering competing accounts of strong sustainability are equally bound to founder. We are thus in need of a moral framework that allows us to give voice to deep-seated intuitions of a non-anthropocentric sort.

In Part I, I shall lay out four accounts of sustainability that are familiar to those who work on the questions of what we are obligated to sustain and why. As I shall demonstrate, these various accounts draw their moral sustenance from our dominant schools of moral thought and are thus hostage to the weaknesses of those theories as much as they are beholden to them for their strengths.

In Part II, I shall explore how theories of so-called "weak sustainability" implicitly ground their tenets in the preference utilitarianism that undergirds modern welfare economics. They thus invite the familiar sorts of counterarguments that can be levied against any theory that takes things to be valuable only if, and only to the extent that, they are valued by humans. As a means of answering these counter-arguments, I shall suggest that accounts of weak sustainability might do well to take seriously the philosophical commitment implicit in utilitarianism to include in measurements of welfare all forms of welfare that can be possessed by entities that can experience pain and pleasure and that therefore have preferences that can be satisfied or thwarted. When so expanded, these theories of weak sustainability are far less anthropocentric, and are thus far less vulnerable to charges that they will permit the continued decimation of the environment in the name of satisfying human greed. Yet as I shall make clear, these theories will still be unable to capture the intuitions of those who take natural resources, systems, spaces, and places that *a fortiori* lack sentience to be valuable in their own right, rather than merely as instruments of welfare.

In Part III, I shall ask whether those who have such residual intuitions, and who are thus prepared to defend a theory of "strong sustainability," would be able to build such theoretical muscle by employing the moral machinery of deontology. Could they predicate strong sustainability on claims that natural entities, both sentient and nonsentient, have rights? And would the invocation of nonanthropocentric rights really generate obligations to conserve the natural world so as to halt our presently voracious consumption of its treasure? As I shall reluctantly argue, the answer to this question is probably no. Deontology has a number of scope limitations that will make it indifferent to a wide array of environmentally exploitative practices and that will thus render it ineffective, even when employed by those who would happily accord rights to nonautonomous, and even nonsentient, entities. Proponents of strong sustainability who hoped for more than instrumental arguments for environmental protection will thus find that deontology gives us grounds to value and protect species, ecosystems, and biospheres for our own sake, but not for their own sakes. And as such, deontology fails to arm strong sustainability proponents with means by which to dispute environmentally destructive practices that will be of net benefit to *persons* (as judged best, perhaps, by their market practices).

In Part IV, I briefly examine the possibility of leaving deontic ethics altogether and seeking the foundation of a strong theory of sustainability in aretaic theory. Perhaps if persons devotedly cultivated dispositions of the sort that would make them persons of good character they would accord both future generations and other species the conditions essential to their own flourishing. As I suggest, however, the defense of an aretaic account of strong sustainability would invite a host of philosophical challenges, not the least of which is that it would constitute an effort to extract a non-anthropocentric ethic from a flagrantly anthropocentric preoccupation with human virtue. While seemingly paradoxical, this approach might have promise, but those who look for non-anthropocentric reasons to protect things of non-anthropocentric value are bound to be disappointed by this last-ditch strategy.

The upshot of my argument, then, is likely to be a distressing one. Our failure to achieve means of living sustainably may ultimately reflect a failure of philosophical imagination—a failure of our ability to stretch our moral concepts so as to allow their protection of the natural world against our own greedy excesses. And inasmuch as law tracks morality—inasmuch as its heftiest demands are justified only when they match the demands placed upon us by our independent moral obligations—it is thus no surprise that environmental law has failed to serve as a bulwark against the kind of environmental exploitation that our own schools of moral thought seemingly permit.

I. Four Concepts of Sustainability

It has become commonplace in the literature on sustainability to lay claim to, and assign to others, one of four positions concerning what we must sustain and why.[2] In turn, these positions are thought to imply various commitments concerning the substitutability of forms of capital, both natural and artificial, and the prioritization of needs and wants both in the present and in the future. The first two of these four positions are thought to be variants of so-called "weak sustainability,"[3] while the second two lay claim to commitments that entail considerably more onerous obligations of conservation, the fourth position constituting a full-throated demand for "strong sustainability."

On what has been termed a "very weak" theory of sustainability, both individuals and organizations (e.g., legislatures, agencies, city councils, corporations, small businesses) have obligations to preserve "total capital." Total capital is comprised of both raw Earthly resources—what many now call "natural capital"—and what I shall call "artificial capital," a term that captures Marx's category of "instruments of labor;" namely, products generated from raw resources by the investment of human ingenuity and labor. On this theory, raw resources can be consumed so long as aggregate social welfare is preserved or enhanced by the goods into which these resources are converted or by other forms of compensation. When the loss of natural capital can be offset by the substitution of artificial resources, there can be no objection, on this theory, to such a substitution, and hence, no objection to the complete exhaustion or elimination of those raw resources. And what constitutes the measure of substitutability? When can our consumption practices comfortably outpace the ability of a natural resource to replenish itself (e.g., by adopting fishing techniques or quotas that will lead to the collapse of a fishery)? The answer, on this theory, is given by the net effect of substitutes on human welfare. If ready substitutes generated artificially will provide the same measure of welfare as did the goods and services that derived from natural capital, then there is no basis for complaining about their substitution. Thus, if the substitution of Krab (made with plentiful Pacific whiting) for crab does not come at a net cost to human welfare, there can be no objection to the continued depletion and ultimate extinction of snow and Russian king crabs. And if the substitution of plastic trees for real trees will not diminish human welfare (because they can be engineered to perform all of the functions valuable to humans), then this concept of

2 For a thorough and illuminating discussion of this taxonomy upon which I leaned heavily, see Andrew Dobson, "Environmental Sustainabilities: An Analysis and a Typology," 5 *Environmental Politics* (1996), 401-428.

3 This much-used terminology was introduced by Herman Daly, *Steady-State Economics*, 2d ed. (Earthscan, 1992), p. 250.

sustainability will deem the substitution of plastic forests for natural ones to be sustainable.

On this first theory, not only are the effects on human welfare the measure of whether forms of resource consumption are sustainable, but those effects are to be weighted more heavily to the extent that they fall on present rather than future generations. "[E]ach generation is allowed to favor itself over the future," writes Robert Solow. "The duty imposed by sustainability is to bequeath to posterity not any particular thing . . . but rather to endow them with whatever it takes to achieve a standard of living at least as good as our own. . . We are not to consume humanity's capital, in the broadest sense."[4] Moreover, successive generations can be expected to have "adapted preferences"—namely, so long as their needs are met, they cannot be expected to miss what they have never known. "How many people lose sleep because it is no longer possible to see a live Dinosaur?" asks Wilfred Beckerman.[5] And thus while our present consumption patterns may drive tigers, rhinos, and blue whales to extinction, they may prove to be weakly sustainable if future generations will not know enough to miss them and if benefits to human welfare accrue that compensate for whatever losses are inflicted upon those who experience these extinctions as losses.

The second account of sustainability that is commonly labelled "weak sustainability," varies from its even weaker sibling only because those who propound it are willing to stipulate that, at this point in human history, there are numerous functions performed by natural systems that cannot be replicated efficiently by artificial technologies. For example, human survival is presently hostage to the Earth's biogeochemical cycles, and these thus count, in David Pearce's terms, as "critical natural capital" which cannot be traded for artificial capital without a loss in human welfare.[6] It may turn out, as well, that certain aesthetic experiences that enhance human welfare cannot be obtained from artificial replicas, and if this is the case, and if other aesthetic experiences that *can* be obtained from artificial

4 Robert Solow, "An Almost Practical Step Toward Sustainability," Address to Resources for the Future, Washington, D.C. (1992) (quoted in Dobson, "Environmental Sustainabilities," 411).

5 Wilfred Beckerman, "'Sustainable Development:' Is It a Useful Concept?, 3 Environmental Values (1994): 191, 194.
Id.

6 David Pearce, *Blueprint 3: Measuring Sustainable Development* (Earthscan, 1993), 16. Pearce also speaks of an "ecological glue." See David Pearce, *Blueprint 4: Capturing Global Environmental Value* (Earthscan, 1995), 52.

replicas cannot fully compensate for the loss of these aesthetic experiences, then the natural sources of these experiences will also count as "critical natural capital." Thus if no amount of realism can make a replica of the Grand Canyon as awe-inspiring as is the real Grand Canyon, and if no degree of artistry can cause a plastic forest of redwood replicas to elicit the same sense of wonder and tranquility as can the real California Coastal Redwoods, and if these aesthetic experiences cannot be off-set by those that can be gleaned from other natural sources or from some set of artificial sources, then the Grand Canyon and the forests of California's Humboldt County must be considered critical natural capital and sustained on this theory of sustainability.

Because life-sustaining ecological processes operate over long time-scales, this version of weak sustainability inevitably weights the needs of future generation over the wants of the present generation. Human welfare is deemed to be contingently but deeply rooted in ecosystem health, and hence, we are not entitled to gratify desires today at the cost of the resiliency of long-term natural processes upon which the satisfaction of future needs will depend. Nature's raw resources and complex systems are solely of instrumental value, but on this account, inasmuch as there is no prospect of crafting artificial substitutes of equivalent value to, say, the watershed protection functions of tropical rainforests or the pollution-cleansing and nutrient-trapping functions of wetlands, their lexical value over non-critical natural goods demands that they be sustained.

The third theory of sustainability, which has earned the term "strong sustainability," calls for the preservation of "irreversible natural capital." Such a theory collapses into the prior theory if what counts as irreversible natural capital is identical to what counts as critical natural capital. But on this theory, there may be many irreversible losses of natural capital that do not impact humans at all, and that thus cannot count as losses of critical capital. As this implies, strong sustainability denies that human welfare constitutes the sole and only touchstone of whether and to what extent natural systems and nonhuman entities have value. It thus marks the transition to accounts of sustainability that seek to sustain more than that which sustains us. To those who despair the past losses of species that made no dent in human welfare, and to those who assign value to works of nature for which there are functionally equivalent substitutes, this theory gives expression to their implicit pluralist convictions that things other than human welfare are of intrinsic value. On this theory, while losses of natural capital can be compensated for by gains in artificial capital, those substitutions cannot come at the cost of natural capital that cannot be replenished, even when such irreversible losses would result in gains to humans. Thus, no amount of Krab can compensate for the loss of Russian crabs, no amount of Yellowfin tuna can substitute for the extinction of Bluefin tuna; and no amount of Pacific halibut can substitute for the collapse of the Atlantic halibut fishery.

On this third account, needs take precedence over wants, and the needs that count include the needs of non-human entities, as well as the future needs of both humans and non-human entities. Artificial substitutions for natural goods and services are legitimate so long as they represent adequate substitutions for all entities of value that depend upon them, and losses are consistent with the sustainability of a resource so long as those losses do not cross ecological thresholds so as to prevent resilience. Thus, natural migratory corridors may be bulldozed if artificial landscaping can restore places for restful stop-overs; tree cover can be eliminated along the thoroughfares of Costa Rica so long as ropes are strung that allow monkeys to swing across lanes of fast-moving traffic; and wetlands can be filled so long as off-sets are purchased elsewhere that prevent a net loss in functionality for both human and nonhuman species that are functionally dependent on their services.

The strongest theory of sustainability—denigrated by some[7] and embraced by others[8] as "absurdly strong"—rejects the description of nature (its raw resources, its ecological systems, its diverse species) as "capital" and rejects the notion that the only check on welfare-enhancing trades that substitute artificial goods for natural goods is the injunction not to cause irreversible losses to nature's bounty. On this view, the value of things that have been produced through billions of years of evolution is not given by the degree to which those things instrumentally advance human welfare. We are, on this view, not entitled to elevate gains to human welfare above the satisfaction of the needs of the other 10 million-plus species with whom we share the planet. And this is true even when our consumption will not cause irreversible losses to the library of evolution. Instead, we must share the Earth's limited resources and sustain its life-supporting ecological

7 Herman Daly, "On Wilfred Beckerman's Critique of Sustainable Development," 4 Environmental Values (1995), 49-55, 49.

8 Alan Holland, "Substitutability: Or Why Strong Sustainability is Weak and Absurdly Strong Sustainability is Not Absurd" (unpublished manuscript, cited in Dobson, "Environmental Sustainabilities").

systems in ways that answer to a theory of distributive justice that takes nonhuman entities to be independently deserving recipients.

Once one appreciates the continuum of positions that lie between very weak sustainability and very strong sustainability, it is tempting to think that accounts that are properly located at the weak end of the spectrum cannot claim to be theories of *environmental* sustainability at all. As Alan Holland observes, "an account of sustainability in terms of non-declining human welfare will not necessarily yield a defense of natural capital on its own."[9] In other words, if human welfare is the sole and only thing of value, then the degree to which natural capital should be valued is purely a contingent function of the degree to which welfare can be sustained and advanced without it. The environment enjoys no place of privilege in a theory that is dedicated to maximizing welfare. Its value is instrumental, and if humans are good at anything, they are good at inventing instruments that progressively supplant the need for the creations of nature that are thought to be comparatively "primitive."

Yet those who are suspicious of the notion that things can have value apart from their ability to be valued through pricing mechanisms within a market that capture human preferences will insist that the accounts of sustainability at the strong end of the spectrum give no guidance as to what and how much we can consume. Do these accounts imply, as Wilfred Beckerman has dismissively charged, that we must "preserve intact the environment as we find it today in all its forms;"[10] that there can be "no mining, and no industry;"[11] that "no species could ever go extinct," nor could "any nonrenewable resources [ever be] taken from the ground, no matter how many people are starving"[12]? Are we to elevate the needs of mice over the wants of humans? And what of the competing needs of animals? Are we obligated to substitute ourselves for the predators we eradicated so as to cull herds? Are we obligated to do battle with species that our own activities have made damagingly invasive? Or does the attribution

9 Alan Holland, "Natural Capital," in Philosophy and the Natural Environment, eds. Robin Attfield and Andrew Belsey (Cambridge University Press, 1994), 169, 176. In Michael Jacob's words: "Once natural capital has been monetized and its benefit stream integrated with that of human-made capital, environmental protection is only contingently connected to the concept of non-declining welfare." Michael Jacobs, "Sustainable Development, Capital Substitution and Economic Humility: A Response to Beckerman," 4 Environmental Values (1995), 57, 61.

10 Beckerman, "'Sustainable Development,'" 194.

11 Id.

12 Dobson, "Environmental Sustainabilities," at 410.

of value imbue non-human entities with claims against such interferences with this "new normal"?

One way to understand the debate between weak and strong sustainability proponents is to recast it as the familiar debate between utilitarians and those who either reject utility as the good to be maximized or reject the claim that morality requires or permits the maximization of what is good. Indeed, weak sustainability has found its most ardent champions amongst economists precisely because weak sustainability appears to be concomitant with the preference utilitarianism that undergirds standard welfare economics. And strong sustainability appears to appeal, in turn, to those who subscribe to a theory that makes certain actions wrongful without regard to their consequences—wrongful because they constitute rights violations or otherwise violate categorical maxims most at home within a deontological moral theory.

But can either weak or strong sustainability proponents defend these implicit moral convictions? Can proponents of weak sustainability defend their exclusive concern for human welfare when humans are but one of 10 million-plus species on the planet? Are there not some nonhuman entities that can be said to have welfare so as to force the expansion of weak sustainability's locus of concern out of respect for the logic of utilitarianism itself? And if so, how would this concession alter the terms of weak sustainability? Inversely, can proponents of strong sustainability do better at defending their claim that nonhuman entities possess intrinsic value of a sort that places moral limits on the ability of humans to satisfy their own needs and wants? Can they equip nonhuman entities with moral weapons that have the power to stop humans in their moral tracks—that have the power to make wrongful acts that would be welfare-enhancing? It is to these two sets of questions that the next two sections are dedicated.

II. Do Nonhuman Entities Have Welfare That Should Count in Calculations of What is Weakly Sustainable?

Classical Nineteenth Century utilitarianism of the sort propounded by Jeremy Bentham and John Stuart Mill has two components. The first is a theory of what is intrinsically good. Utilitarianism is a monistic theory: it takes there to be one thing and one thing only that has intrinsic value or goodness—namely, welfare. Many other things may be good, but they are good only because, and only to the extent that, they instrumentally contribute to welfare.

The notion of welfare has varying definitions within the utilitarian tradition. Bentham's hedonic calculus equated welfare with the presence of pleasure and the absence of pain. Mill's theory of welfare substituted for pleasure and pain the more general notions of happiness and unhappiness. Twentieth century utilitarianism substituted preference satisfaction for happiness and preference frustration for unhappiness and subscribed to the thesis that intensities of preferences cannot be measured cardinally, but only compared ordinally, so as to make stable trade points in costless markets constitutive of welfare-maximizing distributions. And finally, the concept of welfare has sometimes been given an objective interpretation. On such an interpretation, something may be good for someone, even if she does not prefer it, and even if the thing does not give her pleasure or make her happy.

The second component of utilitarianism is its consequentialist principle. Actions are judged to be right if, but only if, they maximize welfare. The animating intuition is that if welfare is good, more is better, and the morally optimal state of affairs is thus achieved when acts or institutions produce the greatest net welfare possible.

So construed, welfare economics is rightly seen as an applied branch of utilitarian ethics. To the classical utilitarianism of Bentham one adds: (1) the substitution of preference-satisfaction for happiness or pleasure as the measure of welfare; (2) the Paretian skepticism about cardinal measures of preference intensity; (3) the substitution of ordinal measures of preference maximization, namely, Pareto-optimality and Pareto-superiority; (4) the behavioral measure of the ordinal criteria in terms of stable trade points in hypothetically costless markets; and (5) the assumption that real markets can sometimes induce those idealized, stable trade points, and when they cannot (because of market failures), guesses at hypothetical market behavior can supply such stable trade points.

It is tempting for those who trace environmental degradation to profit-maximizing practices to assume that if markets were perfect, we would not need to fear for the unsustainable consumption of nature's valuable goods and services. For prices would reflect all the costs of products (many of which are now invisibly externalized), and consumers would then be equipped with accurate information about the environmental implications of their choices. They would then vote with their dollars in ways that would achieve the ratio of consumption to conservation that would be morally optimal.

But market failures are not the embarrassment to welfare economics that many think they are. For the problem with welfare economics does not lie in the failures of actual markets to deliver evidence of what would maximally satisfy human preferences. The problem lies in taking maximally satisfied preferences to be the sole criterion of what is valuable. For notoriously, people can and do have preferences that are short-sighted, self-interested, and even evil. And nowhere is this more apparent than in the environmental arena in which people are demonstrably willing to extract small short-term gains through behaviors that they know will cause devastating long-term losses. So the real problem does not lie in the failure of the market to perfectly express human preferences; it lies in the nature of those preferences themselves. We should fear not that the market only imperfectly realizes our preferences; rather, we should fear that it perfectly realizes our preferences as often as it does!

At the root of the problems courted by a theory of weak sustainability, then, is that it makes *human* preferences the touchstone of valuation. The domain of those whose welfare counts unsurprisingly leads to a standard that overvalues the interests of those who count and undervalues the interests of those who do not. Just as utilitarian defenses of slavery were made preposterous by their exclusion of the pain, preferences, or welfare of slaves, so one should think that weak sustainability is equally preposterous in giving only one of 10 million-plus species exclusive domain over the Earth's natural treasure.

This line of criticism suggests that utilitarianism and the versions of weak sustainability that owe their allegiance to its moral precepts might be more plausible if they enlarged the domain of those whose welfare counts. Could we expand the utilitarian calculus implicit in weak sustainability so that nonhuman welfare counted in computations of what must be sustained in order to maximize welfare? If welfare were translated classically as pleasure and pain, this would expand the domain at least to include animals that are sentient.[13] If welfare were construed as happiness, perhaps the same limited expansion could be justified, so long as happiness were treated as a

13 As Bentham famously wrote:

Other animals, which, on account of their interests having been neglected by the insensibility of the ancient jurists, stand degraded into the class of things. ... The day has been, I grieve it to say in many places it is not yet past, in which the greater part of the species, under the denomination of slaves, have been treated ... upon the same mood or other psychological state. The same is true if welfare is taken to concern itself with preferences, for animals are plausibly thought to have at least simple desires. And, of course, if the domain of those whose welfare counts is extended to include members of future generations of humans and animals, then our welfare calculations might well dictate actions that protect and preserve species, ecosystems, and biospheres which themselves may have no capacities for pleasure, happiness, or preference-satisfaction. In other words, we might arrive at an expanded version of weak sustainability that gives lexical priority to sustaining "critical natural capital" that is critical not only to sustaining human welfare, but also to sustaining the welfare of all nonhuman entities that themselves possess welfare.

But however expansive is the definition of the domain of utilitarian concern, it remains clear that any brand of utilitarianism that correlates moral action with subjective satisfaction cannot vest intrinsic value in entities that do not have subjective experiences. As such their fate is properly at the whim of those of us who can have preferences about them. The only means of answering this perceived shortcoming consistent with the commitments of utilitarianism would be to adopt an objective theory of welfare—a theory that uncouples welfare from subjective well-being. If one can think of something as good for another even if that other does not now think it good for himself and never will think it good, one might be able to insist that utilitarianism demands the maximization of all things that are good for entities that can have a good, including ones that cannot appreciate that they have a good because they have no subjective experiences at all. On such an account, to maximize welfare is to do what is good for all things that can have "goods"—including bacteria, fungi, plants, trees, grasslands, and coral reefs, the goods of which are necessarily objective.

---

footing as ... animals are still. The day may come, when the rest of the animal creation may acquire those rights which never could have been withholden from them but by the hand of tyranny. The French have already discovered that the blackness of skin is no reason why a human being should be abandoned without redress to the caprice of a tormentor. It may come one day to be recognized, that the number of legs, the villosity of the skin, or the termination of the os sacrum, are reasons equally insufficient for abandoning a sensitive being to the same fate. What else is it that should trace the insuperable line? Is it the faculty of reason, or perhaps, the faculty for discourse?...the question is not, Can they reason? nor, Can they talk? but, Can they suffer? Why should the law refuse its protection to any sensitive being?... The time will come when humanity will extend its mantle over everything which breathes... " Jeremy Bentham, *Introduction to the Principles of Morals and Legislation.*

Yet to stretch utilitarianism to require maximization of the objective welfare of entities that do not have any subjective experiences at all is surely to stretch it to the breaking point. For the notion that one can maximize the welfare of a fjord surely strains the notion of welfare beyond practical recognition. Those who are attracted to utilitarianism precisely because it converts moral questions into scientific ones by making what is right a function of what is preferred will surely resist the meaningfulness of the notion of objective welfare precisely because it is not measurable through the use of markets, opinion polls, or other empirical measures. To determine the objective welfare of an entity that itself has no subjective experiences requires an exercise in moral reasoning that is academic in the pejorative to those who are drawn to utilitarianism precisely because it grounds moral judgments in fact rather than theory. It would thus not count as a friendly amendment to suggest to those who espouse weak accounts of sustainability that they should incorporate measures of objective welfare into their calculations when determining the sustainability of our practices.

We are left then with the conclusion that accounts of weak sustainability might be made less anthropocentric if they recognized that many creatures other than humans have subjective experiences that an honest commitment to utilitarianism's essential precepts would make relevant. Inasmuch as all sentient beings experience pain and pleasure, have preferences that can be satisfied or thwarted, and thus are eligible to be considered happy or unhappy, those who are concerned with sustaining welfare when making resource allocation decisions ought to be concerned with the welfare not just of humans, but of all creatures that are sentient. So reconceived, weak sustainability would stand on a stronger moral footing.

While some may fear that such an expansion would convert weak sustainability into a species of strong sustainability, I would view such a fear as misplaced. For weak sustainability, so expanded, would continue to value many natural resources, systems, services, and features not for themselves, but only because, and only so long as, they are of instrumental value. Forests and flowers, mountains and valleys, grasslands and jungles, tundra and taiga—all these should be sustained only if they provide value that cannot otherwise be provided artificially. Perhaps if the category of those whose welfare counts is expanded beyond humans, we will find that these remarkable evolutionary feats of nature do not have, and perhaps never will have, adequate artificial substitutes. But to those who continue to hanker for a theory of sustainability that accords value to Mt. Denali or the Atacama Desert that is not reducible to its value to us or other sentient beings, this assurance falls short of providing them with a theory of sustainability that satisfactorily captures their intuitions about why such largely lifeless places should be sustained.

III. Can Nonhuman Entities Be Said to Possess Rights That Make Actions that Do Not Sustain Them Wrongful?

The most celebrated roll-out of an agenda to implement a strong theory of sustainability was Bolivia's 2010 announcement of legislation granting all nature rights equal to those possessed by humans. The Law of the Rights of Mother Earth[14] purported to establish a set of new rights for nature, including the right to life and to exist; the right to continue vital cycles and processes free from human alteration; the right to pure water and clean air; the right to balance; the right not to be polluted; the right to not have cellular structure modified or genetically altered; and the right not to be affected by development projects that affect the balance of ecosystems and the local inhabitant communities". Bolivia has outlined a framework for establishing a Ministry of Mother Earth and appointing an ombudsman whose charge it is to speak for Pachamama, the earth deity whose independent legal standing has now been established.[15]

One can appreciate that rights rhetoric might have powerful instrumental advantages. Bolivia is struggling to cope with rising temperatures and more extreme weather events including more frequent floods, droughts, frosts and mudslides. As climate change causes Bolivia's vast glaciers to melt, Bolivian glaciologists anticipate that Bolivia will confront devastating water shortages and may be little more than a vast desert within a century. But while it may be rhetorically useful to claim that Mother Nature has rights, the question is, does she? Can proponents of a strong theory of sustainability invoke rights claims on behalf of natural entities to bolster their insistence that we are not entitled to trade off the existence of species or the preservation of old growth forests for gains in welfare?

---

14 The Law of the Rights of Mother Earth (Ley de Derechos de la Madre Tierra), Law 071 of the Plurinational State, enacted on December 2010.

15 The Framework Law of Mother Earth and Integral Development for Living Well (La Ley Marco de la Madre Tierra y Desarrollo Integral para Vivir Bien), Law 300 of the Plurinational State, enacted on October 15, 2012.

There are two types of rights theories, and it must be admitted that neither makes obvious room for the rights of nonhuman entities. On versions of the "will theory," rights are instruments of autonomy that allow one to assert dominion over others' actions.[16] To have a right is (by definition) to be able to waive it, to manipulate it, to dictate the terms of its satisfaction.[17] So on the will theory of rights, there can be no non-waivable rights. And there can be no rights-holders who are not able to waive rights. The will theory thus disqualifies from the category of rights-holders anyone who cannot make the kinds of choices that arefundamental to the possession of autonomy. And so, fetuses, infants, the senile, the insane, and the comatose are without rights. And it follows, *a fortiori*, that animals, plants, species, ecosystems, and biomes cannot be accorded rights, except metaphorically. On the will theory of rights, Bolivia's talk about Mother Nature having rights is just that—talk: it cannot make it so, and it cannot be thought to reflect any discovery of what *is* so.

On the second theory of rights—the "interest theory"—rights reflect powerful interests, and they trigger obligations on the part of others because those whose interests they reflect are made (substantially) better off by the satisfaction of those interests. A right is what one has when one's interests in a matter become substantial enough that one's life will go appreciably better if those interests are served in an obligatory way. Rights, on this account, are instrumental to achieving the good of rights-holders. As Joseph Raz puts it: "[A] person may be said to have a right if and only if some aspect of his well-being (some interest of his) is sufficiently important in itself to justify holding some other person or persons to be under a duty."[18]

On this theory, only beings capable of having interests are capable of having rights; but something may have interests without being an autonomous agent capable of exercising choice about others' actions. The question for

16 As H.L.A. Hart put it in his defense of this view of rights, ""The individual who has the right is a small-scale sovereign." H.L.A. Hart, *Essays on Bentham: Studies in Jurisprudence and Political Theory* (Oxford University Press, 1982), 183.

17 In Hohfeldian terms, it is to have a power over a claim. It is to have the ability to alter one's own or another's "Hohfeldian incidents" (first-order privileges or claims). See Wesley Newcomb Hohfeld, *Fundamental Legal Conceptions*, ed. W. Cook (New Haven: Yale University Press, 1919). See also Michael S. Moore and Heidi M. Hurd, "The Hohfeldian Analysis of Rights," 63 The American Journal of Jurisprudence, 295-354 (2018).

18 William A. Edmundson, *An Introduction to Rights* (Cambridge: Cambridge University Press, 2004), 129.

strong sustainability proponents is whether nonhuman entities can have interests, and if so, on what basis? To answer such a question is to advance a theory of interests—which is not something the interest theory of rights itself does.

It would seem philosophically feasible to advance the claim that animals have interests—and those who write about the moral status of animals have certainly provided ample vindication of this claim. Creatures that are sentient—creatures that have subjective perceptual experiences or "qualia"[19] —are capable of feeling pain and pleasure, and as such they are capable of living lives that are subjectively better or worse *for them.* If the avoidance of pain (beyond a de minimus threshold) is a significant interest—if it is, in Raz's terms, a sufficiently important aspect of well-being—then the interest theory of rights may demand the recognition that fish, fowl, and other fauna have rights—rights, at least, against those who are capable of modifying their behavior so as to avoid causing pain to such creatures. And so such theorists as Tom Regan and Gary Francione have argued.

What is more philosophically challenging is to make out a claim that non-sentient entities might have interests that would support strong sustainability proponents in arguing either for the Bolivian-style recognition of rights in the biosphere itself (the global ecological system that integrates all living beings with one another and with the elements of the lithosphere, hydrosphere and atmosphere, metaphorically called "Mother Nature"), or for the recognition of rights possessed by individual non-sentient entities (particular trees, plants, fungi) or groupings of entities, such as species, ecosystems, or biomes (wetlands, tropical forests, tundra). Some have argued that while things cannot matter *to* individual plants or *to* collectivities such as coral reefs, they can matter *for* them. As one theorist has put it, "matters can be better or worse for the tree, and this amounts to saying that the tree on its own has its goods and harms."[20] What attributes must entities have in order for us to say of them that some things are good for them, and some things are bad? In Von Wright's view, any being that "can meaningfully be said to be well or ill, to thrive, [or] to flourish," is a being of

19 Sentience is distinct from other aspects of consciousness, such as creativity, intelligence, sapience, self awareness, and intentionality (the ability to have thoughts that mean something or are "about" something).

20 Holmes Rolston III, "Value in Nature and the Nature of Value," *Philosophy and Natural Environment*, eds. Robin Attfield and Andrew Belsey, Royal Institute of Philosophy Supplement (Cambridge University Press, 1994), 13-30, 18.

whose good it is meaningful to talk.[21] Thus as he maintains, "The question 'What kinds or species of being have a good?' is . . . broadly identical with the question 'What kinds or species of being have a life?'.[22]

Von Wright's view is echoed by numerous environmental thinkers who are anxious to extend the class of beings who have interests beyond the class of beings who can suffer. In common to all such accounts is the notion that interests are possessed by entities that have teleological ends or are "goal directed". Paul Taylor, for example, accords plants interests on the basis that they are "teleological centers of life;" Kenneth Goodpastor maintains that plants exhibit "self-sustaining organization and integration" worthy of moral concern; Jay Kantor vests interests in plants by virtue of their "self-regulating and homeostatic functions"; and James Mish-alani derives the interests of living things from their possession of "self-ameliorative competence"—that is, "the capacity of a living thing to adjust to its circumstances in a manner to enhance its survival and natural growth." [23]

But these claims—as useful as they may be to those interested in bolstering a strong theory of sustainability—must answer several criticisms. First, by their terms, it would appear that these accounts vest interests in individual living creatures, not in collective entities, and certainly not in non-living entities such as rivers, lakes, or mountains. Such an account thus falls short of promising to vindicate anything like the Bolivian effort to extend rights to ecosystems, biomes, or the biosphere as a whole.

Second, one might think it intelligible to talk about goods for collective entities, without such talk reducing to claims about goods for individual members of those groups. The good of a population of deer, for example, may require the death of a great many of its members. But if collectivities can have interests, they will have to rest on claims other than the ones just canvassed. For while collectivities have tendencies, there is a good deal of consensus amongst scientists of evolution that species or populations

---

21 Id.

22 G.H. von Wright, *The Varieties of Goodness* (London: Routledge, Kegan Paul, 1963), p. 50.

23 I draw all of these quick summaries and their citations from Harley Cahen, "Against the Moral Considerability of Ecosystems," 10 *Environmental Ethics* (1988), 196-216. See specifically Kenneth Goodpastor, "On Being Morally Considerable," 75 Journal of Philosophy (1978); pp. 323; Paul Taylor, The Ethics of Respect for Nature," 3 Environmental Ethics (1981); p. 210-11; Jay Kantor, The 'Interests' of Natural Objects," 2 Environmental Ethics (1980); p. 169; James K. Mish'alani, "The Limits of Moral Community and the Limits of Moral Thought," 16 Journal of Value Inquiry (1982).

are not "goal directed." In Elliott Sober's terms, "Darwinism rejects the idea that species, communities, and ecosystems have adaptations that exist for their own benefit. These higher-level entities are not conceptualized as goal-directed systems; what properties of organization they possess are viewed as artifacts of processes operating at lower levels of organization."[24]

And third, that there may be things that are good for an entity does not mean that it is itself good or that it possesses a good. While there are conditions that enable a virus to do well—to thrive or to flourish—this does not, by itself, suggest that the virus has interests that are of a sort that properly command the moral attention or concern of humans. Put differently, that things can be instrumentally good for an entity is not sufficient to infuse that entity with goodness, and to thereby make its goods into interests that might cumulate to the point of constituting rights. One must not confuse what Holmes Rolston describes as an entity that is "value-able" (able to use things in the service of its own good) with the notion that it is valuable. Or as John O'Neill puts the point:

> That Y is a good of X does not entail that Y should be realised unless we have a prior reason for believing that X is the sort of thing whose good ought to be promoted. While there is not a logical gap between facts and values, in that some value statements are factual, there is a logical gap between facts and 'oughts.' 'Y is good' does not entail 'Y ought to be realised.[25]

This hasty summary should be sufficient to prove the philosophical complexities of employing the interest theory to vindicate the claim that nonhuman entities can be accorded rights of the sort that would make "absurdly strong" sustainability less absurd. Perhaps we can assess the wisdom of further dwelling on such complexities by asking into the implications of recognizing nonhuman entities as rights-holders. What would be the normative implications of concluding that individual living things, or collectivities of such things, have rights? Would the fishing industry around the globe be estopped from bottom-trawling or dynamite fishing or clam dredging or using plant-based poisons toxic to fish? Would we be barred from peeling back Appalachian mountains in order to extract their seams of coal?;

24 Elliot Sober, "Philosophical Problems of Environmentalism," in The Preservation of Species, ed. Bryan G. Norton (Princeton: Princeton University Press, 1986), p. 185. For more sustained criticism of the thesis that groups or species can have interests, see Cahen, "Against the Moral Considerability of Ecosystems," id.

25 John O'Neill, "The Varieties of Intrinsic Value," 75 *The Monist* (1992), p. 132.

from bulldozing tracts of forest for crop lands, grazing lands, or lumber?; from damning rivers for hydro-electric power?; from filling in wetlands for commercial developments?; from using factory-farm techniques to produce meat?; from using animals for medical experimentation?; from culling populations of density-independent animals?

It might seem, on first blush at least, that the virility of rights turns on whether they create categorical obligations (under a deontological account) or can be sacrificed in the name of other rights (under a rights-consequentialist theory). For rights-consequentialists, rights are normatively significant because they define the borders of legitimate utilitarian (or social welfare-based) justifications. Rights bar the ability of others to use the object of a right--one's life, liberty, or property, for example—as a resource for the advancement of others' utility or welfare. For deontologists, in contrast, rights patrol the borders of legitimate consequentialist justifications. Not only can rights not be traded for increases in social welfare; they cannot be traded to protect an even greater number of other (equal or weightier) rights. Thus, for example, if I have a right not to be tortured, then others have a duty not to torture me even if, by so doing, they could prevent many others from being tortured, and many others from suffering other equal or greater rights violations.

Those who argue that animals have rights have never been crystal clear about whether they are rights-consequentialists or deontologists. Tom Regan, for example, insists that inasmuch as animals are "subjects of a life," they each have an inherent worth that is the equal of that possessed by any human, and as such, they have rights "not to be treated as mere means to human ends." Regan thus criticizes those who believe "that we are *sometimes* justified in causing nonhuman animals significant pain, in pursuit of institutionalised human interests," insisting that "animal rightists deny that we are ever justified in doing this."[26] As such, he maintains that animals may not be used for food, cosmetic testing, military research, sport hunting, fur and leather products, or recreation (rodeos, circuses, etc.). Yet he rather clearly leaves open the possibility of justifying the use of animals for life-saving medical research, and he famously insists that if four humans and a dog find themselves in a lifeboat that can only hold four, the humans are justified in casting the dog overboard. He thus appears to stop short of suggesting that animals' lives cannot be taken to prevent others' lives from

26 Tom Regan, Animal Rights: What's in a Name?" Animal Welfare and the Environment, ed. Richard D. Ryder (London: Duckworth, 1992), p. 55 (italics in original).

being lost, and as such, one might plausibly believe that at the end of the day he is a rights-consequentialist, not a deontologist.

Those who find it philosophically incredible to attribute rights to animals (and to other nonhuman entities, as well) will no doubt be relieved to recognize that rights-consequentialism at least permits the sacrifice of such rights in the name of other, weightier (human!) rights. For no one believes that plants cannot be harvested for food and that trees cannot be cut for necessary shelter or warmth; very few believe that species of harmful viruses, bacteria, and disease-carrying pests cannot be altogether eradicated; and the great majority (who eat meat, wear leather, and clamor for cheap electricity) clearly believe that animals can be killed and mountains can be leveled for relatively trivial human comforts. Those who might hope that an attribution of rights to nonhuman entities would put a stop to their exploitation might thus conclude that rights consequentialism is a practical oxymoron. It allows humans to continue to insist that their rights justify the exploitation of nonhumans and other natural resources, even if those are themselves assigned rights.

Strong sustainability theorists who remain hopeful that rights can vindicate their view that human welfare must sometimes, and perhaps often, give way to the protection of the environment might thus want to insist that the rights of nature are of a deontological pedigree: they create categorical duties on the part of humans that cannot be violated in the name of other rights (let alone increased welfare). It would be wrong, however, to suppose that deontology does not permit a fair bit of moral "wiggle room" for those anxious to maximize good consequences at the expense of nature's bounty. While deontological duties may categorically prohibit the intentional causing of harm (pain, loss of life, loss of liberty, loss of living space, etc.), and while some may affirmatively require the prevention of harm or provision of benefits in special circumstances, there are reasons to think that the notions of intentionality, causation, action, and omission that define the content of such rights have built-in limitations that ultimately make these categorical duties less expansive and less onerous then they might first appear.[27]

27 For a rich discussion of the ways in which deontologists themselves constrain the scope of deontological rights and duties in ways that permit the consequential justification of a surprising number of harms, see Larry Alexander and Michael S. Moore, "Deontological Ethics," *The Stanford Encyclopedia of Philosophy*, ed. Edward

First, those who embrace "the Doctrine of Double Effect" insist that the duty correlative of, say, the right to life, precludes one from acting with the purpose of taking a life; but it does not prohibit one from doing an act that one simply knows will cause death. So long as a rights infringement is simply a known side consequence of an act done for a different purpose, that infringement is not a rights violation, and if it produces more good consequences than bad, it is not a wrong. If the distinction between purpose and knowledge can bear the moral weight assigned to it by the Doctrine of Double Effect, one can imagine that it might permit a good deal of environmental damage, for that damage is often not intended; it is simply known to follow from various human activities. Thus, for example, the Doctrine of Double Effect might permit the eradication of the Delhi Sands Flower-Loving Fly, if its extinction is not intended, but is a known side-consequence of converting the coastal sage scrub ecosystem of the Colton Dunes within the Los Angeles Basin into shopping centers, golf courses, and housing developments, the collective benefits of which might be thought to outweigh the elimination of this species of fly. [28]

Second, some maintain, in a somewhat similar vein, that one can often permissibly risk what one cannot knowingly cause. Thus, when the balance of consequences speaks in its favor, one can risk another's death or injury (e.g., by driving to work, by raising children near a lake, by taking a friend tandem skydiving) even as one could not justify doing the same act if one knew it would cause death. And even this claim requires modification, for we regularly take people to be justified in pursuing activities (building skyscrapers, blasting tunnels, and mining coal) that they know, as a statistical matter, will cause others' deaths, when they do not know the specific identity of those on whom such harms will fall (so as to make them mere riskers vis-à-vis each possible victim). If rights protect against being caused harm, but not against being risked, then many activities that risk harm to natural entities, but do not knowingly cause such harm, may remain permissible. And this is particularly so if the rights possessed by natural entities are possessed by individuals, rather than groups, for it must be a

N. Zalta (Fall 2008 Edition), section 2.1. URL = <http://plato.stanford.edu/archives/fall2008/entries/ethics-deontological/>.

28 For a wonderful discussion of the extraordinary obstacles posed to local development efforts, as well as to the operation of I-10 freeway, by the Fish and Wildlife Service's designation of the Delhi Sands Flower-Loving Fly, *Rhaphiomidas terminates abdominalis* as "endangered," see John Copeland Nagle and J.B. Ruhl, *The Law of Biodiversity and Ecosystem Management* (Foundation Press, 2006), Ch. 1, pp. 2-14.

frequent phenomenon for persons to know statistically that they will cause harm to classes of environmental entities (e.g., through water pollution, air pollution, toxic waste dumping, etc.) without knowing, and without being able to know, which individual entities, in particular, will be harmed. All this is to say that the Precautionary Principle (which holds that in instances of doubt, persons must err on the side of caution, and must thus refrain from pursuing activities the environmental implications of which are unclear) may not follow from according environmental entities categorical rights—for caution (the avoidance of risks) is not, itself, morally obligatory, and can thus be cast to the wind when a net gain in good consequences can be anticipated.

Third, it is a common intuition that when the consequential balance favors it, one can permissibly accelerate a harm to a rights-holder that is imminent and non-preventable, even as one could not have purposefully or knowingly set in motion the chain of events that puts the rights-holder in peril. At the root of this intuition is the judgment that one is not a full cause when one simply speeds up, but does not instigate, an inevitable harm. One who accelerates the death of someone who is "already dead" isn't a killer in the full sense of the term. Thus, a climber can cut a rope that is connecting him to a down-rope climber whose fall is inevitable, and whose weight will eventually drag the up-rope climber off the mountain, resulting in two deaths rather than one. Or in the textbook case of *Dudley and Stephens*, the men stranded on the lifeboat were thought to do no wrong when they ultimately used their last strength to kill and eat the languishing cabin boy, Richard Parker, who was sure to die before any rescue effort could save him. If there is moral merit in this notion that good consequences can make deontologically permissible the acceleration of imminent and non-preventable harms, then a number of implications may follow within the environmental context. For example, one might think that certain active efforts to control or stabilize population growth within a species might then be permissible. If in actively culling a population (of deer, elk, feral pigs, etc.), one is targeting animals that are themselves facing imminent death (through starvation brought on by over-grazing, for example), one may not, on this account, be violating any rights, even if rights are possessed by individual animals. More surprisingly (and more troublingly), if rights vest in species, rather than individuals, then perversely it may be permissible to accelerate the extinction of a critically endangered species if so doing achieves a net gain in good consequences, for a critically endangered species might be thought to be "already dead." (Ironically, if rights vest in individual members of a species, and not in the species as a whole, the opposite might follow, for each individual member of a critically endangered species may still have ahead of it a full life, and may not, itself, be in peril.)

Fourth, deontologists frequently place weight on the act-omission distinction, arguing that one can consequentially justify omissions to render life-saving aid when one could not so justify an active killing. One can thus fail to throw a rope to a drowning man in a choice situation in which one can otherwise use that rope to save two others who are also drowning. But one could not forcibly drown the man, even if, by so doing, one could thereby save two others (who might then be able to share his life jacket for flotation). In the environmental context, this distinction proves its worth in answering the argument that anyone who would vest rights in animals, for example, must be committed to preventing their deaths by natural means. If one can morally defend the distinction between causing harm and omitting to prevent harm, one can explain why we need not affirmatively prevent natural predation even as we must avoid actions that cause the death of nonhuman entities through habitat loss, pollution, and global warming.

More troubling, however, is the thought that this distinction may allow many to take moral refuge in their environmental inaction. While it might be said that consumer behavior drives corporate behavior (and corporate behavior drives political behavior!), so that the environmental devastation caused by coal companies, oil companies, large-scale agricultural operations, and so forth, is, in fact, caused by each of us, such a claim founders on the fact that there are a great many intervening causes between a consumer's act of buying a product and an industry's responsive production of more of such goods. On what I take to be the most promising test of proximate causation (the so-called "direct cause test"[29]), intentional, informed, voluntary actions sever causal chains that would otherwise reach back to the actions of others, making those prior actions causally non-proximate. If those who operate the enormous machines that access veins of coal by clear-cutting trees, shaving layers off mountains, and burying streambeds in "overburden" are sufficiently autonomous and informed to count as responsible agents (as they surely are), then our best account of proximate causation will declare them intervening causers. Those whose prior choices may have motivated their actions (consumers, politicians, family members, etc.) are thereby made nonproximate to the ensuing harm. If such prior

29 For the classic unpacking of this test of proximate causation, see H.L.A. Hart and Anthony Honore, *Causation in the Law*, 2d ed. (Oxford University Press, 1985).

actors are to be thought responsible for the harm they have inspired but not caused, it must be by virtue of our thinking that they are blameworthy for omitting to prevent that harm. But if, as a general matter, one violates no rights when one omits to enforce those rights, then our sense of blame will have to derive from some source other than the claim that environmental inaction is deontologically wrong.

Fifth, a somewhat different distinction would be needed to justify the active management of plant and animal populations through indirect means —say, by the (re)introduction of predator species into ecosystems that are unstable without them. To reintroduce wolves into a habitat over-populated by deer is affirmatively to act in a manner that will cause the deaths of individual deer. To introduce biological controls (pathogens, parasitoids, predators, and weed feeders) so as to check the spread of pests or invasive plant species is to act in a manner that will eradicate those species from the habitat. If such an action is not a rights-violation it must be by virtue of finding moral merit in what theorists have called "non-omissive allowings."[30] A non-omissive allowing is an act (not an omission) that allows nature to take its course. There are several kinds of non-omissive allowings, and I will not sketch here the various ways in which all of them might be employed by those who seek to employ consequential justifications in defense of actions that tread very close to violating categorical obligations toward natural entities. But consider just one category—that of being an enabler of another's action.

Many believe that one can consequentially justify an act that enables another to do a deed that one could not do oneself. Thus, for example, it is axiomatic for deontologists to insist that one is prohibited from killing an innocent person, even if so doing will motivate a killer to spare the lives of 20 others. But when asked whether one can simply hand the gun to the killer who himself will pull the trigger, if by so enabling him to kill the one, 20 others will be saved, many agree that such an enabling would not constitute a violation of the rights of the one who is then executed by the killer (even as his execution at the hands of the killer is surely a rights violation by the killer). This intuition that one can enable what one cannot cause is surely at the root of America's willingness to "outsource torture" through the method of extraordinary rendition so as to gain intelligence

30 See e.g., Michael Moore, "Patrolling the Borders of Consequentialist Justifications: The Scope of Agent-Relative Restrictions," 27 Law and Philosophy (2007), p. 70-94 (discussing five kinds of such allowings).

through the efforts of others (e.g., Egyptian interrogators) that it could not itself extract. By so doing, we exploit the notion that those who perform the interrogations are themselves intentional, informed, voluntary actors who break the causal chain extending back to our extradition, making our actions non-proximate to the rights-violations that ensue. If one does not violate another's rights unless one does so proximately, the distinction between enabling and causing creates room for consequentially justified enabling just as the distinction between omitting and causing creates room for consequentially-justified inaction.

If enablings can be consequentially justified, then those who believe that nonhuman entities have rights may nevertheless be able to justify the positive introduction (or reintroduction) of predators and other biological controls in order to check, indirectly, the expansion of populations of plants and animals that themselves, either individually or collectively, have rights to life. Such methods reflect non-omissive allowings for they involve actions that then allow nature to take its course. Of course, we do not normally think of animals, let alone insects or bacteria, as intentional, informed, voluntary actors that break causal chains, so it would surely take some innovative theorizing to adapt this deontological modification to justify the environmental analogue of extraordinary renditions. Still, this notion that we can actively use nature to control nature, even as more direct methods of control may be impermissible, captures common intuitions amongst those who take natural entities to be properly protected by categorical rights.

This non-exhaustive outline of the various ways by which deontologists themselves blunt the protections afforded by rights suggests that those who look to environmental rights as "trumps" of welfare calculations may find themselves disappointed by the enduring moral license that humans will have to manipulate and exploit nature even if nature is recognized as having deontological rights. They thus might conclude that the benefits of rights are not worth the costs of vindicating the contentious claim that nonhuman entities have rights—that is, that nonhuman entities have interests to begin with of a type and weight that generates obligations on our part. And even if nonhuman entities can be shown to satisfy the criteria of the interest theory of rights, and even if the strategies I've discussed to circumscribe the force of those rights can themselves be circumscribed, at the end of the day rights will not provide a promising means of arguing that non-living entities—Mt. Denali and the Atacama Desert, for example—themselves possess moral considerability. One must thus confess that while one might do wrong to humans or other living entities, one would do no wrong *to Death*

Valley by trucking in loads of soil to raise its elevation above sea level; one would do no wrong *to Mt. Everest* by removing its peak (so as to make K2 the highest mountain on Earth); one would do no wrong *to the Moon* by mining it; and we now do no wrong *to the Appalachian mountains* by doing in days what natural processes could do only in millennia. If we are to make sense of the common but philosophically uncomfortable notion that (at least some) nonliving environmental entities deserve protection *for their own sake*, then we will have to look beyond claims of right. But to what?

IV. Can Nonhuman Entities Be Said to Be Objects of Our Virtue?

As I have argued, without some account of the basis upon which nonhuman, nonsentient natural resources, systems, spaces, and places make moral claims upon us in their own right, it is hard to know how strong sustainability proponents can defend their conviction that we are constrained not just by others' welfare interests but by what Alan Holland has called "the units of significance" possessed by the forms and functions of nature.[31] Let me devote this final section to examining the moral promise of one more theory that derives our obligations to sustain the products of millions and billions of years of evolution from considerations about *us*, but that does so in a manner that suggests that if we serve ourselves as morality demands, we will protect nonhuman entities "as if" it were for their own sake.

The theory I have in mind is an aretaic one—one that takes the morality of our relationships with the natural world to derive from our satisfaction of aretaic duties to cultivate virtuous character traits and to suppress vicious ones. This account draws on the view that morality consists of both deontic and aretaic duties. The objects of deontic duties (whether derived from a rights-based or a consequentialist theory) are commissions or omissions at razor points in time, while the objects of aretaic duties are traits of character. Such traits of character are enduring dispositions—habits of thought and action that cumulatively define what sort of person a person is.[32] They function as default responses; as first instincts. They define our essential selves because they assert themselves in moments of crisis, trauma,

31 Holland, "Natural Capital," 178.

32 There is a significant literature on the question of whether aretaic duties can be collapsed into deontic duties or *vice versa*. Is one virtuous when, and only because, one does right actions? Or are one's actions right when, and only because, they reflect

or excitement when our powers to think and act strategically have been suspended or impaired. As such—and this is important to the argument here—character traits tend to creep into circumstances in which reason might rightly exclude them. Those who are virtuous often go beyond the call of their deontic duties, while those who are vicious all too often abuse their deontic rights. And so, deeply honest people tend to be honest to a fault and genuinely courageous people tend to be foolhardy about their own safety. And inversely, those who lie to protect their interests tend to lie even when it does not do so and those who indulge their appetites tend to over-indulge them.

One might plausibly suggest that to be a virtuous person, one must possess character traits that will collectively motivate one to act as a theory of strong sustainability would require. Virtue might demand, in other words, that one treat the environment *as if* it possessed intrinsic value—as if it possessed the independent moral considerability that one might be able to defend were one's philosophical tools less devotedly anthropocentric. What are these personal traits from which we might extract such a strong theory of sustainability?

Put most broadly, it seems to me that to be virtuous is "to know one's place in the Universe." It is to recognize that we are newcomers to a place long occupied by others. ("If you take the history of life as the length of your arm, then one stroke of a nail file erases human history."[33]) It is thus to have a sense that we must make a place for ourselves amongst those whose physical stake in the planet far supersedes our own (even if we cannot force-fit the notion that they have antecedently-existing moral claims into our self-regarding moral theories). This notion that virtue resides, in part, in "knowing one's place in the Universe" is surely not an easy one to

---

virtue? I have argued in some detail that both of these hypotheses are wrong, and that right action and virtuous character are quite independent of one another. *See* Heidi M. Hurd, *Duties Beyond the Call of Duty*, 6 ANN. REV. OF L. & ETHICS 1-36 (1998). After all, one can both be scrupulous in doing the right thing without being a person of good character (think of Inspector Javert in *Les Miserables*), and one can be a person of quite laudable character who at least sometimes, and perhaps often, fails to act rightly (think of the judge who indulges mercy too frequently and who thus fails to treat like cases alike). It is, therefore, open to us to say that persons *aretaically ought* to cultivate certain character traits that will (by their nature) motivate actions that are not *deontically required* and as to which others have no *deontic rights*.

33 This quotation is attributed to Professor Kevin Padian of the University of California at Berkley who apparently uses it to give his students a Deep Time perspective. See John Knoebber and Louie Psihoyos, *Hunting Dinosaurs* (Random House, 1994), p. 5.

unpack. It connotes a number of different judgments and attitudes, many of which smuggle back in notions of rights and interests that we have already found wanting. But, of course, as I have just argued, a virtuous person does just that: she brings, as psychological baggage, her respect for others' rights and her fear of shirking her own duties to arenas in which such concerns may be in moral doubt. She thus feels (non-moral) guilt, for example, even when she has done no moral wrong. And she resists praise (without it being a product of false modesty) even when she has done something genuinely supererogatory. So it should be no surprise that as we unpack the attitudes that a virtuous person has towards those whose claims to the planet's resources predate our own, we should talk in terms of "claims," when to do so is to do so loosely, or only metaphorically (if I am right in the previous sections).

First, to suggest that virtue requires that one know one's place in the Universe is to suggest that one should honor notions of fairness and considerations of equality even before, and probably even after, one can establish with philosophical exactitude the degree to which others are entitled (as a matter of right or as a matter of other defensible moral criteria) to such treatment. On pain of violating the "first come, first served" and "finder's keeper" maxims that even a child learns and finds intuitive at an early age, one should be dispositionally reluctant to displace anything that has already come to rely for its existence upon its present circumstances. As a newcomer, one's first instincts should be to learn and adapt to existing arrangements, rather than to force the redistribution of resources for private gain.

Second, to know one's place in the universe is to exhibit environmental "humility". It is to appreciate how short our individual lives are in comparison to other living things (the oldest living plant on Earth is more than 5,000 years old!) and to the geological formations that form the contours of our world. One who would cut down a 2,000-year old Sequoia tree in less than an hour for pulp, or employ outdated fishing gear that traps and kills an enormous bycatch, or level a mountain within days that has been formed over millennia, or drive a species to extinction in order to build a shopping center, lacks the sort of humility that one considers constitutive of a virtuous person.

Third, a virtuous person is a generous person—one who bestows benefits on others even when they cannot be said to be entitled or deserving. Inasmuch as generosity crosses the boundaries of desert, one would also expect it to be indifferent to the boundaries between humans and animals, between animals and plants, and between species, ecosystems, and biospheres. One would expect that the virtuous person would take all things that could be made better to be worthy objects of generosity, and to thus make sacrifices for the good of environmental entities in the same way (and for the same deontically non-obligating reasons) that she makes sacrifices for other persons.

Finally, to be virtuous is not just to be morally modest, it is to be epistemically modest as well. It is to resist the arrogance of conquerors who destroy what is local before they even know its value. In the absence of full information about how our activities will impact upon delicate ecosystems, virtue would seem to require action in accordance with the Precautionary Principle--the principle that demands that we do not undertake risky ventures without real confidence that we can assure the enduring health of those nonhuman entities with whom we share the planet.

There is much within these brief suggestions with which to find fault, and much to be unpacked. Let me close by raising some of the lines of criticism that would need to be met to advance an aretaic account of strong sustainability. First, while our species is a relative newcomer to Earth as compared to other species, each individual living entity on Earth today is a comparative newcomer (although there is no question that we are each short-lived compared to individual members of many other species). Why are our virtues, as individuals, made relative to the longevity, history, and behavior of our species as a whole? As a general matter, we do not assign guilt to persons by virtue of their mere association with others who are guilty. So why would we think that the aretaic duties that persons have are properly responsive to the (short) history and past behavior of the species *homo sapiens*?

Second, while one can appreciate, as an empirical matter, that virtue is sometimes (and maybe often) "over-inclusive" relative to our deontic duties, so that virtues demonstrate themselves when they are often not required, we require an account of why this *should* be so before we can derive from virtue any moral hope that the environment will be a beneficiary of its promotion. For it is tempting to say, with Aristotle, that virtue becomes vice when taken to an extreme; that it ceases to be virtue at all when it is extended to unworthy objects or exhibited in contexts in which it is inappropriate. Thus, while our own imperfections may prevent us from ever cabining virtue within its appropriate quarters, we should be wary of resting the fate of our environment on the promise that if we cultivate virtue enough, we will cultivate it too much, and only thereby assure the protection of our planet. For while too much virtue is surely not a fear we need have anytime soon, we ought to be nervous about suggesting that we can protect our planet only if we effectively make virtue a vice.

Finally, and most troublingly, I remain unconvinced that an aretaic theory of environmental care can properly explain the intuitions possessed by those who press a theory of strong sustainability. An aretaic theory is unabashedly "all about us." It makes the value of the environment a function of the value we place on our own virtue. While real virtue may require devoted stewardship of the planet and its many entities, I remain unconvinced that the reason we are bound to engage in such stewardship is that *we* will be personally morally worse off if we do not. I take the moral significance of the oceans to be independent of (and far greater than) the significance to be attached to the relative virtue of those who have an effect upon them. While it may be that if we were as virtuous of character as we ought to be, we would act to ensure that the oceans' fish populations were restored, their coral reefs protected, their whales made safe, and their currents unaffected by global warming. But even if we were so virtuous, strong sustainability proponents would surely resist the claim that the moral value of oceans lay in the value of our exhibited virtue toward them.

Conclusion

And thus I end where I began. I fear that our best ethics are not up to the task of vindicating those who seek to protect the global environment from practices that service us at the expense of those in the future and those that are unlucky enough to be members of one of the 10 million other species with whom we share this planet. If moral philosophers cannot devise the theoretical means by which to give voice to deep-seated intuitions about the moral status of the natural world on which we depend, we surely cannot blame market players for failing to reflect the value of the natural world in their economic computations, and we cannot condemn political leaders for failing to keep our markets honest and for refusing to exempt from market practices those aspects of the natural world that might ought not to be commodified at all.

A Relational Approach to Regulating A.I.: Lessons from Environmental Law

Jordan Pascoe

Abstract

As the adaptation and adoption of A.I. outpaces regulatory efforts, legal jurisdictions need expanded strategies for conceptualizing, regulating, and managing the outsize impacts of A.I. on our systems and societies. This chapter proposes a novel approach to A.I. regulation by conceptualizing A.I. as akin to an "invasive species" in our social, political, and economic ecosystems. It develops an ecological approach to A.I. regulation that draws on invasive species management, emphasizing both the direct, causal harms A.I. can have on humans and the systems they inhabit, as well as the indirect, system-wide harms A.I. poses. Finally, it draws on indigenous critiques to propose relational approaches to regulating and managing A.I., taking seriously the ethical challenges posed by the urgency of regulating and managing A.I.

The A.I. revolution is here. As I write, A.I. – largely in the form of large language learning models (LLMs) -- are transforming the economy, education, and multiple facets of everyday life. A.I. is so pervasive that one has to go out of one's way to avoid interaction with it: it responds to our Google searches, answers our customer service calls, screens our job applications, teaches us Spanish, shapes our medical diagnoses and, in some cities, shares the road in driverless cars. A.I. is rapidly transforming the terrain in which we live, in part by playing a significant role shaping the opportunities and resources available to individuals: A.I. may determine insurance premiums and payouts, including how much health insurance will cost us and what medical services will be covered; it may screen our applications for jobs and housing, and determine whether we are eligible for social services and how much financial aid we'll be offered in university. A.I.'s presence in these domains not only transforms access to goods and services, but to jobs themselves. The A.I. customer service chatbot replaces human customer service agents; the A.I. resume screener shrinks H.R.

departments. As A.I. capabilities expand, some studies suggest that A.I. may automate 30% of jobs in the U.S. by 2030, with 60% being significantly altered (Kelly 2025); globally, 400 million workers may be displaced.

The pace of these transformations has significantly outpaced nascent regulatory frameworks, leading to serious concerns about the risks A.I. poses, the forms of discrimination, bias, and exclusion that follow from its widespread adoption, and its rapid transformation of the basic infrastructure of civil society. While the E.U. has developed a framework for assessing and regulating high-risk deployments of A.I., the U.S. has largely failed to develop A.I. regulations. Citing the necessity of encouraging innovation, the Trump administration has aimed to block all potential A.I. regulation.[1] The E.U., on the other hand, has developed a comprehensive, risk-based approach which classifies A.I. systems based on their capacity for causing harm.[2] In doing so, the E.U. has explicitly framed its broad objectives for A.I. regulation by drawing on ecological metaphors, aiming to cultivate "an ecosystem of excellence" as well as an "ecosystem of trust" in its treatment of A.I. (European Commission 2020, 3). In doing so, it emphasized the importance of tracking A.I.'s impact not only on individuals, but assessing its system-wide impacts "from the perspective of society as a whole" (European Commission 2020, 2). This chapter takes up the promise of this explicitly "ecological" approach, exploring how A.I. regulation can draw on the conceptual resources of environmental law in order to orient a more relational approach to A.I.

There are several reasons to draw on environmental regulatory frameworks for developing more comprehensive approaches to A.I. regulation. The most direct, of course, is that A.I. poses significant costs to the envi-

---

1 The Executive Order for Removing Barriers to American Leadership in AI, signed in January 2025, was one of the Trump administration's initial executive orders; the administration also proposed a provision preventing A.I. regulation for 10 years in their signature budget bill, which was ultimately removed (Morgan and Shepardson 2025). While some states, like California and Colorado, have focused on limiting bias and discrimination as well as regulating likeness and deep fakes, there is no comprehensive approach to regulating A.I. in the United States.

2 The E.U. A.I. Act classifies A.I. systems into different risk levels, with corresponding compliance obligations, such that AI with "unacceptable risk" (e.g. "social scoring") are prohibited, while AI that are "high risk" (e.g., AI used as a "safety component" of a product, or AI deployed in education, employment, essential government services, law enforcement, migration, or the application of justice) are subject to the most detailed compliance. Canada, likewise, is developing A.I. regulation that focuses on distinguishing and regulating "high impact" A.I. systems, which determine employment matters or access to basic service provisions, or in biometric, health care, or legal contexts.

ronment, which current regulatory models are poorly designed to address (Hacker 2024). In defending its existing regulatory framework, the E.U. explicitly identified A.I.'s importance for achieving its Sustainable Development Goals while recognizing that "the environmental impact of AI systems needs to be duly considered throughout their lifecycle and across the entire supply chain, e.g. as regards resource usage for the training of algorithms and the storage of data" (EU 2020, 2). This points to the necessity of a broader, more nuanced form of risk assessment, models for which have been developed in ecology and environmental law.

More broadly, many defenders of the A.I. revolution compare it to the Industrial Revolution, which similarly remade not just the global economy, but fundamentally reshaped the conditions of human life, including our relationships with one another and with our environments (Suleyman 2023). Because environmental regulations were designed in response to that revolution, and have emerged as a particularly innovative domain of law, Dennis Hirsch has proposed that environmental law can promisingly orient tech regulation (2006). While early regulatory standards took what Hirsch calls a "command and control" model, through prescriptive and uniform standards, environmental law has included innovative approaches that offer agency to regulated parties in determining how to meet established environmental goals and standards (2006, 8-9). Such approaches often take a risk-based approach oriented through the "precautionary principle", which holds that in cases of scientific uncertainty, preventative regulation is warranted, particularly when potential risks are catastrophic. They have also developed strategies for addressing what is sometimes known as the "responsibility gap", which arises when the systems through which harms are perpetuated are so diffuse that assigning responsibility is itself a regulatory challenge. Both the uncertain potential for catastrophic risk and the responsibility gap are central questions in contemporary debates about A.I. regulation. For example, in their emphasis on risk and "high impact" systems, E.U. and Canadian regulatory frameworks draw on several insights from environmental law, including risk-based assessments, preventative principles that draw on the precautionary principle, and conceptualizations of risk that track harms to both individuals and systems.

Hirsch's environmental metaphor is particularly apt for the proliferation of A.I., which has widely been likened to a kind of pollution of our online and epistemic environments (Wallace Wells 2024). For example, the discourse around "A.I. slop", referring to the saturation of online spaces like You-Tube with low-quality A.I. outputs directly draws on a pollution metaphor. There is a case to be make for regulating A.I. by drawing on existent models for regulating pollution, particularly given that such regulatory problems regularly grapple with both the responsibility gap and the challenges of tracking diffuse and indirect harms. Hirsch explores a variation on this argument with regards to "spam" emails, proposing a pollution-like fee model, wherein spammers must pay some amount per email over some agreed upon minimum (2006). One could imagine drawing on pollution regulation frameworks both to regulate the metaphorical pollution of A.I. slop, as well as the literal strains that A.I. data centers place on the lived and built environment.

However, in this chapter I will take a different tack, which aims to better model the ways that the current A.I. revolution does not just transform our environment, but increasingly displaces us within it. I emphasize not just the pollution-like impact of A.I. outputs, but the ways that A.I. is designed to mimic and replace human functions in our social worlds and political economy (Brynjolfsonn 2022). Thus, my analysis will focus on an area of environmental law that has received little attention in the current debates over regulating A.I.: frameworks for the management and control of invasive species. I'll develop a heuristic for thinking about A.I. as "invasive species" in our human environments, and highlight insights from invasive species management and regulation that might augment and inform A.I. regulation. I'll argue that an ecosystem-based heuristic for thinking about our relationship to A.I. is particularly apt given that ecological approaches have consistently developed tools for recognizing the importance of relationships between humans and "more-than-humans" for our collective survival.

In doing so, I draw on Hirsch's move to recognize the ways that the data revolution is having an impact on what he called "our internal environment" (2006). Hirsch's analysis of the applicability of environmental law to digital regulation focuses on the right to privacy, and is developed at an earlier stage of the information revolution. In this chapter, I'll draw on Hirsch's framework to argue that A.I. is having an impact on our "internal environment" that goes beyond privacy, but concerns a broad range of our epistemic – or knowledge-making -- capacities. In light of this, we need a broader and more nuanced analysis of the ways that A.I. impacts both our literal, living environment, as well as the various ecosystems that we rely on for survival, including our economic, educational, and epistemic ecosystems. With this analysis in place, we can explore the broader potential of environmental law as a model for regulating A.I. and big data.

By drawing on ecological approaches to the management of invasive species, this chapter teases out the promise of such an ecosystem-based approach to conceptualizing and regulating A.I. It proposes that the invasive species case can provide what Katherine McKittrick calls "observational scaffolding" (2021) for contemporary experiences of living with and relating to A.I. In the A.I. era, our economic, educational, and epistemic lives are increasingly impacted by relations with "more-than-human" entities that legal frameworks focused exclusively on human rights and human relationships may struggle to manage and regulate. Thus, this chapter mines environmental law and ecological thinking for relational strategies for regulating A.I. In doing so, it will contend with the relational nature of an ecological approach, and suggest that the heuristic of invasive species may both provide a model for legal approaches to A.I.

1. A.I. as invasive species: An Ecological Approach

In a 2005 essay, pioneer A.I. theorist Nils Nilsson argued that the goal of "human level A.I." was A.I. that could replace humans in a range of employment. This replacement model was dubbed "strong A.I.," while A.I. that aimed to help humans was "weak A.I." As Erik Brynjolfsonn has more recently argued (2022), this "strong" and "weak" terminology helped to incentivize A.I. researchers to prioritize the former, leading to decades of A.I. development that has focused on the goal of automation, or A.I. capable of replacing humans in a wide variety of tasks – rather than augmentation, or the goal of extending or enhancing human capabilities.

This distinction is a useful starting point for thinking about how A.I. has been designed and trained to co-inhabit a variety of ecosystems – from our information ecosystem to our employment ecosystem – with humans. A.I. is not primarily a tool designed to enhance, extend, or augment human capabilities, but an entity designed to automate human functions, and thus to compete with and ultimately replace humans in the ecosystems they inhabit.[3] This need not entail a science fiction-like form of total replacement, like something out of *The Matrix*, although this is certainly a fear that drives longtermist critiques of A.I. (Vallor 2024). We are already seeing

3 There is a strong argument – advanced by Vallor (2024), Brynjolsonn (2022), Alvarado (2023) and others – that an augmentation or enhancement approach to A.I. would be both ethically and epistemically preferable.

Nilsson's "employment test" come to fruition, as a wide range of jobs can now be automated, and A.I. are in fact replacing workers in a huge range of fields – particularly in fields related to knowledge production and data management.[4]

Because "human-level A.I." is defined as A.I. capable of replacing humans, a great deal of innovation and scholarship has focused on the question of whether A.I. has human-like capabilities, including the ability to reason, understand, and know (Ferrario et al 2024). While epistemologists and ethicists have consistently argued that A.I. is not the sort of entity capable of asserting (Frieman and Miller 2021), understanding (Ferrario et al 2024), or reasoning (Vallor 2024), there is consensus that we now interact with many large language models *as if* they were knowers, offering testimony, making assertions, and giving reasons. This is to say that regardless of the epistemic or agential status of A.I., we increasingly treat them as co-inhabitants in our epistemic ecosystems – just as we interact with them *as if* they were agents on customer service calls, as digital assistants and therapists, and even in romantic relationships. This may, as Ori Frieman suggests, reflect our own anthropocentric biases: we treat A.I.s *as if* they were human agents, because we equate human agency and testimony with intelligence (2024) – rather than recognizing, as Shannon Vallor has argued, that we co-inhabit the earth with many other kinds of intelligence that might serve as alternate models for A.I. – and indeed, inspire alternate approaches to A.I. regulation (2024; Godfrey Smith 2016).

Given these features of A.I.'s presence in our lives – that they are explicitly designed to replace, and thus compete with, humans, and that we increasingly treat them *as if* they were human agents and knowers – I suggest that one way to conceptualize our current relationship to A.I. is to understand ourselves as akin to "native species" in an ecosystem now being infiltrated and transformed by "invasive species." In many contexts, we can understand A.I. as an introduced species explicitly engineered to replace and displace humans. Such a framework can give us nuanced tools for examining the harms, risks, and benefits of A.I. – as well as an existing set of legal and management tools to draw on.

---

4 As Brynjolfsonn argues, this replacement strategy is well-incentivized for the technologists whose systems gain unprecedented uptake and influence, the businesspeople who can shrink their workforce and consolidate decision-making power, and the policy makers who have consistently ensured that maintaining a workforce is amongst the tax-burdened options for businesses (2022, 277-280).

One such resource is the distinction ecological models make between the *direct* and *indirect harms* that invasive species pose to other species in an ecosystem. Direct harms include cases where bias or blindness in the A.I.'s programming or training leads to or exacerbates discriminatory harms, through patterns Ruha Benjamin has called "runaway feedback loops", as discriminatory data trains A.I. systems that inscribe unjust patterns more deeply into institutions and practices (2019). Direct harms might also include instances of humans being replaced or displaced by A.I., much as invasive species outcompete native species.

Indirect harms, on the other hand, track the multiple ways that A.I. transforms our norms, expectations, knowledge-production practices, and other modes of production, drastically changing the way our economic, educational, and epistemic ecosystems function. Indirect harms identify the ways that the presence of invasive species can change the "essential functions" of that ecosystem in ways that compromise survival for or require significant adaptation by other species. This emphasis on indirect harms is, I'll argue, an important dimension of risk assessment for A.I. Most current risk-assessment legal models, like the E.U.'s A.I. Act, focus on direct harms: cases where A.I. has a direct impact on individual lives and opportunities (like social scoring), or has the capability to cause direct harms, including endangering lives (as in examples like self-driving cars or medical mis-diagnoses). We see such indirect harms, for example, in the rise of automation bias, as automated knowledge is increasingly privileged not only as more efficient than human-generated knowledge, but also as more unbiased, objective, and neutral (Alon-Barkat and Busuioc 2022). Automation bias can lead to direct harms, as human knowers and workers are replaced by A.I. systems, as well as to indirect harms, as the forms of knowledge that are valued change, undercutting a range of human knowledges that rely on direct experience, reflection, and relationships. Automation bias changes the rules of knowing in ways that indirectly effect all human knowers in the relevant ecosystem. And of course, by incentivizing humans to produce knowledge in ways that mimic A.I. knowledge, automation bias encourages loss of diversity and the development of a monoculture – ensuring, in the long run, that human knowers can be replaced by A.I.

One reason that ecologists emphasize the importance of attending to indirect harms is that changes to an ecosystem's "essential functions" can lead to system collapse or regime change. For example, introduced carp have fundamentally transformed the Mississippi's ecosystem, creating a monoculture in which, in many parts of the Mississippi, carp is the only surviving fish (Hicks and Ling 2015). The sheer scale of A.I. outputs is similarly outpacing human data production on the internet, leading to a situation in which A.I. have run out of human-made data to train on, and are increasingly "cannibalizing" A.I. data, leading to system collapse and increased A.I. "hallucinations." Just as biological "monocultures" threaten the stability of ecosystems, A.I. monocultures threaten the stability of A.I. themselves as well as the ecosystems in which they operate.

To identify both the direct and indirect harms that A.I. poses is not to ignore the possibility that A.I. will transform our economic, educational, and epistemic ecosystems in ways that ultimately benefit humans, nor to deny challenges that remind us of the anthropocentric bias of evaluating A.I. in terms of its effect on humans. One benefit of an ecological approach, however, is that while it encourages us to recognize multiple species – and multiple kinds of intelligence – as features of our ecosystems, it also allows us to recognize ourselves as inhabitants of those ecosystems, with a vested interest in our own ongoing survival and the habitability of those ecosystems (Code 2005). From an ecological perspective, hoping that human knowledge survives, or that human workers remain valued, is not tantamount to hoping that *only* human knowledge survives, or that *all work* is done by humans.

Likewise, identifying A.I. as an invasive species is not to call for its eradication. There are many promising stories of invasive species evolving alongside native ones, of ecosystems adapting to keep invasive and native species in balance, of invasive species playing key roles in both the sustainability and habitability of an ecosystem, and increasing the comfort, convenience, and efficiency of that ecosystem in ways that benefit other inhabitants. This is to say that not all invasive species are what ecologists call "problem species"; in many cases, the benefits of invasive and alien species outweigh the risks. After all, most of what we eat around the world at this point reflects the presence of alien species: that we eat bananas, cinnamon, or lentils in the Americas and Europe or meat in New Zealand reflects the long history of global trade and colonialism, through which we introduced alien species into our ecosystems; globally, 69% of farm production is of introduced alien crops (Cherfas 2016). Most of these alien species are not invasive: they are carefully cultivated in agricultural settings. Only when their spread becomes uncontrollable, leading to direct and indirect harms, does an alien species become invasive. Only when these harms outweigh the benefits the species provides do they become a "problem" species. Both the assessment of harms and benefits and the efficacy of cultivation and management systems are critical to distinguishing invasive species from alien species.

There are parallels in the case of A.I. For example, the adoption of A.I. systems for tutoring purposes within education institutions might be an example of introducing A.I. in a cultivated context, managed by the institution in question. When students begin using A.I. in unauthorized ways, to complete homework and writing assignments, that A.I. is acting like an invasive species, proliferating "uncontrollably" in ways that exceed cultivation and management. The question is at what point A.I. becomes a "problem" species: a species causing substantial direct and indirect harms to its ecosystem in ways that outweigh its benefits. In ecology, species like kudzu and lionfish are "problem species", because they outcompete native species in such a way that they generate a monoculture, straining and changing the "essential rules" of the ecosystem in question.

In the case of both A.I. and invasive species, such designations can be controversial, as stakeholders may disagree both about the harms and benefits in question, as well as about what the "essential rules" of the system in question might be. For example, many college students believe that using A.I. to complete homework and assignments is essential to their wellbeing: some site mental health benefits, while others report both higher grades and the ability to sleep more (Hsu 2025). Professors and administrators worry that the invasive presence of A.I. is drastically changing the "essential rules" of higher education, creating a context in which cheating is inevitable, students are actively resistant to learning, and existing models of education are likely to collapse (Wong 2025). Faculty and administrators recognize A.I. as a "problem species" in the educational ecosystem; for now, students generally treat it as an invasive species whose benefits outweigh the costs. In the workplace, a different dynamic is emerging: employers generally recognize A.I. as an invasive species that offer significant value, both in terms of reducing labor costs and consolidating power (Brynjolfsonn 2022), while employees are more likely to think of it as a problem species, as the short-term benefits of automating dull tasks are outweighed by the likelihood of being outcompeted and made redundant by A.I. Cases like these illustrate the ways that our assessments about the ecosystems we inhabits are partial and never disinterested. The determination of when an invasive species, or an A.I., becomes a "problem" species is thus a complex one with multiple stakeholders and diverse perspectives, which need to be subject to some kind of democratic deliberation. Regulatory frameworks need to be developed in light of substantial and meaningful disagreement about what constitutes the "essential functions" of our existing (epistemic, educational, economic, etc.) ecosystems.

2. Regulatory Strategies: On Risk and Responsibility

A.I. regulation is a rapidly emerging field, with most jurisdictions scrambling to keep abreast of technological developments. As a result, much A.I. regulation occurs through bodies of existing laws, applying established legal frameworks to the risks and transformations posed by A.I. In this, A.I. regulation is quite similar to the regulation of invasive species, which draws a wide range of existing legal structures. This includes commerce and trade law in additional to public health and environmental law; in the U.S., invasive species regulation operates through the coordination of multiple federal agencies, including the Departments of State, Commerce, Health and Human Services and the Interior, and agencies including the Postal Service (Johnson et al 2017). Because of the pervasive and disparate impacts of both A.I. systems and invasive species, regulation necessitates nuanced and multidimensional approaches that incorporate multiple kinds of agencies and both draw on existing and develop new bodies of law.

The regulation of invasive species provides several promising models for A.I. regulation. Invasive species are regulated using risk-based analysis, which orient targeted, single-species approaches. In this approach, species deemed sufficiently risky may be added to a "black list" and blocked from importation or, if already introduced, targeted for eradication or particularly stringent forms of management. Some jurisdictions take a more rigorous "white list" approach, in which *only* species on the white list are free from such regulation. This kind of single-case, risk-based approach is akin to the E.U.'s model for A.I. regulation, which uses a similar kind of risk analysis to designate some A.I. systems, like those that do "social scoring" as "unacceptable risk" (e.g., blacklisted), and others, like those that filter emails, as "minimal risk" (e.g., whitelisted).

Of course, such designations are not static: a difficulty with invasive species is that an invader species if often contained and innocuous in its host environment for an extended period of time – and then, because of mutations or changes to the environment, suddenly proliferate uncontrollably (Crooks and Soule 1996; Simberloff 2006, 5). This necessitates reassessment of risk. Likewise in the case of A.I., relatively innocuous systems or use cases may suddenly pose increased risk, either because of rapid uptake, strains on the surrounding ecosystem, or malfunctions in the system itself, as with A.I. "hallucinations."

The challenges of such assessments illustrate the importance of adopting definitions of harm capable of examining both direct, causal harms and indirect, system-wide analyses. Causal analyses of harms have shown that assessment of harm involves a contrast case: I am harmed by X if there is some other version of events where X does not obtain and I am better off (Beckers et al 2023). System-wide analyses of harm, then, require a standing assessment of the circumstances under which such a system might be "better off." In the case of invasive species, for example, recognizing the emergence of a monoculture as a system-wide risk requires both a valuation of relevant forms of diversity as well as a set of diversity baselines. Recognizing system-wide harms caused by A.I. systems, then, involves the establishment of a set of baselines and norms about what forms of "diversity" are valuable. Such designations of diversity can be either intrinsic or instrumental: we might assert that human knowledge, or human work, is intrinsically valuable as a feature of a habitable ecosystem *for human beings*. Or, we might take an instrumental approach: if human-made knowledge or scientific analysis provides an important baseline for both training A.I. and for assessing the accuracy or methodology of A.I. outputs, then human-made knowledge and analysis is instrumentally valuable for A.I. innovation. In either case, regulatory frameworks would then have a vested interest in promoting human knowledge as a valued form of diversity necessary for maintaining a healthy and habitable ecosystem.

In addition to risk-based, single-species approaches, invasive species regulation has also developed a second, "pathways" approach, which identify the pathways by which species are introduced and spread (Johnson et al 2017; Hulme 2015). In New Zealand, for example, regulation targets the various means by which alien species might enter the country: as contaminants in imported food and crops, as stowaways on arriving vessels, through accidental release, and so on. A "pathways" approach to A.I. regulation might focus on the industries that develop A.I., as well as establishing regulatory norms for industries and institutions that introduce A.I. into new contexts. Of course, because the such an approach targets such systems rather than focusing on the distinct harms of discrete systems or use cases, it's also likely that such an approach could be criticized as aiming to stifle innovation.[5] The "pathways" approach, however, might address an important dimension of the current A.I. "responsibility gap" – namely, that responsibility for A.I.'s potential harms and benefits lie not only with those who develop and train A.I., but also with those who deploy A.I. in novel contexts, creating "pathways" for A.I.'s impact on individuals and transformation of our broader ecosystems.

A.I. regulation must also target the agencies and individuals who invent, program, and train A.I.s – and here again, invasive species regulation offers useful models. If A.I. systems are like invasive species in our varied (technosocioeconomic) ecosystems, there is a sense in which they are like engineered species, specifically designed to outperform and replace "native" species. A persistent problem with engineered species – be they Monsanto tomatoes or A.I. systems – is that they redistribute wealth by creating monopolies, and reshape who has access to a given ecosystem (as when family farms cannot afford genetically engineered crops and are bought out by industrial farms). Regulation of these species, then, includes anti-trust law and appropriate assessment of and accountability for harms following both from flaws in design and this redistribution of wealth and access, as well as legal protections and subsidies to encourage baseline forms of diversity.

Finally, treating invasive species regulation as an instructive parallel for the regulation of A.I. also points to the importance of thinking beyond top-down regulatory frameworks, by also considering resource management, educational efforts, and grassroots resistance – particularly in cases where "problem species" have rapidly transformed existing ecosystems. In the Bahamas, for example, management of invasive lionfish includes widespread educational campaigns designed to teach residents how to catch, cook, and eat lionfish. In Belize, local tour guides are trained to catch and kill lionfish and feed them to sharks and eels to clear local reefs for tourists; some also prepare lionfish ceviche for tourists (Bratspies 2016). Across the Caribbean, lionfish "derbies" mobilize locals and tourists to hunt lionfish en mass (Malpica-Cruz et al 2016). These examples point to both the limits of regulatory frameworks, and the ways that the terms of survival in an invaded ecosystem will involve the agency, resistance, and adaptation of those harmed by both the direct and indirect impacts of invasive species. To be clear, there is nothing just about this distribution of impact, or

5 Such criticisms have played a major role in blocking regulatory frameworks especially in the U.S.

duties of resistance. The lionfish is particularly instructive here. Like the development of A.I., the trade in lionfish is of almost exclusively the purview of the wealthy: the exotic fish trade, driven by those who can afford to spend tens of thousands of dollars on home saltwater acquariums (Bratspies 2016). The lionfish's invasion of the Western Atlantic, Caribbean, and now the Mediterranean is an unintended consequence of laissez-faire regulatory regimes having disproportionate impacts on the ecosystems and economies of poor local inhabitants. International trade and environmental law has been largely ineffective in managing the invasion, leaving jurisdictions and communities most effected to adapt as the ecosystem changes in irreversible ways. In this sense, as Rebecca Bratspies argues, lionfish are an apt metaphor for crises of governance in the era of climate change (2016). They are also, I argue, a metaphor for the transformative impacts of A.I. systems, the drastically unequal distribution of benefits and harms they produce, and the challenges to regulating those systems in ways that recognize and protect the value of diverse socioeconomic, political, and epistemic ecosystems.

3. Regulating at Speed: On Crisis Epistemology and Relational Alternatives

One argument against turning to the invasive species paradigm as a resource for regulating A.I. is that, as indigenous scholars and activists have long argued, the distinction between "native" and "alien" species itself rests on nativist logics both historically and logically bound to discourses of eugenics and racial purity (Wehi et al 2023). Likewise, some scholars have emphasized the anthropocentrism of contemporary discourse on A.I., troubling conceptions of the "human" as itself a Western-colonial product (Wynter 1992), naming the ways that the "human" knowledges A.I. seeks to replicate are in fact a very narrow set of Western, privileged knowledges, and challenging assumptions that human capacities are a useful proxy for intelligence (Vallor 2024).

Instead, in the context of invasive species, indigenous scholars have proposed a relational approach which "honor the complex network of social-environmental relationships" (Wehi et al 2023; see Kimmerer 2020) – and recognize stewardship as the work of protecting these reciprocal relations, including "human and more than human" relations (Whyte 2018). Such arguments challenge environmental and conservationist approaches that seek to preserve the "purity" of an untouched nature, instead honoring a complex web of "human and more than human" relationships as constitutive of the ecosystem in question. This approach holds significant promise in a moment in which A.I. systems, and the transformations they shape, appear to be here to stay, and in which the question becomes not how we protect purely human forms of knowing and agency, but how we adapt in a world in which reliance on and relationships with A.I. is increasingly inevitable.

The relational approach has yielded innovations in environmental law, including frameworks that recognize the standing of environmental entities like the Whanganui River in New Zealand through relationships of stewardship, and those that recognize the standing of all citizens to protect and steward environmental entities (Tanasescu 2017). Accordingly, indigenous scholars and activists have proposed relational regulatory and management structures that focus on relationships and attendant patterns of responsibility, as well as stewarding biodiversity through the development of social institutions that support these relationships and responsibilities (Wehi et al 2023, 1411). As we scramble to adapt our legal frameworks to a new context in which A.I. systems act increasingly autonomously, and in which humans find themselves increasingly imbricated with A.I., either through processes of what Mark Taylor has called "intervolution" (2020), or in emotional relationships, the possibilities of relational regulatory frameworks that recognize us as co-inhabitants in an ecosystem with A.I. will be important resources.

Relational-ecological approaches, moreover, may suggest frames that can shift discourses in the current moment of A.I. radicalization. As AI proponents proselytize a fully automated future, critics are increasingly urgent in their calls for AI regulation and management – sometimes claiming that the threat of A.I. outweighs all other hardships and threat, from disease to climate change (Wong 2025). The urgency on both sides of this debate reflect habits of what Kyle Whyte calls "crisis epistemology", through which claims to "urgency" and "unprecedentedness" are used to justify actions and the implementations of frameworks that run roughshod over moral deliberation and rights, furthering colonial and dominative practices (Whyte 2020). As Whyte argues, crisis epistemology creates contexts in which there is

> "the automatic assumption of imminence. By imminence, I mean the sense that something horribly harmful or inequitable is impending or pressing on the present conditions people understand themselves to be living in. There is a complexity or originality to the imminent events

that suggests the need to immediately become solutions-oriented in a way believed to differ from how solutions were designed and enacted previously." (2020, 3)

This leads to the implementation of urgent actions in which concerns of ethics, rights, and justice can be swept aside, with devastating and destructive impacts. There is little doubt that current moves to regulate and manage A.I. are characterized by such calls to urgency and unprecedentedness – and thus, that a danger of rapid regulation is precisely this kind of crisis epistemology leading to profoundly unethical frameworks.

Given the speed of A.I.'s adaptation and adoption, there are reasons to think this urgency gets something right, and that ecological approaches – which famously call us to "wait another season" (Carson 98, quoted in Code 2006, 46) to better assess both direct and indirect harms – are poorly suited to the moment. As Dennis Hirsch reminds us, environmental law itself adapted, from a command-and-control model necessitated by the urgency of environmental destruction wrought by the Industrial Revolution to more nuanced and reflexive forms of regulation better suited to the rigors and complexity of ecological thinking (2006; Code 2006). If A.I. are emergently invasive in ways that threaten immediate forms of regime change in our economic, educational, and epistemic ecosystems, then there is a case to be made for an immediate push for comprehensive regulation, as the E.U. has done, rather than the largely laissez faire approach the U.S. has taken. The United States's refusal to regulate A.I. has itself been characterized by calls to urgency and unprecedentedness, as well as an assumption of the imminence of a threat of being overtake in the "race to A.I." The urgency implied by such a "race" – and the discourse that positions this "race" within the broader frame of the U.S. facing existential threats from China – produces its own variant of crisis epistemology, in which the federal government justifies the urgent importance of *no* regulation, in order to make way for innovation, no matter how unethical or unjust.

In light of this, democratic deliberation about the project of regulating A.I., as the E.U. has done, is a promising alternative, and it reminds us that comprehensive regulation can nevertheless resist the frames "urgency" attempts to put into place. As Whyte argues, thinking in resistance to such "crisis epistemology" requires the development of what he calls an "epistemology of coordination," which centers relationships – including relationships between the human and "more than human" (2020). The question he poses is what it would look like to move at the speed of relationships, even in moments that seem to require great urgency (2020; Pascoe and Stripling 2024). To do so, Whyte argues, "crisis is interpreted through a deeper history, and traced to the moral bonds of relationships among the diverse beings and entities dwelling together in shared environments" (2020, 7). Relational-ecological approaches go some way towards orienting us in approaching A.I. as co-inhabitants in our shared environment, while providing resources for recognizing when our relationships with it are out of balance, threatening the flourishing of entities and relationships in those environments.

Of course, Whyte's epistemology of coordination assumes that we can draw on "a deeper history", that the kinds of relationships that are constitutive of ecosystems of coordination have long and complex histories of co-habitation. Part of the challenge with A.I. is its very newness, its alien nature, the fact that we do not have long histories on which to draw. A.I. are changing – and are changing our world – so rapidly that it is hard to know how to anchor ourselves in these relationships. This is why, I think, invasive species offer a promising "observational scaffolding" for our contemporary experience: not because of some longed-for ideal of nativist purity, but because we find ourselves in a kind of invasion, wedged into co-habitation with an entity we neither know nor understand, which is transforming our world in ways that fundamentally alter its "essential rules" – with great promise, and great potential for harm.

Works Cited

Alon-Barkat S and Busuioc M, 'Human–AI Interactions in Public Sector Decision Making: "Automation Bias" and "Selective Adherence" to Algorithmic Advice' (2023) 33 *Journal of Public Administration Research and Theory* 153

Alvarado R, 'Opacity, Big Data, Artificial Intelligence and Machine Learning in Democratic Processes' [2020] *Big Data and Democracy* 167

Beckers S, Chockler H and Halpern J, 'A Causal Analysis of Harm' (2022) 35 *Advances in Neural Information Processing Systems* 2365

Benjamin R, *Race After Technology: Abolitionist Tools for the New Jim Code* (John Wiley & Sons 2019)

Bhatia A, 'When A.I.'s Output Is a Threat to A.I. Itself' *The New York Times* (26 August 2024) https://www.nytimes.com/interactive/2024/08/26/upshot/ai-synthetic-data.html accessed 30 August 2024

Bratspies RM, 'Lionfish as a Metaphor for Governance in an Era of Climate Change' (2013) 58 *NYL Sch. L. Rev.* 829

Brynjolfsson E, 'The Turing Trap: The Promise & Peril of Human-like Artificial Intelligence', *Augmented Education in the Global Age* (Routledge 2023)

Cherfas J, 'A Map Of Where Your Food Originated May Surprise You' *NPR* (13 June 2016) https://www.npr.org/sections/thesalt/2016/06/13/481586649/a-map-of-where-your-food-originated-may-surprise-you accessed 9 July 2025

Code L, *Ecological Thinking: The Politics of Epistemic Location* (Oxford University Press 2006)

Couldry N and Mejias UA, 'Data Colonialism: Rethinking Big Data's Relation to the Contemporary Subject' (2019) 20 *Television & New Media* 336

Crooks JA, Soulé ME and Sandlund O, 'Lag Times in Population Explosions of Invasive Species: Causes and Implications' (1999) 24 *Invasive Species and Biodiversity Management* 103

De Almeida PGR, dos Santos CD and Farias JS, 'Artificial Intelligence Regulation: A Framework for Governance' (2021) 23 *Ethics and Information Technology* 505

European Commission, 'White Paper: On Artificial Intelligence: A European Approach to Excellence and Trust' (European Commission 2020) 65 https://commission.europa.eu/system/files/2020-02/commission-white-paper-artificial-intelligence-feb2020_en.pdf accessed 1 July 2025

Ferrario A, Facchini A and Termine A, 'Experts or Authorities? The Strange Case of the Presumed Epistemic Superiority of Artificial Intelligence Systems' (2024) 34 *Minds and Machines* 30

Freiman O, 'AI-Testimony, Conversational AIs and Our Anthropocentric Theory of Testimony' (2024) 38 Social Epistemology 476

Freiman O and Miller B, 'Can Artificial Entities Assert?' [2020] *The Oxford Handbook of Assertion* 415

Grain K, 'We Can Automate Work' (*The Philosophers' Magazine Archive*, 1 April 2018) https://archive.philosophersmag.com/we-can-automate-work/ accessed 2 August 2024

Hacker P, 'Sustainable AI Regulation' (2024) 61 *Common Market Law Review*

Hacker P, Engel A and Mauer M, 'Regulating ChatGPT and Other Large Generative AI Models', *2023 ACM Conference on Fairness Accountability and Transparency* (ACM 2023) https://dl.acm.org/doi/10.1145/3593013.3594067 accessed 8 July 2025

Hicks B and Ling N, 'Carp as Invasive Species', *Biology and Ecology of Carp* (CRC Press)

Hirsch DD, 'Protecting the Inner Environment: What Privacy Regulation Can Learn from Environmental Law' (2006) 41 *Ga. L. Rev.* 1

Hoel E, 'Opinion | A.I.-Generated Garbage Is Polluting Our Culture' *The New York Times* (29 March 2024) https://www.nytimes.com/2024/03/29/opinion/ai-internet-x-youtube.html accessed 20 August 2024

Hsu H, 'What Happens After A.I. Destroys College Writing?' [2025] *The New Yorker* https://www.newyorker.com/magazine/2025/07/07/the-end-of-the-english-paper accessed 9 July 2025

Hulme PE, 'Invasion Pathways at a Crossroad: Policy and Research Challenges for Managing Alien Species Introductions' [2015] *Journal of Applied Ecology* 1418

Johnson R, Crafton RE and Upton HF, 'Invasive Species: Major Laws and the Role of Selected Federal Agencies'

Justo-Hanani R, 'The Politics of Artificial Intelligence Regulation and Governance Reform in the European Union' (2022) 55 *Policy Sciences* 137

Kelly J, 'Jobs AI Will Replace First in the Workplace Shift' [2025] *Forbes* https://www.forbes.com/sites/jackkelly/2025/04/25/the-jobs-that-will-fall-first-as-ai-takes-over-the-workplace/ accessed 8 July 2025

Kimmerer RW, *Braiding Sweetgrass: Indigenous Wisdom, Scientific Knowledge and the Teachings of Plants* (Milkweed Editions 2013)

Malpica-Cruz L, Chaves LCT and Côté IM, 'Managing Marine Invasive Species through Public Participation: Lionfish Derbies as a Case Study' (2016) 74 *Marine Policy* 158

McKittrick K, *Dear Science and Other Stories* (Duke University Press 2020)

Morgan D and Shepardson D, 'U.S. Senate Strikes A.I. Provision from Budget Bill' [2025] *Reuters* https://www.reuters.com/legal/government/us-senate-strikes-ai-regulation-ban-trump-megabill-2025-07-01/ accessed 14 July 2025

Nilsson NJ, 'Human-Level Artificial Intelligence? Be Serious!' (2005) 26 *AI Magazine* 68

Pascoe J and Stripling M, *The Epistemology of Disasters and Social Change: Pandemics, Protests, and Possibilities* (Bloomsbury Publishing PLC 2024)

Petit N and De Cooman J, 'Models of Law and Regulation for AI' [2021] *The Routledge Social Science Handbook of AI* 199

Puzio A, 'Not Relational Enough? Towards an Eco-Relational Approach in Robot Ethics' (2024) 37 *Philosophy & Technology* 45

Simberloff D, Parker IM and Windle PN, 'Introduced Species Policy, Management, and Future Research Needs' (2005) 3 *Frontiers in Ecology and the Environment* 12

Smuha NA, 'From a "Race to AI" to a "Race to AI Regulation": Regulatory Competition for Artificial Intelligence' (2021) 13 *Law, Innovation and Technology* 57

Suleyman M, *The Coming Wave: Technology, Power, and the Twenty-First Century's Greatest Dilemma* (Crown 2023)

Symons J and Alvarado R, 'Epistemic Injustice and Data Science Technologies' (2022) 200 *Synthese* 87

Tanasescu M, 'When a River Is a Person: From Ecuador to New Zealand, Nature Gets Its Day in Court' (*Open Rivers Journal*, 26 October 2017) https://openrivers.lib.umn.edu/article/when-a-river-is-a-person-from-ecuador-to-new-zealand-nature-gets-its-day-in-court/ accessed 11 July 2025

Vitousek PM and others, 'Introduced Species: A Significant Component of Human-Caused Global Change' (1997) 21 *New Zealand Journal of Ecology* 1

Wallace-Wells D, 'Opinion | How Long Will A.I.'s "Slop" Era Last?' *The New York Times* (24 July 2024) https://www.nytimes.com/2024/07/24/opinion/ai-annoying-future.html accessed 20 August 2024

Walsh J, 'Everyone Is Cheating Their Way Through College' [2025] *New York Magazine*

Wehi PM and others, 'Contribution of Indigenous Peoples' Understandings and Relational Frameworks to Invasive Alien Species Management' (2023) 5 *People and Nature* 1403

Whyte K, 'Against Crisis Epistemology' (*Social Science Research Network*, 21 July 2021) https://papers.ssrn.com/abstract=3891125 accessed 11 July 2025

Whyte K, Caldwell C and Schaefer M, 'Indigenous Lessons about Sustainability Are Not Just for "All Humanity."' (2018) 149 *Sustainability: Approaches to Environmental Justice and Social Power*

Widder DG and Nafus D, 'Dislocated Accountabilities in the "AI Supply Chain": Modularity and Developers' Notions of Responsibility' (2023) 10 *Big Data & Society* 20539517231177620

Wong M, 'The AI Industry Is Radicalizing' (*The Atlantic*, 8 July 2025) https://www.theatlantic.com/technology/archive/2025/07/ai-radicalization-civil-war/683460/ accessed 11 July 2025

Writer SLE, 'How Scammers Are Using AI to Steal College Financial Aid' (*Los Angeles Times*, 17 June 2025) https://www.latimes.com/california/story/2025-06-17/how-scammers-are-using-ai-to-steal-college-financial-aid accessed 8 July 2025

Wynter S, 'Unsettling the Coloniality of Being/Power/Truth/Freedom: Towards the Human, after Man, Its Overrepresentation—An Argument' (2003) 3 *CR: The New Centennial Review* 257

V.
International and Transnational Law

Universal Jurisdiction in the Absence of a World State: The Legitimacy of International Criminal Law

Win-chiat Lee

Abstract

I argue that theorizing about International Criminal Law is primarily a normative and philosophical enterprise. This is in part because there is very little by way of facts about the practice in this area of law that is not to be contested. The most central issue concerns universal jurisdiction. It is my contention that universal jurisdiction is essential to international criminal law. While it is controversial, I argue that universal jurisdiction can be justified. But we must admit that the exercise of universal jurisdiction by different states and other entities does not make for a consistent and systematic approach to justice and forestalling impunity. But that may be the best we can do unless we are willing to enter a world-state, which may be even less desirable and riskier from the point of view of justice.

I. Introduction

Legal theory typically involves both descriptive and normative elements. There is a descriptive element because for a particular type of law, such as contract law, to be explained and accounted for, there are facts about an existing practice of a particular legal system that is the subject matter of that body of law. There is also a normative element because legal theory is also to provide a justificatory, evaluative, and critical perspective on the legal practice at hand so as to explain why it is binding on those to whom it applies. Philosophers such as Ronald Dworkin, using what he calls the interpretive approach in legal theorizing, do not think the two can be easily separated.[1] To get the facts about a legal practice correct is in part to be able to cast such facts in good justificatory light. The pre-theoretical description of facts on this approach, however, also acts as a control on the normative/justificatory aspect of legal theory. A theory, no matter how

1 Ronald Dworkin, *Law's Empire* (Cambridge MA: Harvard University Press, 1986).

appealing and plausible as a justification for a legal practice, cannot really be a theory about *that* practice if it fails to bear out a significant portion of the practice as part of the practice. This is what Dworkin calls "the threshold of fit" that a legal theory must cross to qualify as an interpretive account of a practice.

In my view, International Criminal Law (ICL) is an exception and not quite open to this way of legal theorizing. This is because for ICL, there is almost nothing on the descriptive side of things that is not uncontroversial or indisputable and can serve as the facts about the practice that any theory of ICL must be able to "fit" in its account.[2] To answer the question, what ICL is, there is precious little, if any at all, that either can be said without being open to some kind of dispute or skeptical challenge or is not in the process of evolving. Even the law as enforced by the International Criminal Court (ICC) which is established by the Rome Statute – a treaty signed by 137 states and fully ratified by 125– can be disputed as ICL. In part the challenge comes from the fact that the ICC regime is primarily based on voluntary subscription and is *universal* neither in its prescription nor in its enforcement of what counts as a crime under its jurisdiction. In what way can the law under the ICC regime count as *international* criminal law if it is neither universal in its prescription nor universal in its enforcement?

Therefore, it should be clear that theorizing about ICL primarily involves dealing with the normative aspect of the law, most fundamentally concerning its legitimacy. Doubts raised about the legitimacy of international criminal law (ICL) go beyond those concerning international law in general. If we think, as I argue in this chapter, that what makes criminalization by ICL international is its universality, then it is that universality, both in prescription and in enforcement, that needs to be shown to be legitimate, in the face of a general recognition of the equal sovereignty of states in the international arena. In the light of an account of the legitimacy of ICL, then we can give an account of what the practice of ICL should be. This is doing philosophy and particularly political philosophy.

This chapter will be focused on the principle of universality, or what is often referred to as "universal jurisdiction" as one of the three major

2 Dworkin writes, "[Someone interpreting something] needs assumptions or convictions about what counts as part of the practice in order to define the raw data of his interpretation…[T]he interpretive attitude cannot survive unless members of the same interpretive community share at least roughly the same assumptions about this." *Law's Empire*, 67. It is plausible to claim that "the raw data" may also be controversial in ICL.

principles of criminal jurisdiction in international law.[3] This is because universality is what is distinctive, but also highly controversial in ICL. I shall begin in Section II with an account of universal jurisdiction and distinguish between two ways of arriving at universal jurisdiction. I argue that the universal jurisdiction associated with piracy in traditional admiralty law is not really universal jurisdiction -- not in the fundamental way -- and, at any rate, cannot be used to understand the universal jurisdiction associated with modern international crimes. In Section III, to achieve the universality we need for ICL, I argue that we need to return to the idea of natural law or natural justice, albeit in a minimal way. What needs to be accounted for is why the return to natural justice in a world filled with sovereign states exercising their political authority to make laws for their territories and their nationals. An account is given in this section of the nature of international crimes to show that the commission of these crimes will re-create the kind of condition that requires a partial reversion back to the state of nature (in a minimal sense). This partial reversion back to the state of nature will allow universal jurisdiction to be exercised by any state or international entity, and indeed anyone, if capable, to hold the violators accountable for their violations. This, as I shall argue, is really nothing more than the natural jurisdiction that, in the view of modern political philosophers like John Locke, each and every one of us has as the executor of natural law in the state of nature.

The partial reversion back to the state of nature where states or any other entity exercising universal jurisdiction is the situation in which we find ourselves in the legitimate enforcement of ICL. Like the state of nature before we have states, this state of nature has many undesirable aspects. At the very least, the enforcement of justice in that situation is subjective, chaotic, and inconsistent. These features, as I argue in Section IV, will render the enforcement of ICL in this reversion to the state of nature highly problematic and quite dubious as to its claim to be delivering justice. Standardization and codification of the ICL and its enforcement through a central political authority would be the needed solution. But that would require us to enter a world state just as entering the state in general is the

3 The principle of universality is better known as the principle of universal jurisdiction, which is a principle of criminal jurisdiction in International Law. It is important to note that this is both a principle of jurisdiction for both prescription and enforcement, as universal jurisdiction is defined as the jurisdiction that any state may claim over a crime solely because of the *nature* of the crime. However, in most, including my current discussion of universal jurisdiction, it refers to the enforcement aspect.

solution to similar problems in the state of nature. Perhaps for very good reasons, we are reluctant to enter a world state. Is there any alternative way to regulate the exercise of universal jurisdiction in enforcing ICL short of entering a world state? This is what I examine in Section V. Perhaps an international entity, similar to the ICC, i.e., voluntary and without universal membership, but different from ICC, i.e., with claims to universal jurisdiction, is the best we can hope for to achieve some kind of consistency and orderliness in the application of ICL.

II. Universal Jurisdiction

The most serious doubts about ICL concern jurisdiction. If we think of ICL as fundamentally involving the exercise of universal jurisdiction, then where the problem lies is clear. Universal jurisdiction is the jurisdiction that any state can claim over a crime simply because of the nature of the crime (to be specified) regardless of whether the alleged crime is committed on that state's territory (the principle of territoriality) or whether the alleged perpetrator or the victim of the crime is one of that state's nationals (the principle of personality, passive or active). Conceived in this way, part of ICL is to specify which crimes are subject to universal jurisdiction. In this regard, universal jurisdiction has a prescriptive element as well.

There are two questions to be addressed. First, does ICL necessarily involve the exercise of universal jurisdiction? Second, can the exercise of universal jurisdiction be justified? I will address the second question extensively in the following. My initial response to the first question is that the exercise of universal jurisdiction is what makes ICL distinctive and not merely an extension of municipal criminal law. I hope this point will become clear in the following discussion. In any case, as will be clear in the following discussion also, the two questions cannot really be considered separately.

The principle of universal jurisdiction is problematic because it seems to be inconsistent with, broadly speaking, the Westphalian conception of equal sovereign states. More specifically, on this conception, the international arena consists of geographically non-overlapping territorial states with well-defined boundaries which also delineate the scope of their legitimate political authority (sovereignty). On this conception, a state's political authority on its territory is exclusive in the sense that it monopolizes the use of force on that territory, -- such as in the enforcement of law – to the exclusion of all others, including other states, from doing the same on that territory.

It is important to understand this properly. When a state is exercising legitimate political authority as a territorial state, it may exclude others from the use of force on its territory. But that is not equivalent to not having any other states or entities claiming some jurisdiction over the same territory. As we know, modern states' political authority is not merely territorial; they also exercise authority over their members, i.e., their nationals, even when they are not present on their territories. This is what amounts to the aforementioned principle of personality in criminal jurisdiction. However, it is important to note that even though the principle of personality (and perhaps a few other jurisdictional principles mostly connected to a state's interests) affords some extra-territorial jurisdiction, such extra-territorial jurisdiction is quite limited and may be subordinate to the territorial state's own territorial jurisdiction even when it applies. More important, even when a state exercises its jurisdiction over nationals present on another state's territory, it still needs to respect the latter's exclusive use of force on its territory. This can be achieved by either making extradition requests or obtaining permission from the territorial state to apprehend suspects on its territory.

It is, however, important to note that even though the principle of universal jurisdiction expands significantly the claims of extraterritorial jurisdiction, its application may still be limited unless the claims of extraterritorial jurisdiction can also override a state's claim to territorial sovereignty, i.e., its claim to exclusive enforcement within its territory. The easiest case of exercising universal jurisdiction would be for the territorial state on which the accused is present to voluntarily give up the accused to the state exercising universal jurisdiction through honoring an extradition request or some other kind of consent. Otherwise, the state would have to rely on opportunities such as when the accused happens to be on its territory or on the territory of a third-party state that would cooperate with an extradition request. Even when, as I will argue later, the exercise of universal jurisdiction may justify the violation of another state's territorial sovereignty in apprehending the accused for prosecution, it may not be the best policy for any state to do so, with the possible exception in the case of a failed state which has reached the state of anarchy.

There are two different ways of understanding the source of ICL – in fact two different kinds of ICL. One involves the exercise of universal jurisdiction and the other does not. If in fact one thinks that the exercise of universal jurisdiction is essential to ICL, then there is, strictly speaking, only one kind of ICL. Interestingly, this would imply that what the ICC enforces, strictly speaking, is not really ICL for the simple reason that the ICC does not exercise universal jurisdiction.

Universal jurisdiction is the jurisdiction exercised by a state or any other entity over a crime solely because of the nature of the crime, as we have defined earlier. Thus, if the jurisdiction a state or any other entity exercises over a crime is the result of its connection to the crime or if that jurisdiction is transferred to it by a state that has such connections to the crime, then the jurisdiction it exercises is not universal. When France becomes a signatory state of the Rome Statute and as a result hands over some of its jurisdiction over certain crimes to the ICC, the jurisdiction ICC exercises over those crimes committed in France or by or against French nationals is therefore not universal because France has jurisdiction over these crimes which it has handed over to the ICC. If all jurisdiction over international crimes exercised by the ICC is the result of such transfers of territorial or personality jurisdiction by its members, i.e., the signatories of the Rome Statute, none of which is universal, then the ICC does not exercise any universal jurisdiction either. Understood in this way, the ICC's authority is perfectly compatible with state sovereignty under the Westphalian conception.

However, things are more complicated than this. There is also the possibility of referrals by the United Nations Security Council to the ICC for investigation and prosecution of cases that involve states that are not signatories of the Rome Statute. Although such referrals are rare, due to the exercise of veto by the five permanent members of the Security Council, where they are successful, they do not amount to the ICC's exercising universal jurisdiction either because it is arguable that the UN Security Council's authority is over international and regional security and not crimes.[4] It is therefore clear that ICC does not exercise universal jurisdiction and in fact never claims to be doing so.

4 In 2005, for example, the UN Security Council referred the situation in Dafur, Sudan to the ICC for investigation and possible prosecution of the commission of War Crimes, Crimes Against Humanity, Genocide etc., with Sudan not being a signatory state of the Rome Statute. UN Security Councial Resolution 1593, which made the referral, invoked UN's authority under Chapter VII of the UN Charter to deal with threats to peace and security, and not any claim of criminal jurisdiction over the international crimes committed by non-signatory states of the Rome Statute. For the text of the UN Security Council press release, see https://press.un.org/en/2005/sc8351.doc.htm.

The most-often cited historical example of universal jurisdiction is the jurisdiction over piracy in traditional admiralty or maritime law. It has been a traditional practice in international law, going back hundreds of years and even to antiquity, that any state can grab pirates from the high seas, i.e, international waters in modern terminology, and put them on trial even if it is not its ships or nationals who have been robbed or attacked by those particular pirates. One can easily understand why it is in the interest of every state to have piracy subject to universal jurisdiction, insofar as it has any of its vessels sailing the high seas. That is the reason why pirates are considered the enemy of humankind (*hostis humani generis*). For the sake of efficient and effective suppression of piracy and enhancing safety on the high seas, why would any state object to the exercise of universal jurisdiction by any other state to capture pirates from the high seas?

It is not that no one has any other kind of jurisdiction over pirates because, by definition, piracy takes place on the high seas which are not the territory of any particular state. The vessels the pirates attack, however, belong to some nations and are their territories by extension. The people the pirates attack are also nationals of some states. Therefore, the crimes committed by pirates on the high seas are not outside the standard jurisdictional reach of states, theoretically speaking. In practice, however, precisely because piracy takes place on the high seas, it is also extremely difficult for any state to have its law enforcement in the right place at the right time to exercise its jurisdiction and apprehend the pirates who attack its vessels or its nationals. It is more efficient and effective to suppress piracy if any state can apprehend pirates to put them on trial simply because it happens to be in the vicinity, without necessarily having its own vessels or nationals attacked by these pirates. It is therefore in the states' rational self-interest to give up their own jurisdiction over their own vessels and their own nationals and allow each other to exercise it. This creates what I call a "jurisdiction pool" that is the source of the universal jurisdiction associated with piracy.[5]

It is easy to see that this kind of universal jurisdiction should be uncontroversial and can easily be made compatible with respect for the equal

5 See my discussion in the section, "Is Piracy an International Crime?" in the Chapter, "International Crimes and Universal Jurisdiction," in Larry May and Zachary Hoskins (eds.) *International Criminal Law and Philosophy* (New York, NY: Cambridge University Pres 2010), 22-28. I introduce the concept of "jurisdiction pool," also in this chapter, 28-29.

sovereignty of states. It is difficult to see why states would object to this kind of arrangement from an entirely self-interested point of view. If there is to be a proposal to make this kind of arrangement an international agreement, states will gladly sign on to it, especially considering that traditional international law against piracy does not include privateering, i.e., pirate-like operations that are under the employ of or sponsorship by a state. Even without an actual treaty among all states authorizing such universal jurisdiction, one can still presuppose hypothetical consent by states. Such hypothetical consent would not need to load up the counterfactual antecedent with moral or other normative considerations than just "if they were rationally self-interested..."[6] With this account, universal jurisdiction as applied to piracy is quite compatible with the equal sovereignty of territorial states.

Things are quite different, however, when it comes to the universal jurisdiction associated with ICL. ICL criminalizes acts such as crimes against humanity, genocide, torture, disappearance of persons, slavery etc. Unlike piracy, we cannot presuppose that it is in the universal rational self-interest of all states to facilitate the effective and efficient suppression of these crimes. After all, the parties engaged in the commission of these crimes are typically states or state-like entities themselves.

In exercising their sovereign political authority, however, states, if they are interested in the suppression of these international crimes committed on their territory or by or against their nationals, can agree to hand over their territorial and personality jurisdiction and join forces with other like-minded sovereign states to form a "jurisdiction pool" for each other or for an international body to exercise. This is precisely what transpires in the creation of the ICC by the Rome Statute. It is important to note that the jurisdiction pool created for the ICC in this way does not amount to universal jurisdiction for the obvious reason that some states are not parties to the Rome Statute and therefore have not agreed to participate in the jurisdiction pool.

---

6 The ICL jurist and scholar, Antonio Cassese, also argues that there is at best joint interest, but not community values involved in the agreement to suppress piracy universally. This is similar to the distinction I am referring to. For Cassese, community values are human rights and humanitarian considerations "laid down" in international instruments such as the UN Charter and the Universal Declaration of Human rights. See Antonio Cassese, *International Criminal Law* (New York, NY: 2003), 23. My view, however, as will be made clear later, relies less fundamentally, but more derivatively on the importance of the "international instruments" to identify the community values.

It will also be difficult to make the same kind of hypothetical consent argument without resorting to moral considerations, as we do for the universal jurisdiction in relation to piracy, because it cannot be assumed that it is in every state's rational self-interest or perceived by every state to be in its interest to see the suppression of or forestall the impunity for such crimes, as evidenced by the fact that an actual treaty was offered and not every state has signed on to it or has ratified it even if it has signed on to it.

Thus, the conventional approach to ICL or the establishment of ICL by treaties have failed to establish the universality of ICL both in its application as well as its enforcement. One might find the lack of universality to be the reason to reject what is established by the Rome Statute and enforced by the ICC to be truly *International* Criminal Law. To justify the universal applicability and enforceability of ICL, a different approach is needed. I propose that some kind of "naturalist" approach is needed. By that I mean a very minimalist use of the idea of natural law, which involves the use of reason to see that something is wrong -- not only wrong, but wrong in a way that those who commit it can be held criminally liable. One might reject this notion of appealing to reason as too subjective. This is where conventions can be helpful, not as grounds, but as evidence for the universality of the ICL norms.[7] We may have no other *evidence* for their objectivity and basis in reason than the fact that the treaties or conventions against international crimes, such as genocide or torture, are subscribed to by an overwhelming majority of states. This is not to treat conventions and treaties as constitutive of the universality of ICL norms. Treating the majority consensus as evidentiary may still allow us to apply the ICL norms universally even when we lack universal consensus.

III. ICL and Natural Justice

In English Common Law, there is an old distinction between two kinds of crimes – *mala in se* as opposed to *mala prohibita*.[8] The distinction

7 This distinction between gronds and evidence is important for understadning my use of treaties and conventions in the remaining parts of the paper, as well as my disagreement with Cassese in the preceding footnote.

8 I have used this distinction to discuss international crimes and their relation to human rights violation in Win-chiat Lee, "International Crimes and Human Rights," in Borhan Uddin Khan and Md Jahid Hossain Bhuiyan (ed.) *Human Rights and International Criminal Law (*Leiden, the Netherlands: Brill, 2022), 3-22, esp. 10-12.

primarily has to do with the question of whether we need to invoke facts about an act being prohibited by law to understand its wrongness or being a crime. Some acts, such as homicide, can be known to be wrong and should be criminalized without invoking the fact that they are prohibited by law, whereas some acts, such as the carrying of concealed firearms in public, if criminalized, can only be understood to be so by referring to the fact that it is prohibited by law in the relevant jurisdiction. There may not be anything inherently wrong with the latter class of crimes; it is the prohibition by law that makes them so. While the former class of crimes, i.e., *mala in se*, might not rely on their prohibition for them to be crimes, it may still be important to the law to recognize them as crimes and to spell out the finer distinctions and standards to be applied with them, which may be partly conventional. That is part of the function of the state in exercising its political authority to criminalize certain acts by law even if they are *mala in se*.

It is my contention that international crimes, i.e., acts that are criminalized in ICL, would have to be *mala in se* because they are universally applicable. After all, universal jurisdiction is based on the idea that it is the *nature* of certain crimes that gives any state the jurisdiction over them. If they were *mala prohibita*, then they might or might not be universally applicable depending on whether they are prohibited by law by all states. This would require that there be conventions or treaties prohibiting such acts that are universally accepted or agreed to by states and adopted as law by each of them. As *mala in se*, however, international crimes can still use some clarifications and standardization by international treaties and conventions, but their normative force does not fundamentally rely on these international legal instruments and, in that sense, depends on its nature.[9]

We have not yet fully characterized international crimes by simply identifying them as *mala in se* for the obvious reason that not all *mala in se* are international crimes. Some are or should be made into merely domestic or municipal crimes. What is it, then, that makes some acts mere domestic crimes and others to rise to the level of international crimes? In my view, it is not their level of egregiousness or wrongness. Nor is it the case that international crimes are atrocities that "shocks the conscience of civilized society." It is not the case that international crimes are committed across

9 It is important to keep in mind that there are such things as *jus cogens* norms in international law that cannot be set aside by domestic law-making or international treaties.

national boundaries, which are often referred to as "transnational" crimes instead. International crimes such as crimes against humanity, genocide, and torture are often committed well within the boundaries of one state. If we do not adopt a conventionalist account of international crimes, then it is not the case that certain crimes are international crimes only because states *happen* to agree to treat them as crimes for all of them. There must be something about certain crimes, i.e., something about their *nature,* that make them more suitable to be criminalized internationally (i.e., universally) than domestically.

More importantly, in addition to their universal applicability as criminal norms, there is another aspect of universality associated with international crimes, namely, the exercise of universal jurisdiction in enforcement. As mentioned earlier, universal jurisdiction is the jurisdiction over a crime any state can claim simply because of the nature of the crime and not because it is committed on its territory or committed by or against any of its nationals. In arguing that international crimes are *mala in se,* one will still need to point out what that special *nature* about certain *mala in se* is which makes them subject to universal jurisdiction in enforcement. We certainly do not want to think that all *mala in se* should be subject to the exercise of universal jurisdiction in enforcement.

Another thing to keep in mind in giving an account of ICL is that its main purpose is to forestall impunity for (certain) heinous crimes. What this points to is that international crimes are the kind of crimes that would tend not to be prosecuted and agents for such crimes would tend to escape accountability if there were no ICL and no universal jurisdiction associated with it.[10]

---

10 Jiewuh Song aptly coins the term "enforcement gaps" to refer to the problem of impunity in international law. In her argument, universal jurisdiction is important to serve the function of "gap-filling" in enforcing certain international criminal norms. That account applies to both piracy and contemporary international crimes, such as crimes against humanity, genocide etc. See Song, "Pirates and Torturers: Universal Jurisdiction as Enforcement Gap-Filling", *The Journal of Political Philosophy, 23:4 (2015),* 471-490, esp. Section III, 480-486. While I agree with Song that universal jurisdiction serves this function of gap-filling in the case of certain international criminal norms, the source of the *legitimacy* of the universal jurisdiction in modern ICL is different from that in traditional anti-piracy law in my view. For a discussion of the difference between Song's view and mine, see Jovana Davidovic, "Universal Jurisdiction and International Criminal Law," in C. Flanders and Z. Hoskins (eds.) *The New Philosophy of Criminal Law* (London UK: Rowman and Littlefield International, 2016), 113-130, esp. 120-123.

What is distinctive about international crimes, in my view, is that they primarily involve acts of harm committed by state actors or agents against their citizens or others on their territory.[11] Such acts can also be acts condoned or even encouraged by the state even if not committed by state agents. In other cases, it can be that the territorial state is a failed or failing state and cannot act in such a way to bring parties committing such crimes to account. They may also be committed by the feuding parties in the context of a civil war in which they all act like state parties. One can see that typically crimes such as crimes against humanity, genocide, torture, and disappearance of persons fit this description of the situations under which they are committed quite well. If these crimes were not criminalized universally and subject to the exercise of universal jurisdiction, we can see how the impunity for these crimes would follow.

Once a territorial state engages in perpetrating serious harms against its citizens and others on its territory or, as a failed state, fails to provide the protection of them against such harms and to hold the perpetrators to account for the serious harms against its citizens and others on its territory, it has undermined its legitimacy as a political state. As a result, it can no longer claim monopoly in enforcement and thereby exclude others from enforcement. Others may now legitimately claim jurisdiction over the crimes the accountability for which the territorial state may not be able to effectuate either because it is the perpetrating party or, as a failed state, it does not have the ability to do so.

However, this does not fully account for the justification of the exercise of universal jurisdiction over international crimes. If other parties outside of a territorial state's territory never have any jurisdiction over any crimes committed on the territory to begin with, they still would not have jurisdiction even if the territorial state has to relinquish its exclusivity in the enforcement of law. That is, other states must have jurisdiction over these crimes which they are prevented from exercising when there is a legitimate political authority exercising exclusionary enforcement over a territory. Once the legitimacy of that political authority is lost or at least compromised and the territorial state can no longer claim exclusivity over the enforcement of law on that territory, others' jurisdiction over certain crime can now return, be reasserted and be "restored" to that territory as a result. Criminal jurisdiction is a right to enforce. It is important to note

11 I develop this account of international crimes in Lee, "International Crimes and Universal Jurisdiction," 28-34.

that such a right can be a liberty right in the Hohfeldian sense, i.e., it is a privilege or permission, that does not imply duties on the part of others to interfere with its exercise.

What can account for the existence of such a jurisdiction? From what I have discussed, it is a jurisdiction that exists prior to the existence of territorial states whose legitimacy has preempted such jurisdiction from being exercised. Such jurisdiction must therefore exist prior to the existence of states. In political philosophy, that state of affairs is often referred to as "the state of nature." While that term may carry with it theoretical baggage, we can use it, again, in a minimal sense to refer to the logical possibility of a state of affairs where there are no territorial political states wielding political authority to enforce laws exclusively on their territory. Would such a state of affairs, i.e., the state of nature, have laws that apply to it? Traditional natural law theory claims that there are and refer to them as natural law. Again, for our present purposes, we need only subscribe to a minimum sense of such natural law to refer to the fact that there are moral norms that govern people's relation with one another even if they are not subject to the positive laws as members of political states.

However, not all such moral norms can be considered natural *law*. As John Locke, the Early Modern British philosopher, puts it, it would not make sense for natural law to be *law* if it can be violated with impunity. Someone must therefore have jurisdiction as executor of the natural law over its violation. Since the state of nature is a state of equality among individuals in the sense that no one has political dominance, i.e., political authority, over another, if anyone has jurisdiction as executor of the natural law, then everyone will have the same.[12] Let us call this the "natural jurisdiction". It is quite clear that given Locke's argument, this jurisdiction is universal.

It would not make sense to treat all moral norms as *law* in the Lockean sense as explained in the above. If any of them is enforceable and the violator of which should be held to account, it would be the moral

12 In *Second Treatise of Government*, Locke writes, "...the law of nature would, as all other laws that concern men in this world, be in vain if there were nobody that, in the state of nature, had a power to execute that law, and thereby preserve the innocent and restrain offenders. And if any one in the state of nature may punish another for any evil he has done, every one may do so. For in that state of perfect equality, where there is no superiority or jurisdiction of one over another, what any may do in prosecution of the law, every one must needs have a right to do." John Locke, *Second Treatise*, II 7.

norms that prohibit harm committed against a person -- in her life, bodily integrity, and liberty. This is the kind of moral wrongness that is subject to the natural jurisdiction of all human beings. Much needs to be explained, specified, and elaborated on the kind of harm committed against a person and how to exercise the natural jurisdiction to hold the perpetrators of this kind of harm to account.[13] For our purposes, it is sufficient to note that this is what I argue to be the source of international criminal law that is not conventional. On this account, international crimes are universal as *mala in se* and subject to universal jurisdiction. This is the *default* situation that we revert to when a territorial state compromises or loses entirely its legitimacy as political authority in exercising exclusive jurisdiction over its territory. Natural jurisdiction returns where the territorial state may no longer legitimately exclude others from exercising it on its territory.

If this account is correct, we can see that the universal jurisdiction associated with modern international crimes is quite different in its origin than that associated with piracy. The latter has to do with piecing together the jurisdiction that each territorial state has in forming a jurisdiction pool for each other to help itself to in apprehending pirates on the high seas. The universal jurisdiction associated with modern international crimes is a jurisdiction that is more fundamentally universal, i.e., a jurisdiction that all individual human beings have against one another and is excluded or preempted from being exercised when a legitimate political authority is operating on a certain territory and exercising its jurisdiction over it.

It is important to examine the specific international crimes to bear out my claim that they are primarily committed by the state against its citizens or condoned by it when they are committed by others against its citizens. The test would be that if similar acts of harm were committed without the agency, sponsorship, or acquiescence of the state, we would not consider them to be international crimes. Crimes against humanity, genocide, torture, disappearance of persons, for example, will not be international crimes if they are committed by some citizens against others without the participation of the state. Even the attack on a population or the attempt to eliminate members of a group *en masse* because of their membership in that group by private individuals will count only as hate crimes, no matter

13 I have argued for some ethical principles in the exercise of natural jurisdiction in Win-chiat Lee, "Ethical Vigilantism and Natural Justice: Outline for a Theory of International Criminal Law" in Gordon A. Babst and Win-chiat Lee (eds.), *Contemporary Aspects of Injustice* (Switzerland: Springer, 2025), 135-150.

how egregious they are, and not rise to the level of international crimes without the participation of the state in some ways. In such cases, the state can claim exclusive jurisdiction over such cases. However, if the state is unable or unwilling to prosecute such cases, i.e. to assert their territorial jurisdiction over such egregious crimes, then it would be appropriate for others, including states, to assert their universal jurisdiction over them.

War crimes might be more difficult to account for as international crimes along the line we have suggested because they often involve more than one state, with atrocities perpetrated by one state against the citizens of another state and not by a state against its own citizens. The state whose citizens are the victims of war crimes committed by another state in a war that occurs on the former's territory will have territorial jurisdiction over such crimes. There will be relevant territorial jurisdiction to be used to prosecute the perpetrators of war crimes and hold them to account. Unfortunately, in wars, the state which has territorial jurisdiction over war crimes might be the loser in the war or be weakened to the extent that it is unable to prosecute such crimes during or after the war. Therefore, we have a situation where it is not the case that the territorial state lacks legitimate jurisdiction, but rather it lacks the capacity to exercise jurisdiction. There may also be cases in which war crimes are committed against members of an entity that is not a state, thus lacking the jurisdiction (or the capacity) a state would have to prosecute such cases. In all these cases, because there is the lack of an effective legitimate territorial jurisdiction being asserted to keep out the exercise of a natural universal jurisdiction, the latter can be reasserted by default. This is how the impunity for war crimes and other atrocities committed in a war can be minimized.

War crimes and other atrocities are committed not only in wars between states. They often are also perpetrated in a civil war where a formerly unified state is now segmented as feuding factions fighting against each other for dominance or independence. War crimes and other harm can be perpetrated against the territory's civilian population. If in a civil war, there is still a state standing wielding legitimate political authority, then we do not have a difficult or different situation than the standard one we have been discussing. If the state perpetrates war crimes or other harm against its civilian population, then the crimes committed are international and universal jurisdiction may justifiably be exercised over them. If war crimes or other harm committed against the civilian population are perpetrated by a non-state warring party, then the situation is also quite standard. These crimes are domestic and not international because they are subject to the territorial jurisdiction of the legitimate state left standing. However, things are different if the legitimate state in the situation is unable or unwilling to bring the perpetrators of such crimes to account during or after the civil war, then we have a situation that is not all that different from a failed state. Such crimes could then be considered international crimes subject to universal jurisdiction. However, if the state in the territory has collapsed in a civil war or can no longer be considered to be wielding legitimate political authority, then we have a situation of more than one warring party, all of which might act like a state, but none of which has legitimacy as a state. I would argue that the relevant territory is now a state of anarchy in which no party really has the legitimate political authority to ward off the exercise of universal jurisdiction from the outside to hold the violators of natural law to account. Clearly the harm perpetrated against individuals in that situation of anarchy can be considered international crimes.

It is time to take stock of what I have argued for in this account of international criminal law. I begin with the argument that ICL must be universal. There are two aspects to this universality. 1) There are some acts that must be criminalized universally. 2) The perpetration of such crimes is subject to enforcement by universal jurisdiction. Why must ICL be universal? Without universality, there remains the possibility of impunity for serious harm perpetrated against individuals. The world as we know it is divided into geographically discrete political entities that are territorial states. Ideally, if all the territorial states serve their legitimate functions properly, exercise their exclusive territorial (perhaps with the help of a few other limited extra-territorial) jurisdiction, and hold perpetrators of harm against individuals to account effectively, then we do not have any role for ICL to play and hence we do not need ICL. Unfortunately, the real world is not ideal. Impunity for serious harm becomes real possibilities when a territorial state itself is engaged in the perpetration of such harm or has become so dysfunctional that it can no longer exercise its jurisdiction to bring the perpetrators of such serious harm to account. ICL becomes necessary to fill the gapping holes that leave room for impunity.

IV. The Perils of Exercising Universal Jurisdiction without a World State

Given the above account of exercising universal jurisdiction in ICLas similar to exercising natural jurisdiction in the state of nature, it is understandable why the contemporary American legal philosopher David Luban advocates what he calls the "bootstrapping" approach in international criminal law.[14] The example Luban focuses on is the Nuremberg Trial of Nazi officials for Crimes Against Humanity by the International Military Tribunal (IMT). The IMT was constituted by the Allied Forces after WWII specifically to hold high Nazi officials to account. It lacked certain standard jurisdictions presumably, especially in the cases involving Crimes Against Humanity committed against German nationals on German soil, not to mention that Crimes Against Humanity was not a crime in the books either domestically in German law or in international law. In Luban's view, natural justice is ultimately what prosecutions of international crimes, such as the ones in Nuremberg Trial, must rely on and the jurisdiction entities such as the IMT can claim in this kind of situation is universal jurisdiction. By committing Crimes Against Humanity against their own citizens, what the Nazis had done was to create a vacuum of legitimate political authority, which, on my account, is equivalent to the state of nature. Luban considers such exercise of universal jurisdiction akin to "vigilante jurisdiction," which, on my account, is the natural jurisdiction anyone of us has in the state of nature.[15]

To ensure that we are not only replacing one situation of lawlessness or one kind of lawlessness with another, Luban suggests that entities exercising universal jurisdiction, such as the IMT, to hold the violators of international crimes to account, "bootstrapped" themselves into legitimacy by delivering the highest quality of justice possible, including the use of impeccable due process. On this view, the exercise of universal jurisdiction to enforce natural justice can *self-legitimate* simply by delivering justice as much as possible and not every entity or state or tribunal is up to that job.

Luban's view is attractive because there may not be other ways to legitimize the exercise of universal jurisdiction, as I have argued in the above. No doubt there are epistemic problems with the bootstrapping approach

---

14 Luban writes, "Tribunals bootstrap themselves into legitimacy by the quality of justice they deliver; their rightness depends on their fairness." In David Luban, "Fairness to Rightness: Jurisdiction, Legality and the Legitimacy of International Criminal Law", in S. Besson and J. Tasioulas J (eds.) *The Philosophy of International Law* (New York: Oxford University Press, 2010), 579.

15 For Luban's invocation of vigilante jurisdiction and introduction of universal jurisdiction through "the back door", see David Luban, "A Theory of Crimes Against Humanity," *Yale Journal of International Law 29* (2004), 140-146. Luban's authority for the natural right to punish is Grotius instead of (as in my argument) Locke.

because of its reliance on the confidence of the state or any other entity exercising jurisdiction in its judgment of what natural justice requires.[16] There will always be disagreements and skepticism expressed by some states or agencies about the quality of justice delivered in a particular situation. Even the judgment and approach taken by the IMT are not beyond reproach.[17] But that may be the best we can do. Universal consensus in the international community that justice has been delivered in a particular exercise of universal jurisdiction may be hard to come by. A relatively broad-based consensus in the international community may be all that we can hope for to mitigate any criticism that the judgment that natural justice delivered in a particular exercise of universal jurisdiction is subjective. But given the contentious nature of most international criminal cases, even a relatively broad-cased consensus may be hard to come by.

A more serious problem facing Luban's "bootstrapping" approach to prosecute international crimes is the failure to deliver justice systematically. It is important to note that the systematicity we are talking about is only relative. Even the prosecution of domestic crimes within a state to hold perpetrators accountable might involve gaps and inconsistencies. Generally, we do expect similar domestic crimes to be equally prosecuted when discovered. But Luban's bootstrapping approach only deals with how to legitimize the use of universal jurisdiction in a single case where a state or an international entity happens to prosecute the perpetrator of an international crime in that case. It at best prevents impunity in that case. There is no requirement that a state or any other entity step forward and exercise universal jurisdiction where similar or other international crimes are known to have been committed. Nor is there any requirement for an or-

16 Similar problems arise with what is known as the Radbruch's Formula as proposed by Gustav Radbruch after WWII to deal with the question of whether judges could be held accountable for applying unjust laws that were "legally correct" under the Nazi Regime. Radbruch's Formula allows for overriding positive statutes with consideration of justice only if the conflict reaches an extreme and intolerable level. While Radbruch's concerns might also lie elsewhere, clearly in the cases of intolerable conflict, considerations of justice would have reached a high level of confidence. Even so, Radbruch writes, "Not every judge acting on its own initiative should be allowed to invalidate statutes; rather, the task should be reserved to a higher court or to legislation." Gustav Radbruch, "Statutory Lawlessness and Supra-Statutory Law (1946)" Bonnie Litschewski Paulson and Stanley L. Paulson transl., *Oxford Journal of Legal Studies 26(1),* 8. I am grateful to Eckardt Buchholz-Schuster for pointing this parallel with Radbruch's Formula.

17 They are often derided by critics as "victors' justice".

ganized effort to ensure that the commission of such crimes be suppressed or at least minimized. Even if we can be sure that justice would be done if some state or other entity did take on these cases, the overall picture would still be that the actual enforcement of ICL is spotty and inconsistent, perhaps even on a large scale. This can hardly be said to be a practice that prevents impunity for serious harm committed against individuals. Such is the nature of vigilante jurisdiction even if used properly and directed towards justice, to use Luban's analogy for universal jurisdiction.

V. Why Not World-State and What Can Be Done for ICL in Its Place

The need for something may not be sufficient to justify its use. The justification for ICL, on my account, is to invoke a minimum sense of natural law and the natural jurisdiction for its execution as the philosophical background for the normative default to fall back on when the territorial state either is dysfunctional or abuses its political authority. We rely on natural jurisdiction over the law of nature to reach the universality we need to forestall impunity because the conventional or treaty approach might not get us there. It is empirically unlikely that we will have all states sign up to give up their relevant jurisdiction to form a jurisdiction pool that is universal to cover the relevant crimes in all territorial states.

Exercising universal jurisdiction is, however, not without its perils, especially if we consider its source, namely, the executor power (i.e., natural jurisdiction) we each have over the natural law in the state of nature. Although the state of nature is only a heuristic device, it is also quite clear that the delivery of criminal justice in such a state of affairs is haphazard and unreliable. This is due to the fact that individuals in the state of nature, in using this "self-help" approach to delivering justice, can only rely on their subjective views about the specifics of the natural law which can be quite different from one another even if they agree on the general content.[18] There will also be different views about whether and what due process needs to be put in place to exercise one's natural jurisdiction properly. There will also be questions concerning whether a person should defer to another if the latter is a better position to comprehend the case (because

18 For Kant, this subjectivity is the major source of the insecurity in the state of nature even if everyone there is well-meaning and wants to be good and just. Immanuel Kant, *The Metaphysical Elements of Justice,* J. Ladd (transl.) (Indianapolis, Bobbs Merrill 1965), 76.

of fewer cultural or linguistic barriers) or simply being closer-by physically to gather evidence. Generally, there are also questions about whether some individuals may more readily elude detection or apprehension by others because attempts to detect or apprehend would be by individual, unorganized efforts.

The problems in the delivery of justice in the state of nature are notorious and among the reasons why traditional social contract theorists such as Locke and Kant think we must abandon the state of nature and enter civil society or state. For Locke, it is irrational for us to continue this state of affairs as we will never know when a dispute has ended and when we can drop our guards. For Kant, while the state of nature may not be unjust, justice is also not served in the state of nature and we have the natural duty of justice to set up an alternate state of affairs where justice can be delivered. What the state does is to exercise its political authority to standardize, codify, and provide specifications for the norms governing individual rights and impose them on its members. Without it, we will have to rely on individuals' subjective and differing understanding of the content of natural moral norms and the proper procedures for the execution of them. For Kant, the fact that there are multiple norms that can be applied to an individual in the same situation itself is a form of injustice. Furthermore, only when there is a state exercising its power to enforce the law against every member of the state can there be the mutual assurance that one will not disadvantage oneself by abiding by the law and respecting the rights of others.

Where there are states, exercising universal jurisdiction in relation to international crimes, as the reversion back to the default natural jurisdiction executing natural law, re-creates some of the same problems of the state of nature where states do not exist. This is because some of the states have now lost their legitimate political authority to keep out external executors of the natural law from claiming and exercising their jurisdiction on their territory. Exercising universal jurisdiction at this global level, however, contains no less inconsistency and arbitrariness that worry the social contract theorists at the more local level.

What saves this global state of nature from collapsing into anarchy in the exercise of universal jurisdiction is the respect for some territorial sovereignty and non-aggression against the states that still retain some of their legitimacy.[19] So prosecution involving the exercise of universal jurisdiction is mainly in cases where the accused and the accuser are both present in the prosecuting state.[20] Extradition from a third country friendly to the prosecuting state's exercise of universal jurisdiction is also an option.[21] Otherwise, the exercise of universal jurisdiction in international criminal law creates a situation that is as arbitrary, inconsistent, and chaotic as the local situation in the state of nature would be before there are states. Illegal kidnapping of the accused from a third country is not unheard of.[22] Even though there is some enforcement of ICL, the exercise of universal jurisdiction would be so gappy that one can hardly claim that impunity is forestalled even with the actions by the ICC taken into account.

This global situation is hardly one in which justice is done. It is quite arbitrary and very much a matter of the luck of the circumstance who gets prosecuted and held accountable and who does not, not to mention the variety of standards and conceptions of rights and justice that are applied by the different states exercising universal jurisdiction. Because its enforcement is so inconsistent and unpredictable, it is hard to imagine the ICL provides any deterrence for the commission of international crimes.

This situation seems to call for another state to be placed on top of all the other states, exercising superior political authority over them. That would be the world state which functions like a state albeit at the global level. It would standardize and codify international criminal law and provide more consistency and predictability in ICL's enforcement and adjudication. The details of how this world state would work will definitely need to be worked out. The more important point is that no one seems to want to go there. Kant has rejected the idea of a world state and most other philosophers

19 It is important to note that legitimacy is a matter of degree.

20 Recent examples are German Court exercising universal jurisdiction over Syrian nationals who happened to be in Germany, including the most recent conviction and sentencing by Higher Regional Court (OLG) of Frankfurt am Main (judgment of June 16, 2025, ref. 5 - 3 StE 2/21-4 - 2/21) of a former Syrian doctor living in Germany for crimes against humanity committed under the Assad Regime in Syria. Other examples of the exercise of universal jurisdiction include cases tried in Belgian Court over the genocide in Rwanda since 2001.

21 In 1998, Spain attempted to extradite General Augusto Pinochet from UK to Spain for prosecution for crimes against humanity committed in Chile against Chilean nationals.

22 In 1960, Adolf Eichmann, a former high-ranking Nazi official, was kidnapped by Israeli secret agents from Argentina to Jerusalem for trial.

who have considered it have rejected it also.[23] This is particularly curious because all the conditions that Kant considers to be the problems in the local state of nature that require us, as the consequence of our natural duty to be just, to enter the state also exists at the global level. It would therefore be natural for us, following Kant's argument, to enter the world state as a way of fulfilling our natural duty of justice.

One certainly has reason to agree with Kant that, given its size and supreme political power, a world state would be too risky and problematic to have. Regardless of what one thinks of Kant's reasons for rejecting the world state, the single most important concern for our purposes is that even the world state, like any of the smaller states, can turn predatory or dysfunctional and either commit international crimes itself or fail to enforce international criminal law. In that case, the legitimacy of the world state is also compromised, and we again would revert to the state of nature. To forestall impunity in that situation might require the exercise of universal jurisdiction, i.e., the natural jurisdiction as executor of natural law, by the smaller states (if they still exist under the world state) or indeed by any entity or individual. It is difficult to speculate what the situation would be like when the world state fails in its function or abuses its power to engage in serious harm against the citizens or states under its authority. But we cannot rule out that the kind of arbitrariness or even inconsistency that comes with the exercise of universal, i.e., natural, jurisdiction will also return.

As a result of all these arguments, it is hard to see how there can be a systematic approach to international criminal law that is sufficiently close to delivering justice in a general, comprehensive and relatively consistent way. Perhaps we simply have to live with the fact this area of justice and accountability can only be brought about in a spotty, gappy, inconsistent, and unsystematic way, carrying with it inevitably elements of injustice as well. But that should not stop the like-minded states, intending to bring about justice in ICL, from banding together to form some kind of coordinated and relatively organized effort in exercising universal jurisdiction.

---

23 Kant famously rejects the idea of a world-state in *Perpetual Peace*, T. Humphrey transl. (Indianapolis, Hackett: 1983), 76. That argument is, however, constructed unfairly using the idea of a "universal monarchy" which could turn despotic and ineffective. Many contemporary writers on global justice, including John Rawls, follows Kant's lead. Even if the universal monarchy is replaced with a more republican conception of the world-state, Kant's worries about the size and expanse of the power of such an entity are well-taken.

What makes the ICC fall short of living up to the ideal of international criminal justice is the limited jurisdiction it is authorized to exercise, which covers primarily the territorial and personality jurisdiction of its member states. By not claiming or exercising universal jurisdiction in order to have jurisdiction over international crimes committed outside of or unconnected to member states, ICC falls short of universality in the application and enforcement of its laws. We can take a page from Kant's famous work, *On Perpetual Pease,* to propose a different ICC (or an upgrade of the existing ICC) to promote the uniformity, consistency, and, most importantly, the universality of the application of ICL. For Kant, a confederation of republics (but not of every state) is the best we can hope for, when we realize that we should not aim at having a world state, to make peace among states possible.[24] Similarly, like-minded states who feel compelled by their natural duty of justice to prevent impunity in international crimes should form a pact not unlike the ICC. Indeed, the ICC can serve as a basis for such a pact, especially with an expansion of membership. What does this new ICC have that the existing ICC does not? The main thing is universal jurisdiction over international crimes. Such claims of universal jurisdiction would not be hard to come by (theoretically speaking). If, as I have argued in the above, given the nature of international crimes, universal jurisdiction is really nothing other than the return to the natural jurisdiction that everyone has as the executor of the natural law, then everyone has that jurisdiction over international crimes. The ICC members can simply delegate it to the ICC to exercise their universal jurisdiction. Some states, including some who are members of the current ICC, have already provided for universal jurisdiction in their law. In fact, even the ICC, just like the IMT years ago, can claim universal jurisdiction for itself. The other *ad hoc* tribunals before the existing ICC, such as ICTY[25] and ICTR[26], in my view, are already exercising universal jurisdiction without necessarily claiming to have done so.[27]

24 See Kant's proposal in *On Perpetual Peace.* In *The Law of Peoples* (Cambridge MA: Harvard University Press,1999), John Rawls seems to have a similar idea. Not all peoples are parties to the agreement on the Law of Peoples.

25 The International Criminal Tribunal for the Former Yugoslavia.

26 The International Criminal Tribunal for Rwanda.

27 If the existing ICC came into existence to replace all these *ad hoc* tribunals, then it is unclear why it does not claim universal jurisdiction. Without universal jurisdiction, the ICC would not have been able to prosecute and adjudicate the same cases if the former Yugoslavia and Rwanda were not member states of the Rome Statute.

One of the important tasks of the new ICC is to standardize and provide consistencies to the exercise of universal jurisdiction to prosecute and adjudicate either by the ICC or a member state. The existing ICC has already provided some standards and consistency in the prosecution and adjudication of international crimes. It has also codified and provided clarity for what is to count as an international crime that is within the jurisdiction of the ICC. All that is needed for the new ICC might be some additions, but not necessarily much more than the extension of the existing enforcement norms of the ICC to cover the exercise of universal jurisdiction either by itself or by its member states to include cases involving non-member states. Such an ICC, while standardizing the exercising of universal jurisdiction, need not take on every international criminal cases itself. It may prefer the national courts of its member states to exercise their own universal jurisdiction to prosecute and adjudicate certain cases instead. [28]

It is important to note that this new ICC is not related to being a world state and is to be based on a treaty or voluntary agreement among states which are willing to join. As such, it has no authority over non-member states. Whatever norms it comes up with to enhance the consistency and non-arbitrariness of the exercise of universal jurisdiction cannot be imposed on non-member states. The hope is that once such consistent and organized efforts of exercising universal jurisdiction in the new ICC regime are entrenched, non-members will see the merits and adopt the norms as well. They may even join the new ICC. But there will always be recalcitrant states which reject universal jurisdiction or insist on doing it their own way, not to mention rejecting the whole idea of the ICL completely. There is only so much we can achieve without a world state, but there is also so much to fear with one.

VI. Conclusion

ICL, as law, is quite young. In addition, given the kind of subject matter it deals with, there is almost nothing that is settled facts or practice. Almost everything about it needs to be argued for and justified. The most fundamental normative question concerns its legitimacy. This is controversial

28 This preference for the national courts, called "the Principle of Complementarity," has already been put in practice by the ICC. But since the current ICC does not recognize universal jurisdiction, its deference to national courts will only involve states that have traditional, i.e., territorial or personality, jurisdiction over a case.

because of its conflict with state sovereignty, especially when we consider its essential involvement of the idea of universal jurisdiction. In this chapter, I have argued for the legitimacy of ICL and defended the exercise of universal jurisdiction associated with it. While ICL can be shown to be legitimate, I have also argued that unless we can fully systematize and render the exercise of universal jurisdiction somewhat uniform, ICL's claim to doing justice's bidding in preventing impunity for atrocities may be limited. But that may be something we have to live with.

What Makes a Transnational Rule of Law? Understanding the Logos and Values of Human Action in Transnational Law*

*Veronica Rodriguez-Blanco***

Abstract

There are two contemporary theoretical views on the nature of the rule of law. First, a formalistic view says that the rules of law should be clear, consistent, logical, possible to follow, public, not applied to past actions, and stable, but just having these rules doesn't guarantee that the legal system will be fair or just. According to the formalistic view, this set of conditions is contingent upon the moral landscape of the specific legal system. To put it another way, these circumstances can exist in both benevolent and evil regimes. Second, the conditions are not only contingent upon and neutral to a just legal system, but they also embed an ideal that provides the conditions of possibility of any legal system to be just.

According to the latter view, the conditions, albeit refined and conceptualised in more appropriate ways, give shape and make possible a fundamental moral idea that is intrinsic to our understanding of what law is, i.e., the independence from the will of another person. Thus, legal rules and principles that are clear, consistent with action, coherent, possible, knowable, non-retroactive, and constant enable citizens to guide their actions according to them under the warrant that these rules and principles are not the manifestation of the arbitrary will of officials, judges, and legislators, but of a will that possesses a certain 'structure.' This is an important point, but it may be challenging to grasp. How can mere formal conditions generate the power to liberate us from arbitrary will? Simmonds and Fuller describe the idea of law as purposive, and Simmonds adds that

* This chapter was previously published in *Unpacking Normativity*, Kenneth Himma, Miodrag Jovanovic, and Bojan Spaic (eds.), Hart 2018, 209-226. The current version has been revised and modified.

** Professor of Moral and Political Philosophy (Jurisprudence) at the University of Surrey Centre for Law and Philosophy, United Kingdom; LLB, Mg (Caracas), Mjur (*Oxon*), PhD (*Cantab.)*.

it is purposive towards an archetype where the conditions are fully fulfilled. (Note that it is fulfilled only by degrees in defective legal systems).

However, both conceptions of the Rule of Law presuppose law created by the state. The emergence of transnational regulations, which go beyond the borders of state law, poses important questions about their legitimacy and normativity, i.e., their capacity to create reasons for addressees at the transnational level. Transnational regulations seem to go beyond the legitimacy that is provided by the Rule of Law. This paper aims to address this issue. I would like to argue in favour of the possibility of a *Transnational Rule of Law*. I will explore the idea that the 'structure' that constitutes a Transnational Rule of Law enables parties to be free from the arbitrary will of another person. This structure provides legitimacy and normativity to transnational regulations beyond the sphere of the states of the addressees of the regulations. My explanation differs from the one advanced by Simmonds but is not necessarily incompatible with it. However, my proposal goes deeper into the nature of the 'structure' of a Transnational Rule of Law and the distinction between arbitrary will and non-arbitrary will as being key to a conception of liberty. My proposal fully explains why the structure provides a warrant that the will of the arbitrator in applying and interpreting *lex mercatoria* is not arbitrary. In §2 I explain a conception of how human beings produce and transform things in the world and how we can be called 'authors' of the things we bring into the world. I focus on a conception of intentional action that is called 'the guise of the good.' In §3 I argue that a Transnational Rule of Law is no exception to that human way of transforming the world, i.e., human authorship. I explain the interactions between *lex mercatoria* and a Transnational Rule of Law and conclude that my proposal shows how the nature of the 'structure' of a Transnational Rule of Law fits the purpose of the moral value of enabling citizens at the transnational level to be liberated from the arbitrary will of another human being.

§1. Introduction

Despite opposing voices,[1] it is a shared view among legal and political philosophers that the Rule of Law is the most effective mechanism for

1 See Roberto Unger, *Law in Modern Society: Towards a Criticism of Social Theory* (Free Press, 1976) and David Kennedy, "'The Rule of Law', Political Choices, and

controlling the coercion of the state and the arbitrary will that human beings can exercise upon one another. Different characterisations have been advanced to disentangle the nature of the Rule of Law, but two main conceptions can be identified. First, a thin perspective of the Rule of Law that establishes formal conditions for law-making and the exercise of government. These conditions, it is argued, are detached from human rights ideals, justice, freedom, and other substantive values.[2] Secondly, there exists a thicker understanding of the Rule of Law, which interprets it as a pursuit of moral ideals.[3] In the former conception, the Rule of Law guides acts of government through managerial mechanisms, whilst in the latter view, guidance through the Rule of Law is not the final end, but a *by-product* of the final end formulated as a moral aspiration.[4] Within this account the Rule of Law establishes *right* standards of conduct to be followed

Development Common Sense" in *The New Law and Economic Development*, David Trubeck and Alvaro Santos (eds)(CUP, 2006) and "Toward a Critical Phenomenology of Judging" in *Law's Rule-The Rule of Law: Ideal or Ideology*, Allan. C. Hutchinson and Patrick Monahan (eds) (Carswell, 1987). They are sceptical of rules in general and therefore of the Rule of Law. For them there are no rules or principles of law because judges decide according to their biases, prejudices, social and historical perceptions and political ideology. Law is reduced to relations of power and therefore this scepticism also affects the Rule of Law, but mainly the Rule of Law conceived in a 'thin' or formalistic manner. See also Morton Horwitz, "The Rule of Law: An Unqualified Human Good". In: *Yale Law Journal* (1997): 161. Other criticisms come from communitarian fronts. For example, Michael Sandel considers the Rule of Law individualistic. However, this critique of Sandel arguably affects the thin conception of the Rule of Law only. See Michael Sandel, "The Political Theory of the Procedural Republic". In: *Law's Rule-The Rule of Law: Ideal or Ideology*, Allan. C, Hutchinson and Patrick Monahan (eds) (Carswell, 1987).

2 See Charles Montesquieu, *The Spirit of the Laws* (translated by Anne Cohler, Basia Miller, and Harold Stone, CUP, 1989); Albert Venn Dicey, *Introduction to the Study of the Law of the Constitution* (Elibron Classics, 2005, originally published in 1889); Friedrich Hayek, *The Road to Serfdom* (Routledge, 2001); Joseph Raz, "The Rule of Law and Its Virtue" in *The Authority of Law* (Oxford: OUP, 1979) 210-229; Robert Summers, "A Formal Theory of the Rule of Law" in *Ratio Juris* (1993):12; Antonin Scalia, "The Rule of Law as Law of Rules" in *University of Chicago Law Review* (1989) 1175; Richard Posner, *Economic Analysis of Law* (2003) 266-8, 541-2.

3 See Leon Fuller, *The Morality of Law* (Yale University Press, 1964); Ronald Dworkin, *A Matter of Principle* (Harvard University Press, 1986)12-13; John Finnis, *Natural Law and Natural* Rights (Clarendon Press, 1980) 270-281; Nigel Simmonds, *Law as a Moral Idea* (OUP, 2008); Brian Tamanaha, "The Rule of Law For Everyone?" in *Current Legal Problems* (2002):97; Timothy Endicott, "The Impossibility of the Rule of Law" in *Oxford Journal of Legal Studies* (1999):1.

4 For defenders of the thick conception of the Rule of Law the key argument is the need to make law intelligible. See Ernest Weinrib, "The Intelligibility of the Rule of Law" in

that enable legal practice to become closer to a moral ideal of conduct. According to common thought within the transnational perspective, if we correctly delineate the most appropriate conception of the Rule of Law then we are able to transpose the Rule of Law that is defended at the national level to the transnational level. However, finding the right answer for the transnational level is more complex, and supporters of both views miss a key point: we need to properly understand how people act and follow rules, standards, regulations, and principles (which we will call RSRPs). This bottom-up approach is not alien in legal and political philosophy and has an established pedigree in Aristotle and Oakeshott, but is absent in much established thinking of transnational law.[5]

The emergence of transnational laws puts pressure on our most cherished legal and political concepts such as the state, legal authority, and the normativity of law. Such pressure is due to the fact that these concepts have traditionally been shaped and theorised around the idea of state law and within the confinements of single jurisdictions. Furthermore, transnational laws, arguably, make superfluous the debate about the appropriate model of the Rule of Law because there is no state to control and therefore no coercion or arbitrary power to be liberated from. Actors in transnational contexts willingly accept and comply with rules, regulations, and principles and, arguably, the 'coercion question' is therefore dissolved or irrelevant, making the inquiry for the most adequate account of the Rule of Law unnecessary. One might argue, "Why do we need a transnational rule of law if there's nothing to control?"

Lex mercatoria[6] -which operates under conditions of 'raw agency'- illustrates the difficulties of the 'coercion question' and the Rule of Law. This

---

Law's Rule-The Rule of Law: Ideal or Ideology, Allan Hutchinson and Patrick Monahan (eds) (Toronto: Carswell, 1987).

5 In transnational law the methodology is either socio-systemic, e.g., Gunter Teubner, "Global Bukowina: Legal Pluralism in the World Society" in *Global Law Without State* (Ashgate, 1996) and *Constitutional Fragment: Societal Constitutionalism and Globalization* (OUP, 2012); Roger Cotterrell, "What is Transnational Law?" in *Law and Social Inquiry* (2012); William Twinning, *General Jurisprudence: Understanding Law From a Global Perspective* (Cambridge: CUP, 2009); Nico Krisch, *Beyond Constitutionalism: The Pluralist Structure of Postnational Law* (Oxford: OUP, 2010) or neo-Kantian, e.g., see cosmopolitan claims in Claudio Corradetti, "Judicial Cosmopolitan Authority" in *Transnational Legal Theory* (2016); Seyla Benhabib, *Another Cosmopolitanism: Hospitality, Sovereignty and Democratic Iterations* (OUP, 2006).

6 *Lex Mercatoria* is the set of principles and rules that guide the decisions of international commercial arbitration. The participants are non-state actors and state actors but

means that agents or actors comply with regulations, customs, and decisions because they are engaged with the ends of these regulations, custom,s and decisions, which they see as having good-making characteristics or values for them, or so I will argue. They willingly and freely comply with the set of rules, principles, and regulations contained in *lex mercatoria,* and since they do so, the idea of standards of conduct, such as the Rule of Law, does not add much to their already free action. However, contrary to appearances and to this common understanding of the matter, I will argue that the 'coercion question' is also relevant in the context of transnational law.

My aims in this paper are twofold. Firstly, I aim to show that, despite appearances, the 'coercion question' indeed emerges in transnational legal contexts when we thoroughly comprehend the various aspects of coercion. Second, to defend a sound conception of the Rule of Law, which will lead us to the heart of the correct question concerning the Rule of Law, i.e., what is the grounding that enables us to understand how participants of a legal practice comply with regulations, rules, directives, and principles (RRDPs)? Legal philosophers tend to defend one model of the Rule of Law over another, often assuming a particular view on human action without adequately defending this assumption. In this paper, I propose an alternative methodology. I propose to put the horse before the cart, i.e., to explain how human beings comply with RRDPs. This explanation will pave the way to understanding coercion at the transnational level. I will also argue

not *qua* states, but *qua* parties to a commercial contract. States also are indirectly part of this *lex* via international treaties (see for example the Convention on the Recognition and Enforcement of Foreign Arbitral Awards, 1958, "The York Convention"). The contemporary *Lex Mercatoria* includes established customary commercial practices, rules, principles and standards of different States, international organisations and special commissions (UNCITRAL, UNIDROIT, Principles of European Contract Law). See Clive Scmitthoff, "The Unification of the Law of International Trade" in *Journal of Business Law* (1968). International arbitration law is the best example of *lex mercatoria.* It emerges as a result of landmark conflicts due to the nationalisation of oil companies in developing countries. See *Texaco Overseas Petroleum Co. v Lybia,* Int'l Arbitral Award, 104 J. Droit Int'l 350 (1977). As shown by international arbitration rules and principles, transnational law regulates specific activities across borders. Thus, *lex mercatoria* regulates international commercial activities only, but there are many regulations that aim to govern other transnational activities, e.g., insurance (European Standards Alliance), health (Food Standard Agencies and World Health Organisation), forest (Programme for the Endorsement of Forest Certification), banking (Basel Committee on Banking Supervision), advertising (European Advertising Standards Alliance).

in favour of a thick conception of the Transnational Rule of Law. The methodology that I defend establishes that a sound understanding of the Rule of Law entails posing the correct question about the Rule of Law, i.e., how participants comply with the RRDPs of transnational law and how law created by human beings is able to bind other human beings and guide them in their conduct. If we grasp this basic question, we can understand the Transnational Rule of Law's function and necessity. Finally, I discuss some possible objections to this view.

§2. Understanding human action: the Medusa of Coercion

Coercion is characterised by two key features. First, coercion is typically defined as the exercise of violence, psychological or physical, and/or oppression or threats.[7] Second, coercion is defined by arbitrariness. This latter feature is less standard in the literature on coercion[8] but is amply studied in the literature on freedom of the will and practical reason. Coercion as arbitrariness implies that the person who ought to be able to choose and perform an action cannot choose and be guided by any rational standards because the reasons or *logos* that ground the action are confused, muddled, unclear, or contradictory. To understand the latter feature of coercion, we need to understand how voluntary action is possible and how we voluntarily engage and comply with RRDPs.

Aristotle[9] and Aquinas[10] accept that the individual (I) can be blamed or praised only for what she does voluntarily. They also accept that there are two types of voluntary action. First, an action is voluntary if it springs from the will of the agent (V1), if, in other words, the agent is the origin of the

7 For an outstanding contribution of the idea of coercion in this sense in the context of law, see Frederick Schauer, *The Force of Law* (Harvard: HUP, 2015).

8 Exceptions to this trend are Grant Lamond, "The Coerciveness of Law" in *Oxford Journal of Legal Studies* (2000): 39 and "Coercion and the Nature of Law" in *Legal Theory* (2001): 35 and Mark Fowler, "Coercion and Practical Reason". In: *Social Theory and Practice* (1982): 329. For the standard view on coercion see Robert Nozick, *Anarchy, State and Utopia* (Basic Books, 1974). See also Timothy Endicott, "Arbitrariness" in *Canadian Journal of Law and Jurisprudence* (2014): 49 , who distinguishes arbitrary government from arbitrariness *per se*.

9 Aristotle, *Nichomachean Ethics* (trs. Sarah Broadie and Christopher Rowe, OUP 2002) 1109b30-34.

10 Thomas Aquinas, *Summa Theologica* (tr. Thomas Gilby, CUP 2006) I-II, q.21, art. 2.

action. The agent is the *arché,* or principle, of the action.[11] Second, an action is voluntary if the agent wills the end that she sees under the intelligible form of the good and deliberates about the means to obtain the end (V2). In the latter case, we can say that there is full voluntariness, and in this case a voluntary action overlaps with an intentional action.[12] But is it the case that, on some occasions, V1 will be independent from V2? How can there be two types of voluntariness? The idea that the agent is the origin of the action (V1) is possible because the agent is able to grasp the end of the action in the form of good-making characteristics or values and deliberates about the series of actions in terms of a series of reasons that lead to the planned end seen in the form of a good (V2). Allow me to explain. Aristotle says that the agent's desired state of affairs or thing is the starting point of any intentional action. For example, a person might want to take vitamin X because it is considered healthy. Furthermore, the practical syllogism encompasses many intermediate instances, not just two premises and a conclusion. Unlike theoretical syllogism, practical syllogism is not a proof or demonstration of a true proposition, nor is it a proof or demonstration of what ought to be done or what we ought to do. It is a form of *how* and *why* we are bringing something about when we are *actually* bringing it about.

Anscombe presents us with an alternative analysis to practical syllogism and a different way to understand practical reasoning. Thus, the series of responses to the question 'Why?' manifests or reveals the practical reasoning of the agent and enables us to identify whether the action the agent is performing is intentional or not. However, she warns us that the why-question methodology is as artificial as the Aristotelian methodology of practical syllogism. When we act intentionally, we exercise a kind of reasoning that is not theoretical and that is grounded on a desire for that which seems to the agent to have good-making characteristics. You know the thing or state of affairs you are bringing about because you desire the thing or state of affairs you are bringing about, and you are able to desire the thing or state of affairs you are bringing about because you know *practically* the state of affairs. Your desire arises because you represent the thing or the state of affairs to be brought about as valuable or good. Volition and knowledge do not fall apart.[13] For example, if you are

11 Aristotle, (n 9) 1110a16-20 and Aquinas (n 10) q.6, art. 1 and art. 3.
12 For a full development of this conception, see my book *Law and Authority Under the Guise of the Good* (Hart/Bloomsbury, 2014).
13 Elizabeth Anscombe, *Intention* (HUP, 2000) §36.

a painter, you know how and why the shapes and colours on the canvas are what they are; it is because you desire and value the painting you will produce that it should be such and such a colour and shape. But it is also true that because you desire and value *this* and *not that* arrangement of colours and shapes, you are able to know it *practically.* Consequently, moral approbation is irrelevant for practical reasoning and for our practical engagement with the world.[14] This does not mean that there are no instances of objectively justified reasons for actions. On the contrary, we aim at getting it right and finding the genuine good-making characteristics or values that will provide meaning and intelligibility to the movement of our bodies. Therefore, the possibility of hitting the target of genuine good-making characteristics or values resides in our good characters and capacities. However, to understand the basic structure of practical reason and the different scopes of agency, we do not need to begin from fully justified and objective values. Our choosing and deliberative activities are better understood in the progressive form. Therefore, I am the origin of an intentional and voluntary action because I can grasp the end and deliberate about the means as a series of actions that are intelligible because they are connected by underlying reasons (for actions).

One possible way of understanding that V1 and V2 might take separate paths, i.e., that there can be *voluntary actions that are not intentional*, is as follows. It can be argued that if an action is successful and the agent produces the end she intends, i.e., a state of affairs, object, artefact, or activity, then V1 and V2 coincide. However, if the end is not achieved, then we can say that V1 and V2 have become dislocated. The intended end is not achieved, but another end is achieved per *accidens* and not *per se*. In this latter case, V1 results from V2, but V1 takes an independent form. In paradigmatic examples, the agent is forced by circumstances to change her plans to achieve an end that is not what she planned, but she is in some sense the origin (*arché* or principle) of the action because she considers her action as a unity that is caused by her.

Let me put the following example to illustrate the point.[15] A captain might deliberate about the best route to take her ship and its cargo from Southampton to Venezuela, where the cargo needs to be delivered. She hires the best sailors, provides favourable wages, finds the best possible ship, and

14 Ibid. §37-38.

15 See Aquinas (n 10) I-II, Q6, where he says that this kind of action would be "a mixed of voluntary and involuntary, but more voluntary." See also Aristotle (n 9) Book III.

plans the best route that will take the ship, its cargo, and the crew to the planned destination. The captain engages in this activity *because* she aims to earn money and she aims to earn money *to* enjoy a month's holiday with her family. Let us recall that this is her first-person, deliberative stance. She sees this month's holiday as the end of her actions and as having good-making characteristics. When the ship sails close to Bermuda, however, there is a storm that endangers the life of the crew and the captain has no option but to throw the cargo overboard. The captain decides to get rid of the cargo to save her life and the lives of the sailors. This is not what she had planned to do, and it is not the end *per se* when she deliberated and acted upon her deliberations. The circumstances, however, lead her to this other end which in some sense is *per accidens.* She acts voluntarily because the action of hiring the sailors, agreeing to take the cargo to Venezuela, beginning the journey etc. originated with her through her deliberations and the execution of her powers, but in one significant sense, she did not deliberate about throwing the cargo from the ship. This action is voluntary because *'it springs from her will'* but she did not plan or deliberate about it.

Let us suppose an alternative scenario where, in contrast to the former scenario where the plan is thwarted, there is no storm and the captain succeeds in her plan to take the cargo to Venezuela. In this case we can say that the captain had 'enhanced' control of her actions since she knew *what* she was doing and *why,* and there were no impediments to the intended direction of her actions and the production of the planned state of affairs, i.e., the delivery of the cargo. In the first scenario where the ship encountered a storm, the captain was in a position of reduced control because she could not deliberate, and circumstances obliged her to take a different route in her performance, i.e., to get rid of the cargo.

At the other extreme of the range of actions where V1 and V2 are located, we have actions that are neither intentional nor voluntary (V1) or (V2). This phenomenon happens when we have been denied access to the reasons or *logos* of the action that is requested from us. Let us revisit the storm example. I am your captain, and I do not tell you that there is a storm up ahead. When I tell you to throw the cargo overboard, I do not provide any justification for this; I simply demand you throw the cargo overboard. This is a clear case of *coercion as arbitrariness,* where I do not present you with the reasons or *logos* of the action. Rather, I demand that you act. You do not understand 'why' you are doing it. You just do it because I said so. You have been deprived of *your capacity as a chooser or deliberator*, and some authors might say that your dignity has been violated.[16]

How does this all apply to the 'coercion question' in the context of the Rule of Law and transnational law? In the context of national law, judges and legislators provide the necessary justification the state's exercise of coercion and its demands for citizens to obey courts decisions. Judges and legislators provide justifications for why the law requires citizens to perform certain actions in specific circumstances. I have argued that citizens can be bound because legal reasons are formulated as genuine or as having believed good-making characteristics or values. In this way, the grounding of RRDPs are underlying reasons as good-making characteristics or values.[17]

In the transnational context there is no apparent coercion, legitimate or illegitimate, of the state since there is no state at the transnational level. I argue, however, that whilst there is no coercion as violence or repression, *there can be coercion as arbitrariness*. For example, if the arbitrators in an international arbitration case do not provide coherent and adequate legal reasons grounded on values or genuine or believed good-making characteristics for their awards and decisions, or they demand certain conduct or an action to be performed by the parties grounded on muddled, incoherent or confused reasons, then we can say there is *coercion as arbitrariness*.

If this notion is sound, a transnational rule of law would serve as the quintessential mechanism to ensure that agents in the transnational legal context are not subject to the arbitrary will of another, because the transnational rule of law demands that reasons or *logos as values or good-making characteristics* are embedded in the creation of transnational RRDPs, and this enables agents in the transnational context to choose RRDPs because they are grounded in such reasons or *logos*.

But now the question that arises is 'What are the key features of a Rule of Law and Transnational Rule of Law that guarantee agent choice and liberate agents from arbitrariness?' This is the direction I now turn.

---

16 See Immanuel Kant who considers that dignity is grounded on our humanity and therefore capacity to choose our lives. Immanuel Kant, *The Metaphysics of Morals* (translated by Mary Gregor, Cambridge University Press, 2017) 6: 387, 6:392, 6:420, 6:462; *Groundwork for the Metaphysics of Morals* (translated by Thomas Hill and Arnull Zweig, OUP, 1998) 4:435, 4:436; *The Critique of Practical Reason* (translated by Mary Gregor, CUP, 1997) 5:71, 5:87, 5:88). The dignity of humanity is the first step towards the most complete idea of dignity which is the 'dignity of personality'.

17 See my book (n 12).

§3. The Rule of Law and the Thick Conception of the Transnational Rule of Law

There are two contemporary theoretical views on the nature of the rule of law. First, a *thin* conception that establishes the set of conditions that are part of the doctrine of the Rule of Law and according to which the rules of law should be: clear; consistent with action; coherent; possible; public; non-retroactive; and constant. This set of conditions does not necessarily generate a legal system whose key feature is substantive justice.[18] According to the thin view this set of conditions is contingent upon the moral landscape of the specific legal system. In other words, these conditions can be equally present in either evil or benevolent regimes. Second, some believe that the conditions are not only contingent upon and neutral to a just legal system, but that they embed a moral ideal that provides the conditions of possibility for any legal system to be just.[19] According to the latter the conditions, albeit refined and conceptualised in more appropriate ways, give shape to and make possible a fundamental moral idea that is intrinsic to our understanding of what law is, i.e. the independence of one person from the will of another. Thus, legal rules and principles that are clear, consistent with action, coherent, possible, knowable, non-retroactive and constant enable citizens to guide their actions according to them under the warrant that these rules and principles are not the manifestation of the arbitrary will of officials, judges and legislators, but that they manifest a will possessing a certain *logos as good-making characteristics or values.* This is a crucial point, but difficult to understand. How can mere formal conditions generate the power to liberate us from an arbitrary will? Simmonds and Fuller carve the idea of law as being purposive and Simmonds adds that it is purposive towards an aspiring moral archetype where the conditions above are fully fulfilled. (Note that the conditions are fulfilled only by degrees in defective legal systems.)

Both conceptions of the Rule of Law presuppose law created by the state. The emergence of transnational regulations, which go beyond the borders of state law, pose important questions about their legitimacy and normativity, i.e. about their capacity to create reasons for citizens at the transnational level. Transnational regulations seem to go -it is claimed-

18 Raz (n 2) and Matthew Kramer, "The Big Bad Wolf: Legal Positivism and its Detractors" in *American Journal of Jurisprudence* (2004):1.

19 See Weinrib (n 4) and Simmonds (n 3).

beyond the legitimacy that is provided by the Rule of Law. I would like to argue in favour of the possibility of a Transnational Rule of Law that meets the conditions adumbrated by the thick conception of the Rule of Law and explore the idea that the *logos as values* that underlie the rule of law enables us to be free from the arbitrary will of another person. In a similar way, in the case of a Transnational Rule of Law, the *logos as values* that shapes transnational interactions enables citizens in different states to be free from the arbitrary will of another person. My explanation differs from the one advanced by Fuller, Simmonds and Weinrib.[20] My proposal goes deeper into the nature of the *logos as values* of the Rule of Law and the distinction between arbitrary will and non-arbitrary will as being key to a conception of liberty. My proposal fully explains why the *logos as values* provides a warrant that the will of the arbitrator in the case of *lex mercatoria* and transnational law, and the will of officials, judges or legislators, in the national context, is not arbitrary.

Fuller points out that law is a practical craft and proposes that legislation and judging involve developing the skills for a practical craft. We should not be take this idea lightly. It invites us to reflect on the kind of creatures we are and how we produce things in the world and, more specifically, how the will can create something that is not arbitrary, but rather has a certain *logos* that is compatible with and appropriate to the kind of creatures we are. In previous work [21] I have argued that we are '*eudaimonic* creatures' and that the authorship of the law and its key features, i.e. normativity and authority, are rooted in this condition. This means, following the Aristotelian and Thomistic traditions[22], that in our condition of lacking we reach, interact the world and transform it following our visions, conceptions and imaginings of what good-making characteristics or values consist in. We yearn and long for and desire certain things, sometimes apprehending what is correct, right and good, but sometimes catastrophically failing to grasp what is correct, right and good, though we still believe that what we desire and long for does possesses good-making features. We do this not only individually but also collectively.[23] This condition is pervasive and makes the world intelligible beyond its pure materiality. Thus, a piece of

20 Weinrib formulates a similar thick conception, though he focuses on intelligibility, see (n 4).

21 See (n 12).

22 See especially Jonathan Lear, *Radical Hope* (HUP, 2008).

23 See my article "The Myth of the Classical Natural Law Theory: Reflecting on the 'Thin' View of Legal Positivism" in 31 *Ratio Juris* (2018) 9. I rely on the idea of

music becomes more than noise, a speech becomes more than the vocal chords making sounds, a hammer is more than steel and wood assembled in a specific form, a cathedral is more than stone, mortar and glass, and a choreographed dance is more than a group of people moving their bodies. In a similar way the set of legal rules, directives and principles are not the sole expressions of the raw will of judges and legislators, nor mere social facts that become fully intelligible through examination of the beliefs and desires as mental states of judges and legislators. Judges and legislators create legal rules, directives and principles with the aim of bringing about a state of affairs, i.e. compliance with the rules, directives and principles that will either serve or produce good-making characteristics, albeit that they might be mistaken or merely believed.

RRDPs need to be intelligible to the addressee in order for him or her to follow and be guided by them and this intelligibility is only possible when the good-making characteristics or values appear in the scene of our longings, yearnings and desires. In other words, when they *are present or knowable by us*. Judges and legislators do not escape the 'eudaimonic condition' of humankind. What differentiates human actions from the actions of man and women? The latter actions possess an intrinsic aim formulated as a value or good-making characteristic. Other actions such as sneezing, itching your head or yawning are all human actions but not the actions of men and women. This suggests that when men and women transform the world they do it according to an order of reasons or *logos* that they understand and they do it under the rubric of 'actions of men and women'. This order of reasons or *logos* is not merely theoretical but is practical in the sense that it is directed to a future action, to something that will happen. The order of reasons or *logos* is known by the executor or agent of the action and he or she understands why one action ought to follow another until the good-making characteristics or specific value is achieved. The latter makes intelligible the order of reasons and its execution in the world. Thus, make a cappuccino I follow certain procedures and/or possess the know how to make a cappuccino. I switch on the cappuccino machine, put the coffee beans in the appropriate container, press the 'On' button, place the cup in the correct position, open the milk carton, pour the milk into the milk container to be frothed and finally add the milk to the coffee. There

"institutional transparency" advanced by Elizabeth Anscombe in her article "On Brute Facts" in *Analysis* (1958): 69.

is a 'practical craft' in the process because the order of my actions cannot change if I wish to produce a good cappuccino. It has a natural practical character. The performance of any intentional action is parallel to a process of deliberation that involves the exercise of practical reason. This account of intentional action has been misunderstood or confused by contemporary understandings of intentional action which focus on intentional action as a mental state.[24]

It is arguable that the creation of the rule of law is also a 'practical craft', albeit one with a *logos* that can be the subject of discussion and re-conceptualisation. It requires that legal rules and principles are non-retroactive, knowable, clear, consistent in action, coherent, possible, public, and constant. Advocates of the thin view of the Rule of Law have argued that the formal conditions of the Rule of Law do not ensure a just legal system in any substantive way, and that the *logos* consists merely of rules of management that can lead to evil acts such as extra-legal violence. The notion of law as purposive gives us a hint towards a response to the thin view but does not seem sufficient and for a more fulfilling insight we need to go deeper into the nature of this *logos*. My proposal is as follows. *What is missing from Fuller's account is the idea that this logos has a specific subject matter which are values or good-making characteristics and that our will yearns and desires good-making characteristics or values.* This desire is the result of our 'eudaimonic nature'. Thus, if legal rules and principles are grounded on good-making characteristics or values then the consistency is not mere consistency of the will of legislators and judges, but consistency of good-making characteristics or values. If we look in further depth at the thin set of conditions that are part of the doctrine of the Rule of Law we can say that *knowability concerns the knowability of values* that are the basis for legal rules and principles; this does not only mean that the citizens of a state know the texts and words of court legal decisions and statutes, it must also entail that legal rules and principles are grounded on shareable values or good-making characteristics and are therefore knowable by the community. The non-retroactivity of law should also entail that the embedded values or good-making characteristics that ground the rules are non-retroactive. Clarity in the language of the legal rule, directive or principle entails that we *correctly grasp the value or good-making characteristics*

24 In my book (n 12), I extensively criticise this view and will, therefore, in this paper focus only on the account of intentional action under the model of the guise of the good only.

that grounds the legal rule or principle since only in this way will it be possible to formulate in a clear manner RRDPs. The condition of possibility entails that the values are possible to realise and perform under specific social, psychological, cultural and economic circumstances. *The condition of coherence requires that there is coherence in the values* that ground the legal rules and principles, and the condition of constancy demands that grounding or underlying values and good-making characteristics of rules and directives, to the extent that this is possible, remain constant over time. *Consistency in action requires that there is no discrepancy in terms of the values* that are pursued by the law and the actions that guide officials.

Let me provide a metaphor to better explain my point. A good cappuccino is not just the result of my body's movements, the switching on of the machine, and the pouring in of coffee beans and milk and so on. To assert in an intelligible way that I am making a cappuccino is to understand; i.e., know *practically* why I am switching on the machine, filling the machine with coffee beans and milk and so on. Finally, it is to understand that a cappuccino is a warming drink that will pep me up -emotionally and physically- during the day, i.e., the ends of the complex diachronic action provide the complete form or *logos* of my bodily movements. To understand *what* I am making entails understanding *why* I am making it. These two understandings are not independent when we reflect on them from the performer's deliberative point of view. Similarly, the legislator or judge creates RRDPs in the national context, and arbitrators, actors and regulatory bodies at the transnational level create RRDPs, following coherence in values, knowability of values, non-retroactivity of values, consistency in action being guided by the values, clarity in values, and constancy in values, to the extent that this is feasible, and the value is possible to realise. In other words, to understand that we are the authors of something called 'law' entails understanding 'why' we create it. Judges and legislators at the national level, and arbitrators, actors and regulatory bodies at the transnational level, create RRDPs because we all yearn and long for values. But to achieve these values successfully in the world we need to ensure that an arbitrary will is not the creator or author of the law, but rather a will or intention that attains the *logos as* values. The thick conception of the Rule of Law and the Transnational Rule of Law *hinders* the intervention of a will that does not follow the underlying *logos* of RRDPs. *The "structure of values" or logos as values protects me, a citizen, from the arbitrary will of others.* Of course, as I have argued in previous works, the perceived values or good-making characteristics might be mistaken, in error, badly characterised, or even evil.[25]

The power of the proposal lies in the idea that the *logos of the Rule of Law and Transnational Law is able to direct us to the problem of the matter: the values to be pursued and subsequently we are able to choose whether or not to adopt the set of RRDPs.* In other words, the *logos* enables us to see what the genuine or believed value truly is. Consequently, it will be apparent to us what the genuine or believed value that grounds the RRDPs is. In the case of believed values that are not genuine values, the transparency of the *logos* enables citizens to make criticisms of RRDPs grounded on specific values.

The idea advanced in this paper is that the order of reasons or principles of creation lie with legislators and judges at the national level, and with arbitrators, actors or regulatory bodies at the transnational level. However, the Rule of Law or Transnational Rule of Law make apparent the *logos as values* that reveal the order of reasons guiding the creation of RRDPs. Thus, to be more precise, the idea is not that there is a moral ideal that we participate in and that, by degrees, we fulfil.[26] Rather, the approach is that legislators and judges at the national level, and arbitrators, actors and regulatory bodies at the transnational level, already have a set of values that they aim to foster and realise in their respective legal frameworks because we are 'eudaimonic creatures'. Consequently, the Rule of Law and a Transnational Rule of Law provide the best possible mechanism to guarantee the transparency and knowability of these genuine or believed values. When the conditions of the Rule of Law and Transnational Rule of Law fail then it is the transparency and knowability of the values that fail. Therefore, the Rule of Law and the Transnational Rule of Law can be substituted by any arbitrary value imposed by an arbitrary will. In other words, when the conditions of the Rule of Law and Transnational Rule of Law fail, the legislator or judge, arbitrator, actor or regulatory body is guided by his or her own arbitrary order of reasons, even a chaos of reasons, or *for no reasons.* The result is that the citizen or actor cannot guide his or her behaviour rationally and only illegitimate violence or coercion as arbitrariness force the citizen or actors to act and comply with the RRDPs.

When the conditions of the Rule of Law and Transnational Rule of Law are fulfilled, we still need to think hard about the kind of values that ought

25 See Rodriguez-Blanco (n 12).
26 See Simmonds (n 3).

to ground RRDPs. The values that ground RRDPs and the *logos* of the Rule of Law and Transnational Law are not two different phenomena. On the contrary, the *logos* takes as its subject matter values and then brings the form of law to completeness. Analogously, a piece of choreography is not only the bodily movements that follow a certain order, it is also the harmony, agility, grace, and expression of the dance; we can still study the bodily movements but should not forget their subject matter, which is the harmony, agility, grace, and expression of the choreographed piece. This thick conception of Rule of Law and Transnational Law opens the path for a new conception of Transnational Private Law and provides a framework of unity and intelligibility in the context of transnational law.

§4. Possible objections

A.- The conception adumbrated in this paper contradicts the quintessential nature of the Rule of Law, i.e. the pursuit of different ends and values.

It might be argued that the conception defended in this paper contradicts the reasons why we pursue *any ends or goals*. The Rule of Law -the objector might continue- is at the heart of the liberal project. But if legislators and judges, or arbitrators, actors and regulatory bodies create RRDPs following certain ends as good-making characteristics and values, and the citizen or legal participant follows these ends, then the citizen or legal participant *is not really choosing her own ends.*

However, the conception I have defended presupposes the view that ends are already given due to the kind of creatures we are and by virtue of the fact that we take part in certain social practices. Since we have a specific form of life, e.g. we eat, walk, love, play, have friends, write, think, mourn and so on, this form of life can only be understood if we understand the underlying grammar or logic of our activities (*logos*). By contrast, empirical investigations, such as biological, chemical, and physical research, aim to discover their object of study. We must discover the inner logic of such investigations, as it is not inherent in our ordinary actions. *The case of human activities is at variance with this since the internal logic or grammar of our activities is given to us and defines the limits of what we can make intelligible.* However, this view does not contradict the liberal idea that there is a plurality of ends that can be chosen and pursued according to our own life plan; it only proposes that there are limits to our choice of ends and life plans. These limits are the limits imposed by our social practices and the underlying *logos* that demarcates rational from irrational action. It is a pledge of humility that recognises our human nature's richness and limits. This entails that there is plenty of room for imaginative ways of living and participating in the plurality of ends as good-making characteristics or values. Individual purposes can flourish without this being a threat to human practical imagination.[27] The richness of a planned life lies in the determination and creative combination of our shared values.

B.- The redundancy of publicity

If values are embedded in the fabric of society, an objector might argue, then there is no need to make them explicit through the Rule of Law or Transnational Rule of Law; they are already public in our practices. We do not need the publicity of rules and their underlying values.

My response to this objection is as follows. There is a plurality of values and disvalues. All practices involve certain core values, but there is room for different interpretations of the core values of a practice. There is also room for divergence or distortions of the core values of a practice. The publicity of rules and their underlying values enable us to better understand -not only through practice but also reflection- the point of RRDPs. It also encourages the participation of multiple and different cultural perspectives in the practice of compliance with RRDPs due to the pursuit of values. Consequently, it encourages diversity within unity.

C.- The Transnational Rule of Law is too vague to guide behaviour

An objector might argue that the thick conception of a Transnational Rule of Law is too vague and therefore undermines its purpose, i.e., it does not enable us to predict behaviour and protect reasonable expectations in transnational law and, more specifically, in the private sphere.

This objection relies on an empirical conception of agency which presupposes that our intentions are mental events and that we can enact or recreate others's intentions to predict their behaviour. Elsewhere I have argued at length that this conception is parasitic on another model of human actions that relies on values and the good-making characteristics of our

27 Cf. Hayek (n 2) 79.

actions. I cannot fully engage with this objection here due to constraints of space, but I would emphasise that the position does not aim to eliminate agency construed in empirical, economic or social basis. On the contrary, the idea is that the potential power of these explanations is parasitic on a more naïve and intelligible conception of human action that is not based on prediction and theoretical conceptions.

Legal actors who comply with transnational regulations need to recognise each other. I have argued that in order to act and comply with RRDPs legal actors need *to make intelligible the actions of others* and this is only possible under the model of action that I have defended. For example, in the context of transnational arbitration, arbitrators are selected on the basis of their trustworthiness and credibility, and this is not dissimilar from the selection of judges. The arbitrator's capacities to follow *lex mercatoria*[28] and to advance the best possible interpretation of the underlying values of the different RRDPs embedded in *lex mercatoria* depend on his character as a trustworthy person. In this context, trustworthiness may be understood as a commitment to the underlying values of the fabric of RRDPs. Of course, as theorists we can create economic or social models that will enable us to predict the arbitrator's behaviour, but as legal actors in a practice we need to engage with the underlying values of the legal practice and the way that the arbitrator engages with such values.

D.- The thick conception of the Transnational Rule of Law undermines the plurality of goods across pluralistic societies

This objection entails the view that in pluralistic societies, there is disagreement about values and therefore the thick conception of the Transnational Rule of Law presupposes that these disagreements can be dissolved.

The pluralism that I advocate is concerned with values, rather than technical plurality,[29] and this brings about the danger that we can never reach consensus on matters of value. However, the model of human action that I

28 The correct function of a Transnational Rule of Law would need an ample use of the publicity requirement. In the context of international arbitration, for example, it would require the publication of Arbitral Awards.

29 Peer Zumbassen and Gralf-Peter Calliess in their book *Rough Consensus and Running Code: A Theory of Transnational Law* (Hart, 2010) seem to advocate plurality in terms of technical standards. The model of conduct I defend relies on anti-hierarchical structures that emerge and grow from values.

defend as the basis of the Transnational Rule of Law takes the deliberative point of view as the privileged position of human action and presupposes constant engagement and effort to make intelligible the position of the other as *chooser*. Genuine disagreements over values involves taking the matter at hand seriously and earnest attempts to understand how different values can be manifested in legal and social practices. There is no *ex ante* solution that can guide us, and the process is one of constant construction.[30] To abandon our efforts to reach agreement and intelligibility is to abandon our rational capacities.

§5. Conclusion

This paper began with a puzzle about the Rule of Law. If the objective of the Rule of Law is to protect citizens from the coercion of the state, then a Transnational Rule of Law is unnecessary because at the transnational level there is no state and therefore there is no state to exercise coercion. I have shown that this puzzle is misleading because it relies on a misconception of coercion. Coercion is exercised not only through violence, oppression or threats, but occurs when legal actors are deprived of the opportunity to be *choosers* and -therefore- their access to reason is hindered. Consequently, I have argued, a Transnational Rule of Law that has as its subject matter values or good-making characteristics and ensures coherence, knowability, clarity and so on of values or good making-characteristics also ensures the availability of legal reasons to legal actors and shields actors from coercion as arbitrariness. Since we inherited *via* legal positivism a standard conception of the nature of law that is necessarily attached to state law, then any debilitated conception of the state as the source of law generates, it is argued, a *soft* conception of law. I have tried to show that this is a *non sequitur*. Law, *soft or strong*, is not only texts or words that are promulgated by the state and enforced by its organs; promulgated law also entails an underlying *logos* which is translated as the reasons as values or good-making characteristics that ground RRDPs. This understanding of the law opens new avenues for the understanding of transnational and international law. I have shown that the former involves a *logos as values* that underlies RRDPs

30 At the theoretical level a helpful metaphor is provided in 'Neurath's boat'. This metaphor also works at the practical level when we engage in actions and social practices.

and has the form of an intelligible unity when legal actors adhere to the Transnational Rule of Law that ensures a framework of intelligibility and freedom as 'independence from the arbitrary will of another human being'. I have defended the thick conception of the Rule of Law and, *a fortiori,* of the Transnational Rule of Law because it is the only view that understands how we act in the context of the law and serves the key features of the human condition and human actions, i.e., our 'eudaimonic nature'.

VI.
Legal and Judicial Training

Communicational Theory of Law and Legal Text: An Interdisciplinary Approach for Legal Education

Juan Pablo Sterling Casas[1]

Abstract

The Communicational Theory of Law (CTL) is a creation of the Spanish professor Gregorio Robles Morchón that assumes a communicational perspective of the legal phenomenon, this means, a conception of law as a tool for the solution of socio-legal conflicts based on the decision adopted by a legitimate authority. This decision has a characteristic: is communicable through texts, predominantly written, and thus law is a space of textual communication, whose first source is the legal order (ORD) understood as a textual universality that contains the decisions of the authorities (Constitution, law, judicial sentence, administrative act, etc.). The texts that contain the decisions that make up the ORD are special for at least three reasons: first, because they are *writerly* (Roland Barthes), second, because of their *hyper textuality* (Lotman and Landow) and finally, because they are an expression of the *grammar of power* (Deleuze and Guattari). Those reflections on texts are present in CTL and I call it *textual grammar*. The main objective of this paper is, then, to show how legal education can be enhanced from the concept of text, and its characteristics, within CTL by proposing a clear working hypothesis: The teaching of law must give a central role to the study of language based on the recognition that the ORD is a universality of texts that is not precisely ordered and clear, therefore, it is through a hermeneutic and analytical method that the true content of legal texts, that is, the legal system (SIS), is accessed. This method should be used from the first semesters of training. This hypothesis is based on three postulates, first the nature of the legal text, second the analytical-hermeneutic method and finally the teaching of law from narratology and sensibility. At the end, an analysis of how CTL can help with legal teaching in an

1 Professor of Introduction to Law, Philosophy of Law, Logic and Legal Hermeneutics in the Law Program of the Uniautónoma del Cauca, Colombia. Email: juan.sterling.c@uniautonoma.edu.co.

interdisciplinary exercise is illustrated as a proposal and starting point for further pedagogical developments.

Key words

Law philosophy, Legal education, Legal hermeneutics, Communicational Theory of Law, Legal linguistics.

1. Introduction: Short Review of the Communicational Theory of Law

The name Communicational Theory of Law (CTL hereinafter) is a creation of the Spanish professor *Gregorio Robles Morchón* that emphasizes communication processes, since these are its perspective of knowledge. Just as in the iusnaturalist and positivist legal paradigms the analysis falls on the concepts of justice and legal norm, respectively, in the CTL this emphasis will fall on communication. Thus, the communicational theory assumes law as a set of communication processes between the State, its institutions and individuals. But in order to not fall into ambiguities, it should be clarified that since communication is the perspective of knowledge of CTL, the starting point and reference point is language, so it is a theory closely linked to linguistics and its reflections. This is the reason that leads CTL to be considered as a theory that studies the language of jurists. In this section, this theory works has always sought to be juridical, that is to say, it analyzes the phenomena of law and from law without ignoring the necessary contributions from other areas of knowledge; therefore, for a successful approach to CTL, it is necessary to have a previous juridical training.

For the study of two of the central concepts of CTL (legal order and legal system), special attention is paid to the concept of text, insofar as these concepts are textual totalities. Therefore, CTL is the bearer of a theory of texts or textual linguistics. Law manifests itself through language and this, in turn, is susceptible to being manifested in texts (predominantly written). CTL assumes a broad notion of text in which any human work can be elevated to the textual category, whether written or acted. As a consequence of this the CTL turns its analysis on the language of jurists which translates in part into recognizing that there are phenomena of misunderstanding given the duality of two types of language: the natural and the juridical. Therefore, it is the role of the jurist to resort to the tools of language and hermeneutics in order to find a way out of this problem.

This previous reflection allows us to appreciate that the CTL contribution to the study of law is concretized in a theory that conceives it as a hermeneutic-analytical (communicational) exercise, a notion based on the need to abandon the traditional descriptivist legal dogmatics. The starting point here is the idea according to which law is manifested through language, a position that in the early days of CTL Robles called the *weak ontological position* (which today is an anecdote since he no longer uses the term ontological in any sense), therefore, its characteristic is linguisticity (*lingüisticidad*): "*highlighting a fact that does not seem controversial, namely: the fact that the legal phenomenon manifests itself, above all, as a set of processes of communicative interrelation; or, in other words, as a set of communication processes*"[2]. This proposal is vast in literature, analysis and external studies and has as one of its axes the hermeneutic-analytic method which makes it a fertile area for the study of the role of hermeneutics insofar as it presents positions that are not always evident when carrying out a rigorous study of the hermeneutic task, especially with the notion of legal text. Hence, the hermeneutic task starts then from a reflection on the teaching of law insofar as every act of juridicity supposes an act of understanding of its communicational meaning and interpretative consequences; the relationship between hermeneutics and pedagogy is inevitable then in the approach to the problem to be analyzed.

2. The Nature of the Legal Text in CTL

Having made the considerations, which are very general, of the CTL, it is necessary to point that this theory gives great importance to the concept of text, in fact, a second name used by Robles for his theory is *Theory of Legal Texts* insofar as law is concretized in texts in a broad sense (everything that can be read). The particularity of the legal text is that it is verbalized insofar as everything can be put into words and written in a document. This notion of Robles will be decisive later on when addressing the Theory of Texts, based on the concept of hypertext and writerly texts. Suffice it to say for now that CTL idea of legal text is that it is decisional, regulative and institutional: Decision, norm and institution, hence we can speak of a Theory of Legal Decision, a Theory of Legal Norms, and a Theory of Legal Institutions (Legal Dogmatics).

2 Gregorio Robles, *Teoría del Derecho: Fundamentos de Teoría Comunicacional del Derecho*, Vol. I, 6ª edición. Navarra: Thomson Reuters–Civitas, 2015, p. 160.

In this second nomenclature it is important to point out the emergence of one of the most relevant points of the Roblesian theory: The notion of two basic texts: an ordinamental text (describing the legal system) which the CTL designates with the acronym ORD, and a systematic text (which is the hermeneutic result of the ordinamental texts) which the CTL designates with the acronym SIS. The concept of Ordinance refers to the formal sources of law (Colombian law, for example). However, this ordinance "*is organized according to an order, the set of all of them, the global ordering, presents a rather disorganized aspect*"[3], in other words, there is awareness of order, but it is not easily identifiable due to the complexity and defects that are generated when trying to identify it, which is what can be called raw legal text. On the other hand, the system refers to the interpretations and systematization of jurists (experts in legal matters), the system thus seen is a finished text, which can generate other texts, in the words of Robles, the system is created "*through a hard work of interpretation and systematization. This new text, generated by scientific jurists in their treatises and monographs, constitutes the system*".[4] Thus, the ordinance is the result of the decisions of those who create the law (legislators and judges), while the system is the result of the interpretative work of jurists "*who act as true intermediaries between the raw text and the worked text*".[5] In this way Robles begins to outline that law is a hermeneutic exercise that seeks to complete the legal system from the texts that compose it.

It is important to say that regardless of the different conceptions of law (in its essence), it is unquestionable that it appears in the world of life in the form of writing. Again, it should be made clear that this position does not imply that the birth of the legal phenomenon is marked by writing, what it means is that although it is true that not all law is written, its characteristic as a communicational system makes it susceptible of being put in writing, it is potentially writerly, therefore, this being so, textuality appears as one of its most notable properties. Textuality is nothing different from the predominance of writing, something that will be defining in the essence of law and whose consultation allows the recognition, interpretation and justification of legal decisions. The existence of written law is therefore the way to guarantee an open legal system, which provides a certain degree

3 Gregorio Robles, *Introducción a la teoría del Derecho*, 6ª edición. Madrid: Debate, 2003, p. 23.

4 *Ídem.*

5 *Ídem*, p. 24.

of normative security and avoids capricious changes and alterations. But this does not mean that this is always the case; if we turn to the notion of legal system offered by the CTL, we can observe that many times the *ordinamental* text differs from the systemic one.

2.1 The concept of the legal text in CTL

CTL begins to build itself in a detailed and spiral fashion; it starts from the simplest concepts to gradually unveil and teach a broader aspect that in the end allows the appreciation of a vast work with many details, a kind of puzzle.

The elaboration of a formal Theory of Law presents some difficulties that lie in several of the aspects, for example, the necessity to establish a solid concept of law. This first obstacle implies asking what is understood by concept and from there to continue with a more precise elaboration, thus, before offering a concept of law it is necessary to offer an answer to what is understood by concept. This is the reflection that Robles makes, a reflection that will constitute his distinctive feature when addressing the basic elements of the CTL, it works coherently with what in essence is a Communicative Theory: starting from a text, from a word and how it is used in different communicative contexts in order to clarify which is the one that interests law. This procedure is used throughout his extensive work in each and every one of the key concepts in the framework we call law (legal order, legal system, legal scope, legal relations, legal actions, etc.).

In summary, law is a tool that resolves conflicts through decisions made by legitimate authorities. CTL focuses on the concept of authority to establish that within the law it is the authority that can make and generate the decision (act of will). Thus, the authority is the one who decides, it is the one who has the power to make, transmit and execute the decision, in other words, the authority generates the rule.

As previously indicated, there are two relevant textual universalities in the CTL: legal order (ORD) and legal system (SIS), concepts that are treated, in many theories and by many jurists, as synonymous terms, to say legal order and then legal system in the same sense, even in the same discourse or conversation, is so common that it does not even stop to analyze the existence of any difference. But for CTL there is a difference, in fact, it is one of the pillars of its constitution. While the ORD is the decisions of the authorities (which are not necessarily ordered or clear), the

SIS is a kind of elaborated or concluded order, that is, an order that has been arranged or systematized to be more understandable. The SIS is then the result of arranging the legal order (ORD), that is, the raw or unfinished text that is composed of the decisional expressions of an authority (such as the legislator, for example), said order "is just as it comes out of the mouth of the legislator." Then, if the ordinance contains the will through the decisions of the authorities, both ORD and SIS are texts.

In order to make sense of the above, the legal order has a perspectivistic character since it contemplates the legal phenomenon from a special perspective: communication. In the same way, the texts that make up the law have a "*textual perspective*"[6] therefore every legal system is built on a perspective from which the legal world is contemplated and judged. Being the legal text, essentially regulative or prescriptive, with an organizing function through the regulation of social aspects of conduct, its pragmatic function comprises at the same time of a regulation of itself (generating its own elements in an autopoietic attitude) and of the relations with other orders.

As a result of the above, CTL is committed to a broad notion of text, as we have seen, which undoubtedly allows an understanding of the legal world based on the elimination of the ideological hegemony of positivism and its grammatical logic. The text is now a construction that implies an awareness of our presence in the world and is not exhausted simply with positive and codified legal norms, it also appears the conception of jurisprudence as a narrative element, the concept of hypertext (a text connected with others and infinite), even the interesting notion of *writerly texts* can be part of the law, such notion is illustrated by the French author *Roland Barthes.*

The text thus understood represents an interest that raises a question for the interpreter, a question about the historical horizon of the author and his presence in it, which is only perceptible through the text itself and the conversation. A characteristic feature of Gadamerian hermeneutics emerges once again, consisting in the importance of dialogue with the other, insofar as the other is recognized as a valuable subject who can contribute knowledge in order to generate transformation; the other also represents authority insofar as what he wants to say is transcendental for the one who is interested in understanding it. We see how linguisticity is presented as

6 Juan Sterling, Teoría Comunicacional del Derecho y texto: un análisis desde la influencia de Ortega y Gasset in Gregorio Robles (ed) *La Teoría Comunicacional del Derecho: análisis críticos y aplicativos.* Madrid: Civitas, 2023, 217-227, 218.

the essence of the hermeneutic task and the reason lies in the fact that understanding always requires a linguistic framework, not because it comes after words, but because such understanding is consummated in language. It can be concluded then that the *ordinamental* texts require interpretation to be understood and thus create the legal system. The science of jurists or legal dogmatics is in charge of this task by generating systemic text that clarifies, orders and complements the ordinamental and allows its insertion in the legal sphere.

2.2 Legal text as writerly text (Barthes)

Roland Barthes presents the notion of *writerly* texts as opposed to *readerly texts*; a fundamental distinction present in the CTL. The former are characterized by the fact that the reader is encouraged to take an active part in the development of the narrative, allowing his or her decisions about what and how to read to change the ending of the narrative; on the contrary, the latter presents a linear structure in which one can only read in one way with an invariable result.[7] The concept of hypertext added to that of *writable* text is valuable as a complement to the traditional and linear vision, so its exclusion would not be desirable. Basically, *writerly* texts are based on the idea that the reader is not a consumer but a producer of textual meanings. On this point, Barthes states: "*The writable text is a perpetual present about which no consequent word can be posed (which would fatally transform it into the past); the writable text is us at the moment of writing*".[8]

On the other hand, *readerly* texts would be products, the true mass that constitutes literature, but this mass is only achieved through the process of interpretation, as Barthes would say. These texts are not made to be constructed, they are made to be read or consumed as long as the reader has no influence on the story being addressed, conforming only to a mental interpretation that may, or may not, alter their perceptions and ideology.

In this order of ideas, the concept of *writerly* text shows that interpreting a text is not just giving it meaning, it is checking what it is made of. The text is an infinite universe of possibilities that are given to the reader (not just two), who in the end will decide, for himself, which one to choose.

---

7 Roland Barthes, *Image, music, text.* London: Fontana Press, 1977, p. 142.

8 Roland Barthes, *S/Z.* Buenos Aires: Siglo XXI, 2011, p. 14.

These texts have no order or hierarchy, they are a kind of rhizome in which uniformity is not their main characteristic, like *Rayuela* by Julio Cortázar or *The Garden of Forking Paths* by Jorge Luis Borges, we are faced with texts in which the reader participates and decides what to write in order to influence the result, texts like this are not just read, they are written and rewritten with each reader who enters new places and moves at will through a universe of possibilities.

> In this ideal text, the networks are multiple and play with each other without any of them being able to reign over the others. This text is not a structure of meanings, it is a galaxy of signifiers, it has no beginning, it is reversible, it is accessed through multiple entrances without any of them being able to be declared with complete certainty the main one.[9]

The ideas of Barthes are therefore quite useful for understanding the new meaning of text within the CTL proposed by Robles. Barthes presents a vision of the text committed to an attitude of playful reconstruction on the part of the reader. Every reading is an act of subjectivity that develops like a game with rules, but these rules are not set by the author, and therefore he has no control over the interpretation that the reader will give to the message. On the contrary, because every exercise of interpretation of a text is ultimately a narrative practice that contains symbols and traditions, Barthes here presents an idea that is also present in the work of Gadamer: The existence of a reality pre-existing to the interpretative exercise, a reality in which the individual life experience is embedded in the search of meaning. In this way, when a text is approached, it implies freedom to configure, in accordance with a narrative attitude, the meaning that the reader will construct as a game in which the body and all its senses participate, in a kind of spiral (again the hermeneutic circle) that penetrates each sentence.

Finally, the French author also raises the idea that the process of textual interpretation consists of expanding the text in form until it is related to the entire universe, because only then it would make sense. The text gives an account of experiences, stories, feelings, behaviors that occur in a space and time, and the judges approach them and pronounce them with more writable texts that generally refer to other texts (hypertext).

---

9 *Ídem*, p. 15.

2.3 Legal text as hypertext (Lotman and Landow)

The expanded text in its concept allows a different conception from the traditional one and is useful in the understanding of the legal phenomenon. Long gone are the times when the legal text was identified with that expressed in a codification and with no other connections than those that exegesis lavished, of course, few and only with authoritative attributions. The text under the CTL conception can be understood as that which allows communication, the generation of new meanings and a capacity for memory. The text has then some functions that allow to complete the definition of text according to *Iuri Lotman's* thinking.[10]

Lotman combats what he considers the reductionism of Charles Pierce and Chales Morris semiotics (the reduction of all semiotic phenomena to the functioning of isolated signs and chains of these), and he also questions this reductionist practice in the Prague School, follower of Ferdinand Saussure theories, which seeks to reduce speech (texts) to the language system and to a series of isolated communicative acts of message exchanges. Lotman also agrees with the hermeneutic idea that the text is not only a set of isolated signs, but as a message that wants to be transmitted. Thus, there are texts that can be works of art (paintings or sculptures), musical pieces, etc., that cannot be reduced to mere symbols, since this would imply the impossibility of knowing the experience and will of the soul that created them. Lotman, in his semiotic critique, seems to teach the idea that it is impossible to achieve the understanding of a text from the individual analysis of its components, in other words, he raises the need for a hermeneutic circle in the terms in which Gadamer meant it.

> The path taken by semiotic research during the last twenty years allows us to take many things differently. As we can now surmise, precise and functionally univocal systems that really work do not exist on their own in isolation. The separation of these is conditioned solely by heuristic necessity. Taken separately, none of them actually has the capacity to work. They only function when immersed in a semiotic continuum, fully occupied by semiotic formations of various kinds and at various levels of organization.[11]

---

10 Iuri Lotman, *La semiosfera I.* Madrid: Forensis, 1996, p. 86.
11 *Ídem*, p. 22.

Finally, Lotman emphasizes that the reading of a text is an amalgam of traditions, practices and habits that are embedded within the culture, a culture that determines the understanding of the subject and that forms a totality from which the meaning of the texts is accessed.

Now, analyzing *G.P. Landow's* proposal, he constructs a concept of hypertext that is currently relevant in the digital era insofar as it refers to a text that refers to others (hyperlinks). But he also puts forward the idea that the limitations of writing in the West must be overcome insofar as the text can adopt non-traditional forms such as hieroglyphics; this idea is shared by Robles, who states that text (in the legal field) is not only that encoded with letters that form words and propositions, but can also be images or symbols. Landow's contribution is decisive for the interest raised here; it is nothing more and nothing less than assuming hypertext as an infinite text interconnected with other texts of the past, with appendices, clarifications, notes and nuances that are joined to create a uniform, infinite and constantly growing object. This idea of hypertext is the one presented by Robles in law— a varied, non-traditional text that implies symbols, that involves connections necessary to give meaning to the message, that often resorts to past texts and appendices in order to find new meanings in it.

> Although in the distant, or not so distant future all individual texts will be electronically connected, thus forming metatexts and meta-metatexts of a genre only partially imaginable today, much smaller forms of hypertext have already appeared. There are already transliterations into hypertext of poetry, fiction and other subjects originally conceived for book technology.[12]

The text thus understood makes it possible to recover a vision of law as a hermeneutic exercise connected to the world and not as an exercise subject to inflexible rules and to an exclusive vision of the way of understanding the normative statements present in the texts. In the face of the limits of the positivist vision, this new vision of the hermeneutics of law constructed in the CTL appears as a valuable element for the understanding of the legal phenomenon.

12 George Landow, *Hipertexto*. Barcelona: Paidós, 1995, p. 51.

2.4 Legal text and grammar of power (Deleuze and Guattari)

Although there is a diversity of texts, some provide information about reality or about the past (informative or constatative texts) while others are used to express emotions and feelings (emotive), an aspect that should be highlighted in CTL is that the text in law does not have a primary function of informing or transmitting emotions; its primary function is to guide the will of a person to perform a certain action: "*its intrinsic or consubstantial function is to get the addressee, the person to whom the speaker or issuer of the sentence is addressed, to act in a certain way*"[13]. The above is a determining feature of the conception of law and its relationship with language and text in CTL, and this feature obeys the rules of grammar as markers of power, a theory developed by the French thinkers *Gilles Deleuze* and *Félix Guattari.*

In their well-known work *A Thousand Plateaus: Capitalism and Schizophrenia*, Deleuze and Guattari reflect on language and its conception as an informative and communicative element. Using the example of the teacher who teaches, they indicate that when the teacher transmits knowledge to students he "ensigns," that is, he gives orders; under this figure the teacher "*does not inform when he asks a student, nor does he inform when he teaches a rule of grammar or calculus*"[14]. Moreover, the orders of the one who teaches say nothing about knowledge and neither do they reinforce it, for in the end they are acts of will inasmuch as the orders are based on orders and not on information. According to the above, the teaching process (teaching machine according to the authors):

> ... does not communicate information, but imposes on the child semiotic coordinates with all the dual bases of grammar (masculine-feminine, singular-plural, noun-verb, subject of enunciation-subject of enunciation, etc.). The elementary unit of language - the utterance - is the slogan. Rather than common sense, a faculty that would focus information, we must define the abominable faculty that consists of emitting, receiving and transmitting slogans. Language is not even made to be believed in, but to be obeyed and made to be obeyed.[15]

---

13 Gregorio Robles, *Teoría del Derecho: Fundamentos de Teoría Comunicacional del Derecho*, vol. I, 2015, *op.cit.*, p. 97.

14 Giles Deleuze and Felix Guattari, *Mil mesetas: capitalismo y esquizofrenia*. Valencia: Pre-textos, 2008, p. 81.

15 *Ídem.*

From this point of view, when a message is transmitted, what is sought is obedience rather than the transmission of information or the manifestation of emotions. Using a fragment of Georges Darien's L'epaulette when he says: "*The baroness has not the slightest intention of convincing me of her good faith, she simply indicates to me what she would like to see me admit, even if only apparently*"[16], we can conclude that the idea of French thinkers is applicable to the communications of authorities such as the State and its organizations, this can be thought of because the pretension of power as an essential characteristic of language can afford to dispense with credibility or the veracity of the content as long as it is made clear that this is what we want others to do. A kind of legitimacy via authority rather than via argumentation.

Therefore, CTL conceives the text in a similar way to Deleuze and Guattari, insofar as in law the text is designed so that the addressee of the message acts in a certain way, that is, they perform a certain behavior or refrain from performing it. It is prescriptive language, which is directed to action (as J.L. Austin would say), such action can be positive or negative (omission-abstention). Therefore, a legal text (which is the totality of the legal system) can be called a type of prescriptive text insofar as it does not seek to describe reality or to verify specific situations or to make predictions, nor does it seek to reveal truths or establish values. Of course, legal texts offer descriptions and information (for example, it contemplates cases with situations of mode, time and place in which a conduct must occur) but these are not its main functions, they would only be auxiliary or accidental insofar as they serve as a basis or reference. In the same way, law does not seek to accelerate passions or generate emotional impacts (not even rational ones), although when legal issues are addressed, especially those related to delicate criminal, tax or labor matters, or when controversial issues such as minority rights are debated—which often become media spectacles—it is common to react by arousing the most diverse and extreme emotional reactions, from jubilation to indignation, but this is alien to the world of law, as it uses an essentially prescriptive language.

3. The analytical-Hermeneutic Method

The study of CTL implies a deep reflection on the Theory of Legal Dogmatics, which can also be called Theory of the Science of Law, delving

16 *Ídem*, p. 82.

into the hermeneutic-analytic method proposed by Robles to illustrate the process of construction of the constituent elements of this stage. The approach of this method will be determinant to continue the understanding of the role of hermeneutics—in its optimistic vision—in CTL, as well as the pretension of its creator to create an explanation contrary to what most authors maintain: hermeneutics and analytics are essentially opposite fields. It is, therefore, a conciliatory proposal based on complementarity.

In this section, and in a very general way, it can be said that the study of Legal Dogmatics and its role in the CTL starts with a revaluation of the term to later investigate the methods it uses, and that for Robles there have been two main ones: the jurisprudence of concepts and sociological jurisprudence, since these are the ones that best explain the problem of the method in the science of law or science of jurists, the reason? "*Both conceptualist and sociological jurisprudence start from the same purpose, which is none other than to expose the meaning of legal texts*".[17] In addition to the above, Robles indicates that attention should be paid to values insofar as there is usually talk of a third methodological path that corresponds to the postulates of the jurisprudence of values or valuational jurisprudence.

It is important to emphasize at this point that CTL is composed of a Formal Theory of Law, a Theory of Legal Dogmatics and a Theory of Legal Decisions, and dogmatics focuses on the interpretative construction of the system (SIS) based on the hermeneutic-analytic method. This idea of Dogmatics is an open one that incorporates the three parts mentioned above, which are determinant for the understanding of legal texts.

3.1 A new approach: the relation between hermeneutics and analytics

CTL points to the use of a method that he calls hermeneutic-analytic, a novel and conciliatory proposal between two scenarios traditionally considered as opposites: philosophical hermeneutics and analytic philosophy. It is then a method that is the result of the conjunction between analytical or language philosophy (insofar as it seeks the clarification of thought through language with organizational and classificatory functions) and philosophical hermeneutics, which seeks the analysis of the phenomenon of the understanding of the spiritual, cultural or social sciences. This

17 Gregorio Robles, *Teoría del Derecho: Fundamentos de Teoría Comunicacional del Derecho*, vol. II. Navarra: Thomson Reuters–Civitas 2015, p. 19.

hermeneutic-analytic method that CTL uses for concepts such as *action, relationship, situation, institution,* etc., is the proof that the construction of the concept of law is an act of understanding rather than of logical deductive explanation.

Thus, in the first place it must be said that dogmatics is an interpretative discipline, and therefore is the result of the application of hermeneutics. In this section, it follows the philological tradition that deals with finding the understanding of messages through a method that allows differentiating a correct interpretation from others that are not. The relationship between law and literature, for example, comes from this tradition, which is not proper, as many think, to the legal world. Legal dogmatics is confronted with potentially normative legal texts in order to determine their meaning and thus reach an understanding of what the authority that made the decision and originated the text really meant. Besides, CTL is clear in stating that the person who performs this interpretative exercise characteristic of legal dogmatics must have a legal background in order to acquire the techniques and methods offered by the hermeneutics of law. The hermeneutic process, thus understood, is that which allows the choice of one interpretation over others, this process is not exhausted simply with the use of grammar as the only element to obtain meaning, it is necessary to go further, hence interpretation is an activity that requires will, reading is not interpreting, just as seeing something is not representing or interpreting something. The above reflection explains the hermeneutic character of the method proposed by Robles.

Secondly, Legal Dogmatics is a conceptualizing discipline, and therefore, analytical in nature. Analytical philosophy insists that the task of philosophy is to clarify thought through language, therefore, its function will no longer be to scrutinize and explain the logical form of propositions but to understand them, that is, to order the different language games according to the role assumed, thus avoiding misunderstandings (incomprehension), which is nothing different from misuse of language. Philosophical problems are in reality pseudo-philosophical, since they are basically problems of language that must be unraveled in order to clarify them, in this way the analysis of language is the necessary tool to eliminate the problems of philosophy.

In this order of ideas, the influence of analytical thinking in law, specially in CTL, translates into the fact that every dogmatic text seeks to clarify the meaning of the words used (after a hermeneutic process). It is a matter of "*defining the essential terms at issue, i.e., defining concepts*".[18] Legal science must try to give definitions (which are not always precise) just like the other sciences. The conceptualization carried out by dogmatics breaks down the whole into its parts in order to identify the meaning of each one of them in relation to that whole.

In the legal field, the domain of truth must be familiar with the methods proper to the legal field, therefore, one of the tasks of the Theory of Law is to deal with the methodology with questions about whether law is a true science, the existence of various methods and the characteristics of these methods. CTL focuses on the hermeneutic-analytical method it uses. This method should be understood in two senses, one as a *simple hermeneutic* method and the other as *hermeneutic-analytic*. The first is relative to a simply interpretative model in general and that falls on texts. The second sense, the analytical hermeneutic that "*consists in emphasizing the idea that in interpretation there are two sides that need and complement each other*".[19]

3.2 Law as a hermeneutic practice

To maintain that law is a hermeneutic practice, the work of the German author *Wilhelm Dilthey* will be used mainly and it will be assumed that hermeneutics is an exercise in interpreting vital manifestations which have been expressed in writing by the author. In this way we try to understand the individuality from the external signs; for it is these that allow entry into the depths of the mind of the subject who wishes to transmit a message.

The hermeneutic interpretation method then, based on the foundation that Dilthey himself outlined, aims to consolidate itself as one that supports the idea of truth in the social sciences from the understanding of the mentality of the author or creator of a text. In this order of ideas, the method raises the need to distrust grammar as the only source for giving meaning to a proposition. This proposal proposes the abandonment of the grammatical (the perceptible or physical) as the only referent of meaning, to face that often the spirit or intention of the author is not faithfully reflected in the

18 Gregorio Robles, *Teoría del Derecho: Fundamentos de Teoría Comunicacional del Derecho*, vol. II, 2015, *op. cit.*, p. 235.

19 *Ídem*, p. 374.

written text or the speech said: "*on the ground of the physical appears spiritual life*".[20]

Thus, the lived feeling will be the foundation for the development of a hermeneutic that is based on historical reason and so the understanding would be achieved through the analysis of individuality from external signs because in the end every text is the expression of a author, of their feelings and aspirations. Thus, a change in the conception of language is required that adds a generative capacity, in other words, it is not sufficient with the process of understanding alone which is accessed through hermeneutics, but it must also be recognized that this is within a process of communication which is practical because it generates realities and transforms them. When writing or speaking there is always an intention of transformation of reality that transcends the simple externality of the signs used.

Thus, the experiences (*erlebnis*) will be the foundation for the development of law as a hermeneutic practice because given the sources that are analyzed, textual in their entirety, understanding beyond what simple grammar allows is required. Any written expression on CTL is based on intentions that are not always reflected in the text, so the context, history, ideology and local and international circumstances are indispensable elements to be able to carry out a proper comprehensive process. In addition, the need to approach CTL related texts from an emancipatory and constructive perspective implies the recognition of a dynamic notion of text that evolves with various social contexts and has an effective practice. In this section we discuss documents which make it possible to understand the various imaginaries on the human condition and the consequences that in reality it entails to assume such understandings.

Therefore, the teaching of law should aim at optimizing the ideas proposed by CTL and its method, in particular by strengthening the necessary sensitivity and solidarity when interpreting legal texts. When we seek the understanding of the legal system through dogmatic, the need to assume critical positions, but also in accordance with social sensitivity and the defense of shared values, is something essential in the training of future lawyers. It is here that the role of legal education becomes more important, because of its proximity to literature, narratology and the construction of pedagogical curricula containing these visions.

---

20 Wilhem Dilthey, *Dos escritos sobre hermenéutica: El surgimiento de la hermenéutica y los Esbozos para una crítica de la razón histórica*. Madrid: Itsmo, 2000, p. 93.

4. Teaching of Law: Narratology and Sensibility.

As indicated above, the legal dogmatic fulfills its work, which is none other than that of the construction of the system (SIS) which in the end is nothing different from a commentary on texts with certain requirements, this commenting function is what occurs in literature, the relationship between the law and the literary work is therefore important; this idea is closely linked to the theory of texts and the philosophy of language.

Recognizing the closeness between law and literature requires that both areas start from the analysis of individual and social human life, from the simplest sensations to complex perceptions, from momentary happiness to sadness and the most overflowing anger. Therefore, the advantage of linking literature in the teaching of law would be useful and necessary, at least for an improvement in the style and writing of texts, not to mention the empathic capacity that could be generated.

It is sufficient to say that the language of literature allows the limits of legal language to be extended, since the latter being elite and complex does not allow an adequate transmission of images and emotions. The phenomenon of codification and the formal process of linguistic and interpretative pre-requisites to address certain issues reduces the imagination and utopian capacity that literature does offer, in this way, literature and its language shake from lethargy to flat and commonly inexpressive legal language.

4.1 The relation between law and literature: the role of solidarity.

At this point, the work of *Martha Nussbaum* should be introduced, which throughout numerous works has pointed out that the connection between law and literature lies in the possibility of exposing a narrative that allows the construction of empathy from the characters and stories that develop in novels, poetry and jurisprudence. Nussbaum thus tries to create an ethical notion of law committed to the effective realization of justice from a moral philosophy. This is possible by emphasizing the experiences that poetry and literature offer to readers as long as they allow them to evaluate their performances and emotions in order to fit them into the concept of human dignity. Now, although we talk about emotions, this does not prevent a rational analysis of them, the key would be in an ethical analysis that is concrete in the imperative need to act consulting the well-being of others, in other words, putting ourselves in the shoes of the other person is the way to a sense of social solidarity, and this is possible thanks to reading poetry and literature as devices that amplify the essence of the human being from his most genuine emotions. In the end, man's life is told in his actions and decisions, in the end, "*life is never merely presented by a text; it is always represented as something*".[21]

Thus, the communicational and narrative view of law allows for greater sensitivity to social dramas and significant individual experiences. It generates a relationship of emotional empathy that would return humanism to the legal phenomenon and bring it closer to related areas such as public policies, while such sensitivity would allow a better approach to the contexts for which they are created. This is possible as law can be understood as an exercise in narration, since every act of speech (written or oral) is aimed at the transmission of a message and the achievement of ends through the telling of stories and the recreation of individual and collective imaginaries. The narrative of law is then that structure formed by an action, some ends, motives, agents and finally results. All these elements, which are generally present in the court judgments that follow from them, make it possible to understand law on the basis of a concept similar to that of a novel or story. It would be enough to ask basic questions to ignite the plot and set the narrative in motion: "*In short, these terms or other similar ones come up with questions about what, why, who, how, or against whom of the action.*"[22] In the end, every judicial process begins with one narrative and ends with another.

Law, being an instrument that is involved with man's conduct and his judgment, necessarily connects to the ideals and aspirations of the individual. In the same way we find in the judicial judgments such wise positions that it remains only to contemplate them with enormous shock, without forgetting that there will be a few that will make us feel astonished by their untidiness and injustice, each narrative is a life put into text and context: "*the 'lives' are texts ... subject to revision, exegesis, interpretation*".[23]

The previous reflections must bring the legal teaching closer to the community on the basis of the idea of solidarity, as proposed by *Richard Rorty*.

---

21 Martha Nussbaum, *El conocimiento del amor. Ensayos sobre filosofía y literatura.* Madrid: Antonio Machado Libros, 2005, p. 29.

22 Paul Ricoeur, *Tiempo y Narración I.* Buenos Aires: Siglo XXI, 2004, p. 117.

23 Jerome Bruner y Susan Weisser, La invención del yo: la autobiografía y sus formas in David Olson *et al* (eds.) *Cultura escrita y oralidad.* Barcelona: Gedisa, 1995, p. 178.

Solidarity has become the link between the individual and the community, based on the need to improve the quality of life of disadvantaged people by avoiding unnecessary suffering. This implies differentiating between solidarity in the private and public sphere, and this is because our individual values and commitments do not always coincide with those we express in public and this conditions the language that must be more solid, pragmatic and politically sophisticated. Solidarity, in this way, becomes a public issue which translates into concern for others who have not had luck in the lottery of life. Rorty put it clearly: "*Solidarity is to groups what respect is to the individual.*"[24] Therefore, the above reflection implies assuming a notion of history based on contingency (chance) and not as a result of an awareness or repetition together with the abandonment of universal values. Hence, solidarity moves forward as a genuine concern for those who do not have the same luck as us and not as the triumph of human reason as stipulated by Kant.

The challenges facing Law Teaching are becoming increasingly complex, and rethinking the concept of competence (now seen as capacity) is only one step towards solving the social complexity that marks the development of the legal world and training lawyers. For example, the situation generated by the Covid-19 pandemic and its consequences implies that the vision and teaching of law must be reshaped and directed the construction of solidarity. In this context, law acts as an "*element which seeks to convey a message of solidarity based on the recognition of the equality brought by chance: we are all equal because at some point in life and for any reason we can happen a misfortune*"[25].

The result must be the reformulation of competences in the study plans of law programmes under a capacity analysis based on solidarity and implying that the design of learning outcomes has a common thread humanist to guide the practice and achievements of students according to social values. This is possible if one consciously appropriates CTL's subjects, especially those linked to textual linguistics, given its broad view of text, its emancipating and understanding role of human realities and its constructive nature of meaning which moves away from the cold and static descriptivist

---

24 Richard Rorty, *Philosophy as Cultural Politics. Philosophical Papers.* Cambridge: Cambridge University Press, 2007, p. 168.

25 Juan Sterling and Yohana Cárdenas, Enseñanza del Derecho y Resultados de Aprendizaje: prolegómenos a una propuesta desde las capacidades humanas, la solidaridad y la empatía in *Revista Nuevo Foro Autónomo*, 2 (1). Popayán: Uniautónoma del Cauca, 2021, p. 91-112, 97.

view of the world; law as a hermeneutic practice, implies understanding the world, since it is ultimately the sum of the experiences of individual souls expressed in texts.

4.2 Narratology, sensibility and law teaching.

Narratology is the theory of narration. It does not focus on specific narratives as it tries to be a general explanation of what they have in the act of narrating providing rules for it. The concept of narratology is of French origin and prevails over other synonyms such as narrative or semiotic narrative. Originally the term narratology was introduced by *Tzvetan Todorov* in 1969 in his work *Grammar of the Decameron* as "*a science that does not yet exist*"[26], that is, a science of narration.

Like the postulates of CTL, narratology takes a broad position in dealing with the concept of text and deals with the study of its structure and relations both internal and external. Therefore, it can be said that the Communicational Theory has a narratological component, evidenced especially in its pragmatic level; but this does not mean that it is omitted in the other levels, because in the Juridical Dogmatic (semiotic level) can be located as narratology is a subdivision or subset of the semiotic study insofar as it offers analyses on the operative factors in the systems of meaning to influence their practice, in other words, as opposed to the study of the word in the narrative, the narrative language present in the unconscious is studied.

It is important to note that narratology should not be identified as a type of narration, but rather, as indicated, the study of this by adopting the forms of a discipline. Their starting point are the narratives that are mainly found in stories (by their chronicle structure) and that communicate through oral or written language (prose or verse), but also usually fall on sign language or fixed or moving portraits (works of art, gestures, musical pieces or films). Using written language as an example, it can be identified that in the stories there is an order in which facts or events occurring in a space-reality are presentedtime, thus the narratologist is able to identify this order and the events that are told regardless of how they present themselves.

The importance of promoting narratology (understood as the science of storytelling) in law education is aimed at recognizing that the role of

26 Tzvetan Todorov, *Gramática del Decamerón*. Madrid: Taller Ediciones, 1973, p. 10.

of imagination in the cognitive process is relevant as it is related to the person's ability to feel, perceive, recall and project mentally own or foreign situations or emotions and, on the basis of this, to build moral guidelines with based on this capacity to be able to also put oneself in the other's place and to understand their emotions and actions. Moreover, in every society there are feelings or mixed emotions ranging from anger and despair to happiness and optimism; based on this spectrum of emotions the individual is formed through the creation of the early foundations of an imaginative empathic attitude and social compassion that are present in every process of knowledge. Thus, CTL can reflect the contributions of narratology and how it has made the scope of narrative present not only in literary texts but also in technical as well as legal texts when investigating context, the history and philosophy behind rules or judicial decisions, not to mention understanding in the hermeneutic field.

5. Conclusion

CTL as a theory of law, but with notable interdisciplinary approaches to areas such as history, literature, linguistics and philosophy, is a construction that allows rethinking the teaching of law from its broad notion of text, that it is subjected to a hermeneutic-analytical method in order to achieve the comorescence of socio-legal realities (a method that offers a conciliatory proposal which allows the legal dogmatics to be assumed in a broader and deeper way, excluding historical quarrels between these two areas). The above is possible given the special nature of the legal text, which is writerly in addition to responding to the notion of hypertext and being an example of the grammar of power. Thus, the abandonment of a reductionist, traditional and linear view of the legal text opens the way for more solidary and sensitive reflections by law students which objetive must be to understand that interpreting a text means constructing it, changing reality, which is also full of stories, emotions and experiences. Only in this way a more humanistic legal education is possible.

The foregoing reflections, finally, imply that it must be recognized that law as a hermeneutic exercise in a broad, critical and historical way, must have an impact on its teaching, that in many cases it is limited to hermeneutics as the exclusive method of law and what it can offer you. The hermeneutic task then starts from a reflection on the teaching of law as any act of juridical activity presupposes an act of understanding its communicational meaning and interpretative consequences; the relationship between hermeneutics and pedagogy is inevitable.

Finally, and for discussion, a reflection is generated on what the relationship between empathy, solidarity and rationality is in the context of the application of law and legal education? Would not the application of law (and legal education directed at it) be rational if in the future it gave more weight to empathy and solidarity than hitherto? And conversely, does not the search for more empathy and solidarity in law presuppose a rational understanding of law or the search for rationality in legal methodology? To resolve these questions, one must start from the fact that throughout history, human beings have faced countless conflicts, many of them resolved by law. These conflicts reflect a fundamental dichotomy in human nature: the coexistence between rationality and solidarity; the former has often been considered the driving force behind decision-making, while solidarity adds an emotional layer that can significantly influence the behaviors and outcomes of conflicts. Given this situation, spaces must be created to understand how solidarity and empathy can distort the rationality of legal decisions, based, for example, on Jon Elster's extended rationality theory, which is opposed to Rational Choice Theory.

Elster considers that "*between the strict theory of the rational and the broad theory of the true and the good, there is sufficient room and need for a broad theory of the rational*".[27] In this sense, he points out that there are three elements from which human motivations can derive: instrumental rationality, social norms and emotions, the latter being the most important for modifying the classical model in its structure and situating itself as an element that can grant rationality to desires and by which the rational change of preferences can be explained. Thus, in order to harmonize reasons and actions, three characteristics must be satisfied: 1) the beliefs or desires must be elaborated in order to perform the preferred action; 2) the reasons must be the de facto generators of the action; and 3) the reasons must be the de facto generators of the action in the correct way. All these characteristics are in reality what allow people to forge bonds with others, stronger bonds are the result of greater empathy between individuals.

The above explanation is an attempt to harmonize rationality with solidarity and empathy, not only in the field of legal education, but also in

27 Jon, Elster (1988). *Uvas amargas, sobre la subversión de la racionalidad*, trad. Enrique Lynch. Barcelona: Península, p. 15.

judicial decision-making. Although it is a succinct form, it can be a starting point for future work and reflection.

References

Barthes, Roland (1977). *Image, music, text.* London: Fontana Press.

Barthes, Roland. (2011). *S/Z.* Buenos Aires: Siglo XXI.

Bruner, Jerome and y Weisser, Susan (1995). La invención del yo: la autobiografía y sus formas in David Olson *et al* (eds.) *Cultura escrita y oralidad.* Barcelona: Gedisa, p. 177-202.

Deleuze, Giles and Guattari, Felix (2008). *Mil mesetas: capitalismo y esquizofrenia.* Valencia: Pre-textos.

Dilthey, Wilhem (2000). *Dos escritos sobre hermenéutica: El surgimiento de la hermenéutica y los Esbozos para una crítica de la razón histórica.* Madrid: Itsmo.

Jon, Elster (1988). *Uvas amargas, sobre la subversión de la racionalidad,* trad. Enrique Lynch. Barcelona: Península.

Landow, George (1995). *Hipertexto.* Barcelona: Paidós.

Lotman, Iuri (1996). *La semiosfera I.* Madrid: Forensis.

Nussbaum, Martha (2005). *El conocimiento del amor. Ensayos sobre filosofía y literatura.* Madrid: Antonio Machado Libros.

Prince Gerald (2010). Narratología in Roman Selden (ed.) *Historia de la Literatura del siglo XX.* Madrid: AKAL, 2010, p. 110-130.

Ricoeur, Paul (2004). *Tiempo y Narración I.* Buenos Aires: Siglo XXI.

Robles, Gregorio (2003). *Introducción a la teoría del Derecho,* 6ª edición. Madrid: Debate.

Robles, Gregorio (2015). *Teoría del Derecho: Fundamentos de Teoría Comunicacional del Derecho,* vol. I, 6ª edición. Navarra: Thomson Reuters–Civitas.

Robles, Gregorio (2015). *Teoría del Derecho: Fundamentos de Teoría Comunicacional del Derecho,* vol. II. Navarra: Thomson Reuters–Civitas.

Robles, Gregorio (2018). *Cinco estudios sobre Teoría Comunicacional del Derecho.* Santiago de Chile: Olejnik Editores.

Rorty, Richard (2007). *Philosophy as Cultural Politics. Philosophical Papers.* Cambridge: Cambridge University Press.

Sterling, Juan (2020). Teoría Comunicacional del Derecho y hermenéutica: Gregorio Robles y su versión Barthesiana del texto, in Cristina Hermida y Diego Medina (eds.) *La Teoría Comunicacional del Derecho y otras direcciones del pensamiento jurídico contemporáneo.* Valencia: Tirant Lo Blanch, p. 637-659.

Sterling, Juan and Cárdenas, Yohana (2021). Enseñanza del Derecho y Resultados de Aprendizaje: prolegómenos a una propuesta desde las capacidades humanas, la solidaridad y la empatía in *Revista Nuevo Foro Autónomo,* 2 (1). Popayán: Uniautónoma del Cauca, p. 91-112.

Sterling, Juan (2023). Teoría Comunicacional del Derecho y texto: un análisis desde la influencia de Ortega y Gasset in Gregorio Robles (ed) *La Teoría Comunicacional del Derecho: análisis críticos y aplicativos*. Madrid: Civitas, 2023, p. 217-227.

Todorov, Tzvetan (1973). *Gramática del Decamerón*. Madrid: Taller Ediciones.

Philosophy of Law in Professional Ethics Training for Judges

*Derk Venema**

Abstract

Philosophy of law is useful for professional judicial ethics training in several ways. Firstly, different theories focus on different aspects of decisions and actions. Taken together, they help judges form a complete picture of ethical dilemmas in their professional or private lives. Secondly, philosophy presents the insight that ethical "rightness" is a pragmatic category, not an objectively calculable or measurable fact. This contribution shows how philosophy of law and ethics is used in the professional ethics course in the judicial training programme in the Netherlands.

1. Introduction: professional ethics training for judges

Why do judges need their own professional ethics? Isn't it their job to simply apply the law which is the outcome of a democratic procedure, carefully formulated by other professionals? And apart from deciding cases, don't the same ethics apply to their behaviour as to anyone else's? The answer to these questions is: Judges need judicial ethics, because the application of the law is not always straightforward and because judges fulfil a highly specialised and important role in the democratic rule of law State, and thus are are confronted with specific circumstances that make specific norms relevant for their professional conduct. Legal philosophy provides judicial ethics training with structure and depth. This does not explain, however, why judicial ethics trainings and codes of conduct for judges are relatively recent phenomena. That explanation lies in the upsurge of calls on government institutions in general to publicly account for their actions.

* Open Universiteit, the Netherlands.

It takes crises or transitions to cause government institutions to increase their efforts in public accountability.[1] In the US, the Vietnam war (1955–1975) and the Watergate scandal (1972–1974) sparked a call for more public accountability.[2] The latter led the American Bar Association to require law schools to teach legal ethics as a condition for their continued accreditation,[3] indirectly also affecting future judges. Until the Cultural Revolution in the 1960s, judicial authorities in Europe had not felt much need to publicly account for their behaviour inside or outside the courtroom, other than through the selective publication of their decisions. The rise of individualism and public scrutiny and the waning of moral homogeneity, together with the growth of judicial power, caused a growing demand for public accountability from judges which was met with (slowly) increasing attention to professionalism in the form of codes and trainings.[4]

Another crisis was the collapse of communism in Eastern Europe in the 1990s.[5] In new democracies, generally, judiciaries worry more about their public image, as they have an important role in building public trust in the new government.[6] Interestingly, the fall of communism indirectly increased the attention to professional ethics by the judiciary in the Netherlands. According to an anecdote by Dutch judicial ethics pioneer and former judge Gert Vrieze, he visited the Czech Republic with a committee of Dutch judges in 1996 to assist in the drafting of a code of conduct, when at some point a Czech judge asked how a certain question was formulated in the Dutch code. The Czechs were astonished to learn that the Dutch

1 Cf. Iris van Domselaar, 'Where Were the Law Schools? On Legal Education as Training for Justice and the Rule of Law (Against the 'Dark Sides of Legality')', *Netherlands Journal of Legal Philosophy* 2021 (50) 1, p. 3-12.

2 Michael W. Dowdle, 'Public Accountability: Conceptual, Historical, and Epistemic Mappings', in: Peter Drahos (ed.), *Regulatory Theory: Foundations and Applications*, Acton: Australian National University Press 2017, 197-216, at 201.

3 Laurel Terry, 'U.S. Legal Ethics: The Coming of Age of Global and Comparative Perspectives', *Washington University Global Studies Law Review* (4) 2005-3, p. 463-533, at 474.

4 Jonathan Soeharno, *The integrity of the judge. A philosophical inquiry*, Farnham: Ashgate 2009, p. 16-20.

5 Cf. Adam Czarnota Martin Krygier Wojciech Sadurski (eds.), *Rethinking the Rule of Law after Communism*, Budapest: Central European University Press 2005.

6 Cf. Siri Gloppen, Roberto Gargarella & Elin Skaar, 'Introduction: The Accountability Function of the Courts in New Democracies' in: Siri Gloppen, Roberto Gargarella & Elin Skaar (ed.), *Democratization and the Judiciary. The Accountability Function of Courts in New Democracies*, London: Frank Cass 2004, p. 1-6.

judges, having come to lecture them on judicial conduct, did not have one themselves.[7]

Apparently, in the Netherlands, the need for a code of conduct for the judiciary had not been felt by the judiciary nor by society. There was, however, growing public scepticism about the impartiality of judges as long as their ancillary functions were not made public. A statutory obligation for the courts to this effect was enacted in 1997.[8] It took the Dutch judiciary until 2011 to establish a professional ethics code for judges.[9] A code might produce the external appearance of integrity or ethical reliability, but it cannot guarantee that on its own. What matters are the discussions amongst the judges *about* (the drafting of) the code: "A code is nothing, coding is everything."[10] Only a few years before the creation of the judicial ethics code, an obligatory professional ethics course had been integrated into the judicial training programme in the Netherlands.

Codes and courses support judges and other legal professionals in answering the demands of our present critical and authority-sceptical society that expects them to deliver on a wide range of themes— authority, certainty, effectiveness, and critical engagement. This makes the "promise of professionalism... a rather complex promise... ." And because the solving of ethical problems "will require choices by legal professionals", and "this element of choice cannot be overcome on some abstract general level",[11] professional ethics instruction must focus on discussing (the application of codes and ethical theories to) concrete ethical predicaments.

---

7 G. Vrieze, 'Zijn rechters zonder gedragscode nog wel te vertrouwen? (I)', *Trema* 2005-4, p. 139-150.

8 Derk Venema, 'Registers nevenbetrekkingen rechterlijke ambtenaren: rechters en leden OM', in: A. Berlee, S. Devriendt a.o., *Openbare registers, de toegankelijkheid daarvan en het gegevensbeschermingsrecht*, WODC Project number 3457, Open Universiteit 2025, p. 362-374.

9 The English and Dutch versions, together with other (international) judicial codes can be found in *Matters of Principle: Codes on the independence and impartiality of the judiciary*, Eleven International Publishers (2019) <https://www.rechtersvoorrechters.nl/media/nieuws/Matters%20of%20Principle%202019.pdf> accessed 1 November 2025.

10 M. Kaptein & J. Wempe, 'Twelve Gordian Knots When Developing an Organizational Code of Ethics', *Journal of Business Ethics* 1998, nr. 8, p. 853-869.

11 Arie-Jan Kwak, *The Legal Junction. The Complex Promise of Modern Legal Professionalism* (2005) <https://pure.eur.nl/ws/portalfiles/portal/46309092/The%20Legal%20Junction.pdf> accessed 1 November 2025, p. 11, 16.

Professional ethics for judges also serves to maintain the (continued) high public trust in the judiciary,[12] which is especially important in the light of the recent upsurge of populist politics in Europe and America. The 2025 open letter of nine European government leaders complaining about the case law of the European Court of Human Rights (ECtHR) is a case in point. Their claim for "more room nationally to decide on when to expel criminal foreign nationals" and to "keep track of… criminal foreigners" against the ECtHR's limitations to their "ability to make political decisions in our own democracies" is an alarming sign of the growing relativist attitude towards the rule of law and the separation of powers in Europe.[13] The inclination of populist and neo-fascist politicians to disrespect court verdicts and try to compromise the independence of the judiciary as one of the branches of government can be countered only by judges who firmly stand by their independent status in the rule of law state (*Rechtsstaat*).[14]

In this contribution, I will draw on fifteen years of experience as a professional ethics instructor for the judiciary. This one-day course forms an obligatory part of all variants of the initial training programme,[15] and is always led by a team of two instructors: an experienced judge and a professor of legal philosophy. In the latter category the same three persons — amongst them the author of this contribution — have been active for over a decade, while the first group has a much higher turnover. The course is usually planned in the final stage of the training programmes that are tailor-made according to the professional experience of each participant.[16] Every trainee judge is in possession of the book on judicial ethics, authored

12 See the data on the Netherlands and other European countries in: 'Perceived independence of the national justice systems among the general public' <https://europa.eu/eurobarometer/surveys/detail/3193> accessed 1 November 2025.

13 Letter from government leaders of Denmark, Italy, Austria, Belgium, Czeck Republic, Estonia, Latvia, Lithuania, and Poland (22 May, 2025) <https://www.governo.it/sites/governo.it/files/Lettera_aperta_22052025.pdf> accessed 1 November 2025.

14 See e.g. Nils A. Engstad, Astrid Lærdal Frøseth & Bård Tønder (eds.), *The Independence of Judges*, Eleven International Publishing 2014.

15 'Beroepsethiek. Leer beroepsethische dilemma's in de rechterlijke organisatie herkennen, analyseren en bespreken' <https://ssr.nl/cursus/rihlmeth/> accessed 1 November 2025.

16 'Rechter/raadsheer in opleiding' <https://ssr.nl/rio-opleiding/> accessed 1 November 2025.

by two of the three academic instructors, which they have received at the beginning of their training programme.[17]

The course consists of two main parts: a presentation on ethical and/or political theory and a discussion of real-life ethical questions. For the latter, not only ethical theory but also ethical "homework" is required: The participants are asked to send in a brief report of a "hard ethical decision" they have had to make either in their professional capacity or as a private person where their profession is relevant. Until a decade or so ago, the course was half a day longer and included watching and discussing a movie, such as 12 Angry Men or Le 10e Chambre.[18] In addition to documentaries and fiction, history can also contribute to the forming of judges, especially the histories of courts during World War II and communism. I will come back to these disciplines and subjects later in this paper.

Before moving on to the use of moral philosophy in professional ethics training for judges, I will give three examples of ethical questions facing judges, to make clear what kind of issues we are talking about. I will also use these examples in the next sections.[19] Some judges may believe that some judicial decisions are a "purely" legal matter. I do not agree, because law is a form of "practical reason,"[20] being necessarily in the same ballpark as moral or "practical" philosophy, both address human praxis and are therefore always mutually informative.

Example 1

Can I handle this case in the light of a possible appearance of bias? A judge might struggle with this question when one of the witnesses in a case turns out to be the mother of her son's classmate. On the one hand, even when the judge's subjective impartiality is not compromised, the appearance of bias or partiality should be avoided in the interest of public trust in the judiciary. On the other hand, when courts start avoiding every single possible ill suspicion by parties to a case, it may harm its credibility as well as its internal organisation.

---

17 Arie-Jan Kwak & Derk Venema, *De integere rechter. Ethiek en praktijk van het rechterlijk beroep*, Boom Juridische uitgevers, 2nd rev. ed. 2023.

18 *12 Angry Men*, Sidney Lumet (dir.), United Artists 1957; *Le 10e Chambre – Instants d'audience*, Raymond Depardon (dir.), Les Films du Losange (2004).

19 These and many more are discussed in Kwak & Venema 2023.

20 Steven Burton, 'Law as Practical Reason', 62 *Southern California Law Review* 1989, p. 747-793.

Example 2

Can I warn my mother that a building contractor whom she is about to pay a large down payment is on the verge of bankruptcy, which I only know because of my position as a judge? On the one hand, a judge is bound by the confidentiality of that information, while on the other, preventing your mother's financial ruin is a very strong ethical motive as well. Maybe there are ways to persuade your mother to cancel that contractor, or would that risk the real reason coming out in the end? Does it make you a bad judge when you warn her? Is the risk to the image of the judiciary worse than the risk to your mother?

Example 3

Should I acquit a defendant because I think my novel interpretation of the law (which I believe is the only just one) forces me to, when I know that he will probably be convicted in appeal? On the one hand, you alone are responsible for your judicial decisions, while on the other hand you can hardly simply ignore their consequences. Should you take into account that you may be giving the defendant false hope, or is it legitimate to try to persuade the appeal court, in the name of justice, to change its interpretation of the law?

Partly from my experience as an ethics instructor for the judiciary in the Netherlands, I aim to show that the value of ethical theories does not lie in their claims to objective moral truth or superiority, nor in their use as a recipe for the production of morally correct action in any specific case. Rather, the real value of moral and ethical theories lies in their combination which, if used together, help to discover as many relevant perspectives and factors as possible for a well-balanced decision. In this way, they can help to keep an open mind for any possible relevant aspects of an option for action and serve as a tool for systematisation not only in the context of discovery of the "right" decision, but also in the context of its justification. This brings with it a different kind of "rightness" of a decision or action than the ones presupposed in the respective ethical philosophies themselves. I will address that more fully after discussing the different theories.

In what follows, I will make a case for a specific use of moral philosophy in professional ethics training for the judiciary. First, I will show which aspects of decisions and actions are focused on by some of the main moral philosophies (Section 2). In Section 3, I will argue that ethical "rightness" is a pragmatic category, not an objectively calculable or measurable fact.

The content of these sections is more or less corresponds to the first part of my professional judicial ethics course, which is followed by discussing everyone's own ethical cases they sent in beforehand. Section 4 focuses on the rule of law and judicial independence, and Section 5 shows how a combination of philosophy with other disciplines can liven up and deepen the discussion.

2. The limitations of moral theories

I will now very briefly discuss some of the best known and most used ethical or moral theories. Applying them to the examples mentioned above will show the one-sidedness of each of them. This is based on the way I use these theories in my judicial ethics course.

Kantianism

According to Immanuel Kant (1724–1804), the ethical value of an action lies exclusively in the "good will" of the actor. In other words, good intentions make good actions, whatever the consequences. This presupposes a free will which is not determined by external factors, and is solely focused on following the "categorical imperative". That imperative concerns the will as the "faculty of desire considered not so much in relation to action (as choice is) but rather in relation to the ground determining choice in action."[21] Acts or decisions are ethically better the more they conform to the purely rational thing to want, which is determined by the rational grounds for them. Kant provides three different formulations of the categorical imperative, of which the first two are most illuminating for our purposes. The first demands universalisability: "Act only according to that maxim [= principle of your action, DV] whereby you can at the same time will that it should become a universal law."[22] This means that you can want that everyone will always have to act according to that maxim or principle when they are in the same situation. In the second formulation, Kant emphasises human dignity: "Act in such a way that you treat the humanity in your own person as well as in the person of any other, never merely as a means, but

21 Immanuel Kant, *Metaphysics of Morals*, Cambridge University Press, 1996 [1797]; Akademie-Ausgabe (AA) 6:213–4.

22 Immanuel Kant, *Groundwork of the Metaphysics of Morals*, Hackett 1993 [1785], AA 4:421.

always at the same time as an end."[23] Humans are ends in themselves, and must therefore never be treated merely as instruments for higher purposes. The ground for that lofty qualification is every human being's possession of free will, making them able to choose between right and wrong and to be held responsible for their choices.[24]

Material reality does not play any role at all in Kantian ethical assessment. Whether an action itself is a success or not, or whether it harms anyone or has any use at all, is completely irrelevant to its ethical worth. What is more, it isn't even relevant that there is no causal link between the will and bodily movement.[25] This is expressed in the motto *fiat iustitia, pereat mundus* and illustrated by Kant's example of the island society: The last death row inmates have to be executed even when the island society is about to leave the island for good, thus rendering the executions devoid of any practical societal value.[26]

Applied to example 1, the answer is clear: Yes, you can handle the case, because with a good intention you will be impartial, as all judges should always be. You shouldn't worry about image or other consequences. To the second question, the answer is obviously no. Universal just laws always trump individual advantages. Example 3 will be answered in the positive, as it is your good intentioned just interpretation of the law, and it is other people's job to take care of their part of the justice or child protection system.

A typical Kantian guideline in the Dutch judicial code is found in Recommendation 2.5.1, stating it is "the duty of the judge to make [just] decisions even if a strict application of the law would seem to impede this."[27]

Kant has thoroughly and systematically thought through one of the aspects we tend to consider in daily ethical assessments of (options for) actions— our intentions as autonomous individuals. *If* we were to limit ourselves to intentions, then Kant's moral theory would certainly be sufficient. But in real life, we also give weight to consequences.

23 Kant 1785, AA 4:429.

24 Paul Tiedemann, *Menschenwürde als Rechtsbegriff. Eine philosophische Klärung*, Berliner Wissenschaftsverlag 2007.

25 Immanuel Kant, *Critique of Practical Reason*, Cambridge University Press 2015 [1788], AA 5:57-58, 94-99.

26 Immanuel Kant, *Metaphysics of Morals*, Cambridge University Press, 1996 [1797]; AA 6:333.

27 *Matters of Principle* 2019, p. 94.

Utilitarianism

Jeremy Bentham (1748–1832) and John Stuart Mill (1806–1873) developed a method of assessing the moral quality of actions purely by their consequences, which directly contradicts Kant's method. According to the utilitarians, the only criterion for moral rightness can be the amount of pleasure an action causes or the amount of pain it reduces.[28] In short, it is a moral duty to calculate this as well as possible before deciding how to act. This principle of utility Bentham also called the "greatest happiness principle", which states that "the greatest happiness of all those whose interests are involved is the right and proper—and... universally desirable—end of human action; of human action in every situation, and in particular in the situation of functionaries exercising the powers of Government."[29]

Mill regarded individual freedom of fundamental importance to human happiness, and so he famously formulated a utilitarian criterion for when a government may limit an individual's freedom, the so called "(no) harm principle", stating that "the only purpose for which power can be rightfully exercised over any member of a civilised community, against his will, is to prevent harm to others."[30] This is also directly relevant to court decisions.

To answer the question of Example 1, you should try to imagine the possible consequences of both options in terms of changing pain and pleasure levels, such as, if you take the case and it becomes known that you knew the witness personally, how much less trust in the judiciary will how many people have and how much less happy does it make society? And if you don't take the case, what effect will the possible delay have on the parties, or how will it affect your relationship with your colleague who has to step in at the last moment? The best result in expected net social happiness will designate the best moral option. In the second problem, relevant possible consequences are: How probable is it that it will come out if you warn your mother, and how bad will you feel under your colleagues' contempt? Will your mother's being saved from bankruptcy outweigh all downsides? In

28 Jeremy Bentham, *An Introduction to the Principles of Morals and Legislation*, Oxford: Clarendon Press. 1996 [1780]; John Stuart Mill, 'Utilitarianism', in: John Stuart Mill, *Utilitarianism, On Liberty, Considerations on Representative Government, Remarks on Betham's Philosophy* (ed. By Geraint Williams), London: Everyman 1998 [1861], p. 1-67.

29 Bentham 1780, Ch. 1, note 1 (added in 1822).

30 John Stuart Mill, 'On Liberty', in: John Stuart Mill, *Utilitarianism, On Liberty, Considerations on Representative Government, Remarks on Betham's Philosophy* (ed. By Geraint Williams), London: Everyman 1998 [1859], p. 69-185, at 78.

example 3, you will have to weigh, in considering the option of acquittal, the small chance of a more just case law on a certain point (causing more happiness for society in the long run on top of instantaneous and lasting increase of happiness for the defendant) against the higher probability of a short period of happiness for the defendant before being disappointed in appeal, and an increase of happiness for yourself and maybe still having produced another building block for a future change in the case law.

The Dutch "Guidelines for impartiality and ancillary positions in the judiciary" require judges to weigh pros and cons of ancillary positions in a utilitarian way in Recommendation 3: "Ancillary positions, to the extent that they are statutorily permitted, are nonetheless undesirable if they could prejudice the proper administration of justice concretely or harm the confidence in the Judiciary."[31]

Utilitarianism may be directly opposed to Kant's approach, as a material principle versus a merely intellectual one,[32] but nevertheless, both Kant and utilitarian John Stuart Mill view their ethics as universalist and promoting equality, and as an improvement of the Golden Rule, most famous in Jesus' version: "do to others as you would have them do to you" (Matthew 7:12).[33] Although intentions, consequences and universality taken together may already seem to cover every possible ethical consideration, we will look at two more theories shedding light on desirable human conduct yet another way.

Virtue ethics

Aristotle (384–322 BCE) saw the cultivation of virtues as the best way to attain the goal of goals, leading the good life.[34] Virtues, or desirable character traits, cannot be acquired merely by reading an ethics book, but require life-long exercise. That exercise consists of trying to "hit the mean", the golden middle way between too much and too little.[35] In practising the virtue of generosity, for example, one needs to avoid both extremes, or vices: the too-much of wastefulness and the too-little of stinginess.[36]

31 *Matters of Principle* 2019, p. 152.
32 Mill 1861, p. 54-55.
33 Mill 1861, p. 17-18; Kant 1785, AA 4:430.
34 Aristotle, *Nicomachean Ethics* (Loeb Classical Library), Cambridge: Harvard University Press 1982.
35 Aristotle 1982, Book 2, Ch. 6. On virtue ethics, see also Stan van Hooft, *Understanding Virtue Ethics*, London: Routledge 2006.
36 Aristotle 1982, Book 2, Ch. 7, Section 4.

Because it can be quite hard too attain the exact virtuous middle way, Aristotle advises us too approach one of the extremes and then move away from it, and do the same with the other extreme, so as to move closer and closer to the goal.[37] Virtue ethics differs from Kantianism and utilitarianism in three important ways: It is not about recipes for the right decision or assessments in terms of good or bad actions, but about character building, and it takes into account the roles of luck and knowledge.

Which virtues are called upon in our examples? The first example could be an exercise in steadfastness: Not giving in to unwarranted suspicions of bias, avoiding being over-permissive (refusing to handle all cases with even the slightest possibility that unwarranted suspicions of bias might arise) or stubbornness (refusing to excuse yourself even when the appearance of bias is very strong). In the second example, we may find a dilemma between the virtues of trustworthiness and care. When you act on the one virtue, you fail to perform the other. Example 3 is an exercise in the virtue of justice: How do you find the golden mean between being an overzealous justice warrior and giving up on realising justice? What if both options in the case represent both extremes without there being an escape route to the golden mean? Maybe the virtue of honesty is involved as well, and might expediency also be a virtue? In this perspective, this seems like a tough ethical dilemma.

Virtues are called upon in Recommendation 2.5.3 of the Dutch judicial code:

> 2.5.3: "The judge behaves in a prudent and respectful manner and shows this in the way he behaves towards parties in court. The judge treats litigants and other participants in legal proceedings tactfully, politely and fair-mindedly. The judge not only keeps a close eye on his own behaviour but also monitors that of others. Integrity also implies that a judge will confront colleagues if their conduct is not conscientious or upright."[38]

Virtue ethics seems to point even less clearly to a "right answer" in ethical issues than utilitarianism. We now have three aspects of decisions or actions to take into account in ethical assessments: intentions, consequences, and character building. We will take a look at one more ethical approach that is again very different in nature.

---

37 Aristotle 1982, Book 2, Ch. 9, Section 9.
38 *Matters of Principle* 2019, p. 96.

Ethics of care

Although this is, like virtue ethics, not so much a general and abstract formula or recipe for producing good decisions, it does present a substantial ethics that guides behaviour. Originating from feminist authors,[39] care ethics is not gender-specific, but based on a general view of human life and its relation to the world.[40] This view emphasises our dependence on each other and on the cultural and natural environment. From that follows a joint responsibility for one another and for the environment in general. Special attention is due to weaker elements in our surroundings, and alternatives to a confrontational approach should be preferred when solving conflicts.[41] It may be thought of as much less individualist than Kantianism, utilitarianism, and virtue ethics.[42]

When applied to our three examples, an ethics of care would probably not give much more specific guidance than the previous two ethical approaches. In the first example, your attention would be focussed on care for your immediate colleagues in the court and the parties to the case. You might decide to ask the parties at the hearing if they object to your handling the case, being an acquaintance of one of the witnesses, and see if you can solve any reservations. Warning your mother, in the second example, might seem more caring than heeding the interests of a bankrupt building contractor. Nevertheless, care for the court organisation would entail preventing possible backlash from a breach of confidentiality. The third example presents another care dilemma: What would be the caring thing to do for the defendant? If the chance of acquittal in appeal are very slim, you might decide against giving him false hope.

In the spirit of care ethics, the Dutch judicial code in Recommendation 2.4.3 reminds judges to be "mindful of the interests of all those involved in a case. The judge has the ability to listen and approaches parties in a professional way: this gives parties the belief that their arguments have been listened to and that they have been taken seriously."

39 Carol Gilligan, *In A Different Voice*, Cambridge: Harvard University Press 1982.

40 Joan C. Tronto, 'Beyond Gender Difference to a Theory of Care', *Signs* 1987, Vol. 12, No. 4, p. 644-663.

41 See, e.g., Virginia Held, *The ethics of care: personal, political, and global*, New York: Oxford University Press 2006, p. 9-28; Joan Tronto, 'Care as the Work of Citizens. A Modest Proposal', in: Marilyn Friedman (ed.), *Women and citizenship*, New York: Oxford University Press 2005, p. 130-145.

42 Tronto 1987, p. 661-662, Held 2006, p. 34-35.

3. Ethical "rightness" as pragmatic outcome

If there were a fixed hierarchy in ethical theories, we would need only the top theory and could disregard the others. But if there is no hierarchy, and different ethical approaches lead to different outcomes, what's the use of any of them? The answer is quite simple, the reason that they all remain relevant is that each of them focusses on a *different (set of) aspect(s)* of a decision or action. This means that each of them separately is one-sided, but combined they encompass the decision or action in its entirety, or nearly so. It also means that they do not necessarily contradict, but rather supplement each other. On these grounds we can stop believing in the independent existence of objectively right answers that can, in principle, be found by very wise and moral thinkers.

The ethical theory that fits with the observation that the ethical theories discussed above fall short of treating the ethical questions in their entirety is called *pragmatism*. This term expresses the practical nature of the theory, which is focussed on human praxis, making it an obvious candidate to connect ethics or "practical philosophy" with law as "practical reason". For pragmatists, ethics is not concerned with finding "*the* right answer", but rather "*a* practicable and acceptable answer". For principal pragmatist John Dewey (1859–1952), morality is "a matter of interaction of a person with his moral environment."[43] In that interaction, people, individually and as groups, develop regularities in their behaviour, which Dewey calls "habits". Moral norms originate from habits as their ossified intellectual residue, not intentionally created, but the result of long periods of social interaction.[44] To remain relevant, however, moral norms should be useful for current situations, and adaptable to new ones. When habits become routines, it is important to keep questioning their ability to solve present ethical problems, and to adapt them to remain relevant and beneficial to practice. Making the right choice for action is therefore not a matter of applying abstract principles or calculations or virtues, but of solving an actual practical problem by considering different options, being either the

43 John Dewey, *Human Nature and Conduct* [1922], Vol. 14 in: *The Middle Works of John Dewey, 1899-1924*, 15 Vols., Carbondale and Edwardsville: Southern Illinois University Press, 1978, p. 219. On Dewey's ethics, I follow Louis Logister, *Creatieve democratie. John Deweys pragmatisme als grondslag voor een democratische samenleving*, Budel: Damon 2004, p. 174-209.

44 Dewey [1922], p. 57, 159.

practice of an old habit or the beginning of a new one.[45] In the words of Hans Joas:

> "ethics does not elucidate the validity of the ultimate values, but instead attempts to reconstruct empirically the procedure for resolving situations requiring moral decisions in such a way that in it a procedure becomes recognizable that can itself serve as a basis for its own self-perfecting."[46]

All moral judgments are therefore hypothetical and temporary,[47] and the outcome of an ethical discussion or thought process is ideally the selection of a better line of conduct, together with a practical and convincing justification. There is no ethical correctness that can be demonstrated by mere logic or measured by an external standard. What is ethically right, is always a relatively stable, temporary, and not necessarily universal agreement within a social group. It is fitting in this regard that the words "ethics" and "morality" derive from words meaning "habit" (Greek *ethos*) and "disposition" (Latin *mos*), and not from words for "truth".

What can be said for habits and moral principles also applies to codes of conduct, as mentioned at the beginning: The codes are end-points of discussions of practical problems, but should never be regarded as final solutions for all ethical predicaments a judge might find herself in. They are mere guidelines that can be amended, supplemented and replaced. The most important thing for judges, in their professional conduct in handling cases as much as in their private lives, is that they keep a *reflective* and *open mind* for the possibility that successful solutions from the past no longer work. To update their habits and principles, they might use the traditional ethical approaches just to make sure that they do not miss any aspects.[48]

Let's apply these insights to the third example: Should I acquit a defendant because I think my interpretation of the law (which I believe is the only just one) forces me to, when I know that he will probably be convicted in appeal? After applying the four ethical approaches, one will have thought about one's own good intentions and treating all concerned parties as ends in themselves (Kant), calculated the probably best outcome for the

45 Dewey [1922], p. 144, 199.

46 Hans Joas, *Pragmatism and social theory*, Chicago: The University of Chicago Press 1993, p. 252-253.

47 Dewey [1922], p. 146-7.

48 John Dewey, *Ethics* [1932], Vol. 7 in: *The Later Works of John Dewey, 1925-1953* (17 Vols.), Carbondale and Edwardsville: Southern Illinois University Press, 1985, p. 166.

well-being of society (utilitarianism), practised one's virtues of justice and honesty (virtue ethics), and finally sought alternatives for confrontational approaches and looked out for the weaker party (care ethics). Pragmatism proposes to use all of these perspectives, not for their own sake, but for the improvement of one's habits in order to become better at making ethical choices. One of these habits is keeping an *open mind* for new situations and new opinions, in order to be able to adapt to them and act to the advantage of all concerned.[49] A pragmatist ethics does not point towards a specific solution or a specific abstract norm, but it offers the best possible *process* to arrive, individually or as a group, at what would be, all things considered, the best thing to do in the situation at hand and others like it. In short, the best thing to do is what *works well*, in the short and the long term. Pragmatism uses other ethical approaches for the improvement of the process, capturing all relevant aspects, not for receiving instructions to the "correct outcome".

In the example, this might lead to acquittal, when all judges on the panel are convinced that they can give such compelling reasons for their decision that the appeal court cannot but accept them, and if it doesn't, that it will lead to a significant discussion soon tilting the scales in the case law. In other words, the judges' judging habits are challenged by the case and they respond to this challenge by adapting their habit and trying to motivate other courts to adapt their habits accordingly. The judges do this because they have good reasons to believe the new approach to the type of case they are handling will be for the benefit of all concerned.

On the other hand, when the judges expect, with good reason, that their new approach will be universally attacked in the press and the law journals and quashed in appeal, they might decide that a verdict is not (yet) the opportune place to present their ideas. Instead, they may decide to convict the defendant and then write an article in a law journal themselves, putting forward their alternative views. In both scenarios, keeping all the ethical theories in mind may serve to remind the judges of all possible aspects of the case in order to make the reasoning of their judgement more complete and more convincing, which is also a requirement of Article 6 of the European Convention of Human Rights: The right to a fair trial.[50]

---

49 Cf. Kwak & Venema 2023, p. 67-68, 176-178, 120.

50 Ragnar Aðalsteinsson, 'The Right to Adequate Judicial Reasoning', in: Asbjørn Eide, Jakob Th. Möller & Ineta Ziemele (red.), *Making Peoples Heard. Essays on Human Rights in Honour of Gudmundur Alfredsson*, Leiden: Brill 2011, p. 305-321.

4. Rule of law and democracy

Judicial ethics concerns many facets of this fascinating profession, from decisions in difficult cases to dealing with less ethical colleagues to giving legal advice to family members. But there is also an important political dimension to the job. The judiciary's independence as one of the branches of government is crucial to the rule of law (as opposed to the rule of self-interest) and the political system of checks and balances, which is increasingly under pressure in democratic countries. I will very briefly touch upon two complementary approaches to this situation, both relevant for judicial ethics. The first considers something that is already in place: the judicial decision-making process. As Steven Burton very clearly argues, its legal nature acts by itself as a *set of constraints* for judges, because the *types of reasons* they are permitted to use for their decision are restricted to *legal reasons* or "reasons provided by law" (rules, principles, case law, custom, doctrine).[51] This limitation by itself functions as a membrane against undue influences from the executive and legislative branches, and from anyone else, but also in the opposite direction, against undue influence from judges on the political process. It keeps judges in their legal bubble, so to speak. Nevertheless, the nature of a membrane is such that it is never *absolutely* closed, some political reasons may slip through, which cannot be fully ruled out in an interpretative practice like judging.[52]

Finally, recognising the law by itself does not guarantee that judges restrict themselves this way, Burton's model, the "good faith thesis", is a middle position between Dworkin's "one right answer thesis", claiming a duty for judges to find the single right answer in every case, and Hart's "total discretion thesis" in cases where the law does not dictate a clear solution.[53] It makes an appeal to the judicial conscience to practise the virtue of temperance: "Judges, we hope, are disposed by character to fulfil their duty to uphold the law so conceived."[54] This is echoed in the ENCJ working Group Judicial Ethics Report 2009-2010: "Through his knowledge of the realities and of the law, and by his reasonable, fair and prudent behaviour, a judge shows his wisdom."[55]

---

51 Steven Burton, *Judging in Good Faith*, Cambridge University Press 1994, p. 36-37.

52 Cf. Ronald Dworkin, *Law's Empire*, Fontana Press 1986, Ch. 2, 9, 10.

53 Burton 1994, p. 16-17; Ronald Dworkin, *A Matter of Principle*, Harvard University Press 1985, p. 119-146; H.L.A. Hart, *Essays on Bentham*, Clarendon Press 1982, p. 161.

54 Burton 1994, p. 64, 165.

55 'Judicial Ethics: Principles, Values and Qualities', in: *Matters of Principle* 2019, p. 48.

The second approach looks at who the justice system is for: all citizens. In order to protect their rights and address their interests, law and adjudication must be "responsive", as Nonet & Selznick famously put it, instead of "repressive" (supporting executive policies) or "autonomous" (taken as a self-contained system of logic).[56] That entails that justice must be both done and seen to be done. Citizens must feel that they are taken seriously by government institutions. Inspired by care ethics, courts can show this concern in the reasoning of their judgments and their interactions with parties at hearings. In the Dutch Child Care Benefits Scandal, this went terribly wrong.[57] Not only did the highest administrative court, the Administrative Jurisdiction Division of the Council of State[58] refrain from critically assessing the Tax Authority's illegal methods, it actively went along with its false statement of the law, and reasoned its decisions so marginally, that the litigating parents nor the lower courts could comprehend why their arguments were not accepted.[59]

Another case in point for both approaches is global warming, in two different ways, of which the first is public interest litigation against the State. In a landmark case, brought to court by climate activist group the Urgenda Foundation,[60] the Dutch Supreme Court in effect ordered the Dutch State "to reduce Dutch greenhouse gas emissions by 25% by the end of 2020", confirming, ultimately, the initial district court verdict from 2015.[61] The legal grounds for that decision were the UN Climate Convention and the European Convention for the Protection of Human Rights and Fundamental Freedoms (the ECHR), Articles 2 (the right to life) and 8 (the right to respect for private and family life). The court interpreted these rights according to the European Court of Human Rights' (ECtHR)

56 Philippe Nonet & Philip Selznick, *Law & society in transition. Towards responsive law*, Harper Torch Books 1978.

57 Maarten Bouwmeester, 'System failure in the digital welfare state: Exploring parliamentary and judicial control in the Dutch childcare benefits scandal', *Recht der Werkelijkheid* (44) 2, p. 13-37. See also 'Dutch childcare benefits scandal' <https://en.wikipedia.org/wiki/Dutch_childcare_benefits_scandal#> accessed 1 November 2025.

58 'The Council of State' <https://www.raadvanstate.nl/talen/en/> accessed 1 November 2025.

59 Kwak & Venema 2023, p. 13-14, 76-79. In depth: Bouwmeester 2024.

60 <https://www.urgenda.nl/en/home-en/> accessed 1 November 2025.

61 'Dutch State to reduce greenhouse gas emissions by 25% by the end of 2020' <https://www.hogeraad.nl/actueel/nieuwsoverzicht/2019/december/dutch-state-case-reduce-greenhouse-gas-emissions/> accessed 1 November 2025, including links to English translations of the court decisions.

Manual on Human Rights and the Environment.[62] As is the case with the relevant legal rules, a court is not free to choose its facts either, but is restricted to those facts that the parties can prove or agree upon (and facts of general knowledge). In this case, Urgenda and the State agreed on the facts very broadly endorsed by national and international climate scientists (Paragraphs 2.1 and 4.1 of the decision). The Dutch courts were not forced to their decision by shear legal logic, but they did not use extra-legal arguments either, much like the ECtHR in the similar *KlimaSeniorinnen case*.[63] The law provides reasons, not ready-made outcomes.[64]

In its judgment, although the Dutch Supreme Court explicitly addressed the political question and claimed to have remained within its constitutional bounds, it did not merely establish "the unlawfulness of [the government's] failing to act", but went "beyond the common ground in the European case law by replacing politically determined policy targets with policy targets of its own design, and ordering legislature and executive to realise those targets", pointing out the "exceptionality" of the circumstances.[65] Normally, courts deal with the assessment of claims of exceptional circumstances by the executive.[66] The danger of courts invoking "exceptionality" is that it has a tendency to open the membrane of legality allowing extra-legal motivations to pass through and influence judicial decision-making. In turn, with those decisions, courts may encroach upon the political domain. In Nonet and Selznick's terms: Although the court was being very responsive, taking citizens seriously and explaining its verdict meticulously, and clearly anti-repressive and not treating the law as a self-contained system (autonomously), it remains an open question whether or not it limited itself to its constitutional role as a legal decision-maker. Although political reasons are generally understood not to be appropriate reasons for a judge

62 Council of Europe, *Manual on Human Rights and the Environment* (2012) <https://www.echr.coe.int/documents/d/echr/dh_dev_manual_environment_eng> accessed 1 November 2025.

63 ECtHR 9 April 2024, application no. 53600/20 (Verein Klimaseniorinnen Schweiz and Others v. Switzerland).

64 Burton 1994, p. 34.

65 Leonard F.M. Besselink, 'The National and EU Targets for Reduction of Greenhouse Gas Emissions Infringe the ECHR: The Judicial Review of General Policy Objectives: Hoge Raad (Netherlands Supreme Court) 20 December 2019, Urgenda v The State of the Netherlands, *European Constitutional Law Review* (18) 2022-1, p. 155-182.

66 Cf. David Dyzenhaus, 'Schmitt v. Dicey: Are States of Emergency inside or outside the Legal Order?', 27 *Cardozo Law Review* 2006, p. 2005-2040.

to decide upon,[67] they cannot be completely ruled out, not even unambiguously defined, let alone their causal role determined.

The second way in which global warming is a case in point for both rule of law approaches concerns the question how far judges may go *outside* the courtroom in expressing their views on climate change and what the government should do about it. Can they, for example, participate in protest marches in robes? That would certainly bar those judges from handling future cases concerning climate issues, because of the appearance of bias. It may even contaminate the public image of the judiciary as a whole, especially if a large group of judges would protest together, and even more so when the demonstration is not allowed and causes public anger because it blocks a major motorway.[68] Of course, judges have the right, as private persons, to protest, even in a civil disobedient manner, but they are also responsible for the "good administration of justice", which includes guarding the judiciary's public image and public trust in the justice system.[69]

This section can be summarised by the recommendation to judges to use ethical theory to strengthen their resolve to be responsive and transparent towards citizens, and to *close ranks* to undue influence by the executive and legislative branches or other non-legal reasons, including their own political opinions.

5. Combination with other disciplines: Literature and history

One of the main objectives of professional ethics courses, meetings, discussions, textbooks and so forth is to stimulate an open mind concerning the usefulness of all practices and habits (intellectual ones included) of judges, that are in any way connected with their profession. This is not easy, because habits have the tendency to become fixed and questioning them

67 Burton 1992, p. 45.

68 Emma de Ruiter, 'Several arrested as climate activists block major highway in The Hague' (11 January 2025) <https://www.euronews.com/my-europe/2025/01/11/several-arrested-as-climate-activists-block-major-highway-in-the-hague> accessed 1 November 2025.

69 United Nations Office on Drugs and Crime, *The Bangalore Principles of Judicial Conduct* <https://www.unodc.org/documents/ji/training/bangaloreprinciples.pdf> accessed 1 November 2025, p. 4.

often appears as inefficient at the least, and as sabotage at the worst.[70] To stimulate legal professionals' enthusiasm for professional ethics, in other words getting them to exercise their ability to question and usefully adapt their habits, it might help to use other interests they may have to entice them to rethink their professional behaviour. Two of those interests often found in judges are literature and history. Both of these fields offer numerous cases and subjects that are directly relevant to judicial ethics and legal philosophy alike, on which I will elaborate briefly.

The field of "law and literature" has been popular for decades with academics and practitioners alike. The literature is vast and growing and has yielded many useful introductory texts for teaching.[71] Other than textbooks, novels allow the reader to travel in the mind of a protagonist that he would probably never get to know in real life. This gives body to legal philosophical theories of free will, fair trial, crime, privacy, etc. Further themes in literature that are relevant for judicial ethics include attitudes towards those in power, utopian politics, formalism and equity, and meaning and interpretation of texts. Reading literature has not been proven to improve empathy,[72] nor, according to Richard Posner, morality: "The world of literature is moral anarchy; if immersion in it teaches anything in the moral line it is moral relativism."[73] Nevertheless, it may enhance professional ethics in the sense of openness to different values and value systems.

Having to be brief, I will give only one example of a legal philosophical theme which is relevant for judicial ethics and capable of elucidation by literary texts. This theme is free will and responsibility , which may seem a very abstract philosophical subject, but is directly relevant to the aspect of decisions and actions addressed by Kant's categorical imperative: intentions. Take, for example, the poor student Rodion Raskolnikov, who murders a vile old pawnbroker and her sister in Dostoyevsky's 1861 novel *Crime and Punishment*.[74] In his pitiful state of despair and near-madness, he expe-

70 Cf. Roberto Unger, *Passion. An Essay of Personality*, The Free Press New York 1984, e.g. p. 36.

71 To name but a few: Theodore Ziolkowski, *The Mirror of Justice. Literary Reflections of Legal Crises*, Princeton University Press 1997; Kieran Dolin, *A Critical Introduction to Law and Literature*, Cambridge University Press 2007; Richard R. Posner, *Law & Literature*, 3rd Edition, Harvard University Press 2009.

72 A.E. Denham, 'Empathy & Literature', *Emotion Review* 2024-2, p. 84-95.

73 Posner 2009, p. 463.

74 Fyodor Dostoyevsky, *Crime and Punishment* (transl. David McDuff), Penguin Books 2004 [1861].

riences his own actions very differently from "normal" people. Apart from having in mind a theory about the right of exceptionally superior persons to kill for a greater cause, he feels as though his own murder experiment is carried out *with* him, instead of *by* him. From the beginning, the plan does not seem serious to him at all, he doesn't believe he is actually going to carry it out, and at the same time he feels as though he has no freedom of thought and no will, and everything was already decided *for* him.[75] This theme can be pursued further by reading in Camus' *The Stranger* about Meursault, who, having killed a man, doesn't really seem to understand the concept of responsibility and guilt at all,[76] and in Kafka's *The Trial* about Josef K., who is obsessed by the same concept without understanding what he is responsible *for*.[77] Having met these strange characters, a judge may become more open to different ways of experiencing one's own actions, see Kant's theory in a wider perspective, and better understand parties, defendants, colleagues and others she deals with professionally. She might also decide to interpret certain criminal laws pertaining to culpability wider or narrower to accommodate different views or cases.

History provides abundant instances of ethical predicaments for judges. Judges working in times of war and oppression are among the most popular examples in scholarly texts on judges and ethics, and World War II is usually overrepresented. There is even a two-week programme of Fellowships at Auschwitz for the Study of Professional Ethics.[78] Although it can be doubted whether such an extreme case as the Holocaust itself can provide direct guidance for every-day ethics, the wider context of WWII does present more general themes and situations also occurring in times of peace. The example I will address here is the dilemma of the judge under an oppressive regime between remaining in function or resigning. This has become reality again in Hungary, where judges have recently resigned in protest.[79] Even

75 Dostoyevsky [1861], part I, Ch. 1, Ch. 5 and Ch 6.

76 Albert Camus, *The Outsider* (transl. Sandra Smith), Penguin Books 2012 [1942].

77 Franz Kafka, *The Trial* (transl. Idris Parry), Penguin Books 1994 [1925].

78 'FASPE: Promoting Ethical Leadership for Today's Professionals' <https://www.faspe-ethics.org/> accessed 1 November 2025.

79 Laura Szaplonczai, 'Judges in Hungary fight for an independent judiciary', *Deutsche Welle* 24 March 2025 <https://www.dw.com/en/judges-in-hungary-fight-for-an-independent-judiciary/a-72020372> accessed 1 November 2025;
Tamás Matusik, 'Targeting Disciplinary Courts. Why Hungary Is on the Verge of a Full-scale Judicial Capture', *Verfassungsblog* 16 January 2025

in the Netherlands in 2011, when specific minimum penalties for recidivism in serious crimes were proposed, there were judges who announced their resignation in the event such a proposal would become law.[80] The proposed law was never passed by parliament.

The discussion about these problems can be stimulated by a notorious case I regularly use in my professional ethics course: the Dutch Supreme Court's "Review Case" of 1942, under the German occupation of the Netherlands.[81] In its decision, the court refused to review a certain ordinance passed by the occupation regime, because it argued (contrary to their own pre-war case law) that Dutch courts lacked the competence to do so. The real reason was revealed only after the war: The judges had feared being dismissed and replaced by nazis, and that in reaction the whole judiciary might resign and be replaced by nazis as well. In their 1943 correspondence, a Supreme Court judge and a law professor discussed this from two different ethical approaches.[82] The judge argued from his "pragmatic" position that keeping adjudication in "good" Dutch hands was better for all citizens in the end, because it enabled judges to negotiate with the occupiers and use their office to (secretly) help citizens in need. He thought these advantages greater than the disadvantage of making compromises like not reviewing war-time ordinances, which is utilitarian reasoning. The law professor argued from a principled standpoint that it is the duty of every citizen to protect national values, including the law, and that as soon as you make compromises with the enemy, you are guilty of undermining the law, which should be upheld in all situations. He also thought that it was wrong to weigh all consequences, because the enemy's reaction is the enemy's responsibility. This reflects a Kantian perspective.

<https://verfassungsblog.de/targeting-disciplinary-courts/> accessed 1 November 2025.

80 News website nu.nl reported this on 3 November 2011: 'Rechters dreigen ontslag te nemen om plannen kabinet' <https://www.nu.nl/politiek/2658071/rechters-dreigen-ontslag-te-nemen-om-plannen-kabinet.html?referrer=https%3A%2F%2Fwww.google.com%2F> accessed 1 November 2025.

81 The case is explained in Derk Venema, 'The Hoge Raad during the German Occupation of the Netherlands', in: Derk Venema (ed.), *Supreme Courts Under Nazi Occupation*, Amsterdam University Press 2022, p. 187-226, at p. 211-216 <https://doi.org/10.5117/9789463720496> accessed 1 November 2025 (open access).

82 The correspondence is published in Derk Venema, Leny de Groot-van Leeuwen & Thomas Mertens (eds.), *Onder de huidige omstandigheden, De Hoge Raad en het Toetsingsarrest 1942,* Den Haag: Boom Juridische uitgevers 2008.

6. Conclusion: Open minds, closed ranks

The use of philosophy of law, broadly conceived, for professional ethics for judges lies mainly in its ability to assist in keeping an open mind in all situations where ethics come into play, and to keep eyes and ears and communication lines open for relevant information from and in all directions. In ethical decision making, it can be useful to ask oneself, or each other, if every aspect has been taken into account: intentions, human dignity, consequences large and small, good judicial character, shared values and responsibilities, etc. But to uphold and defend this *open and independent attitude*, it is at the same time necessary as a judge to keep the *ranks closed* against undue influence from the executive and legislative powers, commercial parties, the general public, and, last but not least, your own private opinions and values. From practical philosophy, many perspectives and reasons can be drawn that together serve to improve the process of ethical decision making, instead of determining objective outcomes.

List of Authors

Prof. Dr. Eckardt Buchholz-Schuster, Coburg University of Applied Sciences and Arts / Germany

Adela Gąsiorowska, LL.M., Doctoral Candidate in Jurisprudence, University of Warsaw / Poland

Prof. Dr. Daniel Herbe, Coburg University of Applied Sciences and Arts / Germany

Prof. Heidi M. Hurd J.D., Ph.D., M.A., University of Illinois / USA

Dr. Hyungjoon Jun, M.A., Friedrich-Alexander-Universität Erlangen-Nürnberg / Germany

Prof. Dr. Stephan Kirste, Paris Lodron Universität Salzburg / Austria

Dr. Hyun Jung Lee, M.A., Friedrich-Alexander-Universität Erlangen-Nürnberg / Germany

Prof. Win-chiat Lee, Ph.D., Wake Forest University / USA

Prof. John Murungi, Ph.D., J.D., Towson University / USA

Dr. Oche Onazi, Ph.D., (Edinburgh), LL.M. (Warwick), Senior Lecturer in Law, University of Stirling / UK

Dr. Jordan Pascoe, Ph.D., M.A., Binghamton University / USA

Prof. Dr. Veronica Rodriguez-Blanco, Ph.D., MgSc (Caracas), MJur (Oxford), University of Surrey / UK

Prof. Juan Pablo Sterling Casas, Ph.D., Uniautónoma del Cauca / Colombia

Prof. Dra. Leonor Suárez-Llanos, Universidad de Oviedo / Spain

Dr. Derk Venema MEd, Senior Lecturer, Open Universiteit / The Netherlands